Beginning FPGA: Programming Metal

Your brain on hardware

Aiken Pang
Peter Membrey

Apress®

Beginning FPGA: Programming Metal: Your Brain on Hardware

Aiken Pang
Chelmsford, Massachusetts
USA

Peter Membrey
Lai Chi Kok, Kowloon, Hong Kong
China

ISBN-13 (pbk): 978-1-4302-6247-3   ISBN-13 (electronic): 978-1-4302-6248-0
DOI 10.1007/978-1-4302-6248-0

Library of Congress Control Number: 2016962137

Managing Director: Welmoed Spahr
Lead Editor: Natalie Pao
Technical Reviewer: Brendan Horan
Editorial Board: Steve Anglin, Pramila Balan, Laura Berendson, Aaron Black, Louise Corrigan, Jonathan Gennick, Robert Hutchinson, Celestin Suresh John, Nikhil Karkal, James Markham, Susan McDermott, Matthew Moodie, Natalie Pao, Gwenan Spearing
Coordinating Editor: Jessica Vakili
Copy Editor: Lori Jacobs
Compositor: SPi Global
Indexer: SPi Global
Artist: SPi Global

Distributed to the book trade worldwide by Springer Science+Business Media New York, 233 Spring Street, 6th Floor, New York, NY 10013. Phone 1-800-SPRINGER, fax (201) 348-4505, e-mail orders-ny@springer-sbm.com, or visit www.springeronline.com. Apress Media, LLC is a California LLC and the sole member (owner) is Springer Science + Business Media Finance Inc (SSBM Finance Inc). SSBM Finance Inc is a **Delaware** corporation.

For information on translations, please e-mail rights@apress.com, or visit www.apress.com.

Apress and friends of ED books may be purchased in bulk for academic, corporate, or promotional use. eBook versions and licenses are also available for most titles. For more information, reference our Special Bulk Sales–eBook Licensing web page at www.apress.com/bulk-sales.

Any source code or other supplementary materials referenced by the author in this text are available to readers at www.apress.com. For detailed information about how to locate your book's source code, go to www.apress.com/source-code/. Readers can also access source code at SpringerLink in the Supplementary Material section for each chapter.

Printed on acid-free paper

Contents at a Glance

Contents

About the Authors

Aiken Pang was born in Hong Kong in the early 1980s just in time for the home micro-computer revolution. He developed an interest in computers after finding an Apple IIe at his uncle's home; he installed a TV card and a floppy drive and loaded his first game (Pacman) by himself at the age of 10. Since then he has self-taught himself a number of programming languages and built his own computers from scratch.

Aiken followed his passion for computing into more formal studies and holds a BEng in Electronics Engineering and an MSc in Computer Engineering from Hong Kong Polytechnic University and the University of Massachusetts at Lowell, respectively. He has been using VHDL (VHSIC (very high speed integrated circuit) Hardware Description Language) to design hardware in FPGAs (field-programmable gate arrays) for more than ten years.

He lives in the United States with his wife France and their daughter Mayah.

Hailing from the UK, **Peter Membrey** has worked for Red Hat, holds a RHCE certification, and has worked and taught at a number of educational institutions since the beginning of his career. He knows what Linux users like and need and hopes that CentOS will get the kudos it deserves. He lives in Hong Kong and is teaching and consulting on all matters having to do with Linux Enterprise networking, while studying for his master's degree.

About the Technical Reviewer

Brendan Horan is a hardware fanatic, with a full high rack of all types of machine architectures in his home. He has more than 10 years of experience working with large UNIX systems and tuning the underlying hardware for optimal performance and stability. Brendan's love for all forms of hardware has helped him throughout his IT career, from fixing laptops to tuning servers and their hardware in order to suit the needs of high-availability designs and ultra low-latency applications. Brendan takes pride in the Open Source Movement and is happy to say that every computer in his house is powered by open source technology. He resides in Hong Kong with his wife, Vikki, who continues daily to teach him more Cantonese.

PART I

Getting Started with FPGA

CHAPTER 1

■ ■ ■

What Is an FPGA and What Can It Do?

Field-programmable gate arrays (FPGA) are a special type of integrated circuits (ICs) or chip that can be programmed in the field after manufacture and has three basic building blocks: logic gates, flip-flops + memories, and wires. In this chapter we will quickly review what FPGA is and some of the things it can do.

An IC has input and/or output pins (the gray color in Figure 1-1). The black box is the "brain" of the IC and most ICs have white or gray markings on top of the black box. Most of the ICs mention their specific functions in their datasheet (e.g., is it an amplifier, a processor, a counter, an Ethernet MAC, or a combination of the lot). If you read the FPGA's datasheets and are looking for a specific function, you will probably get very frustrated. That's because they don't mention the purpose or any of the FPGA's feature sets. All you will be able to find is how many logic gates, how much memory, and how to program the FPGA, but you won't find functions or features. You just cannot figure them out from the datasheet.

APFS 240416

Figure 1-1. *Integrated circuits, or chip, look like this*

© Aiken Pang and Peter Membrey 2017
A. Pang and P. Membrey, *Beginning FPGA: Programming Metal*, DOI 10.1007/978-1-4302-6248-0_1

FPGAs allow designers to modify their designs very late in the design cycle —even after the end product has been manufactured and deployed in the field. Sound familiar? It should sound a lot like Windows updates or Android/Apple phone software updates. That's one of the most powerful and compelling features of an FPGA but please don't treat FPGA design as a software programming exercise for a microcontroller or processor. An FPGA is not a processor with software. It is an amazing device that allows the average person to create his or her very own digital circuit. You are designing a hardware digital circuit when you are creating an FPGA design. You are going to use a hardware description language (which, incidentally, is used by Intel CPU chip designers too) to design your FPGA. This is a very important concept. We will provide more details when we are putting together some example designs in the later chapters. In the following sections we'll provide a little bit more detail about field-programmable, gates, and arrays and what they can do.

1.1   Field-Programmable

The most valuable FPGA feature is that the end user can program or configure it within seconds. This means that the end user can change the hardware design in the FPGA chip quickly and at will. For example, the FPGA can change from temperature sensor to LED (light-emitting diode) driver within a few seconds. This means that FPGAs are useful for rapid product development and prototyping. This field-programmable magic is done by a configuration file, often called a bit file which is created by a designer (you). Once loaded, the FPGA will behave like the digital circuit you designed!

1.1.1   Configuration Technology

Table 1-1 lists the three types of configuration technologies: static random access memory (SRAM), flash memory, and antifuse.

Table 1-1. *Different Types of Configuration Technology*

	SRAM	Flash	Antifuse
Achronix	YES	--	--
Altera	YES	--	--
Lattice	YES	--	--
Microsemi	--	YES	YES
Xilinx	YES	--	--

Most of the FPGA vendors are using SRAM technology. It is fast and small, and it offers unlimited reprogrammability. One of the drawbacks though is that the FPGA needs time to reload the entire design into SRAM every time you power up the FPGA. This approach also takes more power.

Flash and antifuse technologies are non-volatile (meaning that they can retain data even if the power is turned off) so that they provide the benefit of "instant on" without needing to reload the FPGA bit file every time we power up the FPGA or the system. They also draw less power than the SRAM approach.

Antifuse technology can only be programmed once and can't match the performance of SRAM technology. The only reasons to use an antifuse technology FPGA today is due to its super high reliability and security.

■ **Tips**   The world's largest and most powerful particle accelerator—Large Hadron Collider (LHC)—uses antifuse FPGAs to implement radiation protection digital circuits.

This book focuses on SRAM technology because it is the most common technology and is the easiest to program. Most of the SRAM-based FPGAs have an external EEPROM (electrically erasable programmable read-only memory) for storing the bit file, similar to how a computer stores programs on disk. All you need to do is "burn" your bit file into the EERPOM and the FPGA will autoload the bit file from the EEPROM when it powers up.

1.2   Gates = Logic

The gate is the most basic element in digital logic and is more formally known as a logic gate. All modern digital designs are based on CMOS (complementary metal oxide semiconductor) logic gates. To support complex digital designs, FPGAs contain tens of thousands, hundreds of thousands, or even more individual logic elements which are built by logic gates.

1.2.1   The Basic Gate Design Block No. 1: Logic Element

The logic element (LE) is one of the smallest elements in FPGA design. It basically consists of a look-up table (LUT), flip-flop, and multiplexer (which we will cover shortly). FPGAs are used extensively for compute problems that can benefit from parallel computing architectures—for example, cleaning up images being received from an image sensor, local processing on image pixels, and computing difference vectors in H.264 compression. LEs can form any complex or even simple digital function inside the FPGA. Figure 1-2 shows the basic configurable logic elements. Although different FPGA venders have their own LE designs, they are very similar to the one shown in Figure 1-2. Most of the inputs to a LE are connected to the LUT and followed with a flip-flop (register). The output of the LE is selected by a multiplexer (MUX). The LUT and MUX are the major configurable blocks in the LE. Don't worry, this will all make sense after you read the next section.

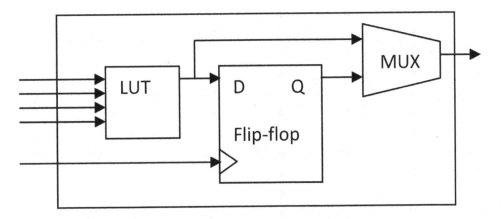

Figure 1-2. *Basic configurable LEs*

1.2.1.1   The Magic Block: LUT

The LUT is basically just a small amount of read-only memory. A four-input, one output LUT, can generate any four-input Boolean function (AND/OR/XOR/NOT) (Figure 1-2). We will provide more details on Boolean function in Chapters 8 and 9. When you configure the FPGA, the contents of the LUT will be configured accordingly. Table 1-2 shows an OR gate with all four possible inputs the LUT supports. The four inputs act as an address bus, addressing one of 16 (2^4) stored bits; therefore it can emulate any Boolean function that can be handled in 4 bits (Figure 1-3). In some FPGA LE designs, LUTs can be combined to form a 16-bit shift register or memory block. There is another similar block, the MUX, in the basic LE. It is used to select the output source from a register or directly from LUT. In reality, the LEs are a bit more complex in that they may very well have more than one LUT and MUX.

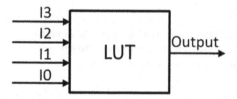

Figure 1-3. *Four inputs, one output Boolean function*

Table 1-2. *Four-Input, One-Output LUT*

Address	I3	I2	I1	I0	Output
0	0	0	0	0	0
1	0	0	0	1	1
2	0	0	1	0	1
3	0	0	1	1	1
4	0	1	0	0	1
5	0	1	0	1	1
6	0	1	1	0	1
7	0	1	1	1	1
8	1	0	0	0	1
9	1	0	0	1	1
10	1	0	1	0	1
11	1	0	1	1	1
12	1	1	0	0	1
13	1	1	0	1	1
14	1	1	1	0	1
15	1	1	1	1	1

If you are serious about FPGA digital design, then you may want to read the LUT datasheet from the FPGA vendor. You can do more with the same FPGA, if you know how to fully use the LUT blocks.

1.2.1.2   The 1-bit storage block: Flip-flop

The flip-flop (or register) is the smallest storage unit in an FPGA. Each flip-flop can store 1 bit of information at a time. Like a light switch, it can either be on (a value of 1) or off (a value of 0). The basic function of a flip-flop is to hold information and make it available to the logic elements for the computing process. This flip-flop is one of the most important blocks in a computer. Figure 1-4 shows the digital design of a D-type flip-flop, which is a basic flip-flop used in FPGA.

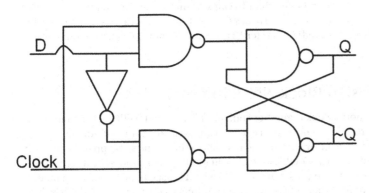

Figure 1-4. Flip-flop logic gate design (D-type flip-flop)

There are two inputs (D and Clock) and two outputs (Q and ~Q) in a flip-flop. The D flip-flop captures the value of the D input at a defined stage of the clock cycle (such as the rising edge of the clock input). That captured value becomes the Q output. At other times, the output Q does not change. The D flip-flop can be viewed as a memory cell, a zero-order hold, or a delay line. Multiple flip-flops connected together can form a shift register.

■ **Tip**   You can go to the following web site for more details about D-type flip-flop: http://electronics-course.com/d-flip-flop.

Most of the FPGA digital designs are synchronous design. It means that all the inputs and outputs are synchronous to one clock or more. All the examples in this book are synchronous design with the rising edge of the clock because most of the FPGAs are built for implementing synchronous design.

■ **Note**   A synchronous circuit is a digital circuit in which the changes in the state of memory elements are synchronized by a clock signal. In a sequential digital logic circuit, data is stored in memory devices called flip-flops or latches. Source: www.wikipedia.org. It is like shooting pictures. Each picture stores the "data" when you hit the shutter button. The picture is the storage elements and the button is the clock signal.

1.2.2   The Basic Gate Design Block No. 2: Configurable IO Block

Another basic logic design element is configurable input/output block (IOB). It is used to connect the LE to the outside world. It can be configured as an input or output, as b-directional, or not connected. The IOB can support different types of electrical input/output (I/O) specifications (e.g., TTL logic, 3.3V CMOS, and PCIe) and add internal pull-up or pull-down resisters. Remember to select the correct I/O specification. It is because different specifications have different driving strength (voltage and current) and most of the time they are **not** compatible. The worst is overload the FPGA IO and break the FPGA.

The latest FPGA IOB can support bandwidth higher than 10 Gbps. Some FPGAs even have direct optical input and output physical connections (Source: www.altera.com/content/dam/altera-www/global/en_US/pdfs/literature/wp/wp-01161-optical-fpga.pdf). Chapter 12 provides a detailed discussion on how to use IOBs.

1.2.3   The Basic Gate Design Block No. 3: Internal RAM

The internal RAM (random access memory) block is another configurable unit in the FPGA. The main configuration parameter is number of read/write ports. You can read and write the same memory with different locations at the same time. It is like one instruction to read and write on the same physical memory with different address. Can you think of a use case of this type of configuration (read and write at the same time/clock cycle)? One possibility is FIFO (first in, first out memory) which is used to pass data from module A to module B. There is an FPGA vendor that puts DRAM (dynamic random access memory) (which is the one you'll find in your computer because of its density—it can pack more bits into the same physical size) inside the FPGA and allows the rest of the logic to access it directly. Some FPGA vendors put flash memory (which is a non-volatile memory such as you'd find in a memory card or USB stick) into their FPGA. If your application needs non-volatile memory, then an FPGA with built-in flash memory would be a good fit for you. In Parts 3 and 4, we will show how to configure internal RAM.

1.3   Arrays Have Many Connections

An array is a large group of things put together with a particular order. At this moment, we know that FPGA has a lot of LE, IOB, and internal memory. All of them can be configured to do whatever you would like them to do. There is a last piece of kit inside the FPGA that can be configured; the connections between the LEs and IOBs. To make the connection efficient, FPGA vendors put the LEs and IOBs into a two-dimensional array (some newer FPGA's have three-dimensional arrays instead). Figure 1-5 shows an FPGA array example. All of the IOBs are close to the IC edge such that it has the shortest distance to the outside world. The wires between each LE and IOB are the configurable connection (wires). These are extremely flexible and easy to use. Most of the time, the FPGA vendor tools take care of all the connections for you.

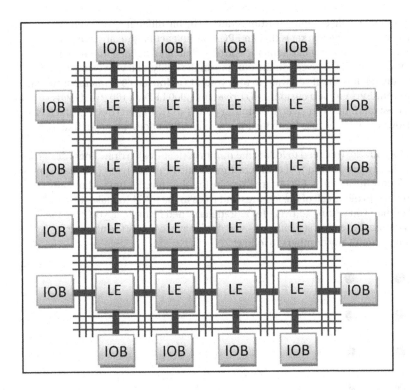

Figure 1-5. *Gate array*

Digital logic theory: If you have enough NAND gates then you can build anything that you want. In an ideal world we don't need to have complicated LE blocks. All we need to have are NAND gates and connections in between.

In the real world: The routing between NAND gates will very quickly run out of room to finish even a simple job. Traditional FPGAs are optimized for more complex configurable logic element blocks with a relatively limited number of interconnections between them. Today, FPGAs have added more interconnections by using 3D arrays. These 3D arrays are stacked like multiple chips with connections between chips.

Keep in mind: It is possible to run out of connections between LEs and IOB and thus fail to generate a viable FPGA design.

1.4 What Can It Do?

Generally speaking, all the FPGA does is generate ones (3.3 V) and zeroes (0 V) which means it can do everything or nothing. That doesn't sound terribly impressive does it? However, you need to ask the right question in order to get the right answer. The right question is, "What you want it to do?" The more you do, the more it can do for you! Think of the FPGA as a piece of clay. You can mold that clay into any number of shapes, make a plate, make a statue, or make a tiny house. Its potential is limited only by your imagination, and that's also true of an FPGA—it has the capability to take on practically any function you can imagine!

It is very difficult to design your own chip completely from scratch. The big difference between an FPGA and every other chip you can buy on the market is that an FPGA doesn't actually do anything. It has no intended function when you buy it. It is not like a microcontroller that has a defined function or a generic process ready to run software. An FPGA gives you the ultimate in flexibility, allowing you to design anything you can imagine in the digital domain. If you want to turn your FPGA into an 8051 microcontroller, you can do it. You can configure your FPGA to be a custom LED driver for 1,000 LEDs, a 100 PWM (Pulse Width Modulator), or a universal asynchronous receiver/transmitter (UART or COM port) device, which is a common computer interface. However, just because it can be done with an FPGA does not mean that it will necessarily be easy to do so.

When you play a join-the-dots puzzle, you need to follow the numbers (features) to draw lines (design). It is like you get a processor; you have a fixed amount of counters, timers, and interface types (features); and you write your code (design) to follow the features. FPGAs are like join-the-dots puzzles but without any numbers at all (Figure 1-6). You need to design all of the features and rules in the FPGA to make it "work." Another way to look at it is rather than you writing software for a predetermined feature set, you have the ability with an FPGA to actually define the feature set yourself—you don't have to follow the numbers because with an FPGA, there simply aren't any numbers to follow!

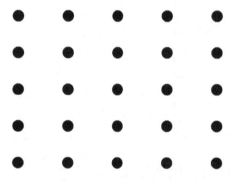

Figure 1-6. *Connect-the-dots puzzles without number*

Some fun: Try to join all 25 dots in Figure 1-6 by drawing no more than eight straight lines. The straight lines must be continuous.

■ **Tips**   Think out of the box. This tip is valid for designing FPGA too!

1.5   It Can Get the Job Done Fast!

FPGAs can get the job done faster than a computer, if you can separate your job into discrete pieces. This is due to order reduction in FPGA tools and parallelism operation in FPGA. The FPGA tool (mention in Chapter 3) is smart enough to reduce complicated operations to simpler ones. This operation is order reduction! The tools can reduce complex operation like multiplying by 2 into an addition which runs faster and uses less energy. An FPGA can parallelize a task that was already much slower to run as software on a CPU (central processing unit). Once the designer starts to realize the following, "I can perform in 25 FPGA clock cycles a task which takes my CPU 200,000 clock cycles, and I can do this task in parallel 5 items at a time," you can easily see why an FPGA could be a heck of a lot faster than a CPU! Reversing the order of bits inside a 32-bit integer is a very good example for order reduction. Computers need to use a FOR loop to do it which will take a number of clock cycles to complete. You can accomplish the same thing in a single cycle with an FPGA.

Data flow into and out of the FPGA is expandable too! So you can send a lot of data to an FPGA to get more jobs done at the same time. Image, video, and Ethernet packet processing all need this kind of high bandwidth data flow.

For example, suppose you want to do some processing work on an image, and let's say you want to rotate it. Let's also say that it takes one second to do this, and you have 10,000 images to do. A single processor would take nearly three hours to process this workload. Of course, modern CPUs are multicore, so let's be generous and assume we have eight cores at our disposal. Now we can do the same work in just over 20 minutes. With the FPGA, though, we might have our "image processing" unit, and maybe 500 of those fit on a single FPGA. If we could keep those units full of data, we'd complete our task in only 20 seconds. If we also consider that it is now being processed in hardware rather than software, we could say that it only takes half a second to process an image, dropping our total time down to ten seconds. Okay, this example is a bit contrived and there are plenty of ifs, buts, and maybes, but it gives you an idea of the power of an FPGA.

1.6 FPGA vs. Processor

The major difference between a processor and an FPGA is that an FPGA doesn't have a permanent hardware configuration; on the contrary, it is configurable according to the end-user needs. However, processors have a permanent hardware configuration which means that all the transistors, registers, interface structures, and all of the connections are permanent. A processor can only do predefined tasks (accumulation, multiplication, I/O switch, etc.). Designers make the processor do these tasks "in a consecutive manner" by using software, in accordance with their own functions.

Hardware configuration in the FPGA is not fixed so it is defined by the end user. Although logic elements are fixed in FPGA, functions they achieve and the interconnections between them are controlled by the user. So tasks that FPGAs can do are not predefined. You can have the task done according to the written hardware description language (HDL) code "in parallel," which means concurrently. The capability of parallel processing is one of the most important features that separates FPGAs from processors and makes them superior in many areas.

Processors are generally more useful for repetitive control of specific circuits. For example, using an FPGA for simple functions such as turning on or off a device from a computer may be overkill. This process can easily done with many conventional microcontrollers. However, FPGA solutions are more reasonable, if you want to process 4K video data on the computer. Table 1-3 compares FPGAs and processors in a few more ways.

Table 1-3. *FPGA vs. Computer*

	FPGA	Processor
Cost	High	Low
Hardware structure	Flexible	Fix
Execution	Concurrent	Sequential
Programming	HDL	Assembly language
Development time	Long	Short
Power	Efficient	Not efficient

There is something that the both have in common and we will find out more about that together in Chapter 2.

1.7 Summary

*F*ield-*p*rogrammable *g*ate *a*rrays have three basic building blocks.

1. Logic gates

2. Flip-flops + memories

3. Wires

FPGAs can do many things, or they can do nothing, with these three building blocks. It all depends on you. You need to design the hardware structure to handle the task you want. FPGAs can concurrently process your tasks and this is the main difference between FPGA and a processor. Chapters 2, 3, and 4 will get you ready to design real digital logic.

In Chapter 2, you will get hands on with the hardware platform we will be using.

In Chapter 3, you will install FPGA digital design environment software.

In Chapter 4, you will create your first digital design in the FPGA world!

As you work your way through this book (Part 2 and Part 3), you will create a number of design blocks; each block can be reused. Each block is like LEGO, you can reuse all the blocks you create in other designs.

"Nothing will work unless you do."

—Maya Angelou**Electronic supplementary material** The online version of this chapter (doi:10.1007/978-1-4302-6248-0_1) contains supplementary material, which is available to authorized users.

CHAPTER 2

■ ■ ■

Our Weapon of Choice

This chapter will briefly review the various FPGAs (field-programmable gate arrays) available and then examine the features of BeMicro MAX 10 board, which is what we are using throughout the book.

Finally, we introduce some tools for simple hardware projects. You will find that they are very useful for this book and for your hardware projects.

2.1   What Weapons (FPGAs) Are Available

You may think FPGAs are expensive things. This was true ten years ago, but right now, you can always find a FPGA fit for your budget and application. A quick browse on one FPGA manufacturer's web sites turns up more than five differently named FPGAs. This is similar to browsing Intel's web site where you'll find a wide range of processors available: Celeron, Pentium, Core, Atom, Xeon, and Itanium. All this choice is great, but what does it really mean for you? Well, just like you need the right processor for a particular job, you'll also need the right FPGA. Don't worry, though, our job is to get you up to speed so that you'll be able to navigate through all the choices with ease.

Most of the FPGA companies don't have that much support for people who are just getting started, so let's begin with a quick look at the different types of FPGAs you can get your hands on:

In general, FPGA manufacturers provide three types of FPGA:

1.   The Aircraft Carrier—System on Chip (SoC): This one comes with pretty much everything onboard (FPGA chip). SoC means that the FPGA has a central processor unit (CPU) and many standard interfaces built-in. An ARM core is one the most common processor designs that you'll find in SoC FPGAs. Because it comes with all these features, a SoC can be used to quickly develop prototypes and they tend to have a lot of custom interfaces wrapped around a CPU for which existing software is already written. This type of FPGA is best suited for your need for software flexibility and hardware speed. One of the hottest examples is Advanced Driver Assistance Systems (ADAS). It is a system to help the car driver in the driving process. The system should improve car and road safety. All of the autopilot cars (Google self-driving car, Telsa Autopilot system, and Volvo's IntelliSafe Autopilot) have ADAS.

2.   The Laser Cannon—High End: It provides high-density computational power and super high-speed digital interfaces in one go. The computational power comes from a specially designed logic element(LE) which is digital signal processing(DSP) blocks that we discussed in the first chapter. One of the super high-speed digital interfaces available is PCIe Gen 3 (close to 8GBs per second. It can transfer one and a half DVDs within seconds). This type of FPGA is designed for consuming a lot of digital data. For example, High-Performance Computing (HPC), Optical Transport Networks, and Software Define Radio are using this type of FPGA.

© Aiken Pang and Peter Membrey 2017
A. Pang and P. Membrey, *Beginning FPGA: Programming Metal*, DOI 10.1007/978-1-4302-6248-0_2

3. The Pocket Knife—Low End: It provides the most cost-effective solution for a general digital interface. This type of FPGA is like a sea of gates which has only basic elements (logic, memory, and clocks). Anything you can think of using logic gate to design, you can finish with this type of FPGA. This type of FPGA is like an 8051 MCU, which has all you need to do basic things. This type of FPGA is best suited for consumer products, low-cost prototyping, and education.

Table 2-1 shows the FPGA names from different FPGA manufacturers. You can use this table to narrow down what FPGA may suit your next project FPGA need.

Table 2-1. *Different Types of FPGA's Name List*

FPGA	SoC	High End	Low End
Achronix	N/A	Speedster 22i	N/A
Altera	Stratix SoC	Stratix/ Arria	Max 10 (used in BeMicro Max 10)
Micorsemi	Smart Fusion 2	N/A	IGLOO 2
Lattice	N/A	ECP/Lattice	iCE40 / MachXO
Xilinx	Zynq	Virtex	Spartan-6

If you're hoping you can simply search for the name of the FPGA and find just the development kit you're looking for, you're probably going to get lost very quickly. The problem is that there are literally thousands of different combinations out there ranging in cost from hundreds to tens of thousands of dollars. Often just looking at the description between two parts, it isn't even obvious why one is five times the price of the other. Once you get a few projects under your belt, you will welcome this bounty of choice—but for now, how do you even know where to start?

That's where the BeMicro Max10 development board comes in: it is small, practical, and reasonably priced. It's powerful enough for you to do a lot of different things and it includes enough hardware built in to start building projects with practical real-world applications straight away. Every component is representative of what you'll find in industry. This board puts you on equal footing with the big boys, but without the big cost.

In subsequent sections we'll look at the BeMicro Max 10 and the other tools you'll need in this book.

■ **Tips** Please go to the following web site to order your BeMicro Max10 development board: http://www.arrow.com/bemicromax10.

2.2 The BeMicro Max 10: Our Weapon of Choice

The BeMicro MAX 10 development board is developed by Arrow. The purpose of this board is to demonstrate any many of the MAX 10 features as possible. Arrow's web site says it best: "A compact and low-cost hardware evaluation platform for a broad range of embedded applications." This makes it a great fit for our purposes. Figure 2-1 shows the BeMicro Max 10.

Figure 2-1. *Altera MAX 10 FPGA board*

The most attractive feature for us is the price. For only US$30 at the time of this writing, it should fit anyone's budget. In terms of price, it is also very competitive with similar boards on the market.

2.2.1   The Master: Altera MAX 10 FPGA

The BeMicro MAX 10 development board is based on a single Altera MAX® 10 FPGA. If you're wondering whether or not Altera offers the MAX 9, 8, 7, then the answer is no. For some reason Altera only has MAX® 10, MAX V (5), and MAX II (2). Strangely though, MAX® V and MAX® II are not even FPGA products, just in case things weren't confusing enough. They are Altera's CPLD (Complex Programmable Logic Device). In the next chapter we will describe what CPLDs are and what the big deal is of changing from a CPLD to FPGA. There are a lot of impressive features offered in the MAX® 10 FPGA, such as an analog-to-digital converter (ADC) block, a temperature-sensing diode, and flash memory. In case you wanted to find out more about the FPGA specifically, the part number of the FPGA on our BeMicro MAX 10 is 10M08DAF484C8G.

Here is a brief summary of the features in this FPGA.

- 8,000 logic elements (LEs)—Look-up table (LUT)/logic array block

- 378 Kbit embedded SRAM (static random access memory). Altera name: M9k

- 256 Kbit user flash memory (UFM)—You can use it to store anything you like

- Non-volatile self-configuration flash memory (CFM)—This is used to store the FPGA configuration file

- Two phase locked loops (PLLs)—Very useful for creating clocks inside the FPGA

- 24 18x18-bit multipliers—DSP block: These are hard (i.e., burned into silicon rather than made up of LEs from the FPGA itself) which means it runs really fast!

- 1 ADC block with 18 channels—17 of them are external inputs and 1 is the FPGA internal temperature sensor

- 250 general-purpose input/outputs (I/O)—You can use them to do a lot of different input and output at the same time

This version of the MAX 10 FPGA brings logic element densities up to 8K logic elements. It looks small compared with all other big FPGAs, but it can provide us with enough logic gates for our needs. Each logic element is equal to around a 25 logic gate design plus one flip-flop. 8k logic elements then are roughly equivalent to 400,000 transistors. Consider for a moment that in the early to mid-1980s a high-end personal computer's CPU had well under 100,000 transistors in it. Can you even begin to imagine what's possible with 400,000 transistor logic gates?

The MAX 10 includes analog block (ADCs and temperature-sensing diodes), which enables the device to be used in system monitoring applications. Figure 2-2 shows the basic blocks location on the chip. It may be easy for you to figure out what the FPGA can do from the figure. The LUT, M9K block ram, and DSP block are very interesting and important basic blocks in Altera FPGAs. In Part II of this book, we will describe these basic blocks in more detail with design examples.

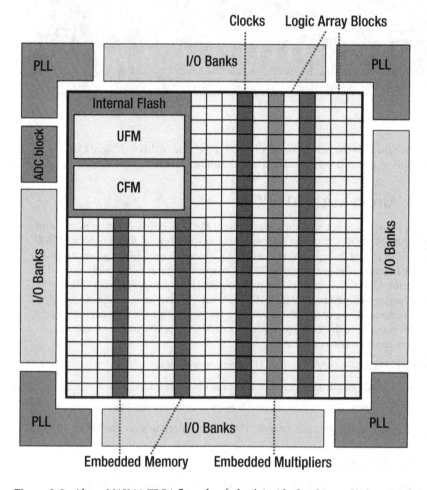

Figure 2-2. *Altera MAX 10 FPGA floorplan (what's inside the chip and where it is located)*

With this kind of density, the MAX 10 can easily integrate an Altera Nios II soft-core embedded processor, turning it into a non-volatile almost instant-on SoC. Today, it can actually integrate "complete system-level designs," at least for a sufficiently modest definition of "system." (system definition: computer with inputs and outputs).

2.2.2   The Emissaries: BeMicro MAX 10 Board Features

The BeMicro MAX 10 board has a lot of features (emissaries) on the board. The board comes with an 80-pin edge connector interface. This interface can be used as input and/or output. The board includes a variety of peripherals such as 8MB SDRAM (synchronous dynamic random access memory), accelerometer, digital-to-analog converter (DAC), temperature sensor, thermal resistor, photo resistor, LEDs (light-emitting diodes), pushbuttons, and several different options for expansion connectivity. The board comes with an Altera USB Programmer (Altera calls it the USB-Blaster). The programmer is used not only for programming the MAX 10 FPGA but also for debugging the FPGA. Figure 2-3 shows all of the function blocks on the board. The way to power this development board is easy. All you need is your computer's USB port, as it only needs a very small amount of juice. Most of these features will be used in Part III and Part IV.

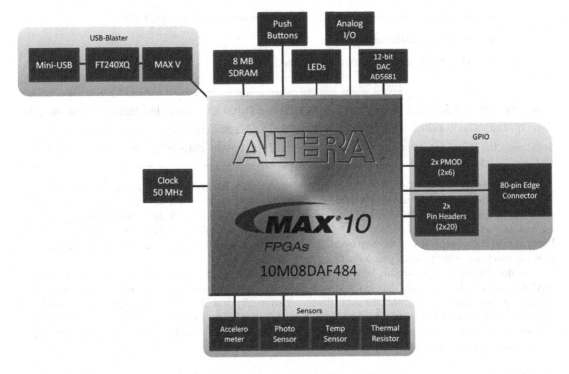

Figure 2-3. *BeMicro MAX 10 Block diagram*

The summary of the features is

- Embedded USB-Blaster for use with the Altera Programmer

- Clocking circuitry: 50 MHz oscillator

- External peripherals

  - 8MB SDRAM (4Mb x 16) (ISSI IS42S16400)

  - Accelerometer, 3-Axis, SPI interface (Analog Devices ADXL362)

  - DAC, 12-bit, SPI interface (Analog Devices AD5681)

  - Temperature sensor, I2C interface (Analog Devices ADT7420)

- Thermal resistor

- Photo resistor

- General user input or output

  - 8 user LEDs

  - 2 user Pushbuttons

- Expansion connectivity

  - Two 6-pin PMOD expansion headers

  - Two 40-pin prototyping headers which provide access to 64 digital I/O

  - One 6-pin analog input header

  - One 80-pin BeMicro card edge connector

■ **History**   The first SoC integrated circuit (IC) was a digital watch. It integrated a timekeeping circuit and LCD driver transistors on to a single Intel 5810 CMOS chip in 1974. Source: `http://www.computerhistory.org/ semiconductor/timeline/1974-digital-watch-is-first-system-on-chip-integrated-circuit-52.html`.

It's excellent for getting started and learning the basics, but at the same time it's ready to be the core of something big. We understand that you may have very good reasons to use another development board. Although the projects in this book are tailored for the BeMicro MAX 10, most of the example designs we use are standard and are applicable to any FPGA. However, if you have the BeMicro MAX 10, you will benefit of being able to follow explicit step-by-step instructions and won't have to worry about converting or adapting those instructions, which causes problems all by themselves.

We do take advantage of the on-board peripherals including the LEDs and ADC, and we use the MAX 10's block RAM for storing data in some projects. If your development board has different on-board peripherals, you can either connect the same device(s) externally or replace the relevant parts of the code with equivalents for the on-board peripherals you have. It's a bit harder to adapt to different internal FPGA features, so it's best to choose a development board based on an FPGA from the MAX 10 family if you want to follow along when we're using the block RAM.

■ **Tips**   The most updated information about BeMicro MAX 10 is in this Altera Wiki web site: `http://www.alterawiki.com/wiki/BeMicro_Max_10`.

2.3   Other Tools

I know the BeMicro MAX 10 module is self-contained, and you can start programming it with no other components, but limiting yourself to eight LEDs as outputs and four buttons as an input is rather restrictive. It's far more fun to hook up your FPGA to the real world. We won't be doing any hard-core electrical engineering—it's all going to be pretty basic stuff—and I don't expect you'll want to set up a workshop, but you will need a few essential tools to get the job done. You may even already have some of them already.

2.3.1   The Place to Connect Everything: The Breadboard

The most important item of all is the solderless electronics breadboard (Figure 2-4). Why is it called a breadboard? You definitely don't want to get bread near it—crumbs in those holes would be very bad. The name is a historical artefact: back when components were bigger, you'd build experimental circuits on a wooden breadboard, drilling holes in it and screwing down wires to make connections. The modern breadboard is a bit more civilized than that, but it still serves the same purpose: letting you build and modify a circuit with minimal effort. Don't forget to get jumper wires for the breadboard to connect things.

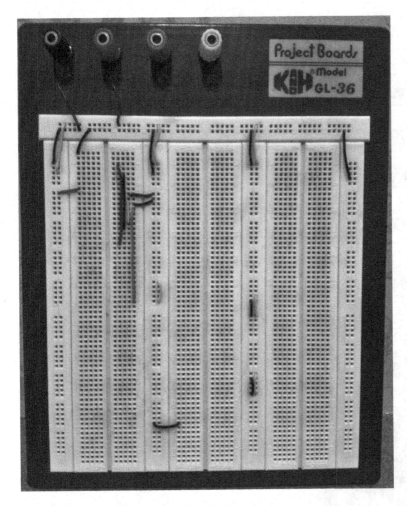

Figure 2-4. *My breadboard: I bought this board when I took my first electronic class.*

■ **Tips**   Use various colored solid-core jumper wire. You can color-code each connection according to its purpose and it is easier to insert in the breadboard's holes.

2.3.2   Making the Invisible Visible: The Multi-meter

A proper multi-meter for regular use around the home or electronic work can be had for less than $20. More expensive meters do not necessarily have more features. They give greater accuracy for professional work, and they are more rugged in their construction and durability. We only need the multi-meter to measure DC voltage, DC current, and resistance in this book's project. Any cheap multi-meter (Figure 2-5) will be accurate enough for all the projects in this book, so don't feel forced to pay more for something that comes with a calibration certificate too.

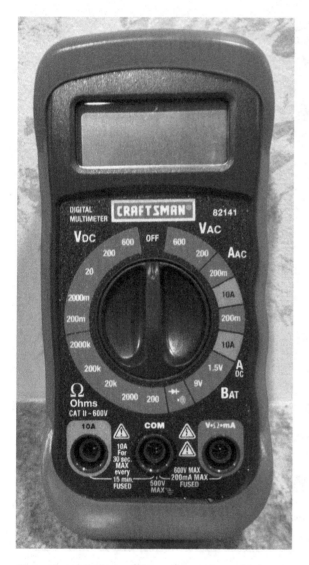

Figure 2-5. *My cheap multi-meter*

2.4   Wrap-up

This chapter briefly presented the features of the BeMicro MAX 10 board—one of the common development boards—and the MAX 10 FPGA. We provided links to some of the key online documentation and to the wiki forum. I recommend you download the MAX 10 FPGA user guide collection from the Altera MAX 10 support page (`www.altera.com/products/fpga/max-series/max-10/support.html`). Please don't read through the whole user guide, as it has more than 500 pages. It is for reference only. The preparation for hardware is done; next comes software!

"People who are really serious about software should make their own hardware."

—Alan Curtis Kay

CHAPTER 3

■ ■ ■

Lock and Load

Before you can begin writing VHDL (VHSIC Hardware Description Language) code for the FPGA (field-programmable gate array), you'll need a few items. To begin with, you'll need an FPGA board (e.g., the "MAX10" FPGA board, which we described in the Chapter 2) and development tools from the FPGA vendor. In this chapter we will walk you through how to download and install the toolchain in Windows.

3.1   Getting the Development Toolchain Up and Running

Nowadays, most of the FPGA companies provide three editions of their development toolchain: free edition, paid edition, and some form of pro edition. Table 3-1 lists them by brand.

Table 3-1. *FPGA Brands*

	Altera	Xilinx	Microsemi
Free edition	**Quartus Prime Lite Edition**	Vivado HL WebPACK	Libero Gold
Paid edition	Quartus Prime Standard Edition	Vivado HL Design Suite	Libero Standalone
Paid more edition	Quartus Prime Pro Edition	Vivado HL System Edition	Libero Platinum

Every few years, the companies' marketing departments need to come up with new names for their new products. The development toolchain gets updated to a new version every year or so, which means it is a new product. In 2015, the new name for the Altera toolchain is Quartus Prime. Previously it was known as Quartus II. This shouldn't pose any problems for you though, just remember to download at least version number **15.1**.

Altera Quartus Prime Lite edition (free edition) is all you need to use in this book. It is Altera's integrated development environment (IDE). The Quartus Prime Lite includes tools for creating and simulating the FPGA design, compiling (Synthesis + Place & Route) your design, and actually programming the FPGA. With this Lite edition, you can use Altera's industrial quality toolchain and development environment for free. The trade-off is that it will only work with the smaller devices and it will take longer to compile. Happily this isn't really an issue for us as by current standards, small means that it can build a microprocessor with memory and some interfaces (e.g., UARTs (**u**niversal **a**synchronous **r**eceiver/**t**ransmitter) and general-purpose input/output) which is still pretty powerful. When Altera says small, it means the MAX® series, Cyclone® series and Arria® II series. Altera's bigger (and thus more powerful) FPGAs are the Stratix® series and Arria 10. One of the reasons we picked the BeMicro 10 FPGA board was that the BeMicro10's FPGA (MAX 10) fits into the small category and thus we can use the toolchain for free. The Quartus Prime Lite Edition supports 64-bit Linux and Windows. When we wrote this book, the latest version of Quartus Prime Lite was v15.1.0. Ideally you should download the same version we are using, but if there is a newer version available, just be aware that there might be some differences between our instructions and what you see on your screen.

© Aiken Pang and Peter Membrey 2017
A. Pang and P. Membrey, *Beginning FPGA: Programming Metal*, DOI 10.1007/978-1-4302-6248-0_3

The Quartus Prime Lite Edition includes the following features that we will use in this book:

- Design—VHDL editor, Altera IPs (MegaCore IP Library), synthesizer, and fitter
- Simulation—ModelSim®-Altera Starter Edition
- Debug—SignalTap II Logic Analyzer (Built-in logic analyzer)
- Programmer—Quartus Prime Programmer

So you've got your development board and you're ready to build stuff, but you're not quite sure how to set up your tools? Or, maybe you've ordered the development board and you want to get everything set up so you're ready to play as soon as it arrives? Well, don't worry if you feel overwhelmed or confused by the Altera web site, it's not the easiest to navigate. The next section will guide you through downloading and installing Quartus Prime Lite edition.

■ **Note** The required toolchain depends on the exact FPGA you are targeting. Altera Quartus Prime Lite edition supports the MAX 10 family of FPGAs, including the device used in BeMicro 10. If you are planning to use a different development board, please ensure you can obtain a toolchain that supports it for an affordable price before you commit to the board.

3.2 Downloading Altera Tools

You'll need an Internet connection and a web browser to begin the download from the Altera web site (www.altera.com).

To get access to the latest and greatest from Altera, you'll need to create a *myAltera* Account. To create your *myAltera* account, just go to Altera web site at. That will bring you to a page similar to the one shown in Figure 3-1. Then follow the steps outlined in the next few sections.

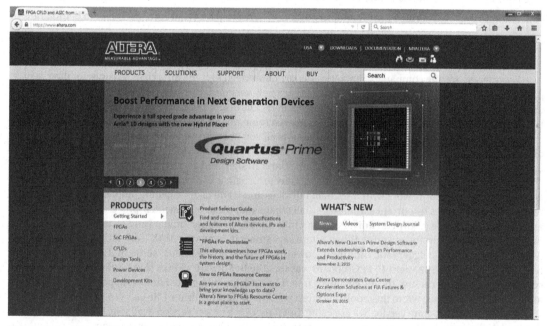

Figure 3-1. Altera web site front page

3.2.1   Altera Toolchains

Let's talk about what we are going to download from the Altera web site before we start the download process. (It may take you few hours to finish.) There are at least three files you are going to download.

- Quartus Prime (IDE + programmer) is the basic tool that you are going to use in this book.

- MAX10 FPGA design support file. Quartus Prime needs this file in order to support BeMicro10's MAX 10 FPGA board.

- ModelSim-Altera Starter edition software supports functional simulation for Altera devices. ModelSim simulator is the most popular choice for FPGA design simulation. The version we get from Altera has a 10,000 executable line limitation and is ideal for simulating smaller FPGA designs like the designs covered in this book.

3.2.2   Create an Altera Account

1. After you arrive at the Altera web site (www.altera.com), click **MYALTERA** in the top right-hand corner. You'll be given the option of either *myAltera Sign in* or *Don't have an account?*. Since you don't have a myAltera account yet, enter your e-mail address in the *Don't have an account?* section and click *Register* (Figure 3-2).

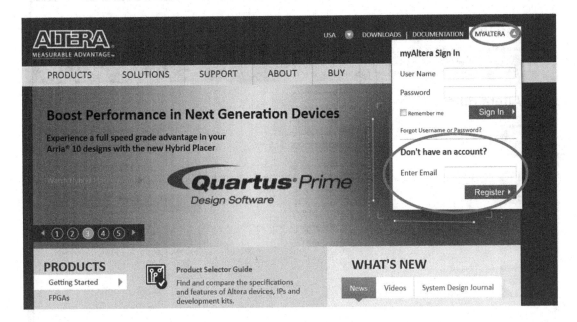

Figure 3-2. *myAltera Sign In*

2. You should then receive an e-mail containing a link to complete the registration process after submitting the form. Click the activation link in the e-mail to prove that you weren't providing a fake e-mail address, and you should be good to go. If you're signed in now, you should see WELCOME, "Your Name," and Sign Out links at the top of each Altera page where you previously saw the MYALTERA tab (Figure 3-3). At this point your myAltera account should ready to download Quarts® Prime Lite edition.

3. If you aren't signed in, click the **MYALTERA**, and enter the login details you chose a moment ago, and click **Sign In**.

4. Once you're sure you're signed in, follow the steps in the next section to download the Altera toolchain.

3.2.3 Download the Altera Toolchains

1. Once you are logged in to the Altera web site with your account, click **MENU** on the top menu. Figure 3-3 shows the login page. There will be a pop-up window as Figure 3-4. Click the top **SUPPORT** and click **Downloads**.

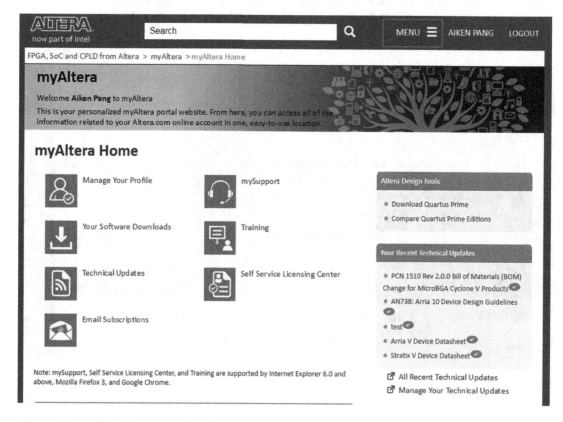

Figure 3-3. *myAltera Home page after login*

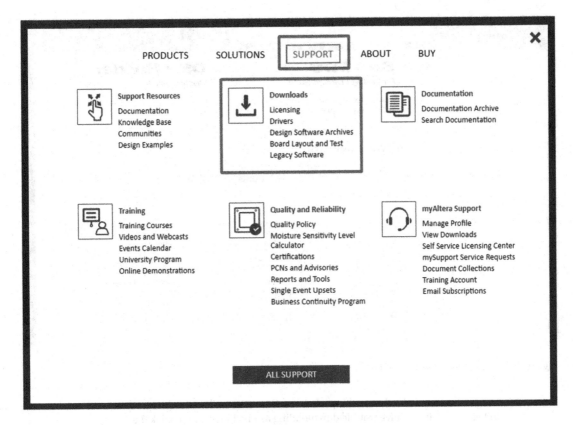

Figure 3-4. *Pop-up window for downloading the tools*

2. You'll be taken to the Quartus Prime edition's selection page. All you need to do is click Version *15.1* and click *Lite Edition* on the right-hand side (Figure 3-5). Or you can use this link (http://dl.altera.com/15.1/?edition=lite) to directly access the download page for the lite edition.

Figure 3-5. *Altera Downloads selection*

3. I suggest you download everything: click the ***Combined Files*** tab which is shown in Figure 3-6. If you have trouble downloading as one big file, then click the ***Individual Files*** tab which is shown in Figure 3-7. Regardless of which method you choose, you must select release version 15.1. Be sure to download the same version we are using.

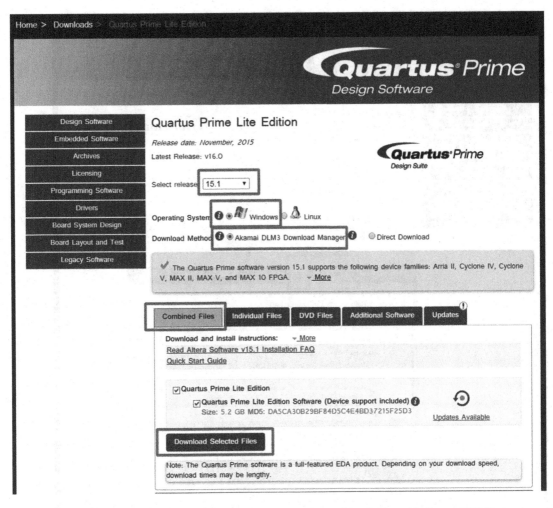

Figure 3-6. *Altera Quartus Prime Lite Edition selection page—Combined Files with Akamai DLM3 Download Manager*

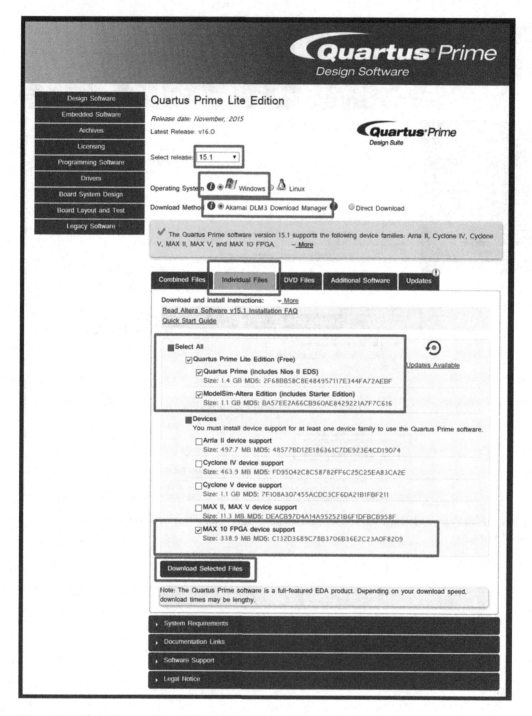

Figure 3-7. Altera Quartus Prime Lite Edition selection page—Individual Files with Akamai DLM3 Download Manager

■ Tips   Altera isn't limited to a single version. You can install newly released versions after you install 15.1 without having to uninstall it. Keep in mind, though, that it will take up to another 13GB of space. It's also possible to use the Akamai DLM3 Download Manager in a Window machine to download the Linux version.

3.2.3.1   Download Select Checklist

Before you click the ***Download Selected Files*** button, please double-check that you are using the same selection as the following list:

- Select release: 15.1

- Operating system: Windows

- Download method: Akamai DLM3 Download Manager (probably faster)/Direct Download

- For Individual Files tab selection: you need to download the following things
    - Quartus Prime (includes Nios II EDS)
    - ModelSim-Altera Edition (includes starter edition)
    - MAX 10 FPGA devices support

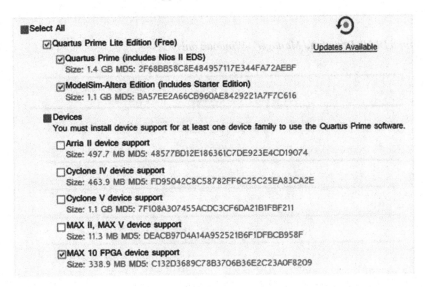

4. If everything looks good, then click Download Selected Files either in the Individual Files tab or the Combined Files tab. After you pick a download location and save, the download manager opens and begins the file download process (Figure 3-8). If you cannot use the download manager, select Direct Download and click the download arrow next to each file (Figure 3-9). You may ask for login to myAltera again in this step.

■ **Tip**   Select the location storage that can handle files bigger than 4GB (e.g., NTFS). It allows you to move the .tar file easily after you've finished the download.

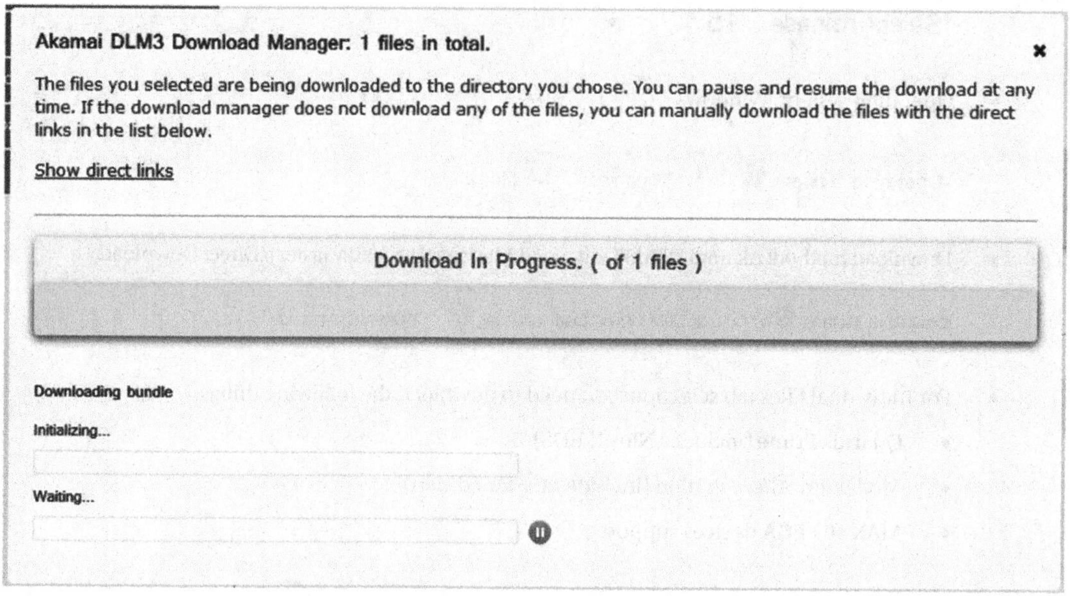

Akamai DLM3 Download Manager: 1 files in total.   ✖

The files you selected are being downloaded to the directory you chose. You can pause and resume the download at any time. If the download manager does not download any of the files, you can manually download the files with the direct links in the list below.

Show direct links

Download In Progress. (of 1 files)

Downloading bundle

Initializing...

Waiting...

Figure 3-8. Akamai DLM3 Download Manager—Windows only

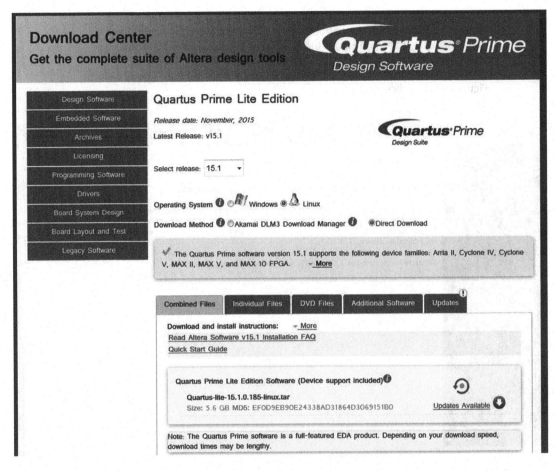

Figure 3-9. Altera Quartus Prime Lite Edition selection page—Combined Files with Direct Download

3.3　Install Altera Quartus Prime Lite Edition

Once you've gotten your hands on the Quartus Lite setup files, you can start to install them on your development machine. The process is fairly similar for Windows and Linux, so we describe Windows here. Make sure you have enough disk space for the installation—a full installation of the Altera tools consumes over 13GB.

If you're installing on Windows, you'll need the 64-bit version of Windows 7, Windows 8.1, or Windows Server 2008, preferably with the latest service pack and security updates. You'll need administrator access to install the software, and an Internet connection and web browser to obtain a license. The screenshots of the Windows installation process are captured on Windows 7.

If you prefer Linux, Altera only supports the use of their products on Red Hat Enterprise Linux 5.10 and Red Hat Enterprise Linux 6.5. If you aren't using one of these officially supported distributions, don't despair: the tools work pretty well on any modern Linux distribution, you just might need to do some tweaking to get it to work.

1. For the individual files method: if you are using Windows, run the file QuartusLiteSetup-<version>-windows.exe. For the combined file method, you must unzip the .tar file to extract the installation files. Examples of unzipping tools: WinZip, 7-zip, or WinRAR. You need to unzip the files on the same directory and run Setup.bat. Both ways will bring you to the Setup Wizard as in Figure 3-10. Just click *Next*.

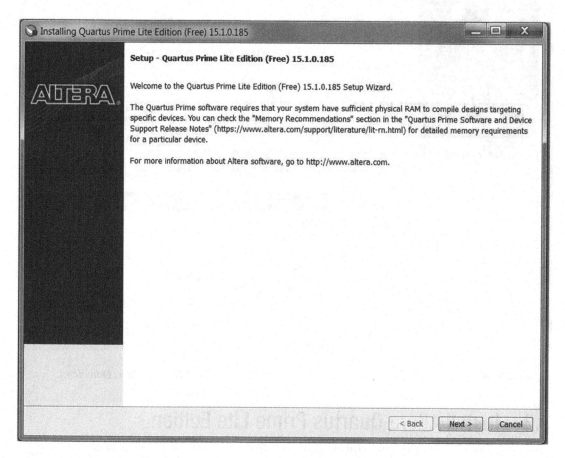

Figure 3-10. *Installing Quartus Prime Lite Edition (Free)*

2. Click "I accept the agreement" and then click *Next* (Figure 3-11).

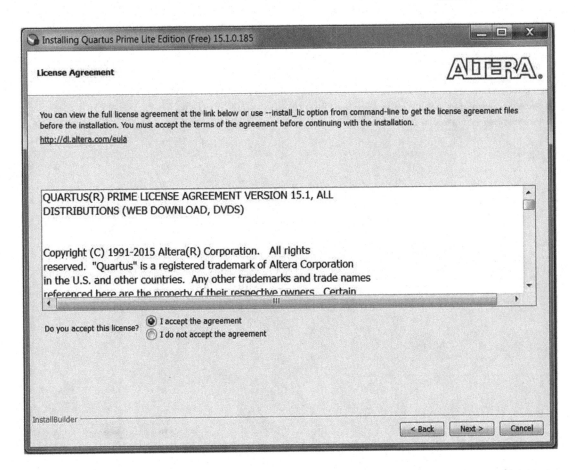

Figure 3-11. *License Agreement*

3. Select the installation location for the giant (>10GB) Quartus Prime Lite edition
   and click *Next* (Figure 3-12).

■ **Tips** You can install the Quartus Prime Lite on your external hard drive to save space from your
C:\, although of course this will mean you need your external drive handy if you want to use it.

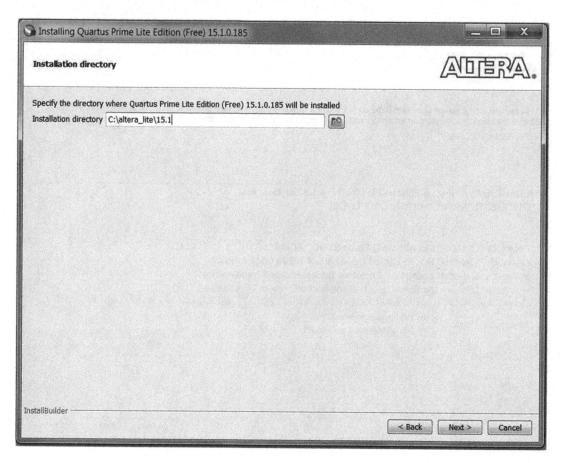

Figure 3-12. *Installation directory*

4. Check Quartus Prime Lite Edition (Free), MAX 10 FPGA, and ModelSim-Altera Starter Edition. It should look like Figure 3-13. Click *Next* to move forward.

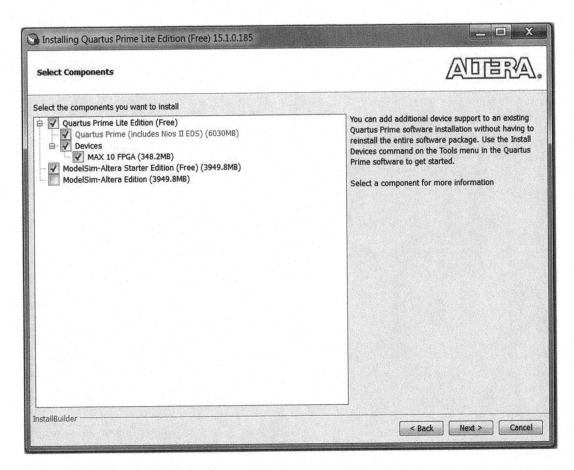

Figure 3-13. *Select components.*

5. This window shows how much space is needed to install the tools and asks for your approval to install (Figure 3-14) by clicking *Next*.

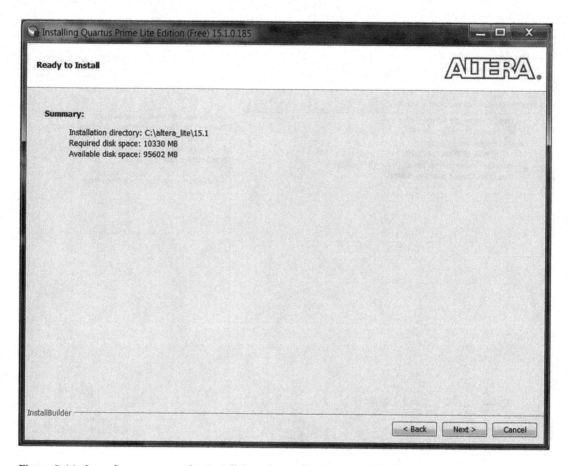

Figure 3-14. *It needs your approval to install the software (Ready to Install)*

6. This step just requires patience. You need to wait for your screen to change from Figure 3-15 to Figure 3-16. At the installation complete page, click **Finish** and you are only a few steps away from completing the install.

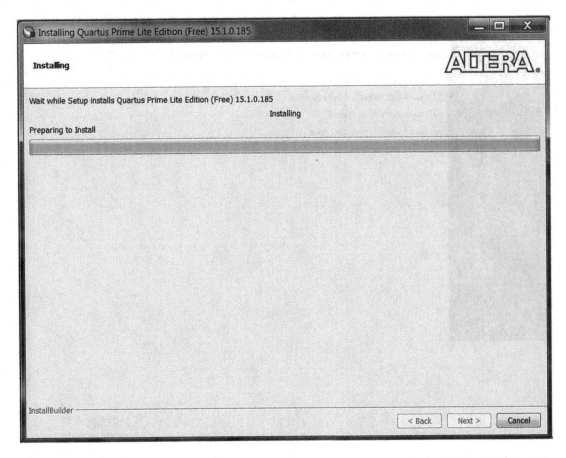

Figure 3-15. *Installing*

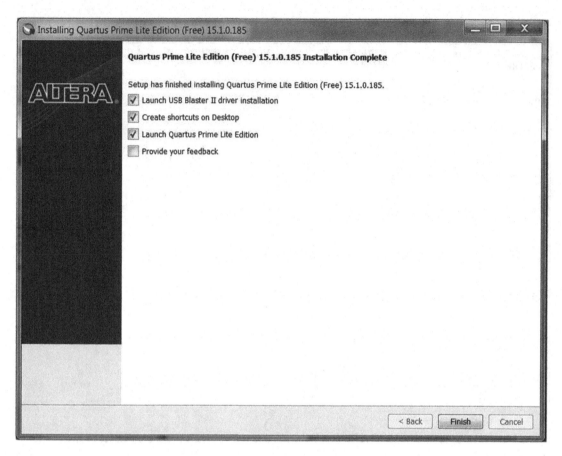

Figure 3-16. *Quartus Prime Lite installation complete*

7. Click **Next** on the Device Driver Installation Wizard (Figure 3-17) and Click **Finish** after it completes the installation (Figure 3-18). This step installs the Altera programmer, USB Blaster II, to your machine. You'll need this to copy your designs to the FPGA.

Figure 3-17. *Programmer Driver Installation Wizard*

Figure 3-18. *Completing the programmer driver installation*

8.   In order to use the free edition, you need to enable sending TalkBack data to Altera (Figure 3-19). Check **Enable sending TalkBack data to Altera** and Click **OK.**

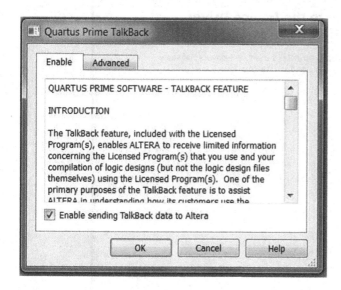

Figure 3-19. *Quartus Prime TalkBack*

9.   Select **Run the Quartus Prime software** and click **OK** in Figure 3-20. It means that you selected the Lite edition. The Lite edition doesn't need any software license to run it.

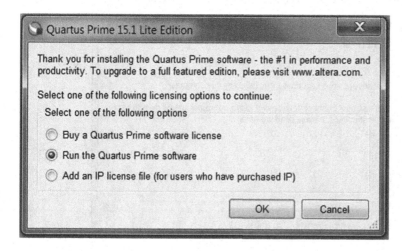

Figure 3-20. *Quartus Prime 15.1 Lite Edition licensing options*

10. Quartus Prime Lite Edition should be brought up in front of you, as in Figure 3-21. If it isn't, you can bring it up from your Start menu. In the Start menu, Quartus Prime 15.1 is your entry point. You should able to find it as in in Figure 3-22.

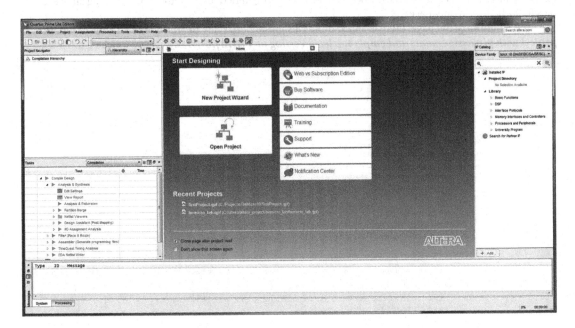

Figure 3-21. *Quartus Prime Lite Edition*

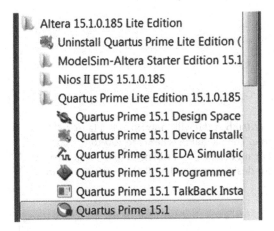

Figure 3-22. *Windows Start menu*

We finally have the Altera toolchain and development environment installed. In the next chapter, I will describe how to use the Quartus Prime Lite Edition.

3.4   Download BeMicro10 files and Documentation

You can download all of the BeMicro10 files and documentation from the Altera Wiki web site at the following link: `www.alterawiki.com/wiki/BeMicro_Max_10`. Altera does a good job of collecting all of the files for its boards in one place.

At the bottom of the page, there is an Example Design section. Click ***BeMicro Max 10 empty Quartus project with pin assignments and empty top level Verilog or VHDL file (Design Store link).*** Figure 3-23.

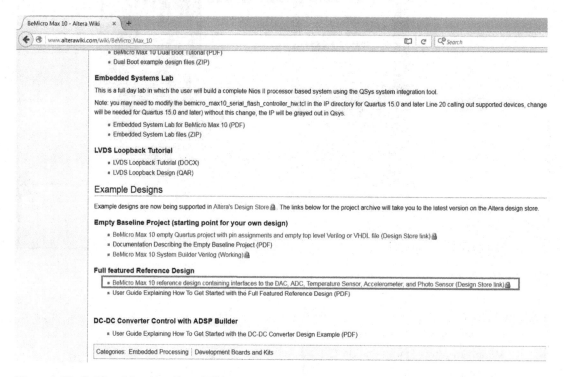

Figure 3-23. *BeMicro Max 10—Altera Wiki page*

It will bring you to the Altera design store. Click the ***15.1.0*** tab and it will show up as in Figure 3-24. Click the ***Download*** button to download the design example. The file name is `BeMicro_MAX10_top.par`. You should save it somewhere where you can easily find it again because you will need to use it in the next chapter. This file forms the basic building block for all of our designs. It includes all of the settings for the Altera Quartus Prime to build BeMicro MAX 10 projects.

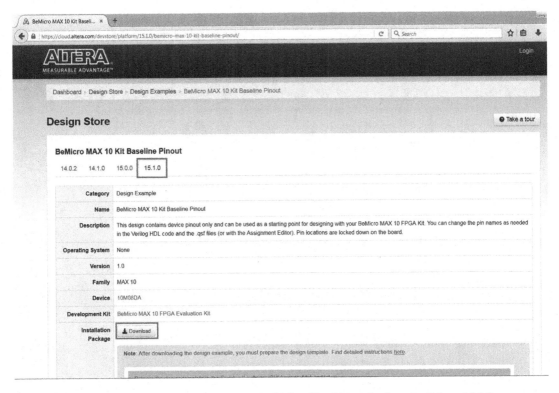

Figure 3-24. *Altera Design Store for BeMicroMax 10 kit baseline Pinout for Quartus Prime v15.1.0*

3.5 Summary

This chapter described different types of FPGA tools which are available from FPGA vendor. If you follow the guide you should know how to download and install the FPGA tools—Altera Quartus Prime. The Altera Quartus Prime will be used for the rest of the book.

Please make sure you get the following things done before moving to next chapter.

- Install Altera Quartus Prime Lite Edition 15.1.0 with support MAX10 devices

- Download BeMicro MAX 10 Kit Baseline Pinout file (BeMicro_MAX10_top.par).

Do you believe you are halfway to starting to compile your first FPGA design?

"Believe you can and you're halfway there."

—Theodore Roosevelt

CHAPTER 4

■ ■ ■

Hello World!

What do Knight Rider's KITT and Battlestar Galactica's Cylons have in common? That's right: undeniably awesome scanning LEDs (light-emitting diodes)! Now that we're set up, we'll recreate this on our development board. We'll go through the steps pretty quickly and then go back and take a look at how we got there in more detail. At this point we're still unfamiliar with the development environment, so the mechanics of each step are covered here. Don't worry, though, you only have to learn to do this stuff once, and I won't be telling you which button to click in every project. The basic steps are writing the code, simulating it to check that it does what we expect, and loading it on to the FPGA board.

Specifically, our example entails the following design steps:

1. Launch Quartus Prime and create a new project

2. Write code

3. Implement design

4. Simulate design

5. Burn it!

4.1   Launch Quartus Prime and Create a New Project

In this section you'll use Altera Quartus Prime to create a new project for your BeMicro MAX 10 FPGA development board. You will do this step multiple times in this book when you walk through all the examples in this book.

1. Click **Start ➤ All Programs ➤ Altera 15.1.x.xxx Lite Edition ➤ Quartus Prime Lite Edition 15.1.x.xxx ➤ Quartus Prime 15.1**, or click the shortcut on your desktop. The Quartus Prime Lite Edition will open. The first time you open Quartus Prime, it look like Figure 4-1.

© Aiken Pang and Peter Membrey 2017
A. Pang and P. Membrey, *Beginning FPGA: Programming Metal*, DOI 10.1007/978-1-4302-6248-0_4

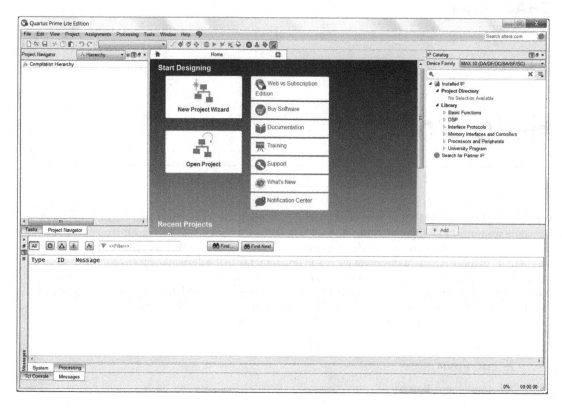

Figure 4-1. *Quartus Prime Lite Edition*

The splash screen will be displayed while it loads, and you'll be presented with the main development environment window. Assuming you haven't gone ahead and created a project already, you should see a toolbar at the top with the usual file, edit, view, and project menu options; the Project Navigator on the left; and the Message pane at the bottom with tabs for errors, warnings, and search results. You can show or hide toolbars and panels with the options in the View menu.

2.   Create a new project by clicking **File ➤ New Project Wizard** or click the **New Project Wizard** on the Home page tab (Figure 4-2).

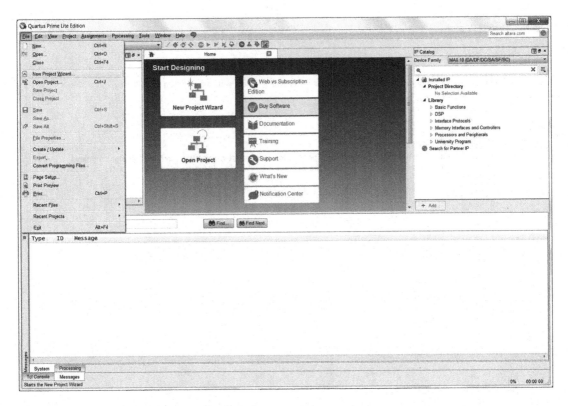

Figure 4-2. *Create a new project from the File tab or Home Page*

3. The new project wizard will open (Figure 4-3), which is where we decide what kind of project we want. The first page is only an introduction. Click **Next**.

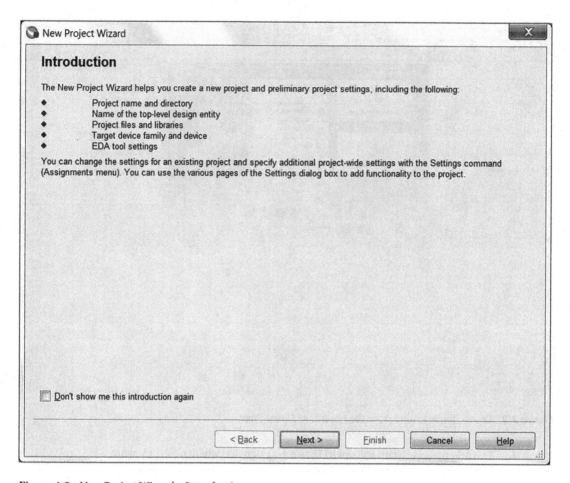

Figure 4-3. *New Project Wizard—Introduction*

4. Enter the information shown in Figure 4-4 on the Directory, Name, Top-Level Entity page of the New Project Wizard and then click **Next.** If the working directory for this project is a new location, the software will ask you "Do you want to create it?" Just click **YES**. This page is where you choose the location and name for the project as well as the name of top-level design entity, which is the name of the design. The Quartus Prime will first search for the top-level design entity in the project folder. Most of the time the project name and top-level design entity are the same.

-   Working directory for this project: **C:/BeMicroMax10/ch04**

-   Name of this project: **scanner**

-   Top-level design entity for this project: **scanner**

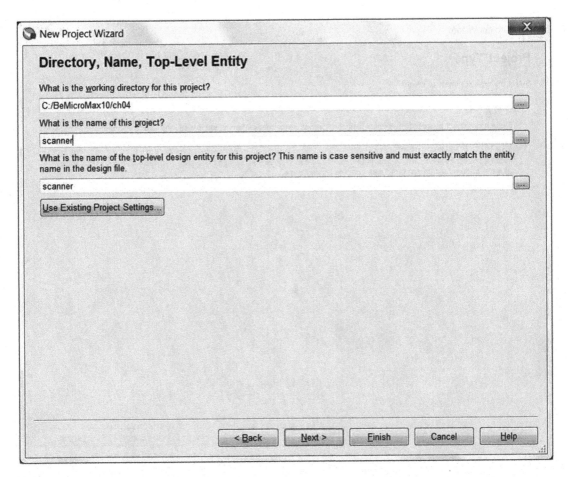

Figure 4-4. *Quartus Prime New Project Wizard dialog box—Directory, Name, Top-Level Entity*

5. Select **Project template** and then click **Next** (shown in Figure 4-5).

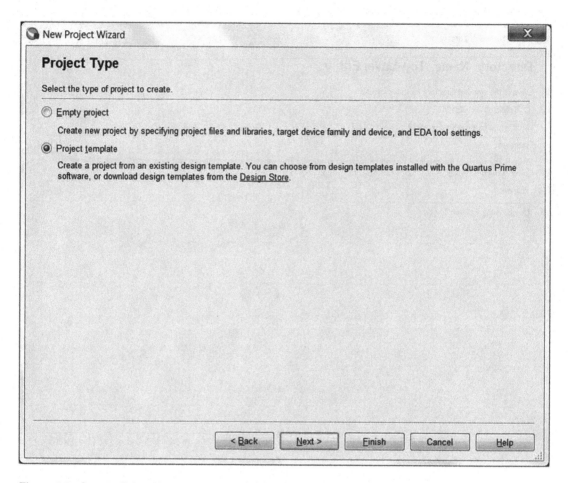

Figure 4-5. *Quartus Prime New Project Wizard dialog box—Project Type*

6. If you downloaded the file BeMicro_MAX10_top.par from Chapter 3, then please go to step 12. Take the following steps to download the project template. Click **Design Store** (Figure 4-6) which will open an Internet browser and access the Altera Design Store. Please follow the steps 7-11 to download the BeMicro Max10 project template from the Altera Design Store. You can use the following project template link to download it directly or download the BeMicro Max10 project template and then go to step 12:

    https://cloud.altera.com/devstore/platform/335/download/

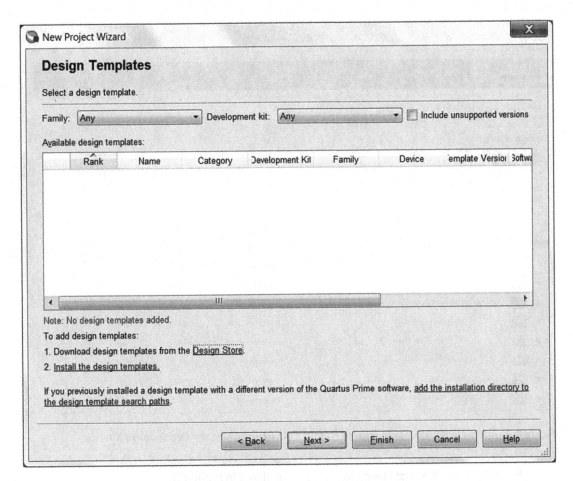

Figure 4-6. Quartus Prime New Project Wizard dialog box—Design Templates

7. Select the information shown in the Design Store web page in Figure 4-7:
   https://cloud.altera.com/devstore/?acds_version=15.1.0

   • Family: **MAX 10**

   • Category: **Development Kit**

8. Click the **BeMicro MAX 10 FPGA Evaluation Kit** in the page as Figure 4-7 shows.

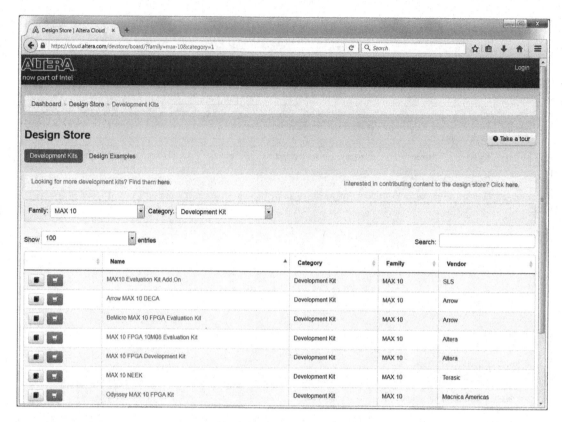

Figure 4-7. Altera Design Store with selected Family: MAX10 and Category: Development Kit

9. Click **View all design examples** in the page as shown in Figure 4-8.

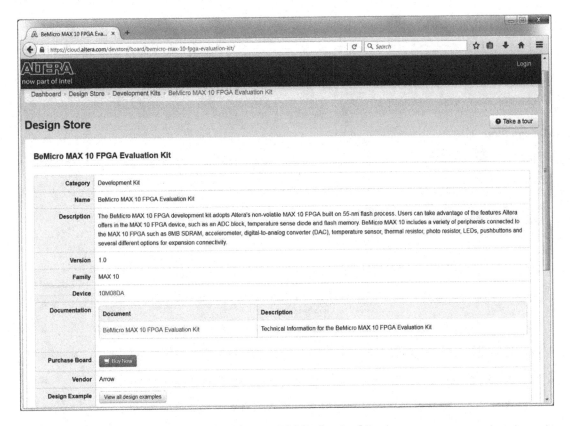

Figure 4-8. *Altera Design Store—BeMicro MAX 10 FPGA Evaluation kit*

10. Select the Category shown in the design examples page. It will look like Figure 4-9. Look for the name: **BeMicro MAX 10 Kit Baseline Pinout** and then click the name to bring you to our final destination.

- Category: **Design Example**

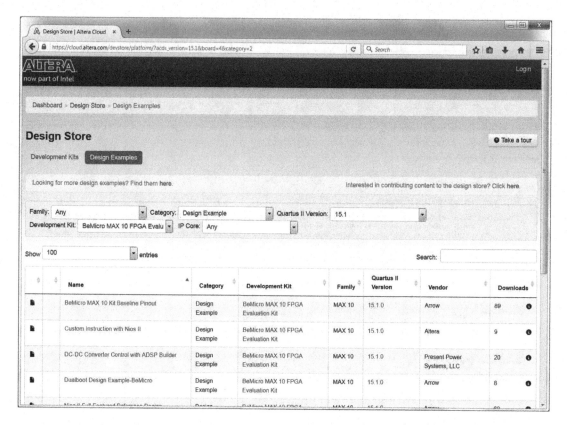

Figure 4-9. *Altera Design Store—Category: Design Example: BeMicro MAX10 Kit Baseline Pinout*

11. Click **Download** on the BeMicro MAX 10 Kit Baseline Pinout page (Figure 4-10). The file name is BeMicro_MAX10_top.par. Go to the next step.

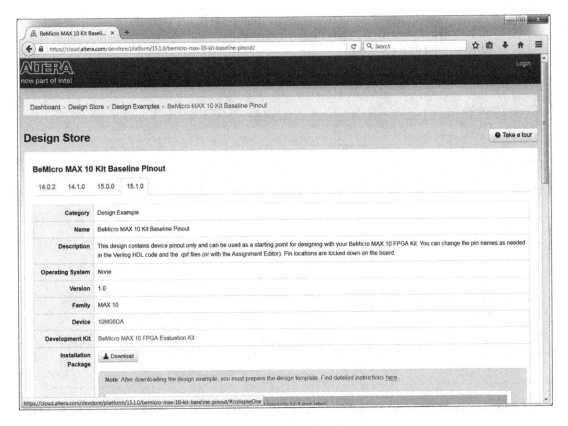

Figure 4-10. *Altera Design Store—BeMicro MAX 10 Kit Baseline Pinout*

12. Click **Install the design template** in the New Project Wizard—Design Templates. Enter the location of the BeMicro_MAX10_top.par and click OK (Figure 4-11).

- Design template file: <Location you store the file>\BeMicro_MAX10_top.par

- Destination directory: no need to change.

Figure 4-11. *Design Template installation*

13. The design templates page will change from Figure 4-5 to Figure 4-12. Click the **BeMicro MAX10 Kit Baseline Pinout** templates (it should highlight the template) and then click **Next**.

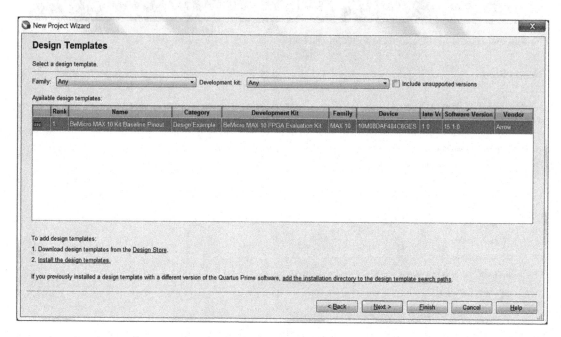

Figure 4-12. New Project Wizard—Design Templates with BeMicroMAX10 kit Baseline Pinout template install

14. This is the last step to set up the BeMicro MAX 10 project. Figure 4-13 shows a summary of the project. Make sure your summary is the same as this one and then click **Finish.**

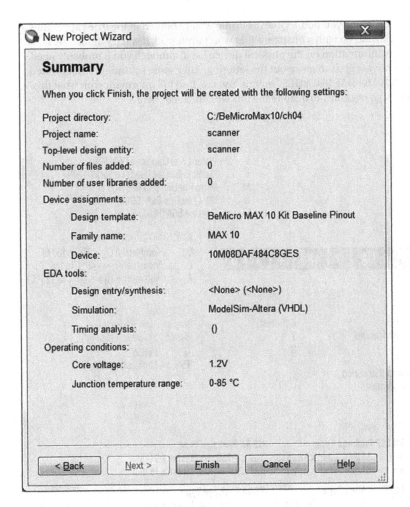

Figure 4-13. *New Project Wizard—Summary*

The summary shows the information we entered previously but also something new. The new things come from the project template. As each FPGA and board is different, it is really important to make sure you've got the right template loaded. If you don't, Quartus will wire things up incorrectly, not only causing strange behavior (assuming it actually does anything) but also giving you a headache as you try to work out why, after following the instructions perfectly, the device refuses to work. You should see the following information in the Summary, if you don't, you can get it from Assignments ➤ Device and Assignments ➤ Settings ➤ EDA Tool Settings ➤ Simulation:

- Device Family: **MAX 10 (DA/DF/DC/SA/SF/SC)**

- Name: **10M08DAF484C8GES**

- Simulation: **ModelSim-Altera (VHDL)**

Again, it's important to get this right: if you don't, Quartus Prime won't know what the true capabilities of the device are, and you're likely to end up with a bitstream that won't even work if you try uploading it. You can read most of the necessary information on the physical device itself, although you'll probably need good light and maybe even a magnifying glass to make out the lettering. After some squinting, I determined that mine says "ALTERA® MAX®10 10M08DAF484C8GES" on top. You can find full information on what this means in Altera's datasheet, but I'll go over how to decode the bits we care about here.

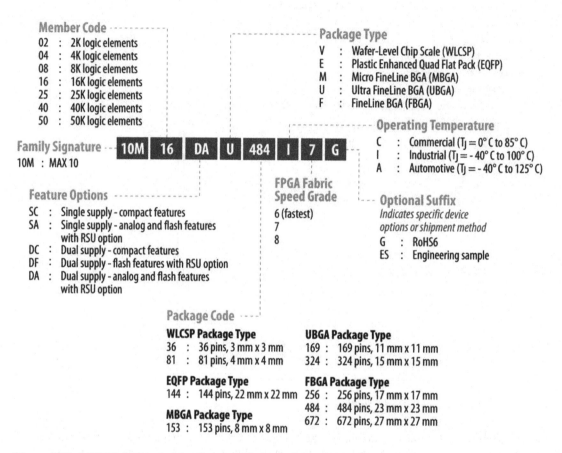

Figure 4-14. *MAX 10 device marking decode table from Altera MAX10 datasheet*

Altera provides a cheat sheet (Figure 4-14) from its datasheet.

- 10M: **MAX 10**

- 08: **8K logic elements**

- DA: **Dual Supply - analog and flash features with RSI option**

- F: **Fine Line BGA (FBPA). It is one of the package type**

- 484: **484 pins,** Package size is **23mm x 23 mm**

- C: **Commercial temperature range** (0° C to 85° C)

- 8: **Slowest speed grade**

- G: **RoHS6**

- ES: **Engineering sample. That's why the BeMicroMAx10 only sale for $30**

We're showing you this here because it's good practice to know and understand the equipment you're actually using, especially if you decide to go it alone and build your systems. However, if you don't understand everything here, don't worry about it.

4.2   Write Code

Now that you've got a project open, you should see the Project Navigator panel on the left (Figure 4-15). The top left shows your project hierarchy (default) with a choice of five views: Hierarchy, Files, Design Unit, IP Components, and Revisions. The Hierarchy view shows how everything fits together; the Files view shows all the files included in the project, which is usually a superset of the Hierarchy. In this example we will only use these two views.

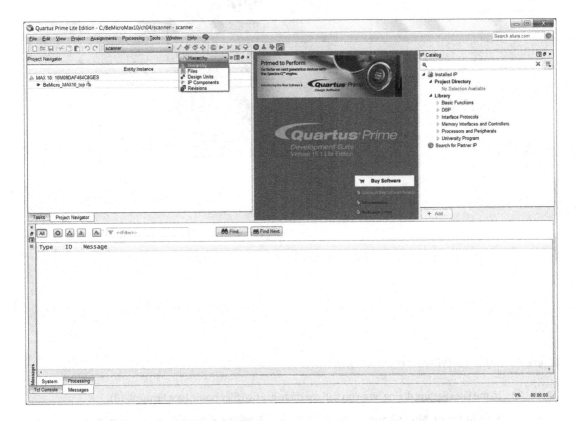

Figure 4-15.   *Quartus Prime—Project Navigator*

This design example will be a stand-alone flashing LED without any user inputs. The design block diagram will look like Figure 4-16. The only input is clock and the outputs are eight LED drivers.

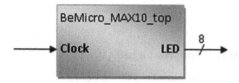

Figure 4-16. *Scanner design block diagram*

1. The first thing to do is add a BeMicro MAX10 vhdl template file. Click **Project ➤ Add/Remove Files in Project…** from the Quartus Prime menu to open the Files Setting dialog box. It should look like Figure 4-17.

Figure 4-17. *Quartus Prime—Project Navigator*

2. In the Files Setting dialog box, you will see there are two files name (see Figure 4-18).

   • **BeMicro_MAX10_top.v**: Verilog HDL file. We will need to replace this file with VHDL file which is provided by the template.

   • **BeMicro_MAX10_top.sdc**: Synopsys Design Constraints file. The Quartus needs this file to know about our development board (e.g., How fast the clock run on this board).

3. Select **BeMicro_MAX10_top.v** and then click **Remove**. Enter **BeMicro_MAX10_top.vhd** in File Name box and then click **Add** (Figure 4-18). Click **Apply.** The completed File Settings should look like Figure 4-19. It has two files. The first one is **BeMicro_MAX10_top.vhd**. The second one is **BeMicro_MAX10_top.sdc**. If the files are included correctly, then click **OK** (Figure 4-19).

■ **Tips .vhd, .vhdl**   are the file extensions used by VHDL. As .vhd is the most common one, we will use .vhd for all the design files used in this book.

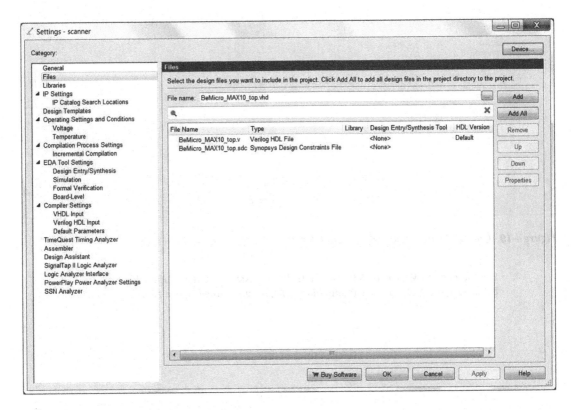

Figure 4-18. *Quartus Prime—Files Settings*

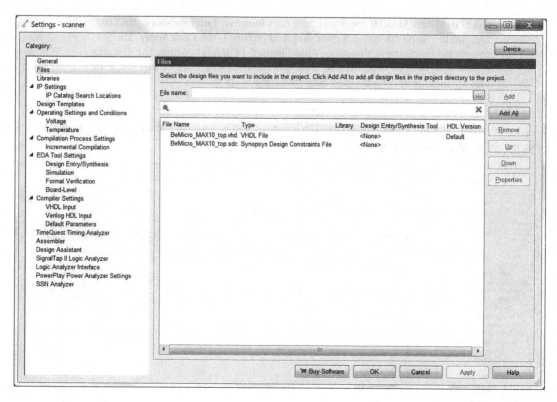

Figure 4-19. *Quartus Prime—Files Settings Completed*

4. Double-click **BeMicro_MAX10_top** in the Project Navigator. It will open the
   BeMicro_MAX10_top.vhd file in the middle of Quartus Prime (Figure 4-20).

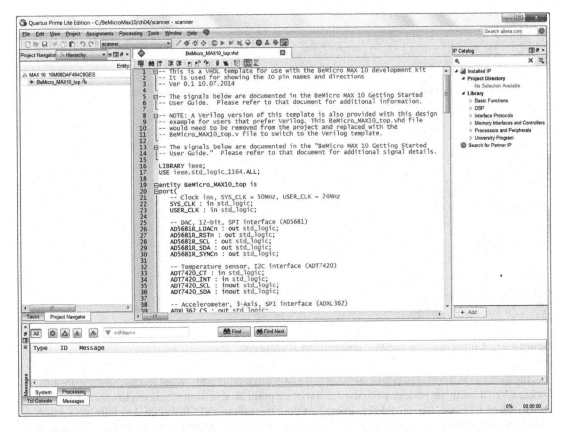

Figure 4-20. *Open BeMicro_MAX10_top.vhd template file*

5. The following steps are going to modify this `BeMicro_MAX10_top.vhd` file (read the following Tips before you start to modify):

a. Delete all the lines from 23 to 70 and 73 to 213.

b. Delete the semicolon at the end of the `USER_LED : out std_logic_vector(8 downto 1)`.

■ **Tips** Back up the BeMicro_MAX10_top.vhd file before you start to modify it. Alternatively, you can recreate the project to get the original .vhdl file back. We will use this backup filter in later chapters.

---

c. Add this `USE ieee.numeric_std.all;` on `line 18`. It should look like Figure 4-21.

```
         BeMicro_MAX10_top.vhd            ⊠

 1  ⊟-- This is a VHDL template for use with the BeMicro MAX 10 development kit
 2     |-- It is used for showing the IO pin names and directions
 3     -- Ver 0.1 10.07.2014
 4
 5  ⊟-- The signals below are documented in the BeMicro MAX 10 Getting Started
 6     |-- User Guide.  Please refer to that document for additional information.
 7
 8  ⊟-- NOTE: A Verilog version of this template is also provided with this design
 9     -- example for users that prefer Verilog. This BeMicro_MAX10_top.vhd file
10     -- would need to be removed from the project and replaced with the
11     -- BeMicro_MAX10_top.v file to switch to the Verilog template.
12
13  ⊟-- The signals below are documented in the "BeMicro MAX 10 Getting Started
14     |-- User Guide." Please refer to that document for additional signal details.
15
16    LIBRARY ieee;
17    USE ieee.std_logic_1164.ALL;
18    USE ieee.numeric_std.all;
19  ⊟entity BeMicro_MAX10_top is
20  ⊟port(
21        -- Clock ins, SYS_CLK = 50MHz, USER_CLK = 24MHz
22        SYS_CLK : in std_logic;
23        -- LED outs
24        USER_LED : out std_logic_vector(8 downto 1)
25      );
26  ⊣
27    end entity BeMicro_MAX10_top;
28  ∟
29  ⊟architecture arch of BeMicro_MAX10_top is
30  ⊟begin
31  ∟end architecture arch;
```

Figure 4-21. Editing BeMicro_MAX10_top.vhd steps a-c finished

Before we go to the next step, let's see what we have in this template file. What you see here (Figure 4-21) is a basic VHDL template which can be used as a starting point for you. Best practice is to only have a single **entity** (Figure 4-21 line 19) per .vhd file. An entity is the basic unit of a VHDL design. An entity has a name and a well-defined interface/**port** (lines 20-25), so it can be instantiated and hooked up to stuff. It also has an **architecture** (line 29) that defines what it does.

The entity name (in our example it's BeMicro_MAX10_top) usually matches the file name. Entity names must be valid VHDL identifiers and must be unique within a project. What's a valid VHDL identifier? It's a string of characters starting with a letter and containing only letters, numbers, and/or underscores. VHDL identifiers are case insensitive, so BeMicro and bEmICRO are the same from the toolchain's point of view. MAX10 is a valid identifier, but 10MAX isn't because it doesn't start with a letter. The architecture name also has to be a valid VHDL identifier, but its value isn't really important as it's local to the entity. You generally use it to indicate the level of abstraction in your implementation. I tend to call it rtl (register-transfer level) from force of habit, but anything sensible will do (the template uses arch as shorthand for architecture).

The template also defined the input and output ports. Our only input (line 22) is a 50 MHz clock signal (not a clock that tells you the time, a clock that just ticks 50 million times a second), and our outputs (line 24) are eight lines driving LEDs.

There are a few things you should be able to pick up about the language just by looking at the template file:

Anything after -- (two hyphens) until the end of the line is a comment and is ignored by the toolchain. The syntax is vaguely reminiscent of Pascal with English-like keywords, parentheses for grouping; and semicolons as statement terminators, and it's relatively insensitive to whitespace (spaces, tabs and line breaks).

> d. All we really need to do in this step is populate the empty architecture with our desired behavior—flashing the LEDs in turn. Fill in the blanks to make it look like Listing 4-1.

Listing 4-1. Architecture for Flashing LEDs in Turn Behavior VHDL Code

```vhdl
architecture arch of BeMicro_MAX10_top is
signal divider_counter : unsigned(23 downto 0) := (others =>'0');
signal state           : unsigned(3 downto 0)  := (others =>'0');
signal scanningLED     : std_logic_vector(8 downto 1);
begin
divider_p: process (SYS_CLK)
    begin
        if (rising_edge(SYS_CLK)) then
            if (divider_counter = to_unsigned(9999999,24)) then
                divider_counter <= (others =>'0');
                if (state = to_unsigned(14,4)) then
                    state <= to_unsigned(1,4);
                else
                    state <= state + 1;
                end if;
            else
                divider_counter <= divider_counter + 1;
                state <= state;
            end if;
        end if;
    end process;
led_driver_p: process (state)
    begin
    case to_integer(state) is
        when 1       => scanningLED <= "10000000";
        when 2|14     => scanningLED <= "01000000";
        when 3|13     => scanningLED <= "00100000";
        when 4|12     => scanningLED <= "00010000";
        when 5|11     => scanningLED <= "00001000";
        when 6|10     => scanningLED <= "00000100";
        when 7|9      => scanningLED <= "00000010";
        when 8       => scanningLED <= "00000001";
        when others => scanningLED <= "00000000";
    end case;
end process;
        USER_LED <= not scanningLED;
end architecture arch;
```

The finished architecture should look like Figure 4-22.

```
15
16   LIBRARY ieee;
17   USE ieee.std_logic_1164.ALL;
18   USE ieee.numeric_std.all;
19  ⊟entity BeMicro_MAX10_top is
20  ⊟port(
21       -- Clock ins, SYS_CLK = 50MHz, USER_CLK = 24MHz
22       SYS_CLK : in std_logic;
23       -- LED outs
24       USER_LED : out std_logic_vector(8 downto 1)
25   );
26
27   end entity BeMicro_MAX10_top;
28
29  ⊟architecture arch of BeMicro_MAX10_top is
30   -- Chapter 4: Scanner Example codes declarations section -- Below --
31   signal divider_counter : unsigned(23 downto 0) := (others =>'0');
32   signal state           : unsigned(3 downto 0)  := (others =>'0');
33   signal scanningLED     : std_logic_vector(8 downto 1);
34   -- Chapter 4: Scanner Example codes declarations section -- Above --
35  ⊟begin
36   -- Chapter 4: Scanner Example codes Part-d -- Below --
37  ⊟divider_p: process (SYS_CLK)
38   begin
39  ⊟    if (rising_edge(SYS_CLK)) then
40  ⊟        if (divider_counter = to_unsigned(9999999,24)) then
41           divider_counter <= (others =>'0');
42  ⊟            if (state = to_unsigned(14,4)) then
43  ⊢               state <= to_unsigned(1,4);
44  ⊟            else
45                  state <= state + 1;
46  ⊢            end if;
47  ⊟        else
48               divider_counter <= divider_counter + 1;
49               state <= state;
50  ⊢        end if;
51  ⊢    end if;
52  ⊢ end process;
53  ⊟led_driver_p: process (state)
54   |      begin
55  ⊟      case to_integer(state) is
56           when 1      => scanningLED <= "10000000";
57           when 2|14   => scanningLED <= "01000000";
58           when 3|13   => scanningLED <= "00100000";
59           when 4|12   => scanningLED <= "00010000";
60           when 5|11   => scanningLED <= "00001000";
61           when 6|10   => scanningLED <= "00000100";
62           when 7|9    => scanningLED <= "00000010";
63           when 8      => scanningLED <= "00000001";
64           when others => scanningLED <= "00000000";
65  ⊢      end case;
66  ⊢end process;
67       USER_LED <= not scanningLED;
68   -- Chapter 4: Scanner Example codes Part-d -- Above --
69   end architecture arch;
```

Figure 4-22. *Editing BeMicro_MAX10_top.vhd step d finished*

4.3 Implement Design

Don't worry if the VHDL code doesn't make sense to you yet; all will be shown in good time. For now, save the **BeMicro_MAX10_top.vhd** file and tell Quartus Prime to try to implement it. You can do the following to implement the design:

1. Click **Hierarchy** and select **Files** in the Project Navigator tab. In Files mode, the project navigator will show you all the files in the project.

2. Right-click the BeMicro_MAX10_top.vhd file and click **Set as Top-Level Entity** from the context menu (Figure 4-23). This step is very important to ensure that Quartus Prime picks the right entity (vhdl file) as the top-level file. This is because Quartus Prime will start to implement the design from the top-level entity. Sometimes people refer to this as the *top module*—the top of the design hierarchy, where submodules are instantiated and linked together (conceptually similar to the main function in a C program).

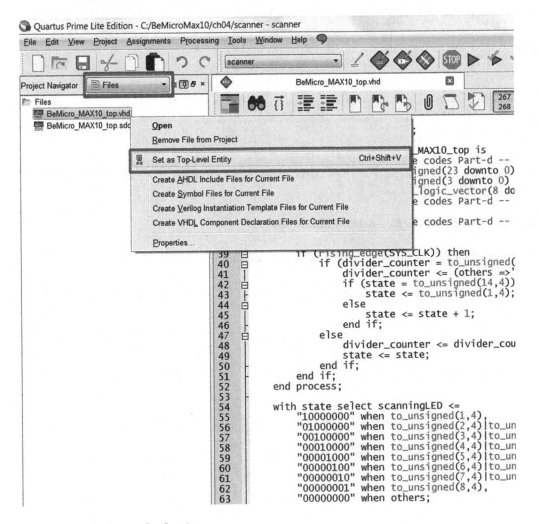

Figure 4-23. Setting top-level entity

3. Double-click the BeMicro_MAX10_top.sdc file which is the timing file for this project. Add # in the beginning of line 14 which comments out an unused USER_CLK and adds **derive_clock_uncertainty** on line 32 (Figure 4-24). This step can eliminate false warnings from Quartus Prime in the compile time.

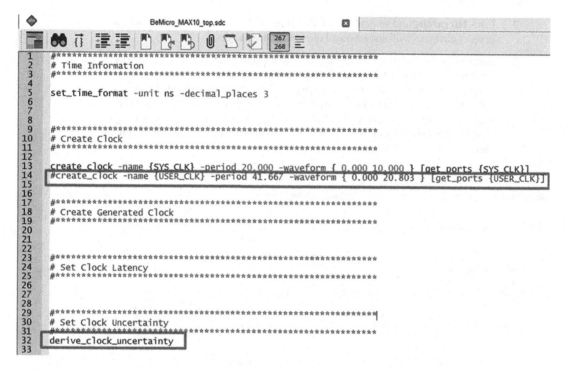

Figure 4-24. *Timing constraint file—BeMicro_MAX10_top.sdc*

4. Click the **Task** tab to switch to the Tasks view. It will look like Figure 4-25.

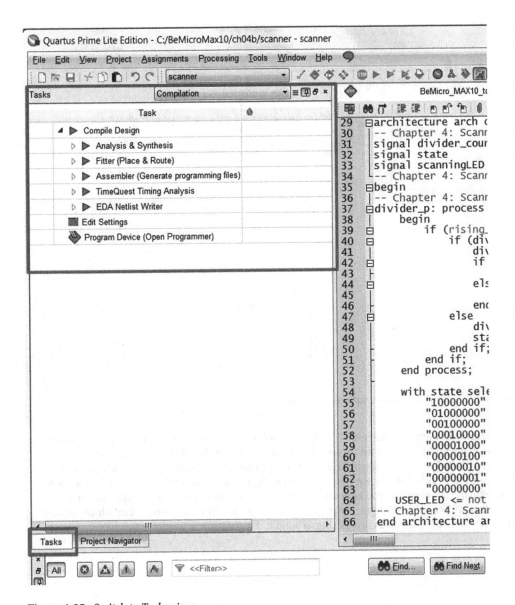

Figure 4-25. *Switch to Tasks view.*

5. To start the implementation process, you can use any of the following methods. Figure 4-26 highlights the locations.

    •   Click **Processing ➤ Start Compilation**

    •   Press keyboard <**Ctrl**> + **L**

    •   Click the **blue "play" triangle icon** in the icon bar below the menu bar

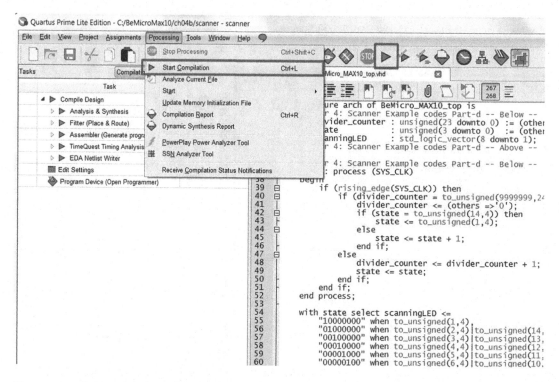

Figure 4-26. *How to start the implementation of the design*

Quartus Prime will change to Figure 4-27 to show the implementation status. The Compilation report tab will show up in the middle of Quartus Prime. The task list on the left-hand side will start to show each task status and its finish time. The Stop icon will "light" up and will allow you to stop the process. In the lower right corner, it will show 100% when it has finished doing the implementation. It may take a while to map the logic onto the target device and generate timing data. This process should not take more than 15 minutes for this project as it's a simple design. The time it takes is related to both the complexity of your design and the specs of the computer you're using to build it.

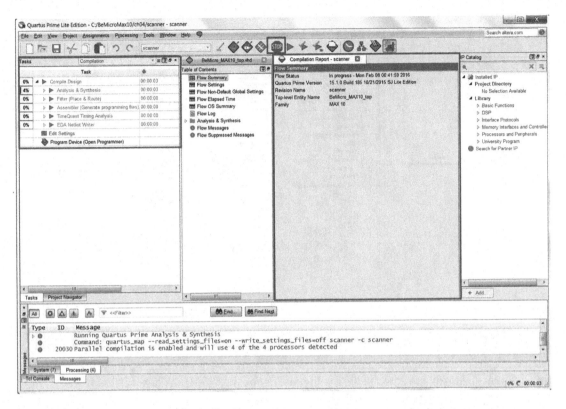

Figure 4-27. *Implement Design in process*

When you see six green ticks show up on the left-hand side of each of the tasks in the Tasks view, Quartus Prime has successfully completed the implementation. You should also see "100%" in the lower right corner. Figure 4-28 shows what it should look like. Please spend some time reading the Compilation report even if you don't fully understand it at this stage. It shows that the Scanner design used 53 logic elements and 9 pins.

You may have found some warnings in your report. It is OK to have some warnings when building this example. (Figure 4-28 shows that my project has three warnings). Let have a look at the warnings by clicking the yellow warning triangle in Figure 4-29. It shows only warning in the message windows. The first warning (ID: 292013) is because we are using the free Quartus Prime version. The second and third warnings are a result of a lot of unused input and output pins which are removed from the design by Write code section step 5a.

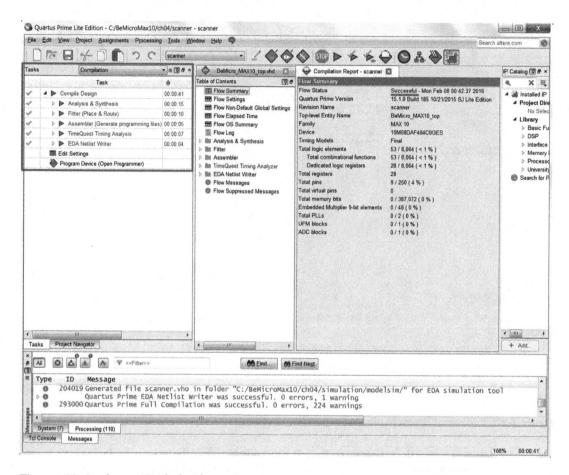

Figure 4-28. *Implement Finished with warnings*

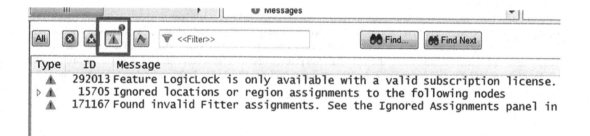

Figure 4-29. *Warning messages are OK to have.*

We should not have any critical warning like **Timing requirements not met**. This critical warning is due to bad, wrong, or incomplete design. If you get a **timing requirements not met** warning, you should review your design files.

Congratulations! You've compiled your first VHDL design! The next step is to work out whether it actually works.

4.4 Simulate Design

Once you have completed the hardware design entry, you may want to simulate your design on a PC to gain confidence that it works exactly as expected before pushing it to your FPGA. Simulation requires a form of input stimulus and then the FPGA simulator software can determine the corresponding outputs. Design simulation is important because we can quickly test our designs under different circumstances, which would either be time-consuming or impossible to test on real hardware.

Altera provides us with industry standard software for simulating and analyzing designs. The name of the tool is ModelSim. As the name suggests, it allows you to simulate your model/design.

There are two ways to create input stimulus:

- Tcl Script in ModelSim (easy)

- Using a test bench (a bit harder but more flexible)

We will pick the harder method for this example, although we will do it with Quartus Prime's help. Let's go build a test bench and run the simulation for our scanner design.

1. Click **Assignments ➤ Settings ➤ EDA Tools Settings\Simulation** to open the simulation settings window. Your setting should look like Figure 4-30.

    - Tool name: **ModelSim-Altera**

    - Output directory: **simulation/modelsim**

    - NativeLink settings: **None**

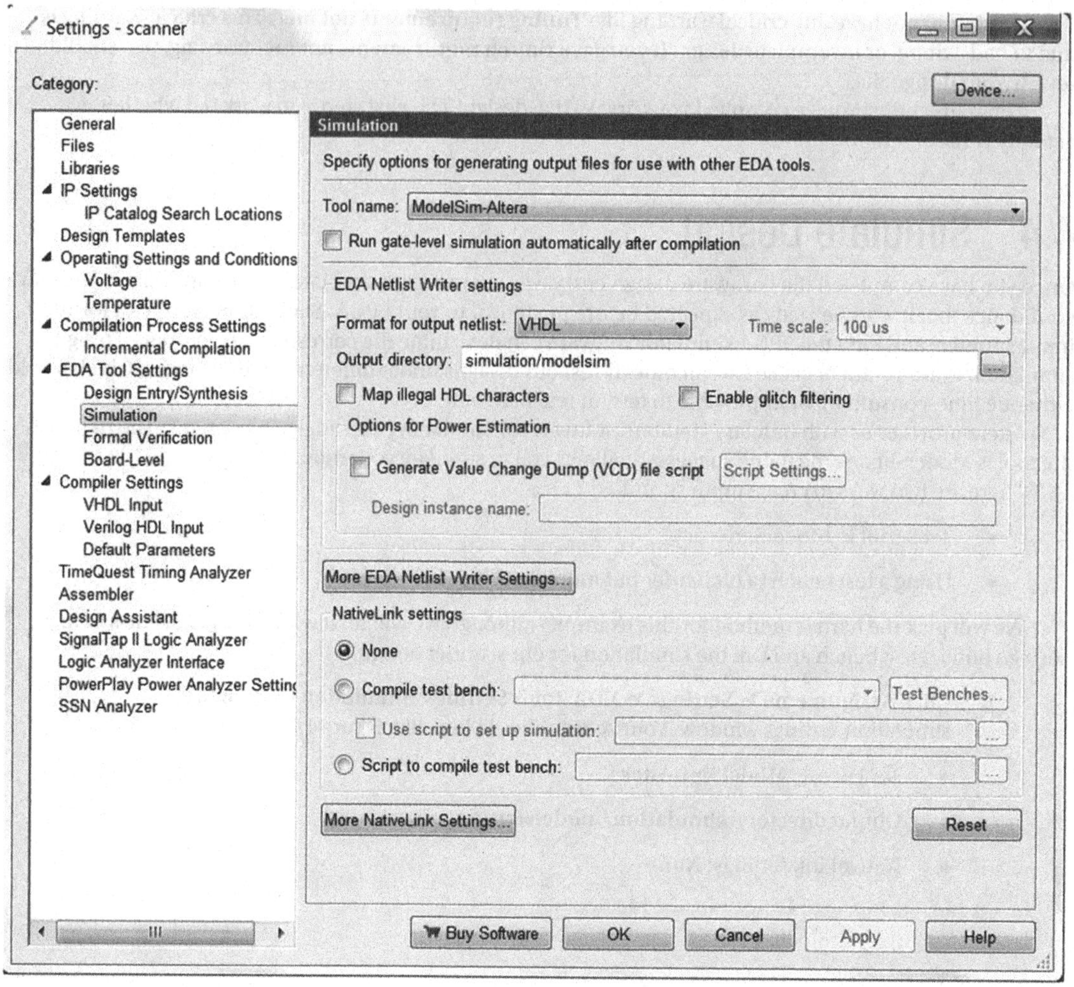

Figure 4-30. *Simulation settings*

2. Create the test bench template: Click **Processing ➤ Start ➤ Start Test Bench Template Writer** from the Quartus Prime menu (Figure 4-31). The test bench template writer is based on your top-level entity module and uses information from that file to generate a test bench for it. It will show the location of the test bench file in the processing message tab (Figure 4-32).

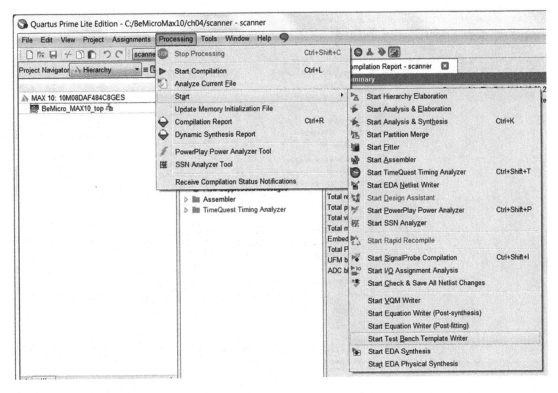

Figure 4-31. *Quartus Prime Test Bench template writer*

■ **Tips** Each module (entity) should have its own test bench to simulate the module. Each module needs to be simulated before it can be connected to other modules. This can save you a huge amount of time when debugging your design later. It also acts like a kind of safeguard for your design.

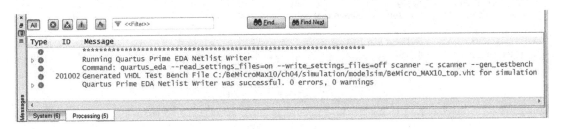

Figure 4-32. *Generated test bench template and the location of the file show in Processing Message tab*

3. Click **Tools ➤ Run Simulation ➤ RTL Simulation** to open ModelSim (Simulation software). It is like Figure 4-33. The first time you run it in a project, it will ask you to select the simulation language. Select **VHDL** and click **OK** (Figure 4-34).

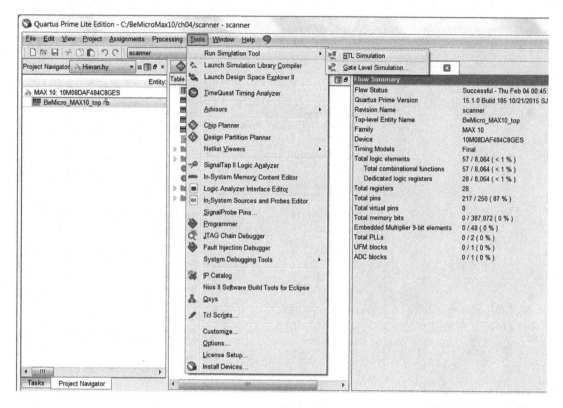

Figure 4-33. *Start the Simulation software—ModelSim-Altera version*

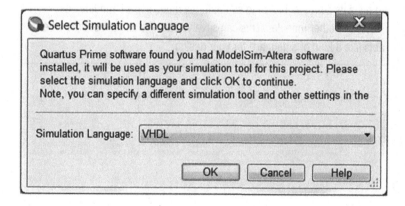

Figure 4-34. *Select simulation language—VHDL*

4. ModelSim ALTERA STARTER EDITION should open (Figure 4-35). In the transcript, you should find the last line is **ModelSim➤**. Enter the following Tcl command and hit Enter. Once completed you should see Figure 4-36 in the Transcript log.

    •   vcom -reportprogress 300 -work BeMicro_MAX10_top.vht

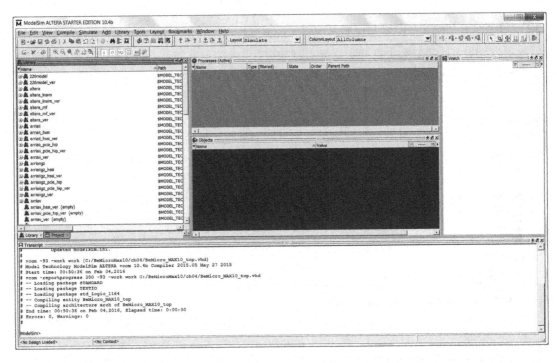

Figure 4-35. *ModelSim ALTERA STARTER EDITION*

```
Transcript
ModelSim> vcom -reportprogress 300 -work work BeMicro_MAX10_top.vht
# Model Technology ModelSim ALTERA vcom 10.4b Compiler 2015.05 May 27 2015
# Start time: 01:28:24 on Feb 08,2016
# vcom -reportprogress 300 -work work BeMicro_MAX10_top.vht
# -- Loading package STANDARD
# -- Loading package TEXTIO
# -- Loading package std_logic_1164
# -- Compiling entity BeMicro_MAX10_top_vhd_tst
# -- Compiling architecture BeMicro_MAX10_top_arch of BeMicro_MAX10_top_vhd_tst
# End time: 01:28:24 on Feb 08,2016, Elapsed time: 0:00:00
# Errors: 0, Warnings: 0
ModelSim>
<No Design Loaded>          <No Context>
```

Figure 4-36. *ModelSim ALTERA STARTER EDITION*

5. You can compile your test bench using the graphical user interface (GUI) too. Click **Compile ➤ Compile...** from the menu (Figure 4-37). It will open the Compile Source Files dialog. Make sure your settings are the same as shown in Figure 4-38, Select BeMicro_MAX10_top.vht and then click the **Compile** icon. Step 4 and step 5 both compile the test bench file BeMicro_MAX10_top.vht into the **work** library. Click **Done** to leave the dialog.

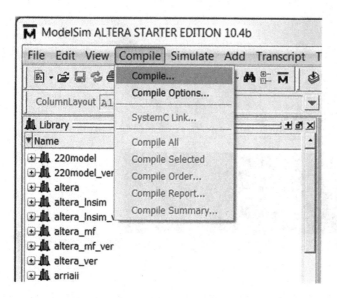

Figure 4-37. *Compile test bench from the GUI*

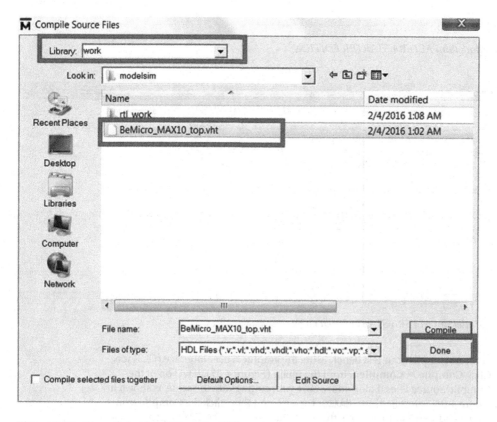

Figure 4-38. *Compile test bench from the GUI*

6. Remember that the test bench is only a template. Let's open it and do some editing. In the top left corner in the Library pane, click the "+" icon next to the **work icon**. You will see two names as follows:

- **bemicro_max10_top**: this is our scanner LED design module

- **bemicro_max10_top_vhd_tst**: this is the test bench

Right-click the bemicro_max10_top_vhd_tst, and click **Edit** (Figure 4-39). This will open an editor as per Figure 4-40.

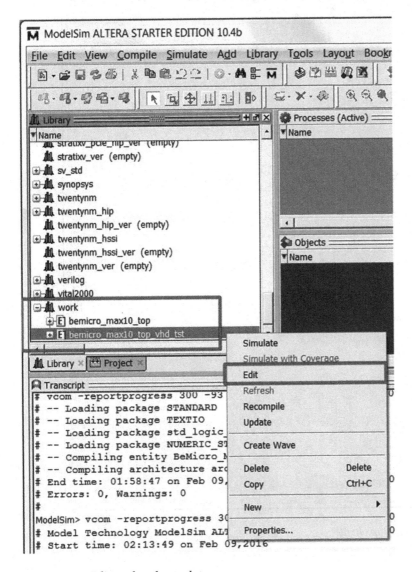

Figure 4-39. *Edit test bench template*

■ **Tips** Quartus Prime and ModelSim both provide VHDL file editors. There are other good VHDL file editors that you can try. For example, you can try Notepad ++ or Emacs with VHDL mode.

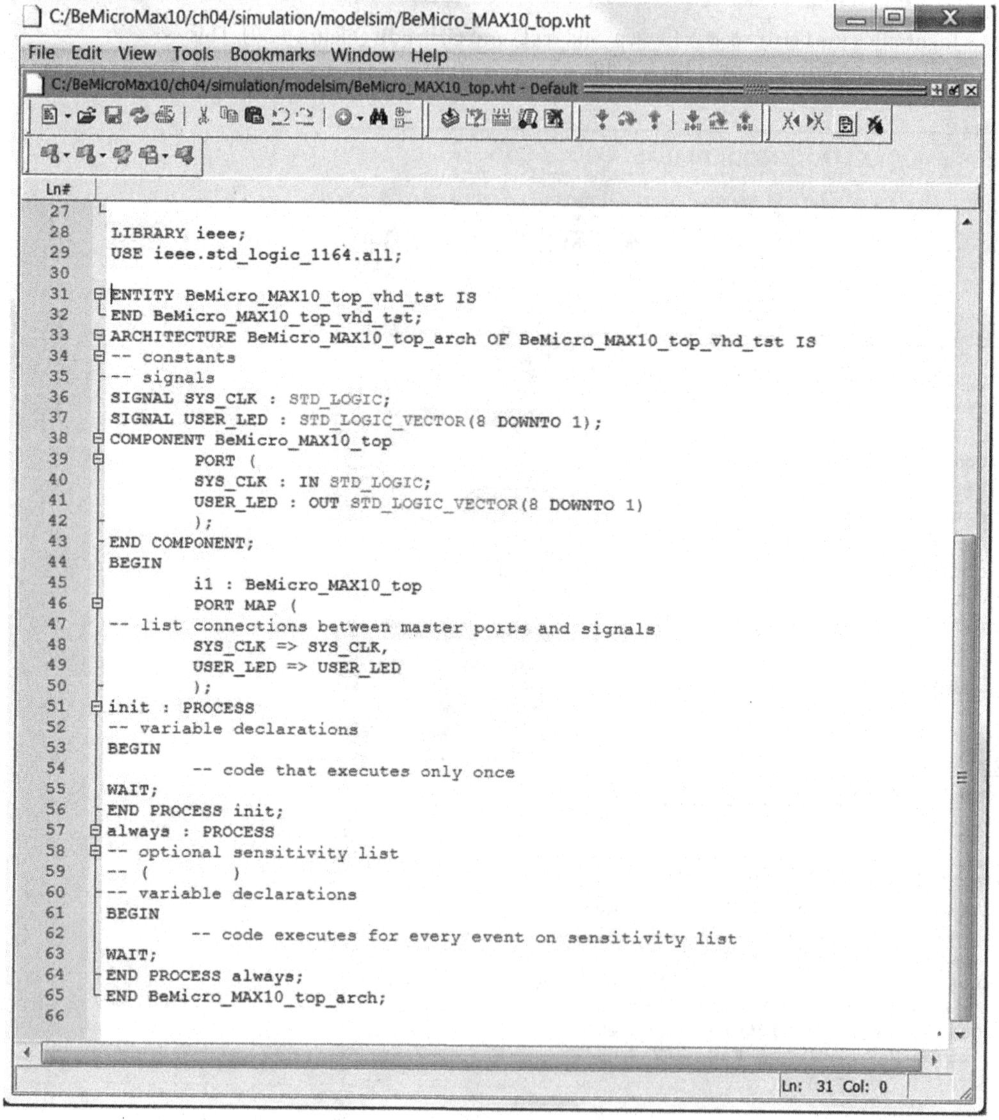

```
Ln#
 27
 28    LIBRARY ieee;
 29    USE ieee.std_logic_1164.all;
 30
 31   ☐ENTITY BeMicro_MAX10_top_vhd_tst IS
 32    └ END BeMicro_MAX10_top_vhd_tst;
 33   ☐ARCHITECTURE BeMicro_MAX10_top_arch OF BeMicro_MAX10_top_vhd_tst IS
 34   ☐ -- constants
 35    ┤ -- signals
 36    │ SIGNAL SYS_CLK : STD_LOGIC;
 37    │ SIGNAL USER_LED : STD_LOGIC_VECTOR(8 DOWNTO 1);
 38   ☐COMPONENT BeMicro_MAX10_top
 39   ☐          PORT (
 40    │         SYS_CLK : IN STD_LOGIC;
 41    │         USER_LED : OUT STD_LOGIC_VECTOR(8 DOWNTO 1)
 42    ┤         );
 43    ┤END COMPONENT;
 44    │ BEGIN
 45    │         i1 : BeMicro_MAX10_top
 46   ☐          PORT MAP (
 47    ┤ -- list connections between master ports and signals
 48    │         SYS_CLK => SYS_CLK,
 49    │         USER_LED => USER_LED
 50    ┤         );
 51   ☐init : PROCESS
 52    ┤ -- variable declarations
 53    │ BEGIN
 54    │         -- code that executes only once
 55    │ WAIT;
 56    ┤END PROCESS init;
 57   ☐always : PROCESS
 58   ☐ -- optional sensitivity list
 59    ┤ -- (        )
 60    ┤ -- variable declarations
 61    │ BEGIN
 62    │         -- code executes for every event on sensitivity list
 63    │ WAIT;
 64    ┤END PROCESS always;
 65    └ END BeMicro_MAX10_top_arch;
 66
```

Figure 4-40. Edit bemicro_max10_top.vht file

Have a quick look through the code, and see if any of it looks familiar. Don't worry if it still doesn't make much sense. One thing that might stand out is that it looks like a different person wrote this template—a lot of reserved words (highlighted in red) that were lowercase in the implementation template are uppercase here (reserved words, like identifiers, are case-insensitive in VHDL). In any case, kudos to whomever it was, because they've managed to almost magically produce a perfect test case for us. Anything that saves us time and helps us to avoid writing the same boilerplate code over and over again is a definite win for us.

7. Edit the test bench and change the following things. The file should look like Figure 4-41 when you're done. Remember to save the file. Click **File ➤ Save**.

    - At the end of line 36: Add **:= '0';**

    - Add a new line after line 50: Add **SYS_CLK <= not SYS_CLK after 10 ns;**

```
Ln#
 28    LIBRARY ieee;
 29    USE ieee.std_logic_1164.all;
 30    |
 31    ENTITY BeMicro_MAX10_top_vhd_tst IS
 32    END BeMicro_MAX10_top_vhd_tst;
 33    ARCHITECTURE BeMicro_MAX10_top_arch OF BeMicro_MAX10_top_vhd_tst
 34    -- constants
 35    -- signals
 36    SIGNAL SYS_CLK : STD_LOGIC := '0';
 37    SIGNAL USER_LED : STD_LOGIC_VECTOR(8 DOWNTO 1);
 38    COMPONENT BeMicro_MAX10_top
 39            PORT (
 40            SYS_CLK : IN STD_LOGIC;
 41            USER_LED : OUT STD_LOGIC_VECTOR(8 DOWNTO 1)
 42            );
 43    END COMPONENT;
 44    BEGIN
 45            i1 : BeMicro_MAX10_top
 46            PORT MAP (
 47    -- list connections between master ports and signals
 48            SYS_CLK => SYS_CLK,
 49            USER_LED => USER_LED
 50            );
 51    -- Add in a free running clock of 50MHz / 20 nS cycles
 52    SYS_CLK <= not SYS_CLK after 10 ns;
 53    init : PROCESS
 54    -- variable declarations
 55    BEGIN
 56            -- code that executes only once
 57    WAIT;
 58    END PROCESS init;
 59    always : PROCESS
 60    -- optional sensitivity list
 61    -- (        )
 62    -- variable declarations
 63    BEGIN
 64            -- code executes for every event on sensitivity list
 65    WAIT;
 66    END PROCESS always;
 67    END BeMicro_MAX10_top_arch;
 68
```

Figure 4-41. *bemicro_max10_top.vht file completed*

8. Right-click the `bemicro_max10_top_vhd_tst,` and click **Recompile** (Figure 4-42). This will recompile the test bench again. Once completed you should see Figure 4-36 in the Transcript log.

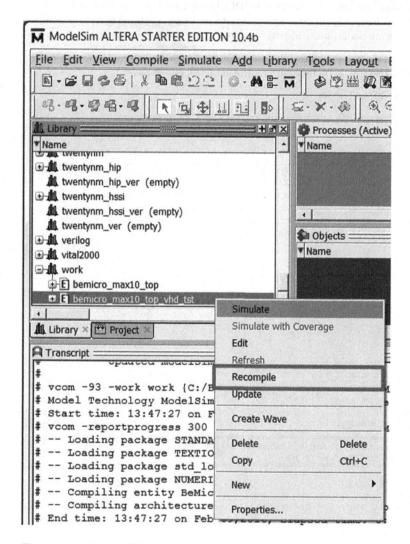

Figure 4-42. *Recompile bemicro_max10_top_vhd_tst*

9. Click **Simulate ➤ Start Simulation...** in the ModelSim menu. It will open the Start Simulation dialog (Figure 4-43).

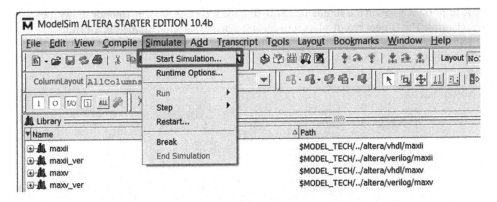

Figure 4-43. *Recompile bemicro_max10_top_vhd_tst*

10. Click the "+" icon next to the **work icon**, select **bemicro_max10_top_vhd_tst,**
    click the black triangle in the resolution box and select **ns**. All the settings should
    look like those in Figure 4-44 within the red box. Click **OK** to start simulation.
    The simulation will look like Figure 4-45.

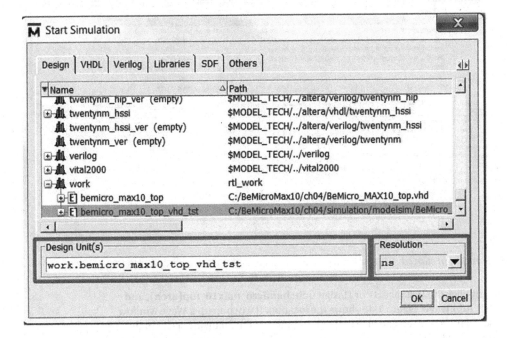

Figure 4-44. *Recompile bemicro_max10_top_vhd_tst*

There are two important boxes in the simulation: **Sim-Default** and **Objects. Sim-Default** shows the design structure relations. The **Object** box displays the object inside the selected (in the sim-Default) module. Figure 4-45 shows that we selected the test bench module (bemicro_max10_top_vhd_tst) and the object box show two objects: SYS_CLK and USER_LED.

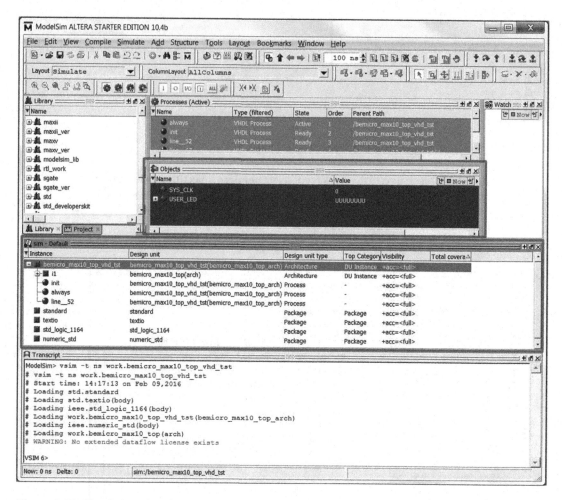

Figure 4-45. *Simulation started*

11. Right-click the Instance :**i1** or Design unit: **bemicro_max10_top(arch), and** click **Add Wave**. Figure 4-46 shows the location. It will pop up a Wave window like Figure 4-47. You can also trigger it by entering the following script in the Transcript box:

- add wave sim:/bemicro_max10_top_vhd_tst/i1/*

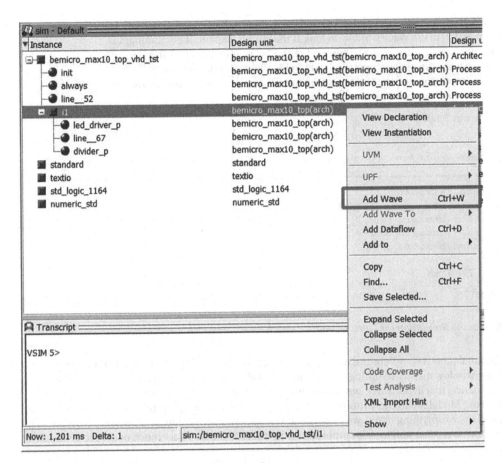

Figure 4-46. *Add all the signals into a Wave display*

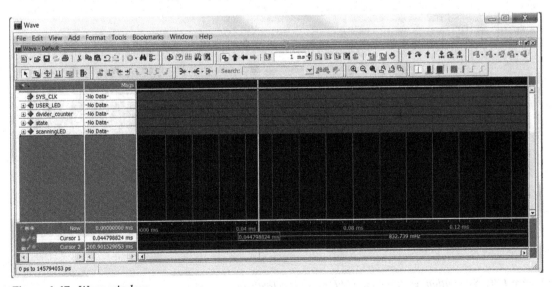

Figure 4-47. *Wave window*

12. Enter the following command in Transcript window and hit enter (Figure 4-48). You can switch to the Wave window to look at the output. Expand the scanningLED bus in the main area of the window (click the "+" next to it to make it "-") so you can see the LED outputs plotted individually. After doing this, wait for the simulation to complete. Depending on how fast your computer is, this may be a good time for a coffee break.

- run 7000 ms

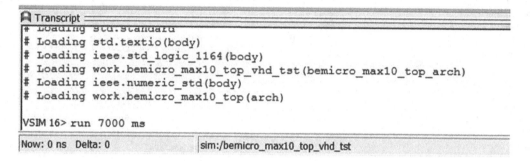

Figure 4-48. Run the simulation for seven seconds

Once the simulation is complete and the simulation time stops counting, click **View ➤ Zoom ➤ Zoom Full** in the Wave window menu. Assuming everything went well, you should see that it's illuminating each of the LEDs in sequence, first in one direction and then going back the other way (Figure 4-49). Pat yourself on the back, and close ModelSim for now (unless you want to do some exploring to find out what else it can do). There's no need to save anything here—we didn't do anything particularly interesting. However, if it doesn't look right, it's time to go back and look for problems in the code. There isn't very much of it, so it shouldn't be too hard to spot the problem.

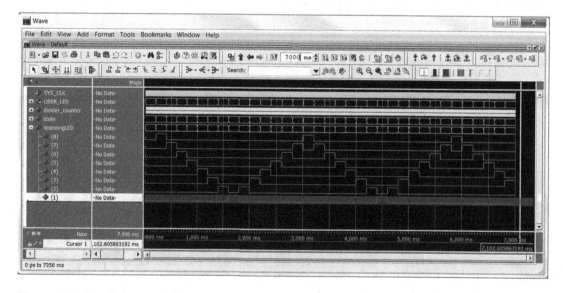

Figure 4-49. Simulation result showing LED outputs activated in sequence

4.5   Burn It!

Now that we're satisfied that our design works in principle, it's time for the moment of truth: running it on real hardware!

4.5.1   Install USB Blaster Driver

You only need to run these steps one time. If you already installed the driver then go the Program Design section.

1. Connect your BeMicro MAX 10 kit to your PC using the provided mini-USB cable.

2. The Installing device driver software pop-up dialog box appears (Figure 4-50).

Figure 4-50. *Windows tries to find a driver for you*

3. The Windows driver installation will NOT find a driver. Click **Close** (Figure 4-51).

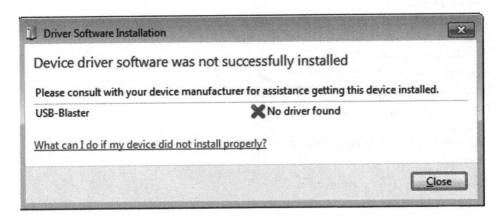

Figure 4-51. *Device driver software was not successfully installed*

1. Launch the Windows Device Manager by clicking the Windows Start button and selecting **Control Panel** then double-clicking the **Device Manager** icon.

2. Right-click the **USB-Blaster** which will be listed under **Other Devices** and select **Update Driver Software...** (Figure 4-52).

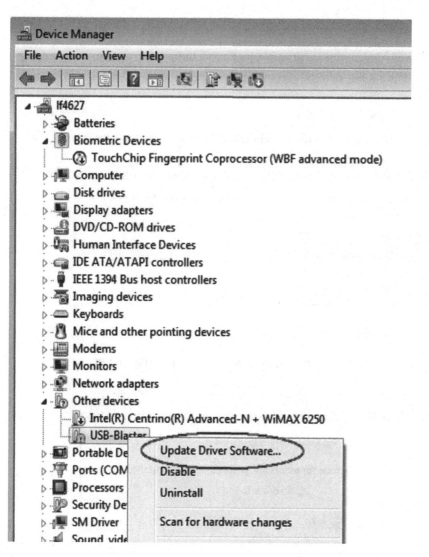

Figure 4-52. Device Manager

3. Do not search automatically. Instead select **Browse my computer for driver software** (Figure 4-53).

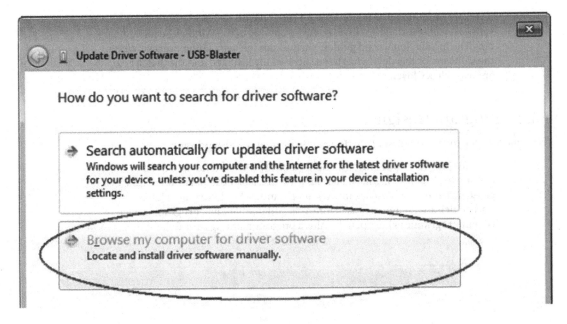

Figure 4-53. Device manager

4. When you are prompted to **insert the disc that came with your USB-Blaster**, select "I don't have a disc. Show me other options."

5. Select **Browse my computer for driver software** (advanced) when you see that Windows couldn't find the driver software for your device dialog box.

6. Click **Browse**, and browse to the C:\altera_lite\15.1\quartus\drivers\usb-blaster directory. Note: Do not select the x32 or x64 directories. Click **OK**. Select the **Include subfolders** option, and click **Next** (Figure 4-54).

Figure 4-54. Update Driver Software - Altera USB-Blaster

7. If you are prompted that Windows can't verify the publisher of this driver software, select Install this driver software anyway in the Window Security dialog box. The installation wizard guides you through the installation process. When the software for this device has been successfully installed and the dialog box appears, click **Close.**

4.5.2   Program Design

This is the last step to put your first FPGA design into the real world-hardware!

1. Back in Quartus Prime, switch to the Task tab. Check that the Assembler (Generate programming files) task has a green check next to it (If there isn't a green tick, then double-click the Assembler and it should run and change to a green tick after it finishes) as Figure 4-55 and double-click **Program Device (Open Programmer)** to open the Altera programmer (Figure 4-55).

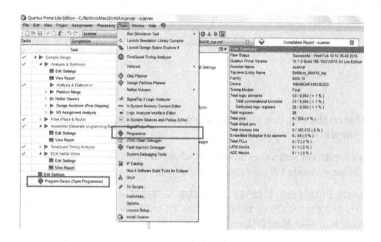

Figure 4-55. *Open Altera USB-Blaster Programmer*

Quartus Prime will grind away for a while as it turns our design into a bitstream suitable for loading onto your FPGA. This takes the form of a file with the filename extension .sof in the project folder. You can find out some interesting statistics about the design, including its utilization of FPGA resources, in the Compilation Report. Unsurprisingly, we're using less than 1% of what the chip has to offer, and our design meets all timing constraints.

2. Click the **Hardware Setup...** icon in the Programmer (Figure 4-56). In the Hardware Setup dialog select **USB-Blaster [USB-0]** and click **Close** (Figure 4-57**).**

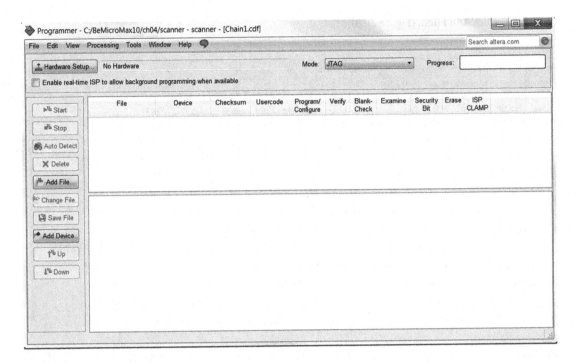

Figure 4-56. *Programmer*

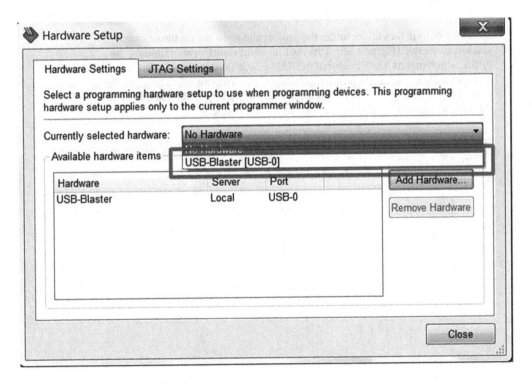

Figure 4-57. *Programmer—Hardware setup*

3. Click **Add File...** (Figure 4-58)

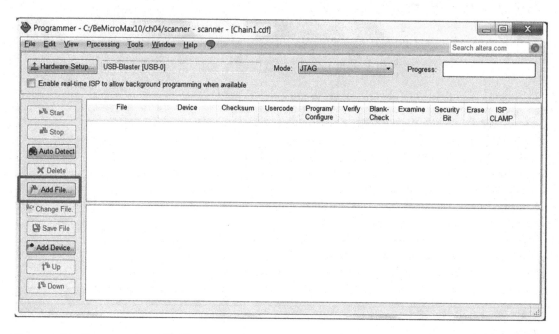

Figure 4-58. *Programmer—Add File*

4. Select the output_files folder under the project and open the bit file scanner.sof you just generated (Figure 4-59). This .sof file is for directly programming the FPGA, which means it will be stored in SRAM (static random access memory) and thus will be erased when you unplug the FPGA. You can select the .pof file instead if you want to upload the bit file to the flash storage inside the FPGA. In this case the program will not get erased by a power cycle.

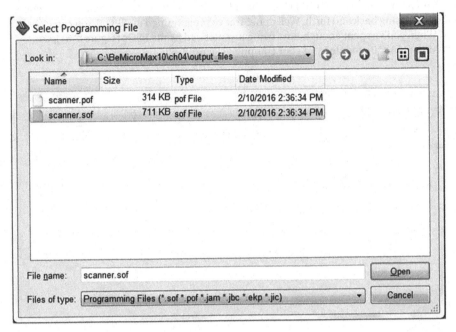

Figure 4-59. *Programmer—Select Programming File*

5. All of the settings should look like Figure 4-60. When you're sure you want to proceed, click the **Start** button and wait while it writes the bitstream to the MAX10's SRAM. The LED (D11) on the board will glow green while this is in progress. Don't disconnect the board while this is in progress or you risk damaging the FPGA.

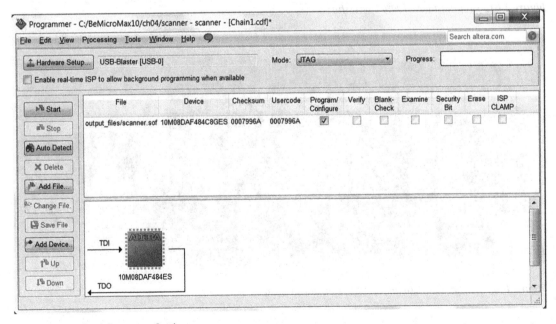

Figure 4-60. *Programmer—Setting*

95

Once the upload has completed, the LED (D11) light should go off, the FPGA should load your program, and the LEDs should start chasing back and forth. Well done! You've programmed an FPGA! You can close the programmer now. When you've spent enough time being mesmerized by the LEDs (Figure 4-61), you can disconnect the BeMicro MAX10 module from your computer (Figure 4-62).

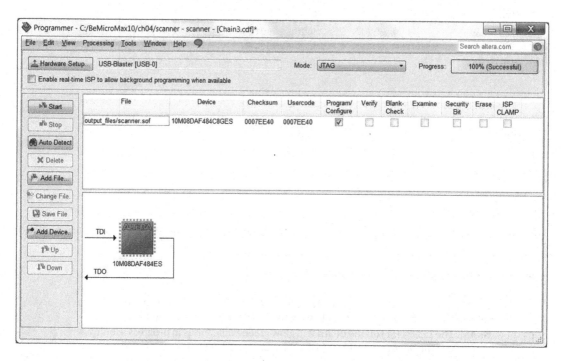

Figure 4-61. *Programmer—100% Successful*

Figure 4-62. *BeMicro MAX10 module running our program*

4.6 Recapping What We Just Completed

So we programmed an FPGA, but how did any of that actually work? What did the code do? Well we're glad you asked because in spite of its small size, this design uses a lot of language features. We'll go through the design step by step in this section.

4.6.1 Timing constraints

Remember the second file from the project template, **BeMicro_MAX10_top.sdc**? We didn't even need to write it as it came straight from the Altera design template for our development board. It's fairly short, but also critical for digital designs:

```
#***********************************************************
# Create Clock
#***********************************************************

create_clock -name {SYS_CLK} -period 20.000 -waveform { 0.000 10.000 } [get_ports {SYS_CLK}]
```

Anything after a hash character (#) to the end of a line is a comment added for your benefit rather than the computer's.

SYS_CLK (one of the pins on the FPGA) is connected directly to a 50 MHz oscillator, and we can work this into the constraints so that our design can be verified to work with it. Why wouldn't it, assuming the chip is rated to run at 50 MHz to begin with? Well, logic elements aren't perfect—they suffer from propagation delays, which means if we get too many of them in a row we may not be able to keep up with the clock signal. The -period tells it that the period of the signal is 20 ns (a 50 Mhz signal triggers 50 million times per second, which is once every 20ns). The -waveform {0.000 10.000} tells it that the signal from time 0 to 10ns is low and 10ns to 20ns is high (10 ns low time and 10ns high. This describes a 50 MHz square wave (Figure 4-63).

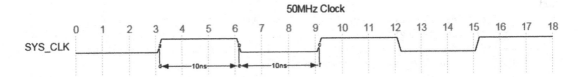

Figure 4-63. 50 MHz square wave

It's possible to create far more complex timing constraints such as specifying maximum propagation delays from one point of a signal to another, defining clock signals in terms of a frequency multiplier, specifying phase offsets from other clock signals, and many other constructs. It's also possible to have constraints that match signals deeper in the module hierarchy, but that's beyond the scope of what we're doing here.

4.6.2 The Implementation

Our design is implemented using a small amount of code, but it contains the core of every VHDL module: an *entity* defining the interface, and an associated *architecture* defining the behavior. VHDL conveniently forces this separation on you, so there's no way to slip into the bad habit of mixing the two together in the source.

4.6.2.1   Library Imports

Before we even get to the entity declaration, there are a couple of lines that tell the synthesizer to import a library:

```
library IEEE;
use IEEE.STD_LOGIC_1164.ALL;
use IEEE.NUMERIC_STD.ALL;
```

Libraries need to be made visible before they can be used, and that's what the library statement does—in this case we want to make the IEEE library visible to our module. (Two special libraries, std and work, are visible by default, but all other libraries must be made visible explicitly.) A library is made up of packages, and you can make their contents visible with the use statement. We want to make everything from the STD_LOGIC_1164 and NUMERIC_STD packages in the IEEE library visible. Why do we need a library in such a simple module? Well, VHDL has a basic BIT type built into the language, but the IEEE1164 standard defines more comprehensive logic called STD_LOGIC, which provides features such as high-impedance, indeterminate, and weak states, IEEE (Institute of Electrical and Electronics Engineers) standard numeric types, and arithmetic functions for use with synthesis tools. This is similar to including "stdio.h" in a C application—it's not technically required, but practically every program you write is going to need it.

4.6.2.2   The Entity Declaration

The entity declaration defines the inputs and outputs of the module (Listing 4-2). The stuff here is all you have access to when you instantiate the module, and the sole means for the module to communicate with the outside world.

Listing 4-2. VHDL Entity Declaration

```
entity BeMicro_MAX10_top is
port(
        -- Clock ins, SYS_CLK = 50MHz, USER_CLK = 24MHz
        SYS_CLK : in std_logic;
        -- LED outs
        USER_LED : out std_logic_vector(8 downto 1)
);

end entity BeMicro_MAX10_top;
```

An entity may define a port containing input and output signals and/or a generic declaration for parameters that supply static values to instantiations of the module. In this simple example, we have a port containing an input and an output. Signals within a port definition take the form of a name, a literal colon (:), the direction, and the data type. Some data types require additional parameters. Semicolons separate signals, and the port definition itself is terminated with a semicolon.

The first signal, SYS_CLK, is a single logic line input: the direction in and the data type STD_LOGIC should be fairly obvious. The USER_LED signal is an eight-bit output bus. There's a STD_LOGIC_VECTOR (8 downto 1) type that represents a one-dimensional bit array with eight elements (from 8 to 1).

There is one other possible signal direction which is used for bidirectional communication lines: inout.

Note that when you close blocks of code with an end statement, you need to indicate what you're closing. This can help you follow where you are if you're looking at the end of some deeply nested blocks. It's a bit inconsistent about whether you need to close things using the name or the type of block, but it's still not a bad idea. The example shows both types of block (entity) and name (BeMicro_MAX10_top).

4.6.2.3   The Architecture

The architecture is divided into two distinct parts: declarations and statements. This is another example of VHDL's strict enforcement of a particular structure. It's rather inflexible, but it also makes it easy to find things, which is extremely valuable when working with code that someone else has written.

4.6.2.3.1   Declaration

Let's start with the declarations—they come between the architecture statement and the begin statement that introduces the statements themselves (Listing 4-3).

Listing 4-3. VHDL Architecture Declarations

```
architecture arch of BeMicro_MAX10_top is
signal divider_counter : unsigned(23 downto 0) := (others =>'0');
signal state           : unsigned(3 downto 0)  := (others =>'0');
signal scanningLED     : std_logic_vector(8 downto 1);
begin
```

Declarations can comprise all kinds of things, including type definitions, constant values, and subcomponents. Here we declare just two internal unsigned signals. Wait a moment, unsigned? Maybe you watched that episode of Futurama where the robot Bender has a nightmare about the number 2: digital electronics only ever deal with zeroes and ones! Well you're right—the FPGA can't directly represent an unsigned number. But the beauty of the modern VHDL synthesizer is that it allows us to use certain high-level abstractions and then let the tools worry about how to implement them on the chip. Signals are only visible inside the architecture, and they can be used for internal state, intermediate values, communication between submodules, debugging values for simulation, or anything else you can think of. They're roughly equivalent to a C++ member variable. Remember, though, these abstractions are a convenience for us developers and do not have a one-to-one equivalent in hardware.

The basic form of a signal declaration is the signal keyword followed by a name, a literal colon (:), the data type, and optionally the initialization operator (=), and an initial value, terminated by a semicolon (;). Two of our signals here are unsigned—we specify a precise number of bits to define the range of the number. We initialize both of the signals to zero.

4.6.2.3.2   Statements

The actual statements that define the behavior of our architecture come between the begin and end statements. First we have a process block (Listing 4-4).

Listing 4-4. divider_p Process

```
divider_p: process (SYS_CLK) -- Sensitivity list
    begin
        if (rising_edge(SYS_CLK)) then -- function call: rising_edges()
            if (divider_counter = to_unsigned(9999999,24)) then
                divider_counter <= (others =>'0');
                if (state = to_unsigned(14,4)) then
                    state <= to_unsigned(1,4); -- assignment
                else
                    state <= state + 1; -- adder
                end if;
```

```
        else
            divider_counter <= divider_counter + 1; -- adder
            state <= state;
        end if;
    end if;
end process;
```

The purpose of this process is pretty simple: the clock source ticks 50 million times per second, which is way too fast to see, so we need to divide it down to something much slower. We do this by counting up to 9,999,999 and then starting over at zero. So, including the zero, there are ten million values, which means we'll complete a cycle five times a second (50 million divided by 10 million is 5). Additionally, each time we start again from zero we move to the next state, or if we're already in the final state 14, we start again at 1.

When we get down to the nuts and bolts of how it works, a process block is a container for *sequential code*. The statements within a process block appear to execute in the order they're written when a specified signal changes state (in practice they're actually executed all at once when a trigger event occurs, but you write the code as though it's executed sequentially). Statements outside process blocks constitute *concurrent code*, and they execute all together all the time. The kinds of statements allowed in sequential and concurrent code aren't quite the same—some things only work in one or the other, while others are valid in both contexts.

The process is named `divider` here so it can be referred to, but this is not strictly necessary—you can create an anonymous process by omitting the name and colon. The part in parentheses following the `process` keyword is the *sensitivity list*: this is where you list the signals that your process needs to react to. This process only reacts to changes in the SYS_CLK input (if your process is sensitive to multiple signals, list them all here separated by commas).

Let's pull apart the first `if` statement. Straight away we can see that the logical operators are English words, they have lower precedence than comparison operators, the equality operator is a single equals sign (=), and outer parentheses aren't required around the condition because it's terminated with the `then` keyword. More subtly, `rising_edge(SYS_CLK)` is an example of *function call*. SYS_CLK is an input to the function `rising_edge()`. The function will output high when the SYS_CLK change from '0' (low) to '1' (high). We won't have to wait long—this happens 50 million times every second.

The remaining `if` statements are pretty straightforward—they just check signals for particular values. Some of them have corresponding `else` clauses that are evaluated if the condition is false. The other statements are assignments: `<=` (left angle bracket, equals) is the assignment operator, and assigns the value on the right to the signal on the left. We can conveniently do arithmetic on unsigned values (there are a couple of additions in there).

The remaining thing to note here is that VHDL code must be unambiguous. The synthesizer must be in no doubt as the expected state of any signal after code is executed. If you don't want to change a value, you can assign it to itself, as we do when we want to preserve the value of the `state` signal near the end of the process block (this isn't strictly necessary in sequential code—it's assumed you want a signal's value preserved if you don't assign to it). If you don't care what the value of a signal is under certain circumstances, you have to make this explicit (you can use the value '-' for STD_LOGIC signals, and the synthesizer will choose a value that minimizes the device utilization).

We finish up with a case statement for obtaining the LED outputs sequences from the `state` signal (Listing 4-5).

Listing 4-5. Case Statement

```
led_driver_p: process (state) --Sensitivity list
    begin
    case to_integer(state) is -- case selection
        when 1      => scanningLED <= "10000000";
        when 2|14   => scanningLED <= "01000000";
```

```
      when 3|13   => scanningLED <= "00100000";
      when 4|12   => scanningLED <= "00010000";
      when 5|11   => scanningLED <= "00001000";
      when 6|10   => scanningLED <= "00000100";
      when 7|9    => scanningLED <= "00000010";
      when 8      => scanningLED <= "00000001";
      when others => scanningLED <= "00000000"; --Another cases fall into this section
  end case;
end process;
```

Remember this is in a concurrent context, so it runs all the time. Any time the state signal changes the LED outputs will change accordingly. The case statement lets us translate from one signal to another using arbitrary tables. There are more than 14 possible output values from state; some of them are mapped to two multiple input values using the | (pipe) operator. Choices are separated with commas, and the statement is terminated with a semicolon. I've organized it with one choice per line, but you can jam it all one line, or divide it up some other way if you like—that's the beauty of whitespace-insensitive languages.

Note that, like everything else in VHDL, a case statement must be completely unambiguous. Every possible input must be mapped to a corresponding output. In this case our input signal is only restricted by the unsigned definition so there are a large number of possible values that you don't want to handle individually. You can make the last choice when others and it will catch any value that isn't handled explicitly.

There's one other thing we can learn by examining this statement: values for STD_LOGIC_VECTOR signals are represented with sequences of characters surrounded by double quotes ("). You use the same characters you would use for STD_LOGIC values, but you need as many of them as there are bits in the vector. The order corresponds to the order used when you declared the signal (MSB first if you used downto, or LSB first if you used to).

The last statement in the code is a concurrent signal assignment. It assigns logical NOT the value of scanningLED to USER_LED. It is because the USER_LED (the onboard LEDs) is active low logic which means logic 0 will turn on the LEDs. USER_LED and scanningLED need to be the same data type (std_logic_vector(8 downto 1)).

```
USER_LED <= not scanningLED;
```

4.6.3   The Test Bench

Despite being generated automatically for the most part, the simulation test bench includes some interesting code. Our implementation was so simple that the simulation test bench is actually more complex than our actual design. Let's pull it apart and see what we find.

4.6.3.1   The Empty Entity

Like every module, the test bench must declare an entity defining its externally visible interface. It's only for simulation purposes, so we can work with internal signals alone, and there's no need for any inputs and outputs. Thus the entity has no port or generic definition. This is as simple as it can get:

```
ENTITY BeMicro_MAX10_top_vhd_tst IS
END BeMicro_MAX10_top_vhd_tst;
```

4.6.3.2   Declarations

Now this looks a bit more interesting—the test bench has to declare the module under test as a component so it can be instantiated (Listing 4-6).

Listing 4-6. Declare Signals and Component

```
-- signals
SIGNAL SYS_CLK : STD_LOGIC := '0';
SIGNAL USER_LED : STD_LOGIC_VECTOR(8 DOWNTO 1);
COMPONENT BeMicro_MAX10_top
    PORT (
                SYS_CLK : IN STD_LOGIC;
                USER_LED : OUT STD_LOGIC_VECTOR(8 DOWNTO 1)
              );
END COMPONENT;
```

The component declaration is a lot like the module's entity declaration, with an equivalent port definition.

There are two internal signals declared, with names and types that match the signals in the port of the component that we plan to test. Note that the USER_LED signal is not initialized—it's unnecessary as it's going to be connected to the output of the unit under test.

4.6.3.3   Statements

In Listing 4-7 we get to see an actual submodule instantiation, and some convenient simulation code that would have no chance of actually being synthesized and run on physical hardware.

Listing 4-7. Test Bench Statements

```
        i1 : BeMicro_MAX10_top
        PORT MAP (
-- list connections between master ports and signals
        SYS_CLK => SYS_CLK,   -- The LEFT one is Port signal, the RIGHT one is Local signal
        USER_LED => USER_LED -- => is a mapper
        );
-- Add in a free running clock of 50MHz / 20 nS cycles
SYS_CLK <= not SYS_CLK after 10 ns; -- this one work in simulation
init : PROCESS
-- variable declarations
BEGIN
        -- code that executes only once
WAIT;
END PROCESS init;
always : PROCESS
-- optional sensitivity list
-- (        )
-- variable declarations
BEGIN
        -- code executes for every event on sensitivity list
WAIT;
END PROCESS always;
```

The first part is possibly the most interesting. This is an instantiation of the scanner component called i1 (short for instance one). Inside the parentheses, the submodule's input/output port signals are connected, or "mapped," to signals in this architecture. The fact that the local signals are named exactly the same way as the signals in the component's port definition doesn't promote clarity here, so you'll have to take my word for how this works. The name of the port signal of the component being instantiated goes on the left of the mapping operator => and the name of the local signal it's being connected to goes on the right. Yes, => (equals, right angle bracket) is the mapping operator, used for associating or connecting things.

Next up we have a concurrent statement that definitely wouldn't work in an implementation module. The first part is a normal logic gate design which is OK for both simulation and design. The after keyword generates delays between each time assignment. As convenient as it would be, there is no hardware component that truly generates arbitrary delays, so as soon as you use an after statement, you're restricting your code to running in simulation. However, it's a very useful tool for building a test bench: NOT the current SYS_CLK, wait for half the SYS_CLK period, NOT the current SYS_CLK, wait for another half SYS_CLK period and repeat forever. This generates a square wave at the clock frequency, which is the perfect input for testing our design.

The last two processes, init and always, would be where we'd generate other inputs for testing our design. It uses wait statements to generate arbitrary delays. Note the final wait statement with no duration specified—this will wait forever, preventing the process from repeating. Our design has no inputs apart from the clock signal, so we didn't have to write anything clever here.

The 10ns is a built-in time type which represents a time interval. You give time signals a numeric value with a unit (valid units are fs, ps, ns, us, ms, sec, min, and hr). The time type is rather abstract, and using it is likely to result in your module only working under simulation. This obviously isn't a problem for a simulation test bench, but you should probably not use time signals in your implementation. The value of 10ns is chosen to correspond to the actual clock half period on our development board.

4.7   Summary

That wraps up the Hello World! project. While it's simple on the surface, there's a lot going on. We've actually seen most of the core concepts of VHDL in action. Where you go next depends on what you want to learn: you can read up on some background and theory in Part II, or jump straight into the projects in Part III of this book.

4.7.1   But I Don't have a Mercury Module!

If you're using a different development board, don't despair. All the code here is standard VHDL, which can be synthesized for and run on just about any FPGA, and even some CPLDs (Complex Programmable Logic Devices). You'll have to make the following adjustments to the process:

- When creating the project, choose your FPGA rather than mine (this is good advice even if you have a BeMicro MAX10—they could change the exact model of FPGA used at some point).

- Use an appropriate timing constraint (.sdc) file for your development board.

- Make the names of the signals in the top module match the names of the clock input and LEDs outputs on your development board.

- Adjust the number 99999999 proportionally if the clock frequency on your board isn't 50 MHz.

- Adjust the 10 ns value in the test bench to match the half period of your clock source (the name may be different if your clock input constraint is named differently).

- Follow the instructions that came with your board for uploading the bitstream file.

"For the things we have to learn before we can do them, we learn by doing them."

—Aristotle, the Nicomachean Ethics

PART II

Time Out for Theory

CHAPTER 5

■ ■ ■

FPGA Development Timeline

We've picked some of the important inventions from the history of electronics world to share with you. These inventions all contributed in some way to modern FPGA (field-programmable gate array) development.

5.1   1847—First Theory—Boolean Logic

With just three operations (AND, OR, and NOT) you can perform all the logic functions for the basic building blocks, not just for an FPGA but all forms of digital computing. If you'd like to know about Boolean logic, you can google *Mathematical Analysis of Logic* by George Boole (1815-1864) (Macmillan, Barclay, and Macmillan, 1847). Today we also refer to this as Boolean algebra, which as we mentioned previously is the foundation of all digital logic. If you love math, I suggest you take a look at this book.

5.2   1935—First Boolean Logic in Real World

Decades later, Boole's concepts finally got someone attention. Claude Shannon (1916-2001) used electromechanical relays to build a Boolean algebra logic circuit. You will use logic gates to build Boolean algebra logic circuits in your FPGA.

5.3   1942—First Electronic Digital Computer

The first vacuum tube (in the 1940s, vacuum tube meant electronic) digital computer was called ABC (the Atanasoff-Berry computer). It was built with more than 300 vacuum tubes and could compute complex algebraic equations. This is the first machine implemented that followed the three key concepts that every modern computer and FPGA digital design relies on.

- All calculations are done using electronics (vacuum tubes) rather than mechanical implementations.

- Binary digits (0 and 1) represent all numbers and data.

- Memory and computation are separated.

A lot of FPGAs are used to compute a specific math model like filtering in digital signal processing (DSP).

© Aiken Pang and Peter Membrey 2017
A. Pang and P. Membrey, *Beginning FPGA: Programming Metal*, DOI 10.1007/978-1-4302-6248-0_5

5.4   1960—First MOSFET

One of the most basic elements in an FPGA is MOSFET (Metal Oxide Semiconductor Field Effect Transistor). In the FPGA world, it is usually referred to as a gate. It is like a light switch. It will either allow the current flow (light is ON) or block the current flow (light is OFF), depending on what value it receives, high (1) or low (0). There are two main types of MOSFETs: P-FETS and N-FETS (Figure 5-1).

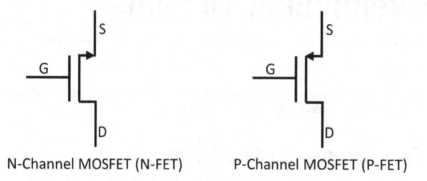

N-Channel MOSFET (N-FET)   P-Channel MOSFET (P-FET)

Figure 5-1. *MOSFET using arrows to designate the type*

N-FETs turn on, when G is high (1). It allows current flow from D to S. P-FETS act in the opposite way. P-FETs turn on, when G is low (0). It allows current flow from S to D.

When you download the bit file to the FPGA chip, the bit file tells the FPGA how to set up all these MOSFETs in the FPGA so they deliver the required output. One example of how they work is in a NAND gate. A NAND gate performs the not-AND operation. Figure 5-2 is the circuit diagram for a NAND gate using two P-FETs and two N-FETs.

Sometimes, N-FETS and P-FETs are shown without the arrows but with a circle on the gate to represent a P-FET. In Figure 5-2, you can see that if A and B are low (0), the two P-FETs on the top will be ON and the two N-FETs on the bottom will be OFF, such that 3.3V will be connected to output which is logical high (1). Since the P-FETs are in parallel, if A or B are low (0), 3.3V will be connected and ground will be disconnected. So this acts as a NAND gate logic element: low (Ground) is connected to output if and only if both A and B are high, another combination of AB input will connect high (3.3V) to output

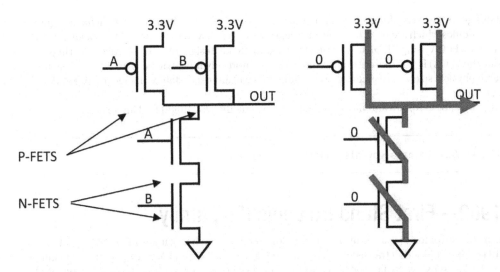

Figure 5-2. *NAND Gate circuit*

5.5   1960—First Practical Commercial Logic IC Module

An IC (integrated circuit) is a small black-colored rectangular-shaped chip that has one or more circuits built into it (Figure 5-3). For example, you can have an IC that has a decoder in it. ICs were an improvement from using transistors to build circuits, because they are the "whole" circuit. This way you can have your entire circuit in one IC, rather than having to assemble the circuit with possibly thousands of transistors. This saves time and space.

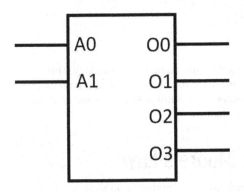

Figure 5-3. *Two- to four-decoder IC module*

When you are writing an FPGA project in VHDL (VHSIC (very high speed integrated circuit) Hardware Description Language), most of the time you are instantiating modules and connecting them. This would be like buying ICs that implement the features you need and then wiring them together on breadboard. The process of wiring is error prone and it's very easy to make mistakes which could burn out your ICs. You will not have this trouble when you are using an FPGA as your "breadboard" because all of the modules are inside the FPGA and the FPGA tools will ensure that the connections are not going to cause any damage. Logic elements are one of the major building blocks in FPGAs for this reason.

Circuit designers use a very long and painful process (physical wires) to build custom digital designs from basic IC modules which are NOT reusable or at least NOT very easy to use reuse without a lot of effort. Compared with an FPGA using VHDL to describe the custom digital design, the whole process (wiring module inside the FPGA) is transparent and automated. One more advantage of using an FPGA is that it keeps the same physical size whereas changing or adding ICs will almost certainly change the size and layout of your circuit.

There is a story about Apollo and the IC in the following link that you might find interesting.

■ **Links**   https://www.hq.nasa.gov/alsj/apollo-ic.html

5.6   1962—First Standard Logic ICs Family

TTL (transistor-transistor logic) is a family of IC technology. Rather than being made of MOSFETs, a TTL is made with BJTs (bipolar junction transistors). The main advantage of TTL over MOSFET is that it consumes less power and is less sensitive to damage from electrostatic discharge. This is one of the most widely used logic standards and most FPGAs support this standard too.

5.7   1963—First CMOS

A CMOS (complementary metal oxide semiconductor) uses a mix of P-FET and N-FET MOSFET technology with a new construction method. The P-FET and N-FET in CMOS circuits are paired such that one and only one FET is ON at a time. This reduces heat as there is no "short circuit" during switching. This construction method improved the circuit yield in the IC manufacturing process too. Therefore, CMOS circuits are widely used in VLSI (very large-scale integration) IC. It means that using CMOS to build a very big IC is cheaper than other technology. It is not surprising then that most FPGAs are built using CMOS technology.

5.8   1964—First SRAM

SRAM (static random access memory) is based on MOS (metal oxide semiconductor) technology. This invention was a huge jump forward compared with previous memory technologies such as drum memory, delay line memory, and magnetic core memory. SRAM can be accessed in random sequence and is smaller than magnetic core memory. SRAM is used in most FPGAs for configuration.

5.9   1965—The Well-Known Law: Moore's Law

Gordon Moore wrote an internal paper to predict "the development of integrated electronics for perhaps the next ten years" ("Cramming More Components onto Integrated Circuits," *Electronics Magazine*, Vol. 38, No. 8 (April 19, 1965)). This became the well-known Moore's Law. This law is based on the prediction that the number of transistors in a circuit doubles every year. This law is now used in industry and research to set goals. Unfortunately, Moore's law is headed for a cliff. Some predict the maximum limit of the law, in which transistor densities continue doubling every 18-24 months, will be hit in 2020 or 2022, around 7nm or 5nm. Think about what it means 5nm (5 billionths of a meter).

5.10   1970—First PROM

PROM (programmable read-only memory) was one of the first types of programmable memory. A user could "burn" the one-time programmable fuse in the PROM to program it. Although PROM was a huge step in programmable technology, there was still improvement to be made, as it wasn't reprogrammable. Once you "burn" the PROM, it cannot be changed. There are some FPGAs that use this technology as it can sometimes be a feature to ensure that the FPGA is not changed after being programmed.

5.11   1971—First EPROM

EPROM (erasable programmable read-only memory) was the second step in programmable memory, in that it could be erased and reprogrammed. To erase an EPROM, you had to bring your EPROM to tanning bed, switch on the UV light, and let it directly shine on the EPROM. This kind of erasing method is clearly not very user friendly.

5.12   1975—First F-PLA

An F-PLA (field programmable logic array) is based on the SUM-OF-PRODUCT form of PROM technology. F-PLA includes a circuit block called a programmable AND gates array and a circuit block called a programmable OR gates array. The F-PLA connected these two blocks to produce a desired output. With this programmable logic you could directly implement POS (product of sums—OR gates and then AND gates) and SOP (sum of products—AND gates then OR gates) in F-PLA. POS and SOP are now only used in teaching tools. POS and SOP are only capable of implementing simple programmable logic like PLA, but they don't come close to the needed complexity for FPGAs.

5.13   1978—First PAL

PAL (programmable array logic) is similar to PLA; however, rather than having two programmable array, it instead has a fixed OR gates array and a programmable AND gates array. Although this only allows PAL to form SOP logic, it can operate faster and cheaper than PLA. Both PAL and PLA are using PROM technology, which means they can be programmed only once.

5.14   1983—First EEPROM

EEPROM (electrically erasable programmable read-only memory) provides a much more user-friendly approach than an EPROM. You don't need to expose the memory under the UV light to erase it. It is the first piece of memory that can be read and write/erase electronically. Erasing an EPROM will erase the entire chip, although you can erase one byte at a time if you wanted to. However, there is a limit on how many times you can reprogram an EEPROM.

5.15   1983—First GAL

GAL stands for generic array logic. Lattice Semiconductor significantly improved the PAL design by making the chips electronically programmable. GALs combine EEPROM and CMOS technology to create a high-speed (at least for 1983), low-power logic device.

5.16   1983—First Programming Language/Tools for Hardware

PALASM (PAL assembler) was the first compiler to convert Boolean equations into a "fuse map" file for PAL.

CUPL (compiler for universal programmable logic) was the first design tool that supported multiple programmable logic device families.

ABEL (Advanced Boolean Expression Language) was the first hardware description language. It included truth table and combinational equation support as well as the ability to describe a state machine. This language is now owned by Xilinx, one of the most famous FPGA companies.

5.17   1985—First FPGA by Xilinx

Finally in 1985, the first FPGA, the XC2064 was shipped! It offered only 800 gates. At that time, you still needed to use a schematic based method to design your FPGA.

5.18   FPGA vs. ASIC

The difference between FPGAs and ASICs (application-specific integrated circuits) primarily come down to $money$, tools, performance, and design flexibility. They each have their own pros and cons. However, the latest developments in the FPGA area are reducing the benefits of ASICs. That's why you see more and more consumer electronic products using FPGA.

5.18.1   FPGA Advantages

- Faster time to market

  - Don't need to have layout, masks, or other manufacturing steps for an FPGA design. Off-the-shelf FPGAs are available and you just need to upload your bit file (which is generated by VHDL) to your FPGA and you're done!

  - FPGA synthesis is much easier than ASIC. FPGA is like using LEGO to build a castle and ASIC is like using sand to build it.

  - Shorter design cycle. This is because the FPGA software can handle a lot of the placement and routing. Modern FPGA design software removes the complex and time-consuming floor planning, timing analysis, placement, and routing from the designer.

  - Reusability of the FPGA is the main advantage. Prototypes of the design can be implemented on FPGAs, which could then be verified to closely replicate how an ASIC would behave. If the design has faults, you just change the HDL code, generate a new bitstream, program the FPGA, and test it again. Modern FPGAs are reconfigurable both partially and on the fly.

- Cheaper to start

  - No NRE (non-recurring engineering costs): This cost is typically related with an ASIC design. There is nothing for FPGA. FPGA tools are cheap or free. We are already using the free one free from Altera. To get started with ASICs you need to commit a large amount of NRE and the tools are expensive—very expensive.

- More predictable development cost: The FPGA design flow eliminates potential respins of the wafer for the project since the design logic is already synthesized and verified in FPGA device.

- If you are going to make less than 500 boards, then using FPGAs is much cheaper. It isn't worth making an ASIC for small runs.

- Faster and cheaper

  - Field reprogram ability: a new design can be uploaded remotely, instantly. FPGAs can be reprogrammed in a snap while an ASIC can take more than $60,000 and at least four to six weeks to make the same changes. Then, of course, you need to ship the new ASIC and physically upgrade the device.

- Buy one get N free!

  - Unlike ASICs, FPGAs have special hardware such as block RAM, clock modules, Ethernet MACs, memories and high-speed I/O, and embedded CPU built in, which can be used to get better performance. High-end FPGAs usually come with phase-locked loops, low-voltage differential signal (LVDS), hardware multipliers for DSPs and microprocessor cores (e.g., Power PC (hardcore), and Microblaze (softcore) in Xilinx and ARM (hardcore) and Nios (softcore) in Altera). There are FPGAs available today that come with built-in ADC (analog-to-digital converter)! Using all these features, designers can build a system on a chip.

5.18.2   FPGA Disadvantages

- Eat too much power!

  - FPGA's consume more power than ASICs. You don't have that much control over the power optimization. This is where ASIC wins the race!

- One size fit all, or doesn't fit at all

  - You have to use the resources available in the FPGA. Thus FPGA limits the design size.

- No one uses FPGAs to build cell phones

  - FPGA are only good for low-quantity production. As quantity increases, the cost per product increases compared to the ASIC implementation.

5.18.3   ASIC Advantages

- Cheaper

  - Lower unit costs: For very high-volume designs the cost comes out to be much less. It can be cheaper than implementing the design using FPGA, at least when you have the appropriate volume of units.

- Faster

  - ASICs are faster than FPGAs: ASICs gives design flexibility. This gives a lot of opportunity for speed optimization.

- Lower

  - Lower in power: ASICs can be optimized for low-power requirements. There are several low-power techniques such as power gating and clock gating that are available to achieve the power target. This is where FPGAs can't compete. Can you imagine a cell phone which has to be charged after every call? Low-power ASICs help extended battery life, which is of course critical for embedded battery-powered devices.

- Mix and match

  - You can implement analog circuits and mixed signal designs in ASIC. This is generally not possible in FPGA.

5.18.4   ASIC Disadvantages

- Time to market

  - ASICs can take a year or more to design. A good way to shorten the development time is to make prototypes using FPGAs and then switch to an ASIC.

- Complex design issues:

  - With ASICs you need to take into account and take care in designing for manufacturability issues, signal integrity issues, and many more. With FPGAs you don't have to deal with these because ASIC designers have already taken care of it. (Don't forget an FPGA is an IC and thus was designed by ASIC design engineer!!)

- Expensive tools

  - ASIC design tools are very expensive. You need to spend a huge amount of NRE.

5.19   Other Technology

5.19.1   CPLD

CPLD (complex programmable logic device) is something between an FPGA and a PAL. CPLD has a lot of PAL and connects them with an array of connections. CPLD purely provide gates. It has another name—SEA of Gates. The biggest difference between CPLD and most FPGAs is the presence of non-volatile memory in CPLD. The MAX10 FPGA in the BeMicro Max10 board has non-volatile memory (flash) too!

5.19.2   Cypress-PSoC

PSoC (programmable system on a chip) architecture contains programmable analog and digital blocks, a CPU, and programmable routing and interconnects. With this technology, Cypress tries to bring everything into one chip. The programmable analog is really cool in that you can program an operational amplifier to be a voltage follower or a voltage diver. You don't need to breadboard the analog circuit anymore.

5.20 Summary

In this chapter you learned about the evolution of technologies that make FPGA technology possible.

1. Digital design theory: Boolean logic

2. Digital logic technology: CMOS

3. Digital storage that can change electrical: SRAM and EEPROM

The differences between an FPGA and an ASIC are shrinking all the time (see Table 5-1). This is driving interest and adoption and is why people like you are getting interested in the technology. The next chapter is going to teach you how to design your own digital design at no cost.

Table 5-1. *FPGA vs. ASIC Summary Table*

	FPGA	ASIC
Initial cost	Nearly free	Expensive
High volume cost	Expensive	Cheaper
Fix bug	Easy	Difficult
Time to market	GOOD	BAD
Power	More	Less
Design method	Easy	Complicated

"Learn from yesterday, live for today, hope for tomorrow"

—Albert Einstein

CHAPTER 6

■ ■ ■

VHDL 101

VHDL (VHSIC (very high speed integrated circuit) Hardware Description Language) is one of the industry's standard languages used to describe digital systems—hardware. It is a powerful language that allows you to describe and simulate complex digital systems. This chapter deals with the basic structure of a VHDL file and how to use it to develop a simple digital design. This chapter is like teaching you how to use a calculator (VHDL) and do math (digital design) at the same time.

6.1   It Is NOT Another Computer Language

Most of the high-level computer languages are used to describe algorithms (e.g., C and JAVA). They execute the code sequentially. VHDL and most of the HDL describe hardware where everything runs in parallel. If you try to write VHDL with a C programing mind-set, then most of the time not only will nobody understand what you're trying to do but also none of the tools will be able to implement your code in FPGA (field-programmable gate array) hardware.

Writing your VHDL code from a hardware point of view will save you a lot of time (and pain) in getting your FPGA design done. It all happens due a somewhat magical process: synthesis. In this process, all of the hardware design VHDL code that you've written is translated to a physical design (the most basic hardware building blocks, for example, CLB, IOB, and Connections). If you write something that's not hardware-like then it will not be possible to make it in hardware. The synthesis process is not "smart" enough to know what hardware you want to implement without you writing it in the VHDL code. Table 6-1 summarizes the differences between VHDL and C.

Table 6-1. *Differences Between VHDL and C Code*

	VHDL	C
Execute sequence	Sequential & Concurrent	Sequential
Knowledge Level	Hardware circuit	Pure logic or algorithmic
Resources Usage	Limited by hardware (FPGA)	Don't care
Language type	Description language	High-level language

We hope you start to think of hardware design when you write your VHDL. To speed up your understanding of how VHDL structure relates to hardware, we will talk about the major components in VHDL for hardware design in this chapter

© Aiken Pang and Peter Membrey 2017
A. Pang and P. Membrey, *Beginning FPGA: Programming Metal*, DOI 10.1007/978-1-4302-6248-0_6

6.2 VHDL File Basic Structure

A VHDL file has two main design units: entity declaration and the architecture body. You can treat the entity declaration as a definition of the input and output signals to connect the architecture body to other VHDL modules. The signals declared here are the only way you can pass information between VHDL modules. It is like the pins on an IC chip or a block symbol in a schematic. It defines how the VHDL module will look like from outside. The architecture body is the function of the module. It defines how the inside of the VHDL will look like and, more interestingly, what it actually does. Figure 6-1 shows a VHDL file containing entity and architecture sections.

▦ **Note**   Good design practice: a VHDL file should contain one and only one VHDL module which in turn has only one entity and architecture.

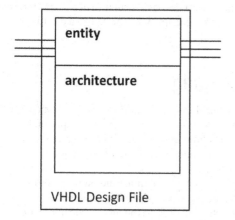

Figure 6-1. *A VHDL design file containing entity and architecture*

▦ **Note**   We are going to use VHDL-93 which is supported by most FPGA tools.

6.2.1   Entity Declaration

Most of the time you will see the entity declaration before the architecture section in a VHDL file because it describes how information flows into and out of the module. Listing 6-1 provides a NAND gate entity example.

Listing. 6-1. NAND Gate Entity Declaration

```
entity NAND is
    port (
                A : in std_logic;
                B : in std_logic;
                C : out std_logic
                );
end NAND;
```

An entity declaration always begins with the keyword **entity**, followed by the module name NAND (which you can name yourself), and the keyword **is**. Next are the port declarations with the keyword **port**. Ports are the connections to other VHDL designs. The port declarations start with **port** and end with **a semi colon**. In this example we have two input ports (A and B) and one output port (C). This NAND gate module implements a two-input NAND gate. The keyword **in** is for the input port and **out** is for the output port. There is another keyword **inout** that defines a bidirectional port. Each entity declaration need to ends with the keyword **end. The module name that follows is optional, however.** In short:

- You can select the name of the entity
- The designer (i.e., you) selects the names of the A, B, and C ports
- The following key words are used to specify the signal direction
  - **in**: input signal to the VHDL design.
  - **out**: output signal from the VHDL design. This signal can only be read by other modules.
  - **inout**: bidirectional signal. Only use this mode when connecting to something outside the FPGA.
- std_logic is one of the built-in signal types. Most of the time, you only use std_logic and std_logic_vector for all simple logic design. We will mention more signal types in later examples.
- Each port declaration ends with semicolon (;), except the last port declaration.

■ **Tips**   You don't have to put input signals before the output signals.

6.2.2   Architecture Body

The internal operation/process of a module is described by an architecture body. In general, the architecture body applies some process on input ports and creates output port values. The NAND gate architecture body looks like Listing 6-2 and Figure 6-3 is how the NAND module actually looks.

Listing 6-2. NAND Gate Architecture Body Declaration

```
architecture behavioral of NAND is
   -- Declartions, e.g. constant declarations, signal etc

begin

  C <= A nand B;

end behavioral;
```

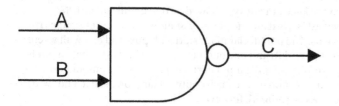

Figure 6-2. *NAND gate module which is implemented by Listing 6-2*

The first line of the architecture body defines the name of the architecture (e.g., behavioral) after the keyword **architecture** and is paired with the NAND entity which was defined earlier in Listing 6-1. The operation of this architecture body is described in between the keywords **begin** and **end**. The keyword **nand** is a built-in NAND function. The <= symbol represents an assignment operator

- You can select the name of the architecture

- You need to pair **architecture** with one **entity**

- The implementation of the architecture is between **begin** and **end**

- If you need extra signals, you can declare them in between **is** and **begin**

■ **Tip** Double hyphen -- is the start of the comment

Let's have one more example. A three-input OR gate digital design has three input ports and one output port. The OR3 gate entity and architecture body look as shown in Listing 6-3 and Figure 6-3.

Listing 6-3. OR Gate with Three-Input Whole VHDL Module Example

```
library ieee;                          -- All of the deisgn need ieee library
use ieee.std_logic_1164.all;    -- Using std_logic_1164 package

entity OR3 is
   port (
            A: in std_logic;
            B: in std_logic;
            C: in std_logic;
            D: out std_logic
          );
end OR3;

architecture behavioral of OR3 is
   -- Declartions, such as type declarations, constant declarations, signal declarations etc
   Signal   X: std_logic;
begin    -- architecture behavioral of NAND

            X <= A or B;
            D <= C or X;

end behavioral;
```

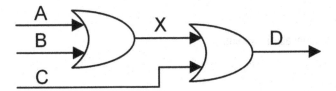

Figure 6-3. *NAND gate module which is implemented by Listing 6-3*

In Listing 6-3, we have two new keywords: **library** and **use**. A library is a place where the compiler keeps data about a particular design. A package is a file that contains declarations of commonly used stuff (e.g., std_logic_1164 contains the data type std_logic) that can be shared with other VHDL models. For most FPGA designs, you'll need to add the ieee library and **use** std_logic_1164.**all**. The .all extension indicates we want to use the entire ieee.std_logic_1164 package. It defines all of the std_logic, std_logic_vector, and so on. The std_logic_1164 is a VHDL file. You can download this file from the following link, but you'll also find it provided by the ModelSim-Altera version.

IEEE web site: www.vhdl.org/rassp/vhdl/models/standards/std_logic_unsigned.vhd

EXERCISES

1. Implement a home security alarm system. A and C are motion sensors. B is a switch that turns on the alarm. The alarm system will trigger when the alarm is turned on (setting B = high) and either motion sensor A or C is set to high. This will set F to high, which will actually trigger the security alarm. Figure 6-4 shows the block diagram.

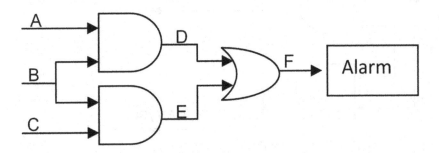

Figure 6-4. *Logic diagram for exercise 1*

2. Implement a 1-bit full adder. It has three inputs, A, B, and C, and two outputs, SUM and Carryout. Go to google 1-bit full adder to get your block diagram. Hints: You only need to use five gates for this design or Figure 6-5.

■ **Tip** Draw block diagrams of what your hardware should look like so that you will have an idea of what you are going to design.

Answers

1. The following code is for a home security alarm system.

```
library ieee;
use ieee.std_logic_1164.all;
entity alarm_system is
   port (
              A: in std_logic;
              B: in std_logic;
              C: in std_logic;
              F: out std_logic
              );
end alarm_system;
architecture behavioral of alarm_system is
   signal   D: std_logic;
   signal   E: std_logic;
begin
              D <= A and B;
              E <= C and B;
              F <= D or E;
end behavioral;
```

2. Full Adder block diagram (Figure 6-5) and digital design.

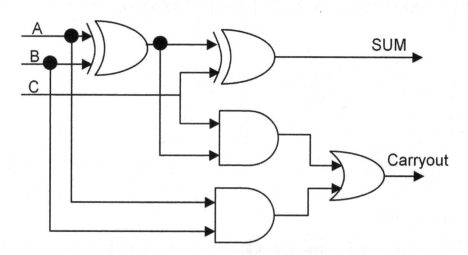

Figure 6-5. *Full Adder block diagram*

```vhdl
library ieee;
use ieee.std_logic_1164.all;
entity fulladder is
   port (
               A: in std_logic;
               B: in std_logic;
               C: in std_logic;
               SUM: out std_logic;
               Carrout: out std_logic
               );
end fulladder;
architecture behavioral of fulladder is
   signal   D: std_logic;
begin
               D <= A xor B;
               SUM <= D xor C;
               Carrout <= ((D and C) or (A and B));
end behavioral;
```

6.3 Summary

VHDL is a hardware description language. It will be much easier for you to design an FPGA when you can start to see things from a hardware point of view. Any complex digital design should be able to be broken down into smaller-size modules for you to implement them in VHDL.

Each VHDL has the following structure:

- library

- entity

- architecture

The chapters that follow will give more detail on how to use VHDL to design more hardware!

▓ **Tip** Notepad ++ is a very good (and free) editor which supports VHDL!

"A person who never made a mistake never tried anything new."

—Albert Einstein

CHAPTER 7

■ ■ ■

Number Theory for FPGAs

Number theory is "the Queen of Mathematics." It is the foundation of mathematics and includes all the basic elements. Don't worry, you did pick up a book on FPGA (field-programmable gateway array) design, but we're going to have to cover just a little math in order for you to be able to actually do anything useful with an FPGA. In this chapter we are going to show you several basic elements of VHDL (**V**HSIC (very high speed integrated circuit) **H**ardware **D**escription **L**anguage), such as identifiers and numbers. All of the stuff shown in this chapter will help you write better VHDL code. You should bookmark this chapter because you will likely come back to frequently when you actually start to write your own VHDL code.

7.1   Vocabulary in VHDL

Vocabulary is the first thing you learn in any new language such as VHDL. There are some basic rules for VHDL words. Listing 7-1 provides an example.

- VHDL is NOT case sensitive

- It doesn't care about how many spaces or tabs in the code

- None of the words can start with number

Listing 7-1. Not Case Sensitive and Doesn't Care About Whitespace

```
NotCaseSensitive <= Spaces Or Tabs;

nOtcAsEsEnsItIvE         <=           spaceS    OR TABS;
```

7.1.1   Identifiers

An identifier is defined by the VHDL designer to name items in a VHDL model (Figures 7-1 and 7-2). Examples of VHDL items are port names and signal names. The rules for identifiers are as follows:

- Can only contain a combination of alphabetic letters (A-Z, a-z), numbers (0-9) and underscores (_)

- Must start with alphabetic letters (A-Z, a-z)

- Cannot end with an underscore (_) and cannot have consecutive underscores

- The identifier should be self-describing

© Aiken Pang and Peter Membrey 2017
A. Pang and P. Membrey, *Beginning FPGA: Programming Metal*, DOI 10.1007/978-1-4302-6248-0_7

■ **Tip** Smart choices for identifiers make your VHDL code easier to read and understand, which in turn means less effort required to find and fix problems in the code.

```
1  reset      --reset
2  clk        --classic clock
3  wen        --classic write enable
4  data_in    --self comment name
5  out_port   --output port
```

Figure 7-1. *Valid identifiers*

```
1  email@apress.com  -- contains illegal characters for an identifier
2  9bit_registers    -- starts with non-alphabetic letters
3  _ABC              -- starts with an underscore
4  ABC_              -- ends with an underscore
5  first__pulse      -- two successive underscores
```

Figure 7-2. *Invalid or bad-style identifiers*

■ **Note** In VHDL-93, VHDL supports extended identifiers, which allows you to use any character in any order. We suggest you don't use these in your design files as they tend to confuse and complicate rather than improve the situation.

7.1.2   Reserved Words—Keywords

Some identifiers, called reserved words or keywords, are reserved for special use in VHDL, so we cannot use them as identifiers for the items we define. Table 7-1 shows the full list of reserved words.

Table 7-1. *VHDL Reserved Words*

Reserved Word	Description
constant, generic, in, inout, map, out, of, port, signal	Entity reserved words: port, in, out, and map are used in the entity section. Inout is another port mode that allows a bidirectional port to be read and updated within the entity model. Signal represents a wire or a placeholder for a value. Signals are assigned in signal assignment statements and declared in signal declarations. Constants can hold a single value of a given type. Generic is similar to port but it is a constant value. It is used to pass environment information to submodules.
if, then, elsif, else, case, select, when, is, end, null	Conditional logic statements: if, then, elsif, else, case, select, and when are used in conditional logic. "End" is used at the end of statement. "is" equates the identity portion to the definition portion in the declaration. "null" is sometimes used with "case". There's an example for it in Chapter 8.
srl, sra, sll, sla, rol, ror	Shift operators: srl, sra, and ror are shift left; sll, sla, and rol are shift right.
and, nand, nor, not, or, xnor, xor	Logic operators: In Chapter 8 we will cover these in more detail too.
abs, mod, rem	Arithmetic operators: Abs = absolute value; Mod = modulus; Rem = remainder
entity, architecture, process, begin, variable, function, component	Most of the VHDL models need to use these reserved words. We used entity, architecture, and begin Chapter 6's full adder example. Process is sequential or concurrent code to be executed. Variable and function are used to define a function in VHDL code.
downto, to, type, subtype, others, array, range, record	These reserved words are used to define signals and types in VHDL code. You will see examples of them later in this chapter.
library, all, use, package, body	All is a suffix for selecting all declarations that are contained within the package or library denoted by the prefix.
after, assert, exit, file, inertial, new, on, open, report, reject, return, severity, transport, unaffected, until, wait	These reserved words are very useful when simulating VHDL code. All of these reserved words cannot be used to generate REAL hardware. Don't use them in your hardware design VHDL code.
for, generate, loop, next, while	for and while loop are very useful when you need to generate multiple identical components.
access, alias, block, buffer, bus, disconnect, guarded, impure, linkage, postponed, procedure, pure, register, shared, units	It's strongly recommended that you don't use these reserved words in your FPGA designs.
attribute, group, label, literal	Attribute reserved words
configuration	When designing for portability, you need to use configuration. We will not talk about this in this book as it's a fairly advanced topic.

There are some VHDL-00 reserved words in the Table 7-1. Most of them are not recommended for use as they are not supported by all tools.

■ **Note**   The following web site descripts each reserved word in detail: `http://www.xilinx.com/itp/xilinx10/isehelp/ite_r_vhdl_reserved_words.htm`.

7.1.3   Signal, Variable, and Constant

Each VHDL module is combined from multiple data objects that store or display information. For example, CONSTANT is used to store fixed information and is a data object. There are three types of data object: signals, variables, and constants. So far, we have seen signals that were used as internal nets (full adder signals D).

When we create a data object, we need to assign a data value and data type to that object. The data value will be different when the object type is different. For example, if the data type is a bit object then the stored value must be either a 0 or a 1. If the data type is a real object then the stored value will be a real number.

7.1.3.1   Signal

Signals in VHDL are like a physical wire. They are used to connect different modules. Signals are declared as shown in Listings 7-2 and 7-3.

Listing 7-2. Signal Declaration

```
signal  signal_name  :  type  [  :=  initial  value  ]  ;
```

Listing 7-3. Signal Declaration Examples

```
signal  Q1  :  std_logic  ;   -- declare Q1 as std_logic data type without initial value
signal  counter  :  natural  :=  0  ;  -- declare counter as natural data type with
                                                    initial value = 0
signal  Data  :  std_logic_vector(  7  downto  0  )  ;  -- declare Data as std_logic_vector
                                                    with 8 bit width
```

Signals can be updated using a signal assignment statement. Figure 7-3 shows an example for the signal data type.

```
1   library ieee;
2   use ieee.std_logic_1664.all;   -- standard IEEE library
3
4   entity signal_example is
5   port(
6           S_in    : in  std_logic;   -- One bit input
7           S_out   : out std_logic;   -- One bit output
8           );
9   end signal_example;
10
11  architecture structure of signal_example is
12
13  signal s_1 : std_logic;
14  signal s_2 : std_logic;
15  signal s_3 : std_logic;
16  signal s_4 : std_logic;
17
18  begin
19  -- The following are the signal assignments
20      s_1 <= not S_in;
21      s_2 <= S_in;
22      s_3 <= s_1 and s_2;
23      s_4 <= (s1 and s_3) or S_in;
24      S_out <= s_4;
25
26  end structure;
```

Figure 7-3. signal_example VHDL module

In the signal_example, signals s_1, s_2, s_3, and s_4 are declared std_logic. All four of them get assigned a value which is a logic operation result from lines 20 to 23. In line 24, the output S_out is assigned the value of s_4.

There is always some delay in the signal assignments. This is different from the variable data type.

7.1.3.2 Variable

Variable data objects, like in C, are used to store local process/function information. They are used to hold temporary data. Variables are declared with the statement shown in Listings 7-4 and 7-5.

Listing 7-4. Signal Declaration

```
variable  variable_name  :  type  [  :=  initial  value  ]  ;
```

Listing 7-5. Signal Declaration Examples

```
variable Q1 : std_logic ; -- declare Q1 as std_logic data type without initial value
variable counter : natural := 0 ; -- declare counter as natural data type with initial
                                          value = 0
variable Data : std_logic_vector( 7 downto 0 ) ; -- declare Data as std_logic_vector
                                                       with 8 bit width
```

In Figure 7-4, variables v_1, v_2, v_3, and v_4 are declared std_logic inside the v_p process. All four of the variables are only allowed to be used within the process. All four of them get assigned a value which is the logic operation result from lines 24 to 27. In line 29, the output S_out is assigned the value of v_4.

```
1   library ieee;
2   use ieee.std_logic_1664.all;  -- standard IEEE library
3
4   entity variable_example is
5   port(
6           S_in      : in  std_logic;  -- One bit input
7           S_out     : out std_logic;  -- One bit output
8       );
9   end variable_example;
10
11  architecture structure of variable_example is
12
13  begin
14
15  v_p:process(S_in)   -- variable process
16
17      variable v_1 : std_logic;
18      variable v_2 : std_logic;
19      variable v_3 : std_logic;
20      variable v_4 : std_logic;
21
22      begin
23      -- variable assignment statements
24      v_1 := not S_in;
25      v_2 := S_in;
26      v_3 := v_1 and v_2;
27      v_4 := (v1 and v_3) or S_in;
28      S_out <= v_4;
29      end process;
30
31  end structure;
```

Figure 7-4. *variable_example VHDL module*

There are two differences between variables and signals. The first one is that variables are only able to assign/update values within a process, procedure, or function. Signals can also be assigned a value by direct assignment (as in Figure 7-3 lines 20-24).

The second example is where the value changes. We will use Listings 7-6 and 7-7 to show the difference.

Listing 7-6. Process Using Signal

```
architecture SIG of delay_example is
    signal   activate, result   :   natural  := 0 ;
    signal   signal_1                :   natural  := 1 ;
    signal   signal_2                :   natural  := 2 ;
    signal   signal_3                :   natural  := 3 ;
begin
    process( activate )
    begin
      signal_1 <= signal_2 ;
      signal_2 <= signal_1   +  signal_3 ;
      signal_3 <= signal_2 ;
      result    <=  signal_1 + signal_2 + signal 3;
    end process;
end SIG
```

Listing 7-7. Process Using Variable

```
architecture VAR of delay_example is
    signal   activate, result   :   natural  := 0 ;
begin
    process( activate )
      variable   variable_1   :   natural  := 1 ;
      variable   variable_2   :   natural  := 2 ;
      variable   variable_3   :   natural  := 3 ;

    begin
      variable_1 := variable_2 ;
      variable_2 := variable_1   +  variable_3 ;
      variable_3 := variable_2 ;
      result    <=  signal_1 + signal_2 + signal 3;

    end process;
end VAR
```

In Listing 7-8, the signals (signal_1, signal_2, signal_3) are computed at the same time that activate is triggered. The signals will get updated as the following: signal_1 = 2, signal_2 = 1 + 3 = 4, signal_3 = 2, and result = 1 + 2 + 3 = 6.

In Listing 7-9, the variables are computed at the time when activate is triggered in sequential order (from top to bottom). The signals will get updated as the following: variable_1 = 2, variable_2 = 2 + 3 = 5, variable_3 = 5, and result = 2 + 5 + 5 = 12.

■ **Tip** For the vast majority of the time use signals in your designs and don't mix signals and variables in the same process

---

7.1.3.3   Constant

A constant is like variable data object, but the value of it cannot be changed. It can improve readability of the VHDL code. A constant is declared as in Listing 7-8.

Listing 7-8. Signal Declaration

```
constant   constant_name   :   type   [   :=   initial   value   ]   ;
```

Listing 7-9. Signal Declaration Examples

```
constant  PEROID : time := 10 ns ; -- declare PERIOD as time data type with value = 10 nano seconds
constant  BUS_WIDTH : natural := 16 ; -- declare BUS_WIDTH as natural data type with value = 16
```

Constants can be declared at the beginning of architecture and can be used anywhere within the architecture. If constants are declared within a process, then they can only be used inside the process.

7.1.4   Literal: Word for Word

There are two main types of literal: characters and numbers. The meaning of the literal though depends on the type of the object. For example, "1" could be the only integer bigger than 0 and smaller than 2, or it could be the character in ASCII code 31 (HEX). Therefore, words in VHDL need to be paired with a data type.

7.1.4.1   Characters

A character is only ONE "character"; it is stored as its ASCII code. To use a character, you need to use single quotation marks, as shown in Listing 7-10.

Listing 7-10. Characters Examples

```
'1', 'Z', 'a', 'f', '$'
```

7.1.4.2   String

A string is a group of characters. You need to use double quotation marks when you want to use a string (Listing 7-11).

Listing 7-11. String Examples

```
"This is a string",
"This is a ""string"" too."
```

7.1.4.3   Bit String

A bit string can treated as a mutation of a string. A string is used to represent characters and a bit string is used to represent binary numbers or a sequence of bit values (Listings 7-12 through 7-14). Examples are show as the following. All of them are showing value 90 and 240 but not the same number of bits for each type: 90 in the binary bit string only uses 7 bit; Octal use 9 bit; and Hexagonal use 8 bit.

Listing 7-12. Binary Bit String

```
b"1011010", b"1111_0000"
```

Listing 7-13. Octal(8) Bit String

```
o"132", o"360"
```

Listing 7-14. Hexagonal(16) Bit String

```
x"5A", x"F0"
```

7.1.4.4 Numbers

Numbers include real and integer numbers. In the IEEE library numeric_std package, numbers can be decimal numbers, negative "-," you can use exponential notation "E," and you can even use underscores "_" to make the number easier to read.

    Integer number range: -2,147,483,647 to 2,147,483,647

    Real number range: -1.0E38 to + 1.0E38

    Following are some examples:

```
3.14
0.7E8
123_456
```

7.1.4.5 Base

Sometimes it is more convenient or easier to read when a base other than 10 is used when representing a number. Here are a couple of examples. The first one is 90 and second one is 240 in decimal.

```
BASE 2: 2#1011010#
BASE 8: 8#132#
BASE 16: 16#5A#

BASE 2: 2#1111_0000#
BASE 8: 8#360#
BASE 16: 16#F0#
```

7.1.4.6 Physical

This is a special word in VHDL which represents time, current, and voltage. In FPGA design, we only use time. Following is an example of 200 Nano seconds.

```
200 ns
```

You will see and use a lot of time words in a test bench. (In Chapter 4, in the section "The Test Bench," we defined the SYS_CLK to toggle every 10 ns) It is a very useful way to generate a clock in test bench. Keep in mind that it is an abstraction and will only work in simulation. As such it can appear in your test bench file but not in your design file. We will talk more about how to create clocks in Chapter 10.

7.2 Grammar in VHDL

VHDL is a strongly typed language. This means that you need to type more (compared with Verilog, which is another HDL language). VHDL is always checking the types of objects to ensure consistency and prevent you from mixing incompatible data types or performing actions that don't make sense. It is needed in hardware design because most of the time hardware needs to be the exact type and size to work. It is like needing to use the correct type and size of screw driver to remove a screw. This section will only cover the most useful grammar, and you will see more of VHDL grammar throughout the next couple of chapters.

7.2.1 Statements in VHDL

Every VHDL statement is terminated with a semicolon. It is quite similar to other computer languages. VHDL statements are easy to create, but what the statement means (and what it ultimately does) is up to you. The semicolons only help you do half of the job.

7.2.2 How to Comment

VHDL only has line comments and doesn't support block comment in VHDL-93. You need to put a double hyphen (--) in front of the comments and rest of the line will be commented out (Listing 7-15).

Listing 7-15. VHDL Comment Example

```
regular_coffee  <=  coffee and cream and sugar  ; -- Here is the comment of how to make a coffee
-- You can start your comment in the beginning of the line
```

7.2.3 <= and := sign

You will see <= and := in VHDL. They mean totally different things. Let's talk about <= first. It is used to assign a value to an object. Remember it is ended by semicolon (Listing 7-16).

Listing 7-16. VHDL Object Assignment Example (Signal and Variable)

```
signal_assignment   <=  value_for_the_signal  ;     -- You will use this for signal assignment
variable_assignment :=  value_for_the_variable ;   -- You will use this for variable assignment
```

In the example, we have <= and :=. We are not suggesting you interchange them. The <= sign is used to assign signals and the := is used to assign variables.

7.2.4 Begin and End

Every time you start with **begin** remember to finish the section with **end.** In the earlier examples (Figures 7-2, 7-3, Listings 7-6, 7-7), you can see that all the begin statements are paired with an end.

7.2.5   Coding Your VHDL with Style

Coding with a convention style can increase readability. If all of your code uses the same style, you will save time hunting for bugs or when you try to reuse code you wrote earlier. A good coding style (guideline) also helps you to avoid certain constructs that often causing bugs. We won't cover all the guidelines here but we would recommend you go to the following link to download a copy for yourself and have a browse through.

1. Do not start writing any VHDL code until you completely understand the specifications.

2. Use only IEEE libraries: std_logic_1164 and numeric_std. Do not use the commonly used Synposys' libraries std_logic_arith, std_logic_(un)signed, numeric_bit, or any other none IEEE library.

3. Comment the general functionality of each section/subsection.

4. The comments written in the code must include valuable and significant information. Avoid unnecessary or trivial comments.

5. Keep the signal names consistent throughout the hierarchy of the design.

6. Write just one statement per line of code, even when doing component instantiation.

7. If possible use lowercase letters for all the code.

8. For synthesizable code do not use 'after' to imply delay: sum <= a + b after 3 ns; The 'after' must only be used in test bench.

■ **Note**   This is a good example that you could follow: `https://wiki.electroniciens.cnrs.fr/images/VHDL_Coding_eng.pdf`.

7.3   Summary

After this chapter you should understand the basic elements in VHDL (signal, variable, and constant) and how to name them (identifiers). You should not use any reserved words for the name of your identifiers. A lot of the reserved words (keywords) will be used in the next chapter. Remember to have enough comment in your code to provide a good description, but don't comment every trivial thing.

In Chapter 8 we are going to employ these basic rules to build some useful designs.

■ **Tip**   **Alt + Shift** in Notepad ++ for block edit is very useful in VHDL coding

---

"God made the integers, all the rest is the work of man."

—Leopold Kronecker

CHAPTER 8

■ ■ ■

Telling the Truth: Boolean Algebra and Truth Tables

In this chapter, we will show you how to use the basic elements (signals) to create combinational logic in VHDL (VHSIC (very high speed integrated circuit) Hardware Description Language). We'll also cover two IEEE (Institute of Electrical and Electronics Engineers) libraries, namely, std_logic_1164 and numeric_std which provide features for more than just Boolean logic in your FPGA (field-programmable gateway array) design. By the end of this chapter you will know how to create a 4-bit adder using two different approaches and then you'll use ModelSim to simulate the 4-bit adder.

8.1 Boolean Algebra

Boolean algebra is like designing switches for turning light bulbs on and off. Figure 8-1 shows a design that uses two switches to control the doorbell. If we would like to ring the bell when either one of the switches is connected (high), then we need an OR gate.

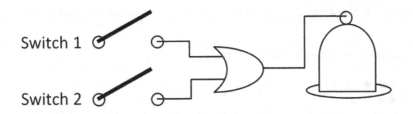

Figure 8-1. *Boolean algebra example 1—doorbell*

In Boolean algebra, we use the following equation to describe what is happening in the doorbell design:

Bell Ring = Switch 1 + Switch 2

The plus (+) sign in Boolean algebra is logical OR. There are two more basic operation signs in Boolean algebra. They are • which is AND and ~ which is NOT. Boolean algebra only has two possible outputs, logical high/true (1) or logical low/false (0) inputs and outputs.

Let's look at one more example. We would like the output (Result) set to high when all inputs (A, B, and C) are low (Figure 8-2). The Boolean algebra equation will be like the following:

Result = ~A • ~B • ~C

© Aiken Pang and Peter Membrey 2017
A. Pang and P. Membrey, *Beginning FPGA: Programming Metal*, DOI 10.1007/978-1-4302-6248-0_8

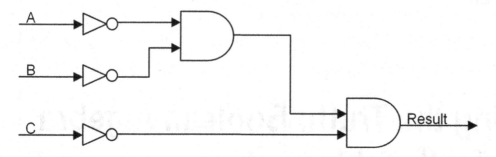

Figure 8-2. *Boolean algebra example 2 in logic gate*

It is very easy to create the logic gates from the Boolean algebra equation. It is like a direct map to the OR, AND, and NOT gates. This gate-level implementation can be easily written in VHDL, as shown in Listing 8-1.

Listing 8-1. Boolean Algebra Example 2 in VHDL Code

```
library ieee;                          -- All of the deisgn need ieee library
use ieee.std_logic_1164.all;     -- Using std_logic_1164 package

entity boolean_algebra_example2 is
   port (
             A: in std_logic;
             B: in std_logic;
             C: in std_logic;
             Result: out std_logic
             );
end boolean_algebra_example2;

architecture behavioral of boolean_algebra_example2 is
   -- Declarations, such as type declarations, constant declarations, signal declarations etc
signal temp : std_logic;

begin    -- architecture behavioral of boolean_algebra_example2

          temp    <= NOT A AND NOT B ;
          Result <= NOT C AND temp;

end behavioral;
```

8.1.1 Simulation Steps for Boolean Algebra Example 2

It is time to do some simulation of this VHDL logic file. Please take the following steps to create the VHDL file and simulate it in ModelSim:

1. Create a Quartus project using the project template (see Chapter 4)

2. Click **File ➤ New...** from the Quartus Prime menu to add a new VHDL file (Figure 8-3).

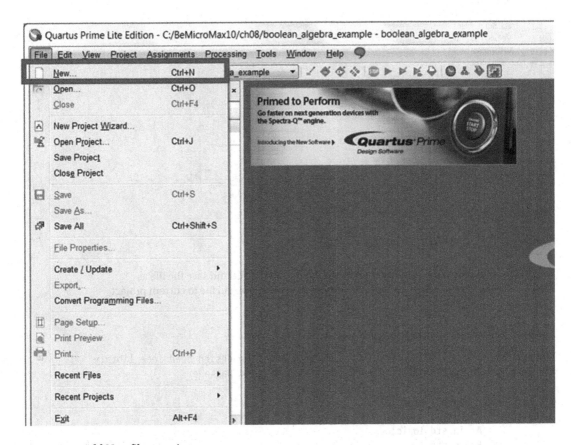

Figure 8-3. *Add New file to project*

3. Select **VHDL File** and Click **OK** (Figure 8-4).

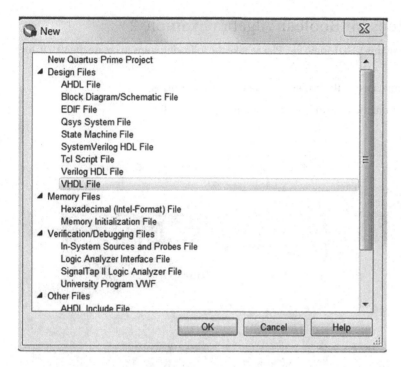

Figure 8-4. *Add New VHDL file in Quartus Project*

4. Copy the code from Listing 8-2 into the new VHDL file and save the file as boolean_algebra_example2.vhd with the check box Add file to current project ticked (Figure 8-5).

Listing 8-2. boolean_algebra_example2.vhd

```vhdl
library ieee;                        -- All of the design need ieee library
use ieee.std_logic_1164.all;   -- Using std_logic_1164 package

entity boolean_algebra_example2 is
    port (
            A: in std_logic;
            B: in std_logic;
            C: in std_logic;
            Result: out std_logic
            );
end boolean_algebra_example2;
```

```
architecture behavioral of boolean_algebra_example2 is
   -- Declarations, such as type declarations, constant declarations, signal declarations etc
signal temp : std_logic;

begin    -- architecture behavioral of boolean_algebra_example2

         temp    <= NOT A AND NOT B ;
         Result <= NOT C AND temp;


end behavioral;
```

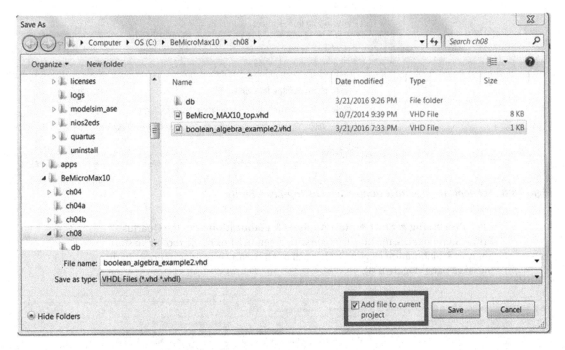

Figure 8-5. Save the VHDL file as boolean_algebra_example2.vhd

5. In Project Navigator, select **Files.** Right-click the file boolean_algebra_example.
    vhd and click **Set as Top-Level Entity** (Figure 8-6).

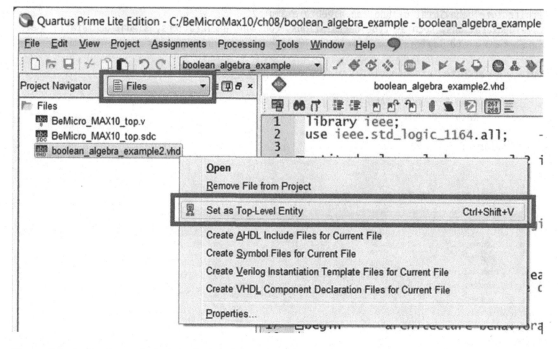

Figure 8-6. *Set boolean_algebra_example2.vhd as Top-Level Entity*

6. Click **Processing ➤ Start ➤ Start Analysis & Elaboration** from the Quartus
   Prime menu or click the blue triangle with green tick box in the toolbar to start
   analysis & elaboration (Figure 8-7). It will not have any warnings or errors in the
   message pane (Figure 8-8).

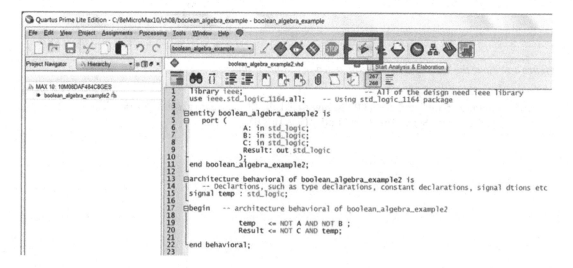

Figure 8-7. *Start Analysis & Elaboration button*

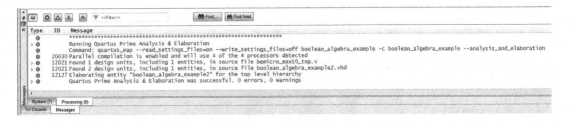

Figure 8-8. *Message after Start Analysis & Elaboration finished*

7. Click **Tools ➤ Run Simulation Tool ➤ RTL Simulation** from the Quartus Prime menu to start simulation (Figure 8-9). The Select Simulation Language box will pop up; select **VHDL** and click **OK** (Figure 8-10).

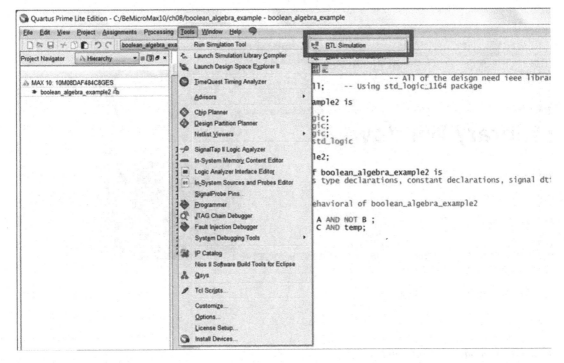

Figure 8-9. *Start RTL simulation from Quartus Prime*

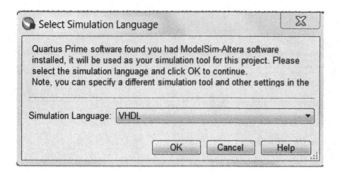

Figure 8-10. *Select Simulation Language*

8. The following two windows should pop up (see Figure 8-11 and 8-12)

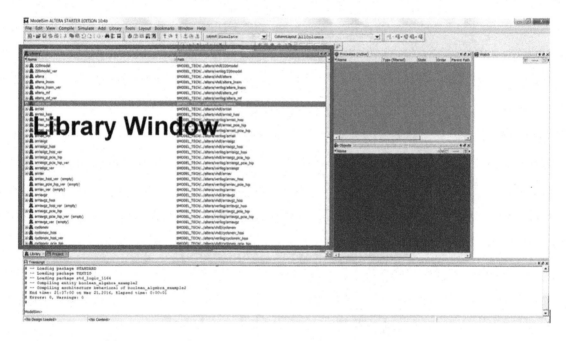

Figure 8-11. *ModelSim Main window*

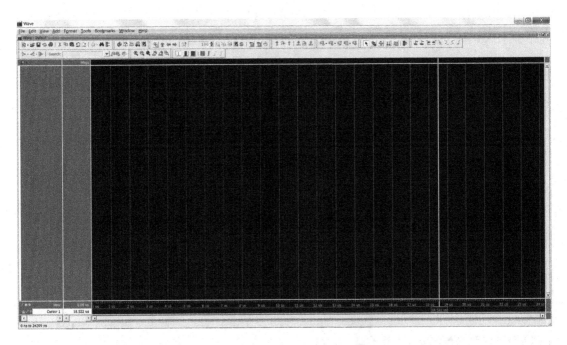

Figure 8-12. *ModelSim waveform window*

9. In the Library Window, click the cross next to the work library and right-click
    on boolean_algebra_example2. Click **Simulate**. Or type **vsim work.boolean_
    algebra_example2** in the transcript box shown in Figure 8-13. ModelSim should
    show something like Figure 8-14. It will have Sim, Transcript, Processes, and
    Objects windows.

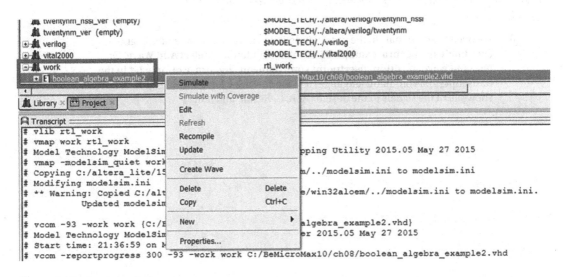

Figure 8-13. *Start simulation*

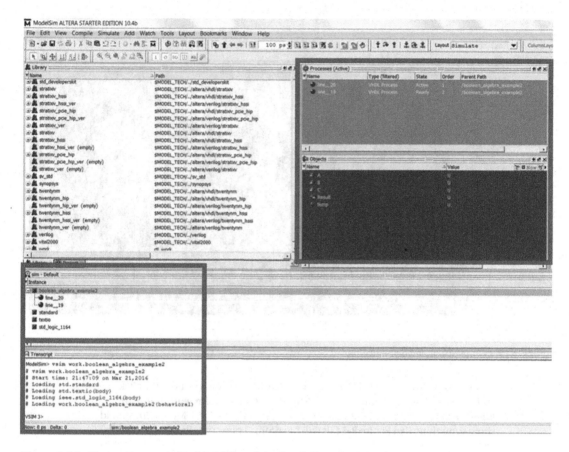

Figure 8-14. *New section started in ModelSim when simulation was started*

10. We need to add signals to the wave windows to see what is happening. Right-click **boolean_algebra_example2** in the sim window and select **Add Wave**. Or type **add wave -position insertpoint sim:/boolean_algebra_example2/*** in the transcript (tool command language (tcl) window). See Figure 8-15. Figure 8-16 shows all of the signals in the design (A, B, C, Result, and temp)

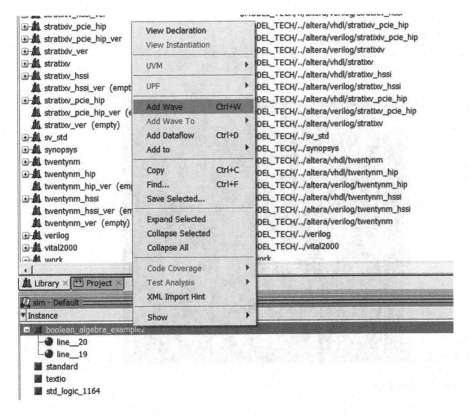

Figure 8-15. Adding signals to the wave windows

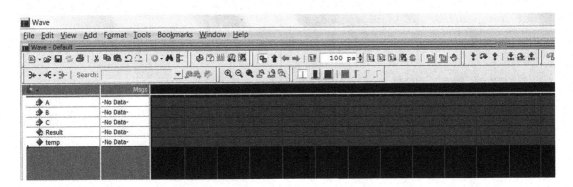

Figure 8-16. Wave window shows all the signals

11. Right-click A signal and select **Force....** Force Selected Signal window pop-up (Figure 8-17). Change the Value from U to 1 (Figure 8-18) and click OK. Or type **force -freeze sim:/boolean_algebra_example2/A 1 0** in the transcript (tcl window).

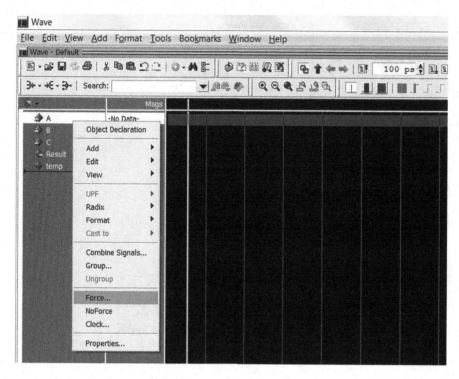

Figure 8-17. *Force signal A to high (1)*

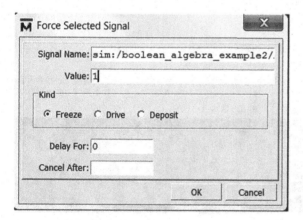

Figure 8-18. *Force signal A to high (1)*

12. To speed up the process, please run the following tcl script (Listing 8-3) in the Transcript window. See Figure 9-19 for the waveform window. This tcl set all inputs (A, B, and C) to high and changes the inputs one by one to low every 100 ns. The output (Result) stays low until 300 ns, when it changes to high. It matches our Boolean algebra equation.

Listing 8-3. tcl for Generating Inputs A, B, and C in Example 2

```
force -freeze sim:/boolean_algebra_example2/B 1 0
force -freeze sim:/boolean_algebra_example2/C 1 0
run 100 ns
force -freeze sim:/boolean_algebra_example2/A 0 0
run 100 ns
force -freeze sim:/boolean_algebra_example2/B 0 0
run 100 ns
force -freeze sim:/boolean_algebra_example2/C 0 0
run 100 ns
```

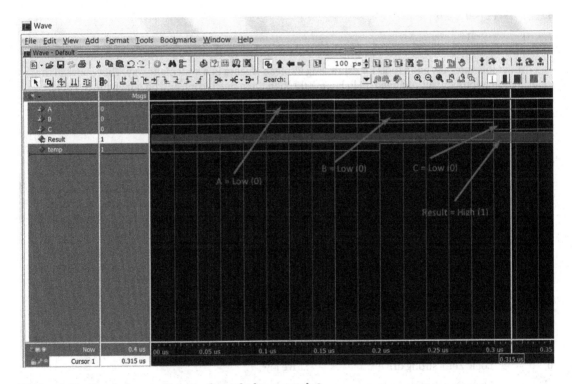

Figure 8-19. *Simulation result on Boolean algebra example 2*

8.1.2 Truth Tables

Truth tables are another way to express Boolean algebra or gate logic. In general, the truth table has 2^n rows where n is the number of inputs. For example, three input will have 2^3 = 8 combinations. Let's use example 2 to demonstrate writing truth tables. In Table 8-1 it's clear that the result is set to high if and only if all inputs are low. This can help you compare the simulation result with the expected behavior.

Table 8-1. *Truth Table for Example 2*

	A	B	C	Result
0	0	0	0	1
1	0	0	1	0
2	0	1	0	0
3	0	1	1	0
4	1	0	0	0
5	1	0	1	0
6	1	1	0	0
7	1	1	1	0

Truth tables are very good tools for expressing Boolean algebra in a systematic way. They show all the input combinations and all you need to do is work through them one by one and fill out all the possible combinations of output. Therefore, the FPGA creates Boolean algebra by using the truth table in look-up tables (LUTs). FPGAs can combine more than one LUT to form a bigger truth table.

8.2   Standard Logic in VHDL

In Boolean algebra, logic states are only defined as high/true (1) or low/false (0). This sounds fine on paper, but there are not enough states to describe real hardware states (high-impedance, unknown, etc.). All the signals in VHDL are wires. We need more than two values to describe a wire status, which is very important for accurate simulation.

IEEE 1164 is a standard logic data type with nine values as shown in Table 8-2.

Table 8-2. *IEEE 1164 Standard Logic Data Type*

Character	Description	Simulate
'U'	Uninitialized	No Driver
'X'	Unknown logic value, strong drive	Unknown
'0'	Logic Zero, strong drive	Drive low
'1'	Logic One, strong drive	Drive high
'Z'	High impedance	Tristate buffer
'W'	Unknown logic value, weak drive	Unknown
'L'	Logic zero, weak drive	Pull-down resistor
'H'	Logic one, weak drive	Pull-up resistor
'-'	Don't care	Don't care

Having these nine values, it becomes possible to accurately model the behavior of a digital system during simulation. The 'Z' is used to model and output enable and the '-' don't care is used to optimize the combinational logic.

The most important reason to use standard logic data types is to provide portability between models written by different designers or different FPGA design tools.

To use this standard logic type in the VHDL file, you need to add two statements in the very beginning of VHDL code.

Listing 8-4. Using IEEE 1164 Standard Logic in VHDL Design

```
library ieee;
use ieee.std_loigc_1164.all;
```

8.2.1 Standard Logic Data Types

There are three data types you need to know in a std_logic_1164 package.

1. std_ulogic

2. std_logic

3. std_logic_vector

The first is one of the most basic data types. The std_ulogic data type is an unresolved type which means that it does not allow two drivers to drive this std_ulogic signal at the same time (Table 8-3). std_logic support resolver two or more drivers to drive the signals. The IEEE 1164 package defines how std_logic resolves multiple drivers' value.

Table 8-3. *Resolution of IEEE 1164 std_logic Data Type*

	'U'	'X'	'0'	'1'	'Z'	'W'	'L'	'H'	'-'
'U'	'U'	'U'	'U'	'U'	'U'	'U'	'U'	'U'	'U'
'X'	'U'	'X'	'X'	'X'	'X'	'X'	'X'	'X'	'X'
'0'	'U'	'X'	'0'	'X'	'0'	'0'	'0'	'0'	'X'
'1'	'U'	'X'	'X'	'1'	'1'	'1'	'1'	'1'	'X'
'Z'	'U'	'X'	'0'	'1'	'Z'	'W'	'L'	'H'	'X'
'W'	'U'	'X'	'0'	'1'	'W'	'W'	'W'	'W'	'X'
'L'	'U'	'X'	'0'	'1'	'L'	'W'	'L'	'W'	'X'
'H'	'U'	'X'	'0'	'1'	'H'	'W'	'W'	'H'	'X'
'-'	'U'	'X'	'X'	'X'	'X'	'X'	'X'	'X'	'X'

The third data type std_logic_vector is an array type. Users need to define the array width in the VHDL code.

8.2.2 4-Bit Adder Examples with Standard Logic Types

This example will demonstrate the std_logic_vector using submodules. The 4-bit adder starts from the Simulation steps for Boolean algebra example 2, step 3 and adds new files.

1. Copy the code in Figure 8-20 (or Chapter 6, Exercise 2 answer code (page 122-123)) into a new VHDL file and save the file as fulladder.vhd with the check box Add file to current project.

```
  boolean_algebra_example2.vhd ☒  |  ◇ Compilation Report - boolean_algebra_example ☒  |  ◆ fulladder.vhd ☒
```

```
 1   library ieee;
 2   use ieee.std_logic_1164.all;
 3
 4   entity fulladder is
 5     port (
 6       A        : in  std_logic;
 7       B        : in  std_logic;
 8       C        : in  std_logic;
 9       SUM      : out std_logic;
10       Carrout  : out std_logic
11       );
12   end fulladder;
13   architecture behavioral of fulladder is
14
15     signal D : std_logic;
16
17   begin
18
19     D        <= A xor B;
20     SUM      <= D xor C;
21     Carrout <= ((D and C) or (A and B));
22
23   end behavioral;
24
```

Figure 8-20. *fulladder .vhd code*

2. Copy the code in Figure 8-21 to a new VHDL file and save the file as four_bit_
    adder.vhd with the check box Add file to current project. Before we can use the
    fulladder inside four_bit_adder (both section A and B show in Figure 8-21), we
    must declare the full adder in section - A.

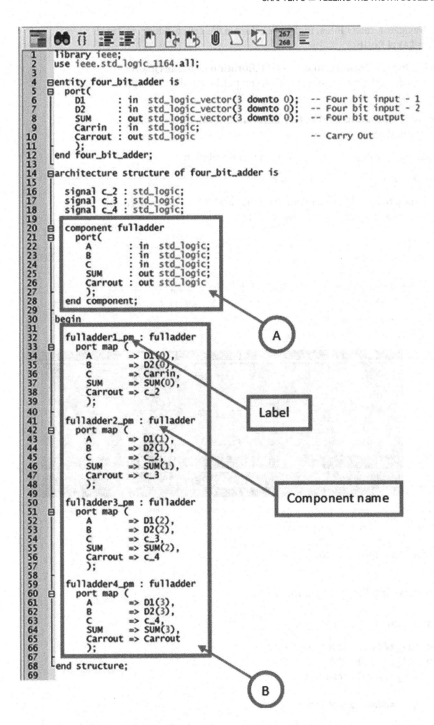

```
1    library ieee;
2    use ieee.std_logic_1164.all;
3
4    entity four_bit_adder is
5      port(
6        D1      : in  std_logic_vector(3 downto 0);   -- Four bit input - 1
7        D2      : in  std_logic_vector(3 downto 0);   -- Four bit input - 2
8        SUM     : out std_logic_vector(3 downto 0);   -- Four bit output
9        Carrin  : in  std_logic;
10       Carrout : out std_logic                        -- Carry Out
11       );
12   end four_bit_adder;
13
14   architecture structure of four_bit_adder is
15
16     signal c_2 : std_logic;
17     signal c_3 : std_logic;
18     signal c_4 : std_logic;
19
20     component fulladder
21       port(
22         A       : in  std_logic;
23         B       : in  std_logic;
24         C       : in  std_logic;
25         SUM     : out std_logic;
26         Carrout : out std_logic
27         );
28     end component;
29
30   begin
31
32     fulladder1_pm : fulladder
33       port map (
34         A        => D1(0),
35         B        => D2(0),
36         C        => Carrin,
37         SUM      => SUM(0),
38         Carrout  => c_2
39         );
40
41     fulladder2_pm : fulladder
42       port map (
43         A        => D1(1),
44         B        => D2(1),
45         C        => c_2,
46         SUM      => SUM(1),
47         Carrout  => c_3
48         );
49
50     fulladder3_pm : fulladder
51       port map (
52         A        => D1(2),
53         B        => D2(2),
54         C        => c_3,
55         SUM      => SUM(2),
56         Carrout  => c_4
57         );
58
59     fulladder4_pm : fulladder
60       port map (
61         A        => D1(3),
62         B        => D2(3),
63         C        => c_4,
64         SUM      => SUM(3),
65         Carrout  => Carrout
66         );
67
68   end structure;
69
```

A

Label

Component name

B

Figure 8-21. *four_bit_adder.vhd*

3. In the Project Navigator, select **Files.** Right-click the file four_bit_adder.vhd and click **Set as Top-Level Entity**.

4. Click **Processing ➤ Start ➤ Start Analysis & Elaboration** from the Quartus Prime menu or click on the blue triangle with green tick box in the tool bar to start analysis & elaboration.

5. Click **Tools ➤ Run Simulation Tool ➤ RTL Simulation** from the Quartus Prime menu to start simulation.

6. In the ModelSim transcript type the following to run simulation

    a. ModelSim ➤ **vsim work.four_bit_adder**

7. Type **add wave -position insertpoint sim:/four_bit_adder/*** in the transcript box. The wave windows should show as Figure 8-22.

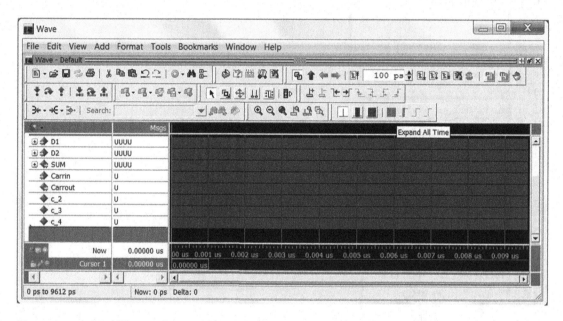

Figure 8-22. *4-bit adder simulation wave windows*

8. Copy the tcl to transcript (Listing 8-5) and hit Enter.

Listing 8-5. tcl for Generating Four-Bit Adder Inputs

```
force -freeze sim:/four_bit_adder/D1 0000 0
force -freeze sim:/four_bit_adder/D2 0000 0
force -freeze sim:/four_bit_adder/Carrin 0 0
run 100 ns
force -freeze sim:/four_bit_adder/D1 0001 0
run 10 ns
force -freeze sim:/four_bit_adder/D1 0010 0
run 10 ns
force -freeze sim:/four_bit_adder/D2 0010 0
run 10 ns
```

```
force -freeze sim:/four_bit_adder/D2 0011 0
run 10 ns
force -freeze sim:/four_bit_adder/D2 0111 0
run 10 ns
force -freeze sim:/four_bit_adder/D1 0110 0
run 10 ns
force -freeze sim:/four_bit_adder/D1 1110 0
run 10 ns
force -freeze sim:/four_bit_adder/D1 0110 0
run 10 ns
force -freeze sim:/four_bit_adder/Carrin 1 0
run 10 ns
```

9.   Wave windows will show all the calculation results from the four-bit adder
     (Figure 8-23). All the input and output are in binary number (Figure 8-24).
     Select D1, D2, and Sum with Ctrl key and then right-click it to select unsigned
     (Figure 8-25).

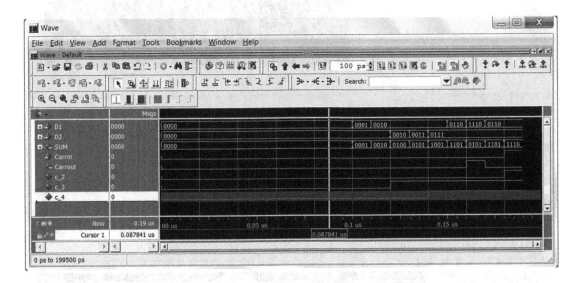

Figure 8-23. *4-bit adder simulation result*

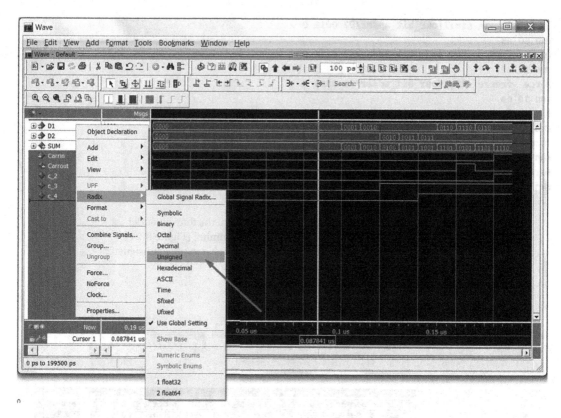

Figure 8-24. *How to change the data radix in simulation*

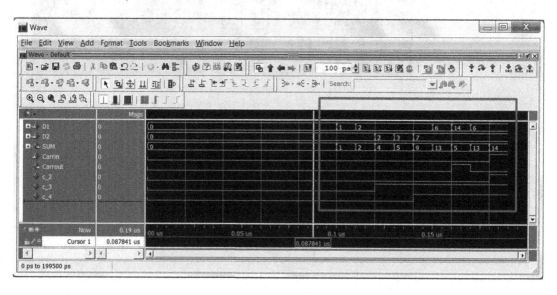

Figure 8-25. *p Data radix in unsigned*

8.3   Combinational Logic Design in FPGA

Combinational logic can be implemented in three different ways: Boolean equations, truth tables, and logic gates. Figure 8-26 shows an example of using the different ways to get VHDL logic.

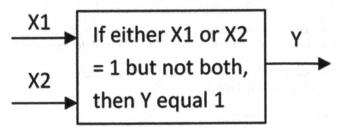

Boolean Equation:

$Y = (X1 \bullet {\sim}X2) + ({\sim}X1 \bullet X2)$

Truth Table:

	X1	X2	Y
0	0	0	0
1	0	1	1
2	1	0	1
3	1	1	0

Gate Representation:

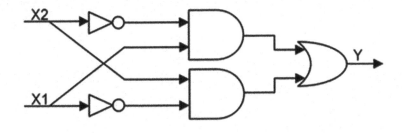

FPGA VHDL:

`Y <= (X1 and not X2) OR (NOT X1 and X2);`

Figure 8-26. *Example Boolean equations*

A FPGA designer usually uses Boolean equations to build combination logic. They are simple and clear; however, they may not provide the best performance (speed) design.

8.4 Summary

Boolean algebra is used to model simple true/false operations with AND/OR/NOT. In VHDL, the IEEE provides a std_logic_1164 library to add more features on Boolean algebra in std_logic and std_logic_vector data types.

This chapter also teaches you how to call modules from another module. It is one of the main reasons you are using HDL to design hardware—you can reuse your modules!

■ **Tip** Break down big problems into small pieces and solve them one small piece at a time.

"Logic will get you from A to B. Imagination will take you everywhere."

—Albert Einstein

CHAPTER 9

∎ ∎ ∎

Simplifying Boolean Algebra for FPGA

Using Boolean algebra to directly describe the combinational logic in VHDL (VHSIC (very high speed integrated circuit) Hardware Description Language) may not be a good idea for a design that has more than four inputs. When the combinational logic design has more than four inputs, the "logic" behind the design tends to become difficult for other designers to understand. Let's do a quick test. Do you know what the code in Listing 9-1 describes?

Listing 9-1. Boolean Algebra in VHDL

```vhdl
library ieee;                          -- All of the design need ieee library
use ieee.std_logic_1164.all;    -- Using std_logic_1164 package

entity code_9_1 is
   port (
            a_input: in std_logic_vector(1 downto 0);   -- 2 bit inputs
            b_output: out std_logic_vector(3 downto 0)    -- 4 bit outputs
         );
end code_9_1;

architecture behavioral of code_9_1 is

begin    -- architecture behavioral of  when_else_combination

         b_output(0) <=  NOT a_input(0) and NOT a_input(1);
         b_output(1) <=  a_input(0) and NOT a_input(1);
         b_output(2) <=  NOT a_input(0) and a_input(1);
         b_output(3) <=  a_input(0) and a_input(1);

end behavioral;
```

Listing 9-1 is a 2-to-4 decoder. Table 9-1 shows the decoder function. You can easily understand the function of the design when you see the contents of Table 9-1. This is why VHDL provides a couple of ways to make it easier for humans to understand the combinational logic/Boolean algebra design. Some call these methods "Concurrent statements." Following are the most frequently used concurrent statements. As a quick reminder, there are **only** two types of statements that you will see a lot in FPGA design. One type is the concurrent statement and the other is the sequential statement which we will discuss more in Chapter 10.

© Aiken Pang and Peter Membrey 2017
A. Pang and P. Membrey, *Beginning FPGA: Programming Metal*, DOI 10.1007/978-1-4302-6248-0_9

Table 9-1. *Truth Table for Listing 9-1 Code*

	a_input(0))	a_input(1)	b_output(3 downto 0)
0	0	0	0001
1	1	0	0010
2	0	1	0100
3	1	1	1000

■ **Tip**   You can use Quartus to show the VHDL in logic gate view. See the following steps.

1.   Save the code from Listing 9-1 into a code_9_1.vhd file and add it to the Quartus project (Please see Chapter 8 on how to create a project and how to add files)

2.   Set code_9_1.vhd as Top-Level Entity, as shown in Figure 9-1

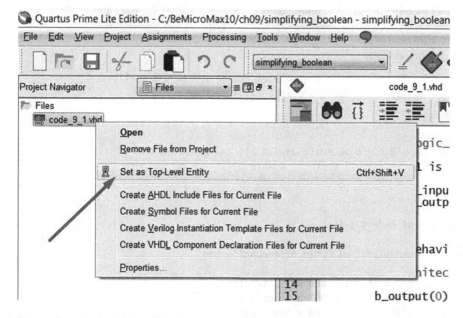

Figure 9-1. *Set as Top-Level Entity*

3.   Click **Processing** from the menu and click **Start compilation** (CTRL +L)

4.   After the compilation is done, switch to **Hierarchy** mode in the Project Navigator (A in Figure 9-2)

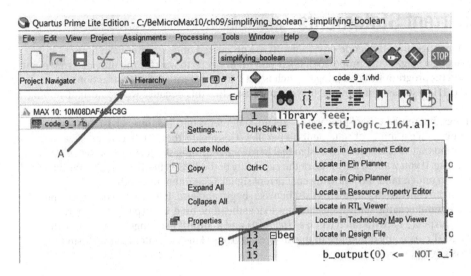

Figure 9-2. *Locate in RTL viewer*

5. Right-click the **code_9_1** design, click **Locate Node,** and select **Locate in RTL Viewer** (B in Figure 9-2)

Figure 9-3 is the RTL Viewer for the gate logic described in Listing 9-1.

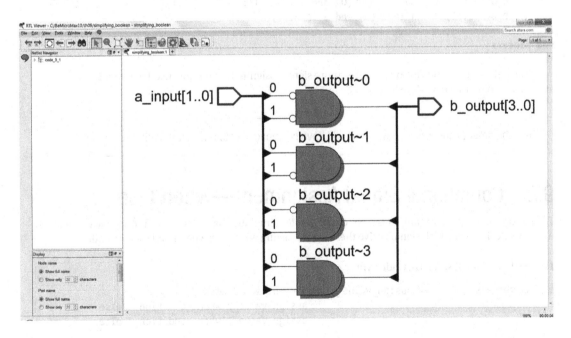

Figure 9-3. *Listing 9-1 RTL view in gate level*

9.1 Concurrent Statements

In a programming language, program code or statements are processed one statement at a time (assuming you are using a single-core processor). Each statement needs to wait for the previous statement to finish. This is good for programming language, which is used to represent a list of instructions for a processor to execute. It is also easy for humans to write programs like this because we are normally doing one thing at a time.

VHDL does things differently. Where processors execute statements one at a time, VHDL has the capability of executing a huge number of statements in parallel. This means that VHDL can run statements in parallel. Keep in mind that VHDL is used to design real hardware. Running statements (hardware) in parallel is a piece of cake. If you want to fully unlock the capability of the FPGA (field-programmable gateway array), then you need to understand the following concurrent signal assignment methods.

In VHDL, most of the concurrent statements exist between **begin** and **end**. It is like the code in Listing 9-2. All four statements are running at the same time. It means that at the same time, b_output(0), b_output(1), b_output(2), and b_output(3) are updated when a_input(0) and **a_input(1)** change. The order of these four statements will NOT create any difference in the final result. These kinds of statements are using concurrent signal assignment.

Listing 9-2. Concurrent Statement: Process in VHDL

```
process(a_input)
begin
        b_output(0) <= NOT a_input(0) and NOT a_input(1);
        b_output(1) <= a_input(0) and NOT a_input(1);
        b_output(2) <= NOT a_input(0) and a_input(1);
        b_output(3) <= a_input(0) and a_input(1);

end process;
```

The following sections introduce three more signal assignment operators used in concurrent statements: When-Else, With-Select, and Case.

■ **Tip** The order of concurrent statements will have no impact whatsoever on the final result.

9.2 Conditional Signal Assignment—When/Else

The conditional signal assignment is a concurrent statement that is based on the condition (**when/else**) to make the decision of which signals drive the outputs. Listing 9-3 shows what it looks like in code.

Listing 9-3. When Else VHDL Code Syntax

```
signal_get_assignment <= assign_value_1 when condition_1 else
                                 assign_value_2 when condition_2 else
                                 assign_value_3 when condition_3 else
                                 ...
                                 assign_value_n;
```

If the first condition (condition_1) is fulfilled, then the assign_value_1 will be assigned to the signal_get_assignment. If the first condition is **not** fulfilled and the second condition is fulfilled, then the assign_value_2 will be assigned and drive the output signal_get_assignment. Follow this logic, until all of the conditions (n-1) are **not** met, and then assign_value_n will drive the signal_get_assignment. Now let's see how to use when/else to do the same thing as the code in Listing 9-1.

Listing 9-4 is an example of using WHEN ELSE to create the same multiplexer as Listing 9-1. Figure 9-4 is the RTL view of the WHEN ELSE design. If you compare it with Figure 9-3, then you will find they are not the same hardware but similar logic function.

Listing 9-4. WHEN ELSE Combination in VHDL Code

```vhdl
library ieee;                          -- All of the design need ieee library
use ieee.std_logic_1164.all;     -- Using std_logic_1164 package

entity when_else_combination is
    port (
                a_input: in std_logic_vector(1 downto 0);   -- 2 bit inputs
                b_output: out std_logic_vector(3 downto 0)   -- 4 bit outputs
                );
end when_else_combination;

architecture behavioral of when_else_combination is
    -- Declartions, such as type declarations, constant declarations, signal dtions etc

begin    -- architecture behavioral of  when_else_combination

            b_output <= "0001" WHEN a_input = "00" ELSE
                              "0010" WHEN a_input = "01" ELSE
                              "0100" WHEN a_input = "10" ELSE
                              "1000" WHEN a_input = "11" ELSE
                              "0000" ;
end behavioral;
```

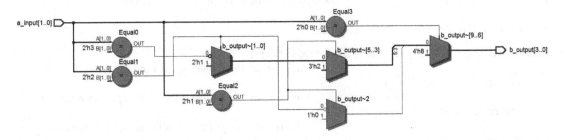

Figure 9-4. *RTL view of WHEN ELSE combination code in Listing 9-4*

There is another example code which is using a WHEN ELSE statement. It is a multiplexer (MUX) with four 8-bit input selection and one 8-bit output.

Listing 9-5. WHEN ELSE MUX in VHDL Code

```
library ieee;                           -- All of the design need ieee library
use ieee.std_logic_1164.all;      -- Using std_logic_1164 package

entity when_else_mux is
   port (
                mux_sel: in std_logic_vector(1 downto 0); -- 2 bit MUX Select
                a_input: in std_logic_vector(7 downto 0);
                b_input: in std_logic_vector(7 downto 0);
                c_input: in std_logic_vector(7 downto 0);
                d_input: in std_logic_vector(7 downto 0);
                m_output: out std_logic_vector(7 downto 0)
                );
end when_else_mux;

architecture behavioral of when_else_mux is
   -- Declartions, such as type declarations, constant declarations, signal dtions etc

begin    -- architecture behavioral of when_else_combination

             m_output <= a_input WHEN mux_sel = "00" ELSE
                         b_input WHEN mux_sel = "01" ELSE
                         c_input WHEN mux_sel = "10" ELSE
                         b_input WHEN mux_sel = "11";
end behavioral;
```

9.3 Select Signal Assignment—With/Select

Based on several possible values of a single condition_variable, it assigns a value to signal_get_assignment. You only need to type the condition_variable(a_input) one time in here. You can compare Listings 9-4 and 9-7. Listing 9-7 show that a_input only needs to be typed one time and Listing 9-4 must be typed four times. The official name for this VHDL with/select assignment is the selected signal assignment.

Listing 9-6. WITH SELECT VHDL Code Syntax

```
with condition_variable select signal_get_assignment <=
                                        assign_value_1 when condition_1, -- condition_
variable equal to condition_1
                                        assign_value_2 when condition_2, -- condition_
variable equal to condition_2
                                        assign_value_3 when condition_3, -- condition_
variable equal to condition_3
                                        ...
                                        assign_value_n when others;
```

Listing 9-7 shows the exact same function as Listing 9-1 but using With/Select.

Listing 9-7. WITH SELECT Combination in VHDL Code

```
library ieee;                          -- All of the design need ieee library
use ieee.std_logic_1164.all;    -- Using std_logic_1164 package

entity with_select_combination is
   port (
            a_input: in std_logic_vector(1 downto 0);   -- 2 bit inputs
            b_output: out std_logic_vector(3 downto 0)   -- 4 bit outputs
            );
end with_select_combination;

architecture behavioral of with_select_combination is
   -- Declartions, such as type declarations, constant declarations, signal dtions etc

begin    -- architecture behavioral of when_else_combination

           with a_input select b_output <=
                             "0001" when "00",
                             "0010" when "01",
                             "0100" when "10",
                             "1000" when "11";
end behavioral;
```

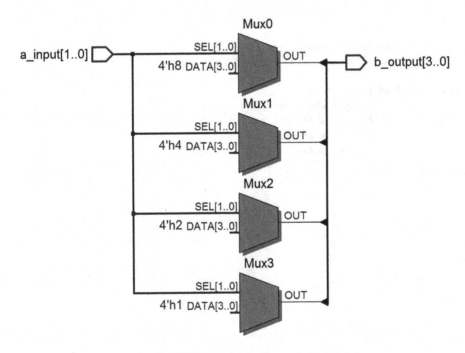

Figure 9-5. *RTL view of WITH SELECT combination code Listing 9-7*

From the differences between Figure 9-4 and Figure 9-5, you can tell that there is something different between the two concurrent statements approach. The first one (WHEN/ELSE methods) added a priority condition in the input. The logic will check condition_1 first. If it passes then the result will send to the output (the Equal3 condition from Figure 9-4). For the WITH SELECT combination code, it uses MUX to implement the design without any priority decoding. The WITH/SELECT statement can ONLY depend on the value of a single expression. WHEN/ELSE statements, however, can depend on the values of multiple expressions.

Listing 9-8 uses the same example for MUX with a four 8-bit input selection and one 8-bit output, this time using a select statement. Figure 9-6 shows the RTL of the MUX design using WITH SELECT design.

Listing 9-8. WHEN ELSE Combination in VHDL Code

```vhdl
library ieee;                              -- All of the design need ieee library
use ieee.std_logic_1164.all;    -- Using std_logic_1164 package

entity with_select_mux is
   port (
             mux_sel: in std_logic_vector(1 downto 0);   -- 2 bit inputs MUX select
             a_input:  in std_logic_vector(7 downto 0);
             b_input:  in std_logic_vector(7 downto 0);
             c_input:  in std_logic_vector(7 downto 0);
             d_input:   in   std_logic_vector(7 downto 0);
             m_output: out std_logic_vector(7 downto 0)
             );
end with_select_mux;

architecture behavioral of with_select_combination is
begin    -- architecture behavioral of when_else_combination

          with mux_sel select m_output <=
                              a_input when "00",
                              b_input when "01",
                              c_input when "10",
                              d_input when "11";
end behavioral;
```

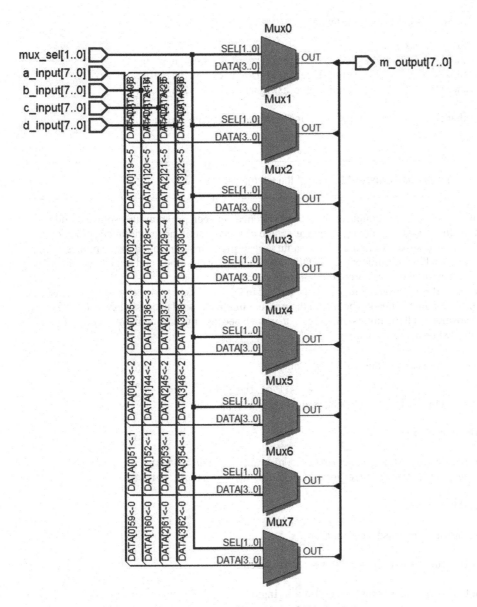

Figure 9-6. *RTL view of WITH SELECT combination code Listing 9-8*

9.4 Process with Case Statement

Case statements are very similar to the WITH SELECT statement. At the start of the case statement is the selector expression, between the keywords **case** and **is** (Listing 9-9). The value of the condition_variable is used to select which statements to run. The body of the case statement contains a list of alternatives. Each alternative starts with the keyword **when** and is followed by one or more condition values and assignment statements. There MUST be exactly one condition value for each possible value. The last alternative is using the keyword **others,** which include, all other condition values that the foregoing alternatives do not cover.

Listing 9-9. Case Statement in VHDL Code Syntax

```
case condition_variable is
        when condition_value1 =>  signal_get_assignment <= assign_value_1;
        when condition_value2 =>  signal_get_assignment <= assign_value_2;
        when condition_value3 =>  signal_get_assignment <= assign_value_3;
        ...
        when others           =>  signal_get_assignment <= assign_value_n;
end case;
```

■ **Tip** Remember to add **when others** at the end of the alternative list.

The case statement is a good example to show the difference between programming software and designing hardware. In the C programming language, switch case statements are examined from top to bottom. In VHDL, all the cases are examined at the same time. C programs are limited by the processor only allowing comparison of a limited number (most of the time it is one) of condition and branch locations. In hardware design, we can design as many conditions and branches as we want.

Listing 9-10 shows the exact same function as described in Listing 9-1 except here we are using case statements. The case statements need to be within the **process begin** and **end process** keywords. The process must be sensitive to all the inputs (in this case a_input), because the output of the decoder (b_output) must change when a_input changes.

Listing 9-10. Process Case Combination in VHDL Code

```
library ieee;                            -- All of the design need ieee library
use ieee.std_logic_1164.all;    -- Using std_logic_1164 package

entity case_combination is
   port (
            a_input: in std_logic_vector(1 downto 0);  -- 2 bit inputs
            b_output: out std_logic_vector(3 downto 0)   -- 4 bit outputs
          );
end case_combination;

architecture behavioral of case_combination is

begin    -- architecture behavioral of case_combination

process( a_input ) -- process sensitive list: a_input
begin
        case a_input is
                when    "00" =>  b_output <= "0001";
                when    "01" =>  b_output <= "0010";
                when    "10" =>  b_output <= "0100";
                when    "11" =>  b_output <= "1000";
                when others =>  b_output <= "0000";  -- output default state
        end case;
end process;

end behavioral;
```

■ **Tip**   You MUST include all inputs within the process in the **process** sensitive list

---

Listing 9-11 is an example code for the same MUX with four 8-bit inputs and one 8-bit output. You will find that the process-sensitive list includes all of the inputs ports. It is due to the output(m_output) will change value when mux_sel or all other inputs chnage.

Listing 9-11. Process Case MUX in VHDL Code

```vhdl
library ieee;                           -- All of the design need ieee library
use ieee.std_logic_1164.all;    -- Using std_logic_1164 package

entity case_mux is
   port (
            mux_sel:  in    std_logic_vector(1 downto 0);  -- 2 bit inputs  MUX select
            a_input:  in    std_logic_vector(7 downto 0);
            b_input:  in    std_logic_vector(7 downto 0);
            c_input:  in    std_logic_vector(7 downto 0);
            d_input:  in    std_logic_vector(7 downto 0);
            m_output: out std_logic_vector(7 downto 0)
            );
end case_mux;

architecture behavioral of case_mux is
   -- Declartions, such as type declarations, constant declarations, signal dtions etc

begin    -- architecture behavioral of case_mux

process(mux_sel, a_input, b_input, c_input, d_input ) -- you need to include all inputs in
here
begin
        case mux_sel is
                when    "00"   =>  m_output <= a_input ;
                when    "01"   =>  m_output <= b_input ;
                when    "10"   =>  m_output <= c_input ;
                when    "11"   =>  m_output <= d_input ;
                when others => null ;   -- Don't define anything
        end case;
end process;
end behavioral;
```

This case statement process is very easy to use because it can design any truth table combinational logic. You will see more case statements in other example designs.

■ **Tips**   You can use **null** as the assignment for the **when others** condition (see Listing 9-11).

9.5 Summary

In this chapter, you learned how to use the Altera Quartus Prime's RTL viewer to "see" what you designed in the FPGA. It is a good tool for checking your VHDL design.

After this chapter, you should not fear to write your own Boolean algebra in VHDL. VHDL provides more than one way (four ways) to write Boolean algebra/combination logic. Now you should able to build any kind of combinational logic in the FPGA and understand the logic in the design from other designers.

- Concurrent assignment
- Case statement
- When/Else
- With/Select

The concurrent assignment (the method in Chapter 8) is easy for small combinations which only need to use one to two gates of logic (max. 4-input bit). This is because anything more than four inputs tends to be non-trivial for the human mind to keep track of: one K-Map is only able to solve logic with four inputs).

Most of the time you will use a case statement for complicated combinational logic with a lot of input bits. When-Else statements are generally used for priority combination logic.

A null statement can be used not only in the case statement but also as a temporary place holder in a process (Listing 9-12). Null process is really handy when developing the model.

Listing 9-12. Null Process

```
process( your_sensitivity_list)
begin
      null;
end process;
```

Within the architecture, the locations of any declaration, process, and signal assignment will not affect the order of executions. Although you can place the declaration, process, and signal assignment in whatever order you like, the statement inside the process may need to consider the sequence. In Chapter 10 we will talk more about the sequential statement.

"K-I-S-S: Keep it Simple, Stupid"

—Kelly Johnson

CHAPTER 10

■ ■ ■

Sequential Logic: IF This, THEN That

All of the sequential logic needs to be put within a process, but not all logic in a given process is sequential. In Chapter 9, we discussed concurrent logic (Process with Case statement). Inside a process, the sequential statements (NOT logic) start to execute from top to bottom when a change in a signal in the process sensitivity list happens. Most sequential logic is about changes in the CLOCK. This clock is the digital time tick. Most of the timing in FPGA (field-programmable gate array) digital design is related to the clock.

In this chapter, we will mainly look at IF statements and how to use them to describe digital designs other than logic gates. Listing 10-1 shows the if statement syntax in VHDL (VHSIC (very high speed integrated circuit) Hardware Description Language).

Listing 10-1. If Statement Syntax in VHDL

```
lable: process(sensitivity list) is
begin
if   (condition1) then
    <signal assignment statement>; -- when condition 1 happened
elsif  (condition2) then
    <signal assignment statement>; -- when condition 1 NOT happened and condition 2 happened
else
   <signal assignment statement>;  -- when condition 1 NOT happened and condition 2 NOT happened
end if;
end process lable;
```

10.1   IF Statement

The IF statement is used to create a branch in the execution of sequential statements. Depending on the conditions listed in the body of the IF statement, either the instructions associated with one or none of the branches is executed when the IF statement is processed. Listing 10-1 shows the general form of the IF statement. The IF statement MUST be within a process with sensitivity list. In Chapter 9, we used process statements for combinational logic (case statements). In this chapter, IF statements are used within the PROCESS statement. This creates a digital design which will be triggered by some external events (e.g., clock signal and reset). Let's look at the digital logic design equivalent of "Hello World!"—the flip-flop. A D flip-flop is one of the most basic design blocks in an FPGA's logic elements.

© Aiken Pang and Peter Membrey 2017
A. Pang and P. Membrey, *Beginning FPGA: Programming Metal*, DOI 10.1007/978-1-4302-6248-0_10

10.1.1   D Flip-Flops with Clear and Preset

Flip-flops are a form of sequential logic. Sequential logic, unlike combinational logic, is affected not only by the current inputs but also by previous history. In other words, sequential logic remembers past events. That is why we define flip-flops as a storage element. It is based on the gated latch (another name is SR-Latch), which can have its output state changed only on the edge of the clock signal. You can get a more detailed description of the SR-Latch from the following link.

■ **Tips**   www.circuitstoday.com/flip-flops

Flip-flops are often used for implementation of circuits where the circuit's output not only depends on current input values but also on current status (past events) of the circuit. The following design example is based on the 7400 series of integrated circuits, specifically the 7474. You can find the datasheet for this IC (integrated circuit) from the TI web site (www.ti.com/lit/ds/symlink/sn74ahct74.pdf). This type of flip-flop was widely used in digital design and we will have two more examples in this chapter. In Chapter 1, we mentioned that an FPGA's logic elements include one D flip-flop. The reason for the FPGA vendor to include a D flip-flop in a logic element is because most sequential logic can be built from a D flip-flop. Figure 10-1 shows a D flip-flop from the Altera MAX FPGA. Positive-edge-triggered D flip-flop with Clear and Preset is another, more formal, name for this flip-flop.

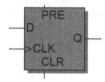

Figure 10-1. *Basic design element in FPGA—D flip-flop with preset and clear*

We can get the truth table for the 7474 from its datasheet. Table 10-1 shows the design requirements. The PRE_N and CLR_N have a higher priority than CLOCK and D inputs. This affects the IF statements' order in Listing 10-1. The rising_edge(CLOCK1) is used in the last if statement because both PRE_N and CLR_N need to be high to allow CLOCK to take effect. The rising_edge() is a function which has been defined in the std_logic_1164 library. Under the rising edge condition, the D (input) value will transfer to Q (output).

Table 10-1. *Truth Table for 7474*

		Inputs		Outputs	
PRE_N	CLR_N	CLOCK	D	Q	Q_N
0	0	x	x	1	1
0	1	x	x	1	0
1	0	x	x	0	1
1	1	Rising edge	0	0	1
1	1	Rising edge	1	1	0
1	1	0	x	Q0	Q0_N
1	1	1	x	Q0*	Q0_N

*Q0 is the value of Q before the rising edge of the clock

When PRE_N and CLR_N are not both 1, then Q(output) only depends on PRE_N and CLR_N value. The Q(output) latch (copy) the D(input) when PRE_N = 1 and CLR_N = 1 and rising edge of the CLK happen.

Listing 10-2. 7474 IC Model in VHDL

```
library ieee;                   -- All of the design need ieee library
use ieee.std_logic_1164.all;    -- Using std_logic_1164 package

entity d_flipflop_7474_example is
   port (
                -- First D-Flip Flop  --
                CLOCK1: in  std_logic;
                PRE1_N: in  std_logic;
                CLR1_N: in  std_logic;
                D1    : in  std_logic;
                Q1    : out std_logic;
                Q1_N  : out std_logic;
                -- Second D-Flip Flop --
                CLOCK2: in  std_logic;
                PRE2_N: in  std_logic;
                CLR2_N: in  std_logic;
                D2    : in  std_logic;
                Q2    : out std_logic;
                Q2_N  : out std_logic
            );
end d_flipflop_7474_example;

architecture behavioral of d_flipflop_7474_example is

begin   -- architecture behavioral of d_flipflop_7474_example

-- The first D-Flip Flop sequential process
-- Only execute this process when CLOCK, PRE_N or CLR_N changes state
d_ff_1_p: process(CLOCK1, PRE1_N, CLR1_N)
```

```vhdl
begin

        if ( PRE1_N = '0' and CLR1_N = '0') then
            Q1   <= '1';
            Q1_N <= '1';
        elsif (PRE1_N = '0' and CLR1_N = '1') then -- Preset the output Q as High(1)

            Q1   <= '1';
            Q1_N <= '0';

        elsif ( PRE1_N = '1' and CLR1_N = '0') then -- Clear the output Q as Low(0)

            Q1   <= '0';
            Q1_N <= '1';

        elsif ( rising_edge(CLOCK1) ) then -- PRE_N and CLR_N are inactive (both are 1) and
                                           -- rising edge of clock happen
            Q1   <= D1;
            Q1_N <= not D1;

        end if;
end process;
-- The second D-Flip Flop sequential process
-- Only execute this process when CLOCK, PRE_N or CLR_N changes state
d_ff_2_p: process(CLOCK2, PRE2_N, CLR2_N)
begin
        if ( PRE2_N = '0' and CLR2_N = '0') then
            Q2   <= '1';
            Q2_N <= '1';
        elsif (PRE2_N = '0' and CLR2_N = '1') then -- Preset the output Q as High(1)

            Q2   <= '1';
            Q2_N <= '0';

        elsif ( PRE2_N = '1' and CLR2_N = '0') then -- Clear the output Q as Low(0)

            Q2   <= '0';
            Q2_N <= '1';

        elsif ( rising_edge(CLOCK2) ) then -- PRE_N and CLR_N are inactive (both are 1) and
                                           -- rising edge of clock happen
            Q2   <= D2;
            Q2_N <= not D2;

        end if;

end process;

end behavioral;
```

■ **Tips** d_ff_1_p and d_ff_2_p are labels for the individual processes. This is not required by VHDL, but the labels can improve the description of the process and make it easier for other designers to read and understand.

10.1.1.1   D Flip-Flop with Clear and Preset Simulation

In this chapter we use script to simulate most of the design. Following are the steps for getting the result in Figure 10-2. You can use step 1 to add all of the example design from this chapter to the same Quartus project and use step 2 to switch the design as top level for simulation.

1.   Create a new project from BeMicro MAX10 template or copy the Chapter 4 project. Add a new VHDL design file named d_flipflop_7474_example.vhd with the code from Listing 10-2.

    a.   Click File ➤ New in the Quartus project

    b.   Select ➤ Design Files/VHDL file and click OK

    c.   Copy Listing 10-2 to the new file and save as d_flipflop_7474_example.vhd with add file to the current project check box checked.

2.   Set the d_flipflop_7474_example as Top-level Entity. **Right-click** the d_flipflop_7474_example.vhd and **click** set as Top-level Entity in the Project Navigator (Files).

3.   Running ModelSim from Quartus Prime. **Click** Tools ➤ **Click** Run Simulation Tool ➤ **Click** Run RTL Simulation. Figure 10-2 shows the result. There is the error of "No extended dataflow license exists." It is because we are using the free version of the ModelSim. It does not affect our simulation.

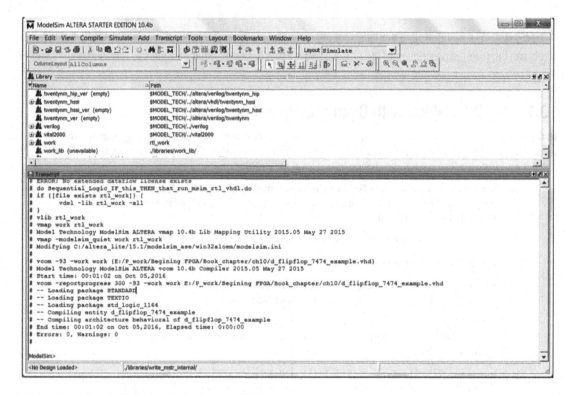

Figure 10-2. *ModelSim bring up by Quartus Prime*

4. Type the following script in the ModelSim Transcript window. The first one runs the simulation and the second one adds all the signals to the window.

    a. vsim work.d_flipflop_7474_example

    b. add wave -position insertpoint sim:/d_flipflop_7474_example/*

5. Create two separate clocks for two different flip-flops

    a. force -freeze sim:/d_flipflop_7474_example/CLOCK1 1 0, 0 {50 ps} -r 100

    b. force -freeze sim:/d_flipflop_7474_example/CLOCK2 1 0, 0 {35 ps} -r 70

6. Initialize all of the input signals

    a. force -freeze sim:/d_flipflop_7474_example/PRE1_N 0 0

    b. force -freeze sim:/d_flipflop_7474_example/CLR1_N 0 0

    c. force -freeze sim:/d_flipflop_7474_example/D1 0 0

    d. force -freeze sim:/d_flipflop_7474_example/PRE2_N 0 0

    e. force -freeze sim:/d_flipflop_7474_example/CLR2_N 0 0

    f. force -freeze sim:/d_flipflop_7474_example/D2 0 0

7. Run the simulation for 275 ps (all three letters (run) are NOT capital letters)

   a. run 275 ps

8. Set both preset values to high

   a. force -freeze sim:/d_flipflop_7474_example/PRE1_N 1 0

   b. force -freeze sim:/d_flipflop_7474_example/PRE2_N 1 0

9. Run the simulation for 125 ps (all three letters (run) are NOT capital letter)

   a. run 125 ps

10. Change preset and clear value

   a. force -freeze sim:/d_flipflop_7474_example/PRE1_N 0 0

   b. force -freeze sim:/d_flipflop_7474_example/CLR1_N 1 0

   c. force -freeze sim:/d_flipflop_7474_example/PRE2_N 0 0

   d. force -freeze sim:/d_flipflop_7474_example/CLR2_N 1 0

11. Run the simulation for 125 ps

   a. run 125 ps

12. Set the Preset to high

   a. force -freeze sim:/d_flipflop_7474_example/PRE1_N 1 0

   b. force -freeze sim:/d_flipflop_7474_example/PRE2_N 1 0

13. Run the simulation for 225 ps

   a. run 225 ps

14. Set both D inputs to high

   a. force -freeze sim:/d_flipflop_7474_example/D1 1 0

   b. force -freeze sim:/d_flipflop_7474_example/D2 1 0

15. Run the simulation for 125 ps

   a. run 125 ps

In Figure 10-3, the two flip-flops in the d_flipflop_7474_example are driven by the same input except CLOCK1 and CLOCK2 are different. The red arrow (A) in the figure shows that Q1 and Q1_N change on the rising edge of CLOCK1. Q2 and Q2_N change on the rising edge of CLOCK2 (red arrow B). This dual flip-flop design shows that sequential statements ONLY execute when the IF condition is true (which is the clock input). The Q output also depends on the D input. Q1 and Q1_N follow the D1 input on the rising edge of CLOCK1 (red arrows C and D). Q2 and Q2_N follow the D2 input on the rising edge of CLOCK2 (red arrows E and F).

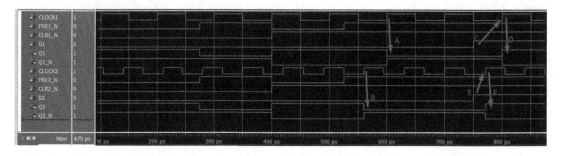

Figure 10-3. *7474 FPGA Timing diagram*

10.1.2   Shift Registers

In the last example, one D flip-flop only stores one bit of data (the Q output). When a group of n flip-flops is used to store n bits of data, we say these flip-flops are a register. Using different ways to group flip-flops together will form a different type of register which provides different functions. Shift registers are one of the commonly used types of registers.

In this section, we will show you the simplest shift register example: the serial in serial out shift register. It works like a time delay module. When anything happens on the input, it will happen on the output after x amount of time. The unit of time is the clock period on the clock input. It provides a discrete delay of the digital signal. A clock synchronized signal is delayed by "n" discrete clock cycle times, where "n" is the number of flip-flops in the shift register. Therefore, an eight flip-flop shift register delays input data by eight clock cycles.

■ **Note**   Shift registers are used in many places (e.g., pseudo random generator, serial communication, delay input, and storage).

Four-bit shift registers can be built by four D flip-flops. They are connected serially as in Figure 10-4. The data bits are loaded into the shift register in a serial fashion using the SERIAL_IN input. The values of each D flip-flop are sending to the next D flip-flop whose Q output is connected to D output, at each positive edge of the CLOCK.

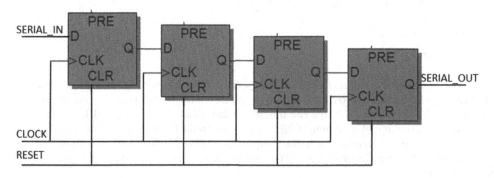

Figure 10-4. *Shift registers circuit (4-bit version)*

Let's build a bigger shift register using VHDL. The following example is an 8-bit serial in serial out (SISO) shift register. The reset values for the shift registers output (Qs) are all reset to all zero (LOW) when reset is one (HIGH). It will start shifting SERIAL_IN on the rising edge of CLOCK. Listing 10-3 is an 8-bit SISO shift register implemented using VHDL code and Figure 10-5 is the block diagram from Quartus Prime after compiling Listing 10-3. You can add the code from Listing 10-3 to the Quartus project with .vhdl file name shift_register_8bit.vhd.

Listing 10-3. 8-Bit Shift Register Example

```
library ieee;                    -- All design needs ieee library
use ieee.std_logic_1164.all;     -- Using std_logic_1164 package

entity shift_register_8bit is
   port (
             CLOCK      : in  std_logic;
             RESET      : in  std_logic;
             SERIAL_IN  : in  std_logic;
             SERIAL_OUT : out std_logic
           );
end shift_register_8bit;

architecture behavioral of shift_register_8bit is

signal shift_registers : std_logic_vector(7 downto 0); -- Internal 8 bit register with name
shift_registers

begin   -- architecture behavioral of shift_register_8bit

-- 8 bits shift register sequential process
shift_p: process(CLOCK, RESET) -- Only execute this process when CLOCK or RESET changes state
begin

        if ( RESET = '1' ) then  -- when RESET is HIGH, all of the internal registers reset to LOW(0)

           shift_registers <= (others =>'0');

        elsif ( rising_edge(CLOCK) ) then -- rising edge of clock happen

           -- This statement define shift_registers(n) <= shift_registers(n - 1) , when n not equal 0
           --                                 shfit_registrs(0) <= SERIAL_IN
           shift_registers <= shift_registers(6 downto 0) & SERIAL_IN;

        end if;

end process;

SERIAL_OUT <= shift_registers(7); -- Concurrent statement: defined SERIAL_OUT is the 8th
shift register

end behavioral;
```

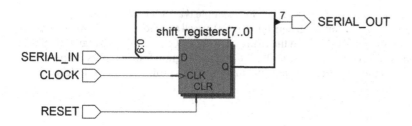

Figure 10-5. *Shift register Quartus Prime v.block diagram*

In Listing 10-4, shift_registers is defined as an 8-bit std_logic_vector. We know that each bit in the shift register needs to be connected to the next bit of the register. You can use the following statement to connect the bits:

Listing 10-4. 8-Bit Shift Register v.1

```
if ( rising_edge(CLOCK) ) then -- rising edge of clock happen
    shift_registers(0) <= SERIAL_IN      ; -- SERIAL_IN send to bit 0
    shift_registers(1) <= shift_registers(0); -- bit 0 send to bit 1
    shift_registers(2) <= shift_registers(1); -- bit 1 send to bit 2
    shift_registers(3) <= shift_registers(2); -- bit 2 send to bit 3
    shift_registers(4) <= shift_registers(3); -- bit 3 send to bit 4
    shift_registers(5) <= shift_registers(4); -- bit 4 send to bit 5
    shift_registers(6) <= shift_registers(5); -- bit 5 send to bit 6
    shift_registers(7) <= shift_registers(6); -- bit 6 send to bit 7
end if;
```

You can use a much simpler way to describe the 8-bit shift register. Listing 10-5 shows the VHDL code used in the example design.

Listing 10-5. 8-Bit Shift Register Version 2

```
if ( rising_edge(CLOCK) ) then -- rising edge of clock happen
This statement shift_registers <= shift_registers(6 downto 0) & SERIAL_IN;
end if;
```

10.1.2.1 Shift Register Simulation

In Quartus Prime, save Listing 10-3 as `shift_register_8bit.vhd` and add the file to the project. You need to set the file as Top-Level Entity before running the simulation tool. You can go to Chapter 4 to review how to set the `.vhdl` design file as Top-Level Entity.

■ **Tip** Ctrl+Shift+J can set the current open file as Top-Level Entity

---

Here are some simulation scripts for testing the shift register. Run Listing 10-6 in the ModelSim after you add `shift_register_8bit.vhd` to the project and **Click** run RTL simulation from Quartus Prime with the top-level entity as shift_register_8bit. Run the following script in the ModelSim:

Listing 10-6. tcl Script for Simulating the 8-Bit Shift Register

```
vsim work.shift_register_8bit
add wave -position insertpoint sim:/shift_register_8bit/*
force -freeze sim:/shift_register_8bit/CLOCK 1 0, 0 {50 ps} -r 100
force -freeze sim:/shift_register_8bit/RESET 1 0
force -freeze sim:/shift_register_8bit/SERIAL_IN 0 0
run 175 ps
force -freeze sim:/shift_register_8bit/RESET 0 0
run 100 ps
force -freeze sim:/shift_register_8bit/SERIAL_IN 1 0
run 200 ps
force -freeze sim:/shift_register_8bit/SERIAL_IN 0 0
run 100 ps
force -freeze sim:/shift_register_8bit/SERIAL_IN 1 0
run 100 ps
force -freeze sim:/shift_register_8bit/SERIAL_IN 0 0
run 1000 ps
```

Figure 10-6 shows the 8-bit SISO shift register simulation result. In the first (1) clock cycle, the SERIAL_IN is High and the bit 0 in shift_registers changes to High after the rising edge of the first (1) clock cycle. SERIAL_OUT output is exactly the same as SERIAL_IN after eight clock cycles.

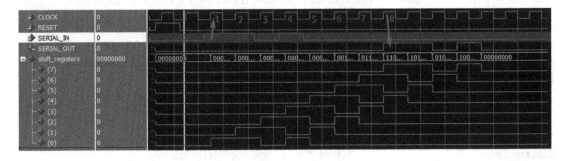

Figure 10-6. Simulation result for 8-bit SISO Shift register

10.1.3   4-Bit Up Counter Design Example

In Chapter 8, a 4-bit adder example is used to perform arithmetic operations in VHDL. In this chapter we demonstrate special types of adder, which are used for the purpose of counting. Counter circuits are used everywhere in digital systems. They can be used for counting events, generating timing intervals (Pulse Width Modulation), or keeping track of time (watch dog).

There are at least two types of counters.

1.   Asynchronous counter

2.   Synchronous counter

Asynchronous counters are also known as ripple counters. The good thing about an asynchronous counter is that it is simpler than a synchronous counter design as it requires less combinational logic than a synchronous counter. There is one drawback, however, which is that the counter's output from the first flip-flop is connected to the next flip-flop's clock input. Using the output of a register as a clock is NOT considered good practice for FPGA digital design. It is because FPGA tools need to calculate all the connection timing with respect to a constant frequency and duty cycle clock, and using output of a register as a clock will create a non-constant frequency and/or duty cycle clock. It means that it is too hard for the tool to create a working design for you and therefore the synchronous type of counter is widely used in FPGA.

The synchronous counter is a synchronous design (all of the flip-flops are driven by the same clock signal) which is the best fit for an FPGA. This is because FPGA's are designed primarily for synchronous digital design hardware.

■ **Tip** FPGA is a design for synchronous digital logic design. This means that all of the clock inputs to the flip-flops should be constant frequency and duty cycle clocks.

This chapter's registers and Chapter 8's adder can be used to build a counter. Following is the example VHDL code for a 4-bit counter. The reason for 4-bit only is that it is easier to show the counter values. You can easily increase the counter size to any size you like.

We would like to design a circuit that can increment a count by 1 when enable is High in every clock cycle. We would need to use the Chapter 8 adder and this chapter's registers to build a counter. Listing 10-7 shows the example VHDL code for a 4-bit counter. Figure 10-7 shows the block diagram in Quartus.

■ **Tip** The bigger the counter size, the bigger the challenge for Quartus to compile it. 64-bit counters are still okay for the current FPGAs, but although Quartus may build a 256-bit counter, it's unlikely that once in hardware it will be able to operate correctly.

Listing 10-7. Counter Example

```vhdl
library ieee;              -- All of the deisgn need ieee library
use ieee.std_logic_1164.all;   -- Using std_logic_1164 package
use ieee.numeric_std.all;      -- Using numeric_std package

entity counter_4bit is
   port (
            CLOCK     : in  std_logic;
            RESET     : in  std_logic;
            ENABLE    : in  std_logic;
            COUNTER : out std_logic_vector(3 downto 0) -- 4 bit counter output
          );
end counter_4bit;

architecture behavioral of counter_4bit is

signal counter_reg : unsigned(3 downto 0); -- Internal 4 bit register with name counter_reg
                                 -- !! Remember to include ieee.numeric_std package !!
begin   -- architecture behavioral of counter_4bit
```

```
-- 4 bits counter register sequenal process
counter_p: process(CLOCK, RESET) -- Only execute this process when CLOCK or RESET changes state
begin
        if ( RESET = '1' ) then  -- when RESET is HIGH, all of the internal registers reset to LOW(0)
              counter_reg  <= (others =>'0');
        elsif ( rising_edge(CLOCK) ) then -- rising edge of clock happen
                  if ( ENABLE = '1') then    -- counter_reg will increment by 1 when ENABLE = 1
                      counter_reg <= counter_reg + 1; -- when counter_reg = 1111 (0xF), it
                                                        will roll over to 0000 (0x0)
              end if;
        end if;
end process;
COUNTER <= std_logic_vector(counter_reg); -- using std_logic_vector() function to convert unsigned value
                                                                --to std_logic_value

end behavioral;
```

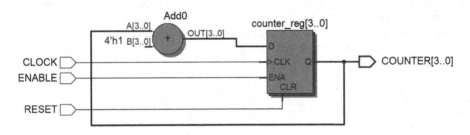

Figure 10-7. *4-bit counter block diagram*

10.1.3.1   Numeric_std Package and Unsigned Data Type

There are three new things in Listing 10-7 that we would like to discuss. First, the package section includes a new package: ieee.numeric_std (**use** ieee.numeric_std.**all**) and declares a new type: unsigned (**signal** counter_reg : **unsigned**(3 **downto** 0)) in the signal section. The ieee.numeric_std package is a very powerful package for arithmetic calculation design in VHDL. It defines two data types: signed and unsigned. It also defines arithmetic, comparison, and logic operators for both data types. Signed and unsigned data types are used to represent numeric values. Table 10-2 shows each data type value range.

Table 10-21. *Signed and Unsigned Numeric Values*

Data Type	Value	Notes
unsigned	0 to $2^N - 1$	N is number of bit
Signed	$-2^{(N-1)}$ to $2^{(N-1)} - 1$	2's Complement number

Figure 10-8 shows the difference between signed and unsigned signals. In the example, all three of the example signals are four-bit registers and are assigned the same bit value to all high (1). The example_unsigned "1111" is defined as 15. The example_signed "1111" is -1. There is an online calculator to help you convert decimal to 2's complement: www.exploringbinary.com/twos-complement-converter.

```
-----------
signal example_unsigned : unsigned(3 downto 0) ;
signal example_signed   : signed  (3 downto 0) ;
signal example_slv      : std_logic_vector(3 downto 0) ;
-----------
example_unsigned <= "1111" ;    = 15 in decimal
example_signed   <= "1111" ;    = -1 in decimal
example_slv      <= "1111" ;    = four bit high
```

Figure 10-8. Signed and unsigned signal examples

10.1.3.2   Arithmetic Operation

The second is a new way to do adding. The reason for using the ieee.numeric_std package is that we can directly using add (+), subtract (-), multiplication (*), and divide (/) arithmetic operators. In Listing 10-7, we are using the adder (+) to increment the counter value, which is the same as the 4-bit full adder in Chapter 8 without the complicated full adder VHDL files. You only need to use one line of VHDL code. Another good reason is that you can easily overload a signed or an unsigned value with an integer value. Figure 10-9 provides simple rules for signed and unsigned value overloading.

```
Signal uv_A, uv_B, uv_C, uv_D, uv_E : unsigned(7 downto 0) ;
Signal sv_F, sv_G, sv_H, sv_I, sv_J : signed (7 downto 0) ;
Signal slv_K, slv_L, slv_M : std_logic_vector(7 downto 0) ;
signal sv_N : signed(8 downto 0) ;

-- Permitted
uv_A <= uv_B + uv_C ; -- Unsigned + Unsigned = Unsigned
uv_D <= uv_A + 1 ;     -- Unsigned + Integer = Unsigned
uv_E <= 1 + D_uv;      -- Integer + Unsigned = Unsigned
sv_F <= sv_G + sv_H ; -- Signed + Signed = Signed
sv_I <= sv_H + 1 ;     -- Signed + Integer = Signed
sv_J <= 1 + sv_F;      -- Integer + Signed = Signed

]-- Illegal Cannot use arithmetic operator in std_logic_vector
-- J_slv <= K_slv + L_slv ;

]-- Illegal Cannot mix different array types
-- Solution persented later in type conversions
-- Y_sv <= A_uv - B_uv ;   -- want signed result
```

Figure 10-9. VHDL ieee.numeric_std overloading examples

In the example in Listing 10-7, we use one overloading in the following code:

```
counter_reg <= counter_reg + 1;
```

On every rising edge of the clock where enable is equal to 1 (High) this overloading code will get run. It means increment by one.

10.1.3.3   4-Bit Up Counter Simulation

Let's run ModelSim to simulate this counter. You can follow these steps to do so:

1. Create a new project (refer to Chapter 4)

2. Create a new VHDL file in the Quartus, copy Listing 10-7, and save as
    `counter_4bit.vhd`

3. Set the new added file (`counter_4bit.vhd`) as Top-Level Entity (shortcut: Ctrl +
    Shift + V)

4. Start compilation (Shortcut: Ctrl + L)

5. **Click** Tools ➤ Run Simulation Tool ➤ RTL Simulation from the Quartus Prime
    Menu

6. In ModelSim run the following script in the Transcript window

    a. vsim work.counter_4bit

    b. add wave -position insertpoint sim:/counter_4bit/*

    c. force -freeze sim:/counter_4bit/CLOCK 1 0, 0 {50 ps} -r 100

    d. force -freeze sim:/counter_4bit/RESET 0 0

    e. force -freeze sim:/counter_4bit/ENABLE 0 0

    f. run 25 ps

    g. force -freeze sim:/counter_4bit/RESET 1 0

    h. run 100 ps

    i. force -freeze sim:/counter_4bit/RESET 0 0

    j. run 100 ps

    k. force -freeze sim:/counter_4bit/ENABLE 1 0

    l. run 200 ps

    m. force -freeze sim:/counter_4bit/ENABLE 0 0

    n. run 100 ps

    o. force -freeze sim:/counter_4bit/ENABLE 1 0

    p. run 1600 ps

7. After step 6 (a-p), the ModelSim Wave window should show Figure 10-10 as the
    result. If both the COUNTER and counter_reg value did not show as Hexadecimal
    and unsigned number, then right-click on the waveform signal name. It will pop
    up a menu on the left-hand side ➤ Radix ➤ click the Radix you would like to
    show (like COUNTER use hexadecimal and counter_reg uses unsigned).

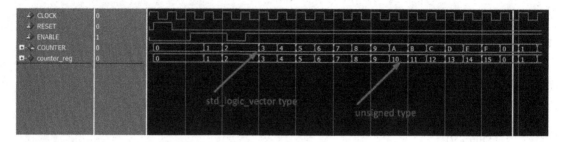

Figure 10-10. *4-bit counter simulation result*

10.1.3.4 Type Conversion Between Types

The third thing is using type conversion in the last line of the Listing 10-7. It is converting an unsigned type (counter_reg) to std_logic_vector (COUNTER). VHDL depends on overloaded operators and conversions. You need to use conversion when you go between the following types:

- signed & unsigned (1 bit) <=> std_logic

- signed & unsigned <=> std_logic_vector

- signed & unsigned <=> integer

- std_logic_vector <=> integer

There are two types of VHDL built-in conversion function in the ieee.numeric_std package: the automatic type and conversion by typecasting.

10.1.3.4.1 Automatic Type Conversion

It only happens between std_logic (1 bit) and signed/unsigned (1 bit). Figure 10-11 shows an example.

```
Signal uv_A       : unsigned(7 downto 0) ;
Signal slv_A      : std_logic_vector(7 downto 0);
Signal sl_A, sl_B : std_logic;

sl_A <= uv_A(0) ; -- assign 1 unsigned element to std_logic
uv_A(1) <= sl_B ; -- assign std_logic to 1 unsigned element
slv_A(2) <= uv_A(2) ; -- assign 1 unsigned element to 1 std_logic_vector element
```

Figure 10-11. *Example of automatic type conversion*

10.1.3.4.2 Typecasting Conversion

You can use typecasting to convert equal-size arrays of unsigned/signed and std_logic_vector. Figure 10-12 shows an example.

```
Signal uv_A        : unsigned(7 downto 0) ;
Signal sv_B        : signed(7 downto 0) ;
Signal slv_C       : std_logic_vector(7 downto 0);

slv_C <= std_logic_vector (uv_A); --convent unsigned to std_logic_vector
slv_C <= std_logic_vector (sv_B); --convent signed to std_logic_vector
uv_A  <= unsigned(slv_c);         --convent std_logic_vector to unsigned
sv_B  <= signed(slv_c);           --convent std_logic_vector to signed
```

Figure 10-12. *Example of typecasting conversion*

10.1.3.5   Mixed with Sequential Statements and Concurrent Statement Design

This 4-bit up counter example is mixed with sequential statements (the counter_p process) and the last type conversion concurrent assignment statement. You can see a lot more of this kind of design in Chapter 11. It is a very common way to develop sequential (synchronous) designs for FPGA. Figure 10-13 shows a block diagram of it.

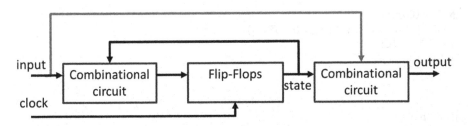

Figure 10-13. *The standard form of a sequential design*

Most of the synchronous sequential designs use combinational logic and one or more flip-flops. It looks like Figure 10-13. The sequential design has a set of inputs (Listing 10-7 has ENABLE and Reset as input) and generates a set of outputs (Listing 10-7 has COUNTER).

The output values of flip-flops are defined as state (Listing 10-7). Figure 10-13 shows that the flip-flop outputs (state) depend on the combination of input and current state of every clock (Listing 10-7 is the rising edge of the CLOCK) such that the state changes from one to another (Listing 10-7 the counter value).

The output of the sequential design is a function of the current state and input. Listing 10-7 shows that the output COUNTER only depends on the current state (counter_reg). Remember that the output of a sequential design MUST depend on current state and it does not necessarily need to depend on input. The green arrow in Figure 10-13 does not necessarily exist, if the outputs are only depend on inputs after one clock cycle. This concept is important for Chapter 11, which covers Finite State Machines (FSM).

10.2   More Than Sequential Logic—Sequential Statements

The IF statement is not the only sequential statement in VHDL. In VHDL, **WAIT** and **AFTER** are sequential statements too! You will only use them in test bench VHDL design. Test bench is a file for testing your actual FPGA digital design. Test bench is NOT FPGA dependent. It doesn't need to follow any rules from the FPGA hardware. You can use the FULL set of VHDL code. WAIT and AFTER are part of the VHDL for test bench VHDL.

Let's create a simple test bench VHDL file to test the 4-bit up counter design. Listing 10-8 shows the test bench VHDL file. Please save this file as counter_4bit_vhd_tst.vht (.vht stand for VHDL test bench) under the <counter 4-bit project folder>/simulation/modelsim and run "vcom -work work counter_4bit_vhd_tst.vht" in ModelSim Transcript.

Listing 10-8. 4-Bit Counter Test bench VHDL Code

```
LIBRARY ieee;
USE ieee.std_logic_1164.all;


ENTITY counter_4bit_vhd_tst IS
END counter_4bit_vhd_tst;
ARCHITECTURE counter_4bit_tb OF counter_4bit_vhd_tst IS

-- signals
SIGNAL CLOCK : STD_LOGIC := '1';
SIGNAL COUNTER : STD_LOGIC_VECTOR(3 DOWNTO 0);
SIGNAL ENABLE  : STD_LOGIC;
SIGNAL RESET   : STD_LOGIC;
COMPONENT counter_4bit
        PORT (
        CLOCK : IN STD_LOGIC;
        COUNTER : BUFFER STD_LOGIC_VECTOR(3 DOWNTO 0);
        ENABLE : IN STD_LOGIC;
        RESET : IN STD_LOGIC
        );
END COMPONENT;
BEGIN
        i1 : counter_4bit
        PORT MAP (
-- list connections between master ports and signals
        CLOCK => CLOCK,
        COUNTER => COUNTER,
        ENABLE => ENABLE,
        RESET => RESET
        );

-- CLOCK --
CLOCK <= not CLOCK AFTER 50 ps;

reset_p : PROCESS
BEGIN
        -- code that executes only once
RESET <= '0';
WAIT FOR 25 ps;
RESET <= '1';
WAIT FOR 100 ps;
RESET <= '0';
WAIT; -- RESET stay Low forever
END PROCESS reset_p;

enable_p : PROCESS
```

```
BEGIN
        -- code that executes only once
ENABLE <= '0';
WAIT UNTIL falling_edge(RESET);
WAIT UNTIL rising_edge(CLOCK);
WAIT FOR 25 ps;
ENABLE <= '1';
WAIT FOR 200 ps;
ENABLE <= '0';
WAIT FOR 100 ps;
ENABLE <= '1';
WAIT;
END PROCESS enable_p;

END counter_4bit_tb;
```

Script "vsim work.counter_4bit_vhd_tst" will use the test bench VHDL file to generate stimulus to test the 4-bit up counter. The test bench generates exactly the same as the script we used in the last section. Run the following two scripts after the simulation is started by "vsim."

```
add wave -position insertpoint sim:/counter_4bit_vhd_tst/*run 2 ns
```

Listing 10-8 uses three types of WAIT statement. WAIT FOR is used to add delays with specific times between two sequential statements (e.g., WAIT FOR 25 ps mean add a 25 pico second delay). WAIT UNTIL "X" is used to add a delay until "X" event happens and then continue to the next sequential statement. If the "X" event never happens then it will wait forever. There is another way to WAIT forever (it means the sequential statements stop there). You can just use WAIT. The execution sequence will stop there.

AFTER is another sequential statement. It is used to generate a periodic signal. Clock signals are one of the examples of a periodic signal. Listing 10-8 CLOCK will invert itself every half clock cycle.

For more details on test bench review please visit the following web site:

```
www.alterawiki.com/uploads/d/d2/Testbenches_public.pdf
```

■ **Tip**   The order of sequential statements, will impact the final result.

10.3   VHDL Architecture Review

Let's take some time for a quick review of the VHDL architecture before we move on to Chapter 11. Architecture is a description of the digital design implementation. It can have local variables (signals). There are three types of architecture.

- Structural

- Dataflow

- Behavioral

Structural architecture assembles existing modules or your own modules to form a larger design. This kind of architecture only has connections between blocks, inputs, and outputs. Structural design is very easy to debug because all you need to do is to connect the blocks correctly. It doesn't include any additional logic design. You will use this type of architecture more often in the top-level modules which connect different modules together to form the final system.

Dataflow architecture is a description of the flow of data (e.g., logic functions and assignments). This architecture uses simple logic designs which are like the examples in Chapter 9.

Behavioral architecture is a VHDL architecture including one or more processes. All processes are run in parallel and the process is triggered by signal change. This is like the examples in this chapter.

You will use a lot of structural and behavioral architecture in your design and implement digital circuits.

10.4   Summary

In this chapter, you learned how to use IF statements within a PROCESS to create basic sequential logic, the D flip-flop. The `ieee.numeric_std` package was introduced in this chapter and the unsigned data type was used in 4-bit up counter design examples to show how to do arithmetic operations in VHDL.

You now know that most of the synchronous digital design's output is based on the current state. The output may or may not depend on the current input. Sometimes we refer to the flip-flop or register's output as the design's state.

Because synchronous designs need to "store" the current state, it needs storage elements. The general storage element in an FPGA is the D Flip-Flop or Register.

Chapter will talk about Finite State Machines which are probably the most fun in digital designs. This is because they can solve most of the problems you need to solve in digital design.

"Success is sequential, not simultaneous."

—Gary W. Keller

■ ■ ■

## CHAPTER 11

Combinatorial Logic: Putting It All Together on the FPGA

11.1   Introduction

In this chapter, we will show you how to combine what we learned in Chapters 7 to 10 to form a finite state machine (FSM). The finite state machine is sequential logic with "special" logic to control what is the next state. The special logic depends on the FSM's task.

In Chapter 10, we showed you a 4-bit up counter, which is a very simple FSM. The counter state is the counter value and the special logic is that the next state will be the current state's value plus one. Figure 11-1 shows the state diagram of the 4-bit up counter.

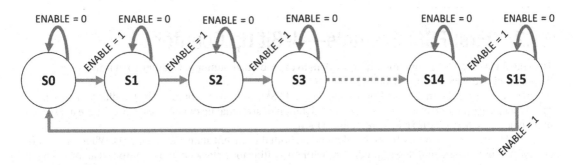

Figure 11-1.   *4-bit up counter state diagram*

In the 4-bit up counter example, we know that the counter state will increment by one when ENABLE = 1 happens. If ENABLE = 0 occurs in any state, then the next clock cycle will NOT change the state. This matches exactly what an up counter should do. In Chapter 10, we mentioned a simple state machine that not only has an input (ENABLE in this example) but also has an output from the FSM. The output of this counter ONLY depends on the value of the state. Table 11-1 shows the output combinational logic. We need to translate the state diagram to the actual digital design. We need to translate the S0, S1 . . . S15 to digital logic first. We used a 4-bit unsigned data type which can store values from 0 to 15 to represent S0 to S15 (see Table 11-1) in Chapter 10's design. We can also define our state data type (see Listing 11-1). We are using a 4-bit std_logic_vector for the output of the counter. In Chapter 10, we used the function std_logic_vector() to translate the unsigned value to std_logic_vector and this is the "special" logic for this 4-bit up counter. In the Listing 11-1 process fsm_p3, we used combinational logic to translate state values to an output counter value.

© Aiken Pang and Peter Membrey 2017
A. Pang and P. Membrey, *Beginning FPGA: Programming Metal*, DOI 10.1007/978-1-4302-6248-0_11

Table 11-1. *Truth Table for 7474*

State	Counter output
S0	0000
S1	0001
S2	0010
S3	0011
S4	0100
S5	0101
S6	0110
S7	0111
S8	1000
S9	1001
S10	1010
S11	1011
S12	1100
S13	1101
S14	1110
S15	1111

11.2   First FSM Example—4-Bit Up Counter

The code in Listing 11-1 is functionally equivalent to the 4-bit up counter in Chapter 10. It is useful for demonstrating the FSM design structure.

If you ask ten different people how to build a good FSM, you will be confused by ten different answers. This is because everyone has a different preferred design or style that he or she likes to use. There are two main types of state machine styles: Mealy and Moore.

The Mealy machine has outputs that depend on both the current state and the inputs. When the inputs change, the outputs are updated immediately, without waiting for a clock edge. The outputs can be changed more than once per state or per clock cycle.

The Moore machine has outputs that are dependent only on the current state but NOT on the inputs. The outputs are changed only when the current state changes.

There is a very good example on the Altera and Xilinx web sites for both types of state machine.

www.altera.com/support/support-resources/design-examples/design-software/vhdl/vhd-state-machine.html

www.xilinx.com/support/documentation/university/Vivado-Teaching/HDL-Design/2015x/VHDL/docs-pdf/lab10.pdf

It doesn't matter which type you use. The more important thing is how you write your FSM in VHDL (VHSIC (very high speed integrated circuit) Hardware Description Language). Listing 11-1 is a Moore-style state machine. In the code, we separate the state machine into three process statements (fsm_p1, fsm_p2, and fsm_p3) (see Figure 11-2). The first part (fsm_p1) only takes care of updating the current_state flip-flops (registers) to next_state value when there is a rising edge on the input clock. The second part (fsm_p2) takes care of all of the decision making for the next state condition. The last part (fsm_p3) is used to create the output combinational logic. This three-part FSM style can help you to design your FSM.

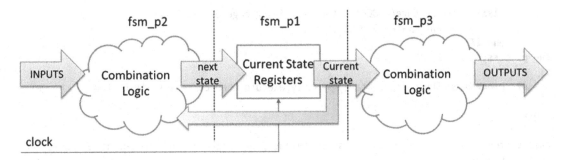

Figure 11-2. *Moore-style FSM block diagram*

■ **Tip**   We suggest you add a flip-flop after each of the combinational logic outputs. The flip-flop outputs works like a camera to take a snapshot of the combinational logic output every clock cycle. Therefore, all the flip-flop output values are changed at the same time and going stable for the whole clock cycle. This can avoid glitches in the outputs. We will show you how it's done in the next example.

Listing 11-1. Using FSM to Design 4-Bit Up Counter

```
library ieee;                  -- All of the design need ieee library
use ieee.std_logic_1164.all;   -- Using std_logic_1164 package
use ieee.numeric_std.all;      -- Using numeric_std package

entity counter_4bit is
   port (
            CLOCK    : in  std_logic;
            RESET    : in  std_logic;
            ENABLE   : in  std_logic;
            COUNTER  : out std_logic_vector(3 downto 0) -- 4 bit counter output
            );
end counter_4bit;

architecture behavioral of counter_4bit is

-- define our own data type state for the 4-bit up counter state machine
type state is (S0,S1,S2,S3,S4,S5,S6,S7,S8,S9,S10,S11,S12,S13,S14,S15);

signal current_state : state; -- Current state value
signal next_state     : state; -- Next clock cycle state value

begin   -- architecture behavioral of counter_4bit

--   FSM state register sequential process
fsm_p1: process(CLOCK, RESET) -- Only execute this process when CLOCK or RESET changes state
begin
        if ( RESET = '1' ) then  -- when RESET is HIGH, the FSM set to S0
             current_state  <= S0;
```

```vhdl
        elsif ( rising_edge(CLOCK) ) then -- rising edge of clock happen
            current_state <= next_state;
        end if;
end process;

fsm_p2: process(ENABLE,current_state) -- Only execute when current_state or ENABLE changes
state
begin

case current_state is  -- in this case statements, we define all of the possible transitions
between states
        when S0 =>
            if ( ENABLE = '1') then
                next_state <= S1;
            else   -- ENABLE = '0'
                next_state <=  current_state;
            end if;

        when S1 =>
            if ( ENABLE = '1') then
                next_state <= S2;
            else   -- ENABLE = '0'
                next_state <=  current_state;
            end if;

        when S2 =>
            if ( ENABLE = '1') then
                next_state <= S3;
            else   -- ENABLE = '0'
                next_state <=  current_state;
            end if;

        when S3 =>
            if ( ENABLE = '1') then
                next_state <= S4;
            else   -- ENABLE = '0'
                next_state <=  current_state;
            end if;

        when S4 =>
            if ( ENABLE = '1') then
                next_state <= S5;
            else   -- ENABLE = '0'
                next_state <=  current_state;
            end if;

        when S5 =>
            if ( ENABLE = '1') then
                next_state <= S6;
            else   -- ENABLE = '0'
                next_state <=  current_state;
            end if;
```

```vhdl
when S6 =>
    if ( ENABLE = '1') then
        next_state <= S7;
    else   -- ENABLE = '0'
        next_state <=  current_state;
    end if;

when S7 =>
    if ( ENABLE = '1') then
        next_state <= S8;
    else   -- ENABLE = '0'
        next_state <=  current_state;
    end if;

when S8 =>
    if ( ENABLE = '1') then
        next_state <= S9;
    else   -- ENABLE = '0'
        next_state <=  current_state;
    end if;

when S9 =>
    if ( ENABLE = '1') then
        next_state <= S10;
    else   -- ENABLE = '0'
        next_state <=  current_state;
    end if;

when S10 =>
    if ( ENABLE = '1') then
        next_state <= S11;
    else   -- ENABLE = '0'
        next_state <=  current_state;
    end if;

when S11 =>
    if ( ENABLE = '1') then
        next_state <= S12;
    else   -- ENABLE = '0'
        next_state <=  current_state;
    end if;

when S12 =>
    if ( ENABLE = '1') then
        next_state <= S13;
    else   -- ENABLE = '0'
        next_state <=  current_state;
    end if;

when S13 =>
    if ( ENABLE = '1') then
        next_state <= S14;
```

```vhdl
            else   -- ENABLE = '0'
                next_state <= current_state;
            end if;

    when S14 =>
            if ( ENABLE = '1') then
                next_state <= S15;
            else   -- ENABLE = '0'
                next_state <= current_state;
            end if;

    when S15 =>
            if ( ENABLE = '1') then
                next_state <= S0;
            else   -- ENABLE = '0'
                next_state <= current_state;
            end if;

end case;
end process;

fsm_p3: process(current_state) -- this counter output ONLY depends on current_state
begin

case current_state is  -- in this case statements, we define all of the possible transition
between states
        when S0  => COUNTER <= "0000";
        when S1  => COUNTER <= "0001";
        when S2  => COUNTER <= "0010";
        when S3  => COUNTER <= "0011";
        when S4  => COUNTER <= "0100";
        when S5  => COUNTER <= "0101";
        when S6  => COUNTER <= "0110";
        when S7  => COUNTER <= "0111";
        when S8  => COUNTER <= "1000";
        when S9  => COUNTER <= "1001";
        when S10 => COUNTER <= "1010";
        when S11 => COUNTER <= "1011";
        when S12 => COUNTER <= "1100";
        when S13 => COUNTER <= "1101";
        when S14 => COUNTER <= "1110";
        when S15 => COUNTER <= "1111";
end case;
end process;

end behavioral;
```

11.2.1   Using Altera Quartus to Understand the FSM

You can use the Altera Quartus tools to help you better understand the design. You'll need to compile the code in Listing 11-1 in Altera Quartus and open the RTL viewer (Figure 11-3).

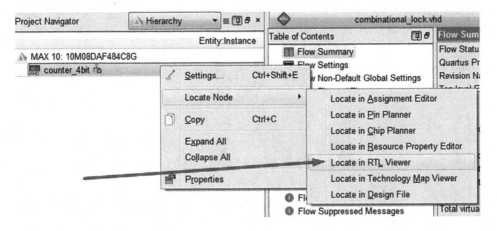

Figure 11-3. *How to open the RTL viewer*

The RTL viewer should look something like Figure 11-4. In the viewer, there are output combination logic and finite state machine logic which is inside the "yellow" box. Double-clicking the "yellow" box will open the state machine viewer (Figure 11-5). It shows all the states in the FSM and all the relationships between the states.

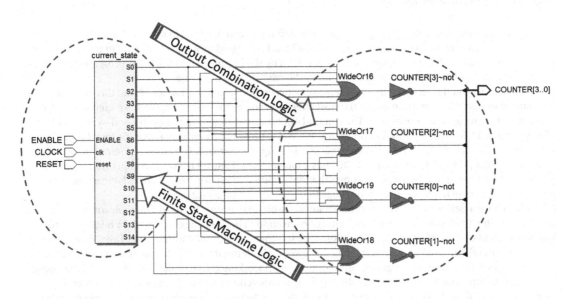

Figure 11-4. *Quartus RTL view of 4-bit counter—FSM version*

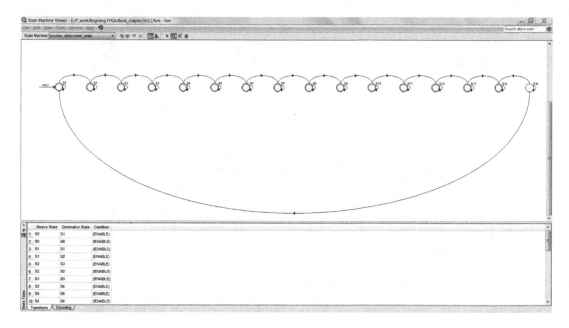

Figure 11-5. *Quartus State Machine viewer*

In here you may become rather excited and think that you can use FSM to solve all your digital problems. Yes, you are 100% correct. You can solve all kinds of digital problems with FSM in the simulation world. In the real world, however, we are all constrained by the hardware—FPGA (field-programmable gate array). Everything depends on how many resource you can use for your design.

Let us show you the resource usage difference between the design in Chapter 10 and this chapter's 4-bit up counter design. There is a compilation report after each compilation. In Chapter 1, we mentioned the basic gate design block: logic element. You can find out how many logic elements are used by the compiled design. Figure 11-6 is the compilation report for the FSM 4-bit adder. You can see that the total logic elements is 17/8064 (<1 %). 17/8064 means that the 4-bit up counter with FSM uses 17 logic elements out of 8064. The FPGA (MAX10 10M08DAF484C8G) has a total of 8064. Figure 11-7 is the compilation report from Chapter 10's 4-bit up counter design. It shows that the Chapter 10 version only used six logic elements. The FSM version used nearly three times more logic than the normal up counter design.

If you have a design need to create more than 500 4-bit up counters in the FPGA, then you need to use the Chapter 10 version; otherwise you will not have enough logic elements (500 x 17 = 8,500). There is another benefit to using the Chapter 10 version, which is that the counter can run faster (assuming a faster clock). In general, the smaller the design (i.e., the fewer logic elements used), the faster the clock it can use.

Please don't use FSM to design a simple counter when working on a real design. It would be like using the Titan (US supercomputer) or the Tianhe-2 (Chinese supercomputer) to do the elementary maths. You can use VHDL to design a real counter that's far smaller, faster, and simpler (only a few lines of code compared with two pages of code). If your design only has a linear sequence, you can use a simple up counter to help you "count" the states.

■ **Caution**   Don't use FSMs to design a simple counter or linear design, even though an FSM can certainly do it.

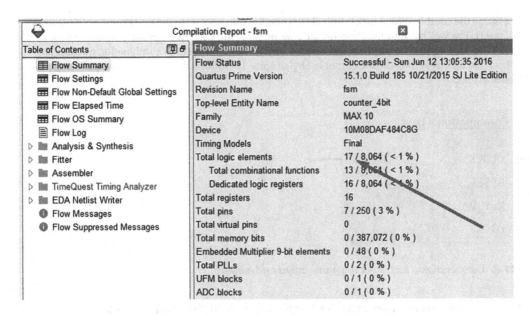

Figure 11-6. *Compilation report for 4-bit up counter with FSM*

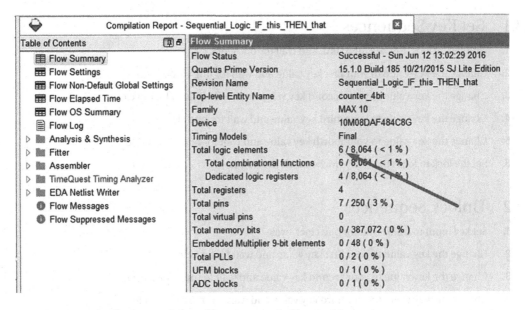

Figure 11-7. *Compilation report for 4-bit up counter in Chapter 10*

11.3 Combinational Lock Example

This combinational lock works like a simple state machine. It has different states (Lock, Unlocked, Key, etc.), inputs (key numbers and lock), and an output lock condition (unlock = Low or High). Different companies have their own ways to design a combinational lock. Let's try to design a combinational lock with a FSM in VHDL.

We assume the combinational lock is unlocked when the user uses it for the first time (the FPGA has just been reset). The lock has four numbers for the combination and each number ranges from 1 to 15. Number 0 is not included as it is used to represent the unlock state. The default combination number is 1-2-3-4. Lock the lock by setting the lock input to High. Figure 11-8 shows the inputs and output for the combinational lock.

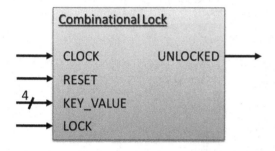

Figure 11-8. *Combinational lock block diagram (inputs and output)*

There are two operation sequences for this design—set key and unlock. Figure 11-9 shows the sequences in state diagram form.

11.3.1   Set Key Sequences

1.   Unlock the lock, the key input is 0, and wait for one clock cycle

2.   Change the key value to your first key value and wait for one clock cycle

3.   Change the key value to your second key value and wait for one clock cycle

4.   Change the key value to your third key value and wait for one clock cycle

5.   Change the key value to your fourth key value and wait for one clock cycle

6.   Set the lock to lock (the lock is locked with the new keys)

11.3.2   Unlock Sequences

1.   Set key input to 0 and wait for one clock cycle

2.   Change the key value to your first key value and wait for one clock cycle

3.   Change the key value to your second key value and wait for one clock cycle

4.   Change the key value to your third key value and wait for one clock cycle

5.   Change the key value to your fourth key value and wait for one clock cycle

6.   Set key input to 0 and wait for one clock cycle

7.   Lock is unlocked

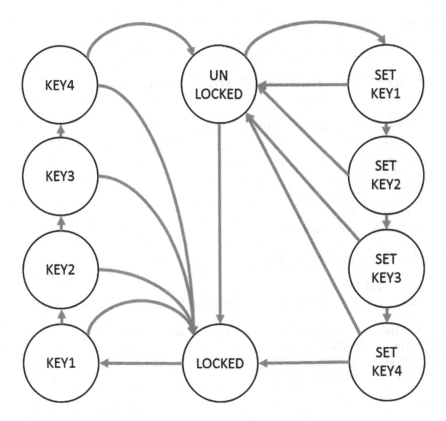

Figure 11-9. *State diagram for combinational lock design*

11.3.3   Code for the Combinational Lock Design

Based on the foregoing requirements for the combinational lock, the code in Listing 11-2 is an example of how to implement the combinational lock. You can copy the following code and save it as combinational_ lock.vhd. You need to create a new project as we showed in Chapter 4—create a new project and add the combinational_lock.vhd file to the new project and set the VHDL file as top level.

Listing 11-2. Combinational Lock FSM Design in VHDL

```vhdl
library ieee;                    -- All of the design need ieee library
use ieee.std_logic_1164.all;     -- Using std_logic_1164 package
use ieee.numeric_std.all;        -- Using numeric_std package

entity combinational_lock is
   port (
            CLOCK       : in  std_logic;
            RESET       : in  std_logic;
            KEY_VALUE   : in  unsigned(3 downto 0); -- only from 1 to 15 is valid key number
            LOCK        : in std_logic; -- 1 mean lock the lock
            UNLOCKED    : out std_logic -- 1 mean locked 0 mean open
         );
end combinational_lock;
```

```vhdl
architecture behavioral of combinational_lock is

-- define our own data type state for the combinational lock state machine
type state is
(UNLOCK,SET_KEY1,SET_KEY2,SET_KEY3,SET_KEY4,LOCKED,KEY1,KEY2,KEY3,KEY4);


signal current_state : state; -- Current state value
signal next_state    : state; -- Next clock cycle state value
signal save_key      : std_logic;
signal shift_key     : std_logic;
signal key_shifter   : std_logic_vector(15 downto 0);
signal stored_key1   : unsigned(3 downto 0);
signal stored_key2   : unsigned(3 downto 0);
signal stored_key3   : unsigned(3 downto 0);
signal stored_key4   : unsigned(3 downto 0);


begin   -- architecture behavioral of combinational lock

--  FSM state register sequential process
fsm_p1: process(CLOCK, RESET) -- Only execute this process when CLOCK or RESET changes state
begin
        if ( RESET = '1' ) then  -- when RESET is HIGH, the FSM set to S0
                current_state  <= UNLOCK;
        elsif ( rising_edge(CLOCK) ) then -- rising edge of clock happen
                current_state <= next_state;
        end if;
end process;

fsm_p2: process(LOCK, KEY_VALUE, current_state , stored_key1, stored_key2, stored_key3,
stored_key4)
begin
case current_state is  -- in this case statements, we define all of the possible transition
between states
        when UNLOCK =>
                if  (LOCK = '1') then
                    next_state <=  LOCKED;
                elsif (KEY_VALUE /= 0) then -- Only allow to set key when it is in OPEN state
                    next_state <= SET_KEY1;  -- The first non-zero value will NOT use as KEY
                else
                    next_state <=  current_state;
                end if;

        when SET_KEY1 =>
                if  (LOCK = '1') then
                    next_state <=  LOCKED;
                elsif (KEY_VALUE /= 0) then
                    next_state <= SET_KEY2;
                else
                    next_state <=  UNLOCK;
                end if;

            when SET_KEY2 =>
```

```vhdl
            if  (LOCK = '1') then
                next_state <=  LOCKED;
            elsif (KEY_VALUE /= 0) then
                next_state <= SET_KEY3;
            else
                next_state <=  UNLOCK;
            end if;

    when SET_KEY3 =>
            if  (LOCK = '1') then
                next_state <=  LOCKED;
            elsif (KEY_VALUE /= 0) then
                next_state <= SET_KEY4;
            else
                next_state <=  UNLOCK;
            end if;

    when SET_KEY4 =>
            if  (LOCK = '1') then
                next_state <=  LOCKED;
            elsif (KEY_VALUE = 0) then
                next_state <= UNLOCK;
            else
                next_state <=  SET_KEY1;
            end if;

when LOCKED =>
            if (KEY_VALUE = stored_key1) then
                next_state <= KEY1; -- First key is correct
            else    -- ENABLE = '0'
                next_state <=  current_state;
            end if;

    when KEY1 =>  --
            if (KEY_VALUE = stored_key2) then
                next_state <= KEY2; -- Second key is correct
            else
                next_state <=  LOCKED;
            end if;

    when KEY2 =>
            if (KEY_VALUE = stored_key3) then
                next_state <= KEY3; -- Third key is correct
            else
                next_state <=  LOCKED;
            end if;

    when KEY3 =>
            if (KEY_VALUE = stored_key4) then
                next_state <= KEY4; -- Fouth key is correct
            else
```

```vhdl
                    next_state <=   LOCKED;
            end if;


        when KEY4 => -- after all four keys are match, it need KEY_VALUE to unlock it
            if ( KEY_VALUE = 0 ) then
                    next_state <= UNLOCK;
            else
                    next_state <=   LOCKED;
            end if;


end case;
end process;


fsm_p3: process(current_state, KEY_VALUE,LOCK) -- output depends on current_state and
inputs.
begin
-- Defualt output values
UNLOCKED <= '1';
save_key        <= '0';
shift_key       <= '0';


case current_state is   -- in this case statements, we define all of the possible transition
between states
        when UNLOCK     =>
                                        UNLOCKED<= '1';
                                        if (KEY_VALUE /= 0) then
                        shift_key <= '1';
                                          end if;
        when SET_KEY1 =>
                                        UNLOCKED <= '1';
                                        if (KEY_VALUE /= 0) then
                        shift_key <= '1';
                                          end if;
        when SET_KEY2 =>
                                        UNLOCKED <= '1';
                                        if (KEY_VALUE /= 0) then
                        shift_key <= '1';
                                          end if;
        when SET_KEY3 =>
                                        UNLOCKED <= '1';
                                        if (KEY_VALUE /= 0) then
                        shift_key <= '1';
                                          end if;
        when SET_KEY4 => -- After all four key are set, it need LOCK = '1' to save the key
                                        UNLOCKED <= '1';
                                        If (LOCK = '1') then
                        save_key <= '1';

                                        end if;
        when LOCKED     => UNLOCKED <= '0';
        when KEY1              => UNLOCKED <= '0';
```

```
        when KEY2          => UNLOCKED <= '0';
        when KEY3          => UNLOCKED <= '0';
        when KEY4          => UNLOCKED <= '0';

end case;
end process;

-- This process manage the key for unlock the lock
internal_key_p: process(CLOCK, RESET)
begin
        if ( RESET = '1' ) then   -- when RESET is HIGH, keys set to "1234"
                stored_key1 <= "0001";
                stored_key2 <= "0010";
                stored_key3 <= "0011";
                stored_key4 <= "0100";
        elsif ( rising_edge(CLOCK) ) then -- rising edge of clock happen
                if ( shift_key = '1' ) then
                        key_shifter <= key_shifter(11 downto 0) & std_logic_vector(KEY_VALUE);
                end if;

            if ( save_key = '1') then
                        stored_key1 <= unsigned(key_shifter(15 downto 12));
                        stored_key2 <= unsigned(key_shifter(11 downto  8));
                        stored_key3 <= unsigned(key_shifter(7  downto  4));
                        stored_key4 <= unsigned(key_shifter(3  downto  0));
                end if;
            end if;
end process;
end behavioral;
```

In the Quartus's state machine viewer, you can see how the states relate to each other. Figure 11-10 shows the combinational lock design FSM.

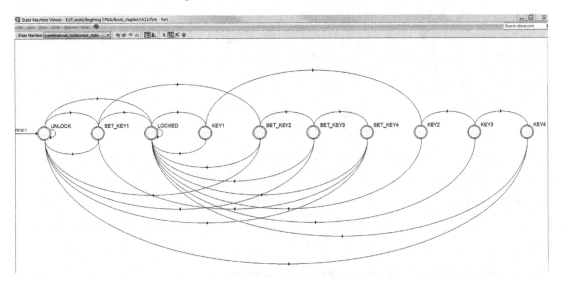

Figure 11-10. State diagram for the combinational lock FSM

11.3.4   Simulate the Combinational Lock with ModelSim Script

We will walk you through how to simulate the FSM with simple ModelSim script.

11.3.4.1   Steps to Start ModelSim and Run Simulation

1.   Set ModelSim-Altera ver. as the default simulator in Quartus Prime. **Assignments** ➤ **Settings** ➤ Tool name: ModelSim-Altera (shown in Figure 11-11)

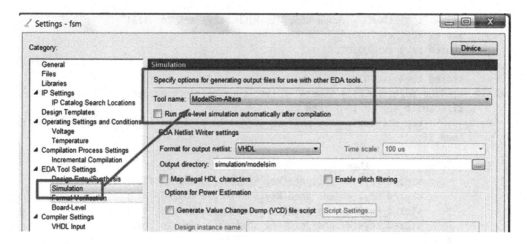

Figure 11-11. *Set ModelSim-Altera as simulation tool in Quartus*

2.   Click Tools ➤ Run Simulation Tool ➤ RTL Simulation (Figure 11-12)

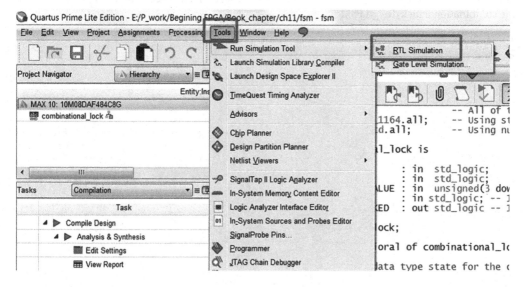

Figure 11-12. *Set ModelSim-Altera as simulation tool in Quartus*

3. ModelSim Altera Starter Edition main window (Figure 11-3) and wave window (Figure 11-4) will bring up. The ModelSim transcript Window should show Error:0, Warnings: 0 in the last line of the Transcript window (Figure 11-14)

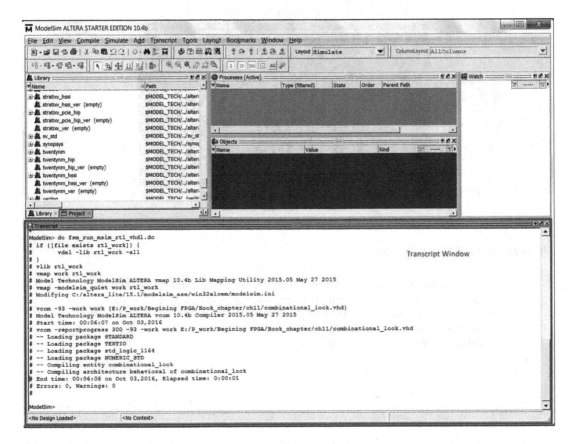

Figure 11-13. *ModelSim-Altera started from Quartus Prime*

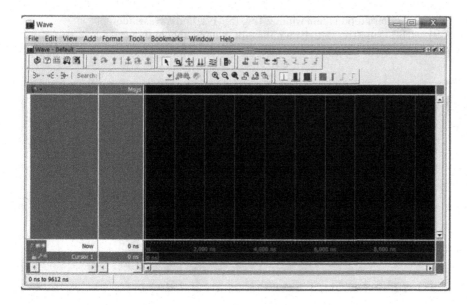

Figure 11-14. *ModelSim-AlteraWave window*

4. Type the following in the Transcript window after ModelSim> and then hit Enter
    (Figure 11-15). The text color in the Transcript window will change to blue and
    ModelSim> will change to VSIM 3> (Figure 11-16). The ModelSim is now in the
    simulation mode. The combinational_lock design simulation is started at time
    equal to 0. vsim work.combinational_lock

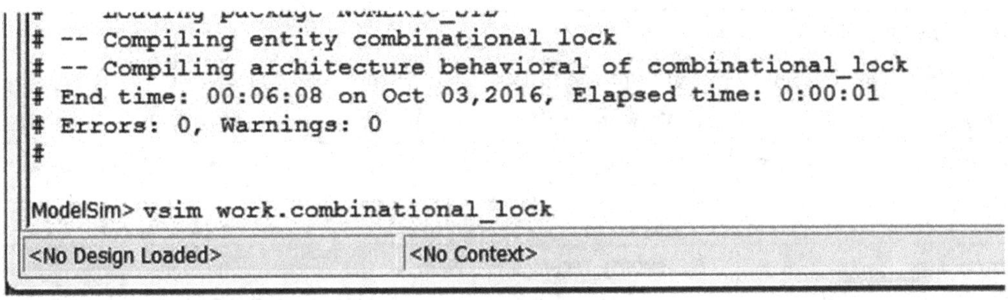

```
# ──────── package NUMERIC_STD
# -- Compiling entity combinational_lock
# -- Compiling architecture behavioral of combinational_lock
# End time: 00:06:08 on Oct 03,2016, Elapsed time: 0:00:01
# Errors: 0, Warnings: 0
#

ModelSim> vsim work.combinational_lock
```

<No Design Loaded>	<No Context>

Figure 11-15. Start combinational lock simulation in ModelSim

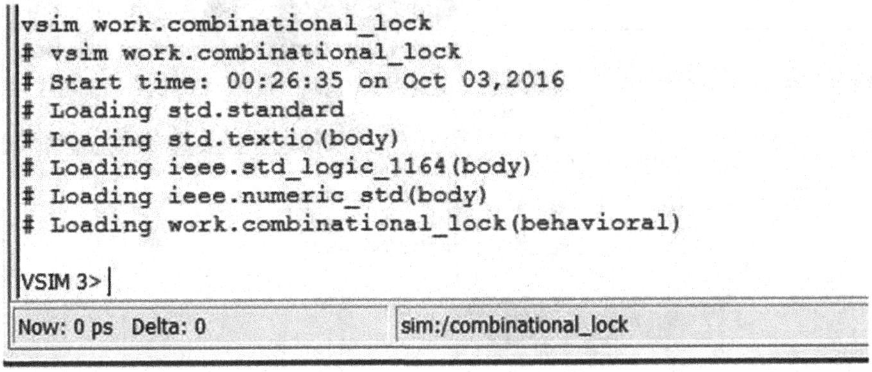

```
vsim work.combinational_lock
# vsim work.combinational_lock
# Start time: 00:26:35 on Oct 03,2016
# Loading std.standard
# Loading std.textio(body)
# Loading ieee.std_logic_1164(body)
# Loading ieee.numeric_std(body)
# Loading work.combinational_lock(behavioral)

VSIM 3> |
```

Now: 0 ps Delta: 0	sim:/combinational_lock

Figure 11-16. Simulation started

5. Add all of the combinational_lock signals to the wave window by right-clicking
    the combinational lock in the Sim box in the ModelSim window (Figure 11-17)
    or run the following script in the Transcript window. The wave window will be
    updated as in Figure 11-18

    • add wave -position insertpoint sim:/combinational_lock/*

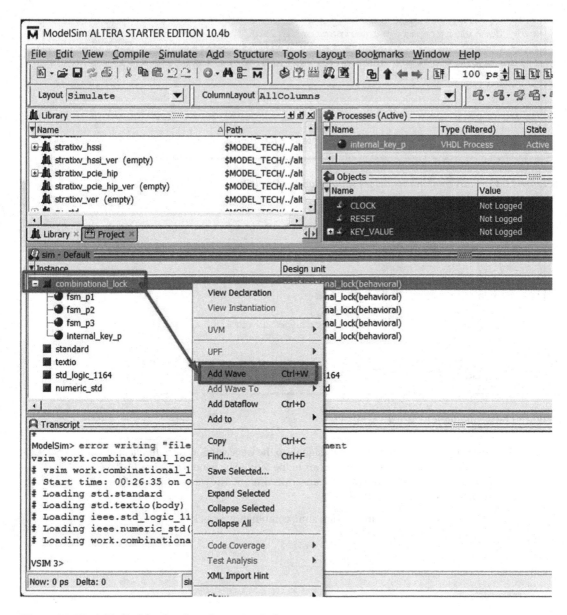

Figure 11-17. *Add all of the signals to the wave window*

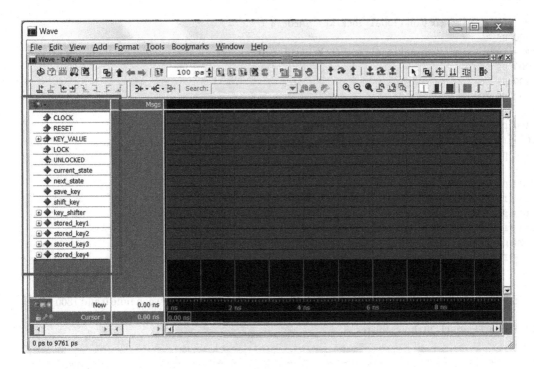

Figure 11-18. *Wave window with all the signals of combination lock design*

11.3.4.2   Simulate the Design with ModelSim Script

After you are in ModelSim and have run the simulation by vsim work.combinational_lock and added all of the signals to the waveform window, run the following script Listing 11-3 to try to LOCK the lock, unlock, and rekey the lock.

Listing 11-3. Combinational Lock simulation Script

```
force -freeze sim:/combinational_lock/CLOCK 1 0, 0 {50 ps} -r 100
force -freeze sim:/combinational_lock/RESET 1 0
force -freeze sim:/combinational_lock/KEY_VALUE 0000 0
force -freeze sim:/combinational_lock/LOCK 0 0
run 200 ps
force -freeze sim:/combinational_lock/RESET 0 0
run 100 ps
force -freeze sim:/combinational_lock/LOCK 1 0
run 100 ps
force -freeze sim:/combinational_lock/LOCK 0 0
run 100 ps
force -freeze sim:/combinational_lock/KEY_VALUE 1 0
run 100 ps
force -freeze sim:/combinational_lock/KEY_VALUE 2 0
run 100 ps
force -freeze sim:/combinational_lock/KEY_VALUE 3 0
run 100 ps
```

```
force -freeze sim:/combinational_lock/KEY_VALUE 4 0
run 100 ps
force -freeze sim:/combinational_lock/KEY_VALUE 0 0
run 100 ps
run 100 ps
run 100 ps
force -freeze sim:/combinational_lock/KEY_VALUE 8 0
run 100 ps
force -freeze sim:/combinational_lock/KEY_VALUE 9 0
run 100 ps
force -freeze sim:/combinational_lock/KEY_VALUE A 0
run 100 ps
force -freeze sim:/combinational_lock/KEY_VALUE B 0
run 100 ps
force -freeze sim:/combinational_lock/LOCK 1 0
run 100 ps
force -freeze sim:/combinational_lock/LOCK 0 0
run 100 ps
```

When the script is finished, the wave window will show all of the signals between time 0 and 1800 pS. Figure 11-19 shows the updated wave window. Click the Magnifying glass (shown in Figure 11-19) to zoom in to the time. Figure 11-20 shows the result.

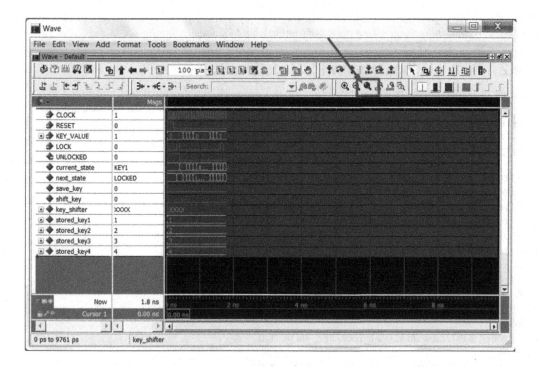

Figure 11-19. *Wave window with simulated signals*

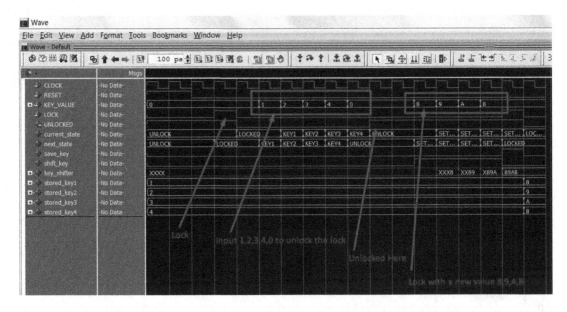

Figure 11-20. Wave window with simulated signals—Zoom in

EXERCISE TIME

The script will NOT test all of the state's transitions. It is time for you to write a test bench VHDL file for this combinational lock.

Please try to create one that will generate exactly the same results as the script. The answer for this task is in the next two pages. You can try to modify the basic test bench to be more advanced if you are feeling up for a challenge. Figure 11-21 shows the simulation result.

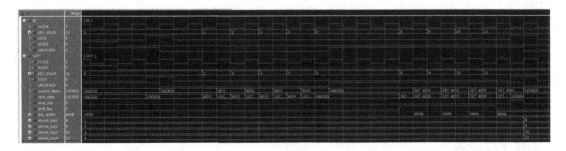

Figure 11-21. Combinational lock simulation result from script/vhdl test bench

Exercise Answer

```
1    LIBRARY ieee;
2    USE ieee.std_logic_1164.all;
3    use ieee.numeric_std.all;        -- Using numeric_std package
4
5    ⊟ENTITY combinational_lock_vhd_tst IS
6    └END combinational_lock_vhd_tst;
7    ⊟ARCHITECTURE combinational_lock_arch OF combinational_lock_vhd_tst IS
8    ⊟-- constants
9    ├-- signals
10   SIGNAL CLOCK     : STD_LOGIC;
11   SIGNAL KEY_VALUE : unsigned(3 DOWNTO 0) := "0000";
12   SIGNAL LOCK      : STD_LOGIC := '0';
13   SIGNAL RESET     : STD_LOGIC := '1';
14   SIGNAL UNLOCKED  : STD_LOGIC;
15
16   ⊟COMPONENT combinational_lock
17   ⊟   PORT (
18         CLOCK     : IN STD_LOGIC;
19         KEY_VALUE : IN unsigned(3 DOWNTO 0);
20         LOCK      : IN STD_LOGIC;
21         RESET     : IN STD_LOGIC;
22         UNLOCKED  : BUFFER STD_LOGIC
23   ├    );
24   END COMPONENT;
25
26   BEGIN
27
28       uut : combinational_lock
29   ⊟   PORT MAP (
30   ├-- list connections between master ports and signals
31         CLOCK     => CLOCK,
32         KEY_VALUE => KEY_VALUE,
33         LOCK      => LOCK,
34         RESET     => RESET,
35         UNLOCKED  => UNLOCKED
36   ├    );
37
38   -- genrate 100ps period clock --
39   CLOCK <= not CLOCK after 50 ps;
40
41   ⊟reset_p : PROCESS
42   │ BEGIN
43   │ RESET <= '1';
44   │ WAIT for 200 ps;
45   │ RESET <= '0';
46   │ WAIT;
47   │ END PROCESS reset_p;
48
49   ⊟lock_p : PROCESS
50   │ BEGIN
51   │ LOCK <= '0';
52   │ WAIT for 300 ps;
53   │ LOCK <= '1';
54   │ WAIT for 100 ps;
55   │ LOCK <= '0';
56   │ WAIT for 1200 ps;
57   │ LOCK <= '1';
58   │ WAIT for 100 ps;
59   │ LOCK <= '0';
60   │ WAIT for 100 ps;
61   │ WAIT;
62   │ END PROCESS lock_p;
63
64   ⊟key_p : PROCESS
65   │ BEGIN
66   │        -- code that executes only once
67   │ KEY_VALUE <= "0000";
68   │ WAIT for 500 ps;
69   │ KEY_VALUE <= "0001";
70   │ WAIT for 100 ps;
71   │ KEY_VALUE <= "0010";
72   │ WAIT for 100 ps;
73   │ KEY_VALUE <= "0011";
74   │ WAIT for 100 ps;
75   │ KEY_VALUE <= "0100";
76   │ WAIT for 100 ps;
77   │ KEY_VALUE <= "0000";
78   │ WAIT for 300 ps;
79   │ KEY_VALUE <= "1000";
80   │ WAIT for 100 ps;
81   │ KEY_VALUE <= "1001";
82   │ WAIT for 100 ps;
83   │ KEY_VALUE <= "1010";
84   │ WAIT for 100 ps;
85   │ KEY_VALUE <= "1011";
86   │ WAIT for 100 ps;
87   │ WAIT;
88   │ END PROCESS key_p;
89
90
91     END combinational_lock_arch;
```

Figure 11-22. Combinational lock simulation VHDL code answer

11.4   A Little Bit More About FSM in Digital Design

You may also hear about different encoding for state machines in digital design. The encoding means how the hardware interprets the state. In our combinational lock example, we have ten states. We can use 4-bit registers to interpret all ten states (e.g., "0000" is UNLOCK, "0001" is SET_KEY1..., "1001" is the last state KEY4). This is called full encoding. We can also use 10-bit registers to represent ten states. One bit of the register is mapped to exactly one state. This is so-called one-hot encoding. There is only one bit of the register set HIGH for any current state. All other state bits are set LOW. There is another approach called gray code encoding.

In general applications, you can let the FPGA tools help you to pick the encoding method. It is usually good enough. If we really need to pick one, we will select one-hot encoding because it uses minimum logic to decode each state which can run faster than other types of encoding. You can force the Altera tools to use one-hot. It is under menu: Assignments ➤ setting ➤ Compiler Settings ➤ Advanced Settings (Synthesis). You can follow Figure 11-23 to set the state machine processing to One-Hot.

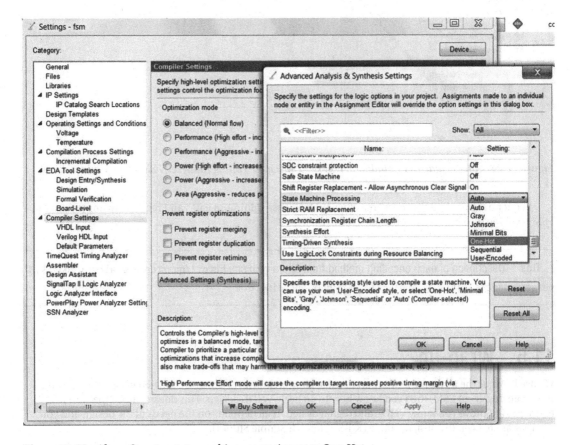

Figure 11-23. *Altera Quartus state machine processing set to One-Hot*

To show you that one-hot encoding can run faster than most of the other methods, we compiled the combinational_lock design with four different encoding methods: one-hot (362.19 Mhz), sequential (326.69 Mhz), gray code (333.33 Mhz), and minimal bits (328.19 Mhz). You can find the maximum clock speed of the design in the Compilation report ➤ TimeQuest Timing Analyzer ➤ Slow 1200mV 0C Model (Figure 11-24).

From high speed to low speed order: one-hot maximum clock speed is 362.19MHz. Gray code maximum clock speed is 333.33MHz. Minimal bits maximum clock speed is 328.19MHz. Sequential maximum clock speed is 326.69MHz.

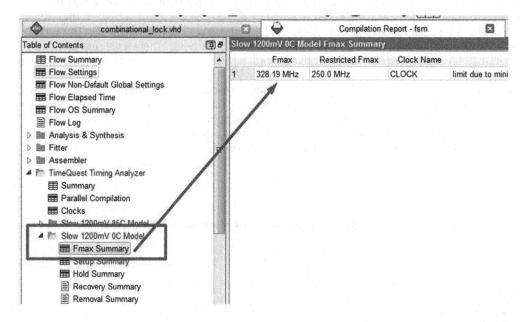

Figure 11-24. *Altera Quartus Compilation report—TimeQuest Timing Analyzer(FSM set to Minimal Bits)*

Sequential encode is the most area efficient. It will use minimum gates and registers to implement the FSM resulting the smallest overall area in FPGA.

■ **Tips**   Description of each encoding method from Altera web site `http://quartushelp.altera.com/15.0/ mergedProjects/hdl/vhdl/vhdl_file_dir_enum_encoding.htm`.

11.5   Wrap-up

We use FSMs as the last topic in this part because they include everything we learned in Chapters 6 to 10. If you can design an FSM, then you know how to do basic VHDL design. This doesn't mean that you need to use FSM to prove you know VHDL and digital design. It all depends on the needs of the design and you always want to keep the design simple (K-I-S-S, Keep It Simple Stupid).

11.5.1   Review FSMs

Complex circuits may be constructed using FSMs. FSMs are easily specified using three processes and the CASE statement. Let's review the steps for designing an FSM.

1. Define all of the inputs and outputs (it needs a clock and a reset)

2. Define the number of states for the design and draw a state diagram

3. Write VHDL code with three separate processes:

   a. Sequential register state process (current_state <= next_state)

   b. Next state decoding process with CASE statement which is used for making the decision for the next_state

   c. Output decoding process: The output it generates depends on current_state and may depend on the input.

■ **Tip**   Always explicitly define behavior for all states and outputs.

Keep in mind of that that all of the design to solve the problems is in step 2, NOT step 3. Step 3 should be straightforward to implement what step 2 asks for, if the state diagram is well defined. It is similar to writing software. If you have a flow chart (step 2) before you start coding (step 3), then you will have a better code than you will without a flow chart. You can get a lot of FSM examples or templates from the Internet. The following link is from Altera:

www.altera.com/support/support-resources/design-examples/design-software/vhdl/vhd-state-machine.html

"It depends."

—A professor at Hong Kong Polytechnic University

## PART III

Let's Make Something!

■ ■ ■

## CHAPTER 12

Light Sensors: Turning a Laser Pointer into a Hi-Tech Tripwire

12.1 Introduction

In Chapters 12 through 14, we will start to bring in the BeMicro Max10 board as a platform to show you how to really do something fun with FPGAs (field-programmable gate arrays) and hardware. In this chapter, we will show you how to use some hardware on the BeMicro Max10 board, the analog-to-digital converter (ADC), the photo resistor to build a light sensor, some LEDs (light-emitting diodes), and a button. Figure 12-1 shows the location of the ADC, which is built into the FPGA, and Photo resistor, which is in the top left corner. This chapter will show you what FPGA IP (Internet Protocol) is and how to use it.

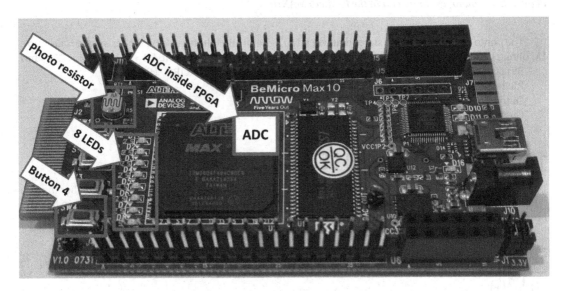

Figure 12-1. *BeMicro MAX10 board—photo resistor, LEDs, and ADC locations*

© Aiken Pang and Peter Membrey 2017

A. Pang and P. Membrey, *Beginning FPGA: Programming Metal*, DOI 10.1007/978-1-4302-6248-0_12

12.2   Photo Resistor Circuit 101

A photo resistor is a light-controlled variable resistor. Its resistance decreases with increasing incident light intensity; in other words, a phoo resistor exhibits photoconductivity (https://en.wikipedia.org/wiki/Photoresistor). In plain English, this simply means that the more light there is, the higher the voltage drop through the photo resistor.

Figure 12-2 shows the circuit for connecting the photo resistor to the FPGA's internal ADC.

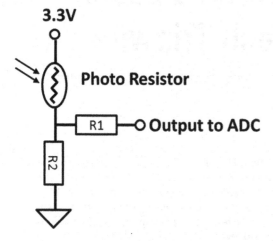

Figure 12-2. *Photo resistor circuit in the BeMicro MAX10*

The photo resistor datasheet states that when NO light hits the photo resistor, the resistance is around 1M ohm. The resistance will change to around 8~20k ohm when light falls on it. R2 = 1k ohm, R1 = 12.7 ohm.

By using the voltage divider equation: Output Voltage equal to 3.3V x [R2 / (R2 + PR)]

PR: resistance of photo resistor

Output Voltage equal to 0.366V when light is on

Output Voltage equal to 0.003V when light is off

12.3   BeMicro MAX10 LED Circuit

The BeMicro MAX10 has eight LEDs. Figure 12-3 is a LED symbol. If the voltage on (+) side is higher than (-) side by at least 0.8 V, then the LED will light up. The user LEDs are all green color on the BeMicro MAX10 board. We will use these LEDs to show how many times the tripwire got crossed.

Figure 12-3. *LED symbol*

Have some fun: Do you know what the first LED color is and what color was missing before we had LED light bulbs?

■ **Note** The world's first LED color is RED. It was built by GE physicist Nick Holonyak in 1962. We need a blue color LED to build a white color LED. It is because we need primary colors (red, green, and blue) to form white.

The LED (+) side is connected to 2.5V (Logic High) in series with a resistor R3. The (-) side of the LED is directly connected to an output from FPGA. We know that the (+) side needs to be higher than (-) by at least 0.8V to turn on the LED. Therefore, 0V (Logic low) output from the FPGA will turn on the LED and 2.5V (Logic High) output from the FPGA will turn off the LED. It is kind of inverting the normal logic. Figure 12-4 shows the circuit on the BeMicro MAX10 board.

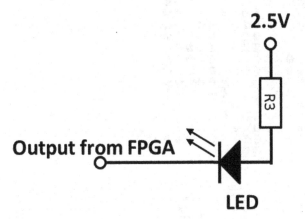

Figure 12-4. *BeMicro MAX10 LED circuit*

You may start to think, How can I define that 2.5V is logic high and 0V is logic low? The project template from the Altera store for the BeMicro MAX10 defined all of the inputs and outputs. You can read or modify the I/O (input/output) definitions in the Altera Quartus Prime—Pin Planner (Figure 12-5). Open the pin planner: Open/Create a BeMicro MAX10 project, click Assignments menu, and then click Pin Planner or Ctrl + Shift + N.

Figure 12-5 shows that all of the USER LED I/O standards are 2.5V.

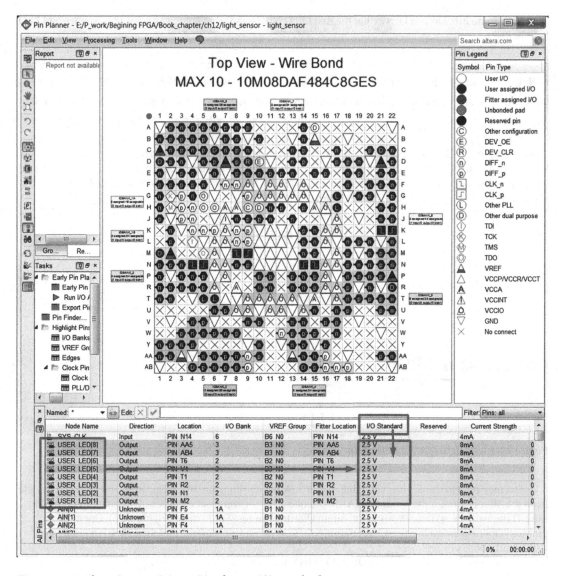

Figure 12-5. Altera Quartus Prime—Pin planner I/O standard

12.4   FPGA IP—Altera ADC IP (Hard IP and Soft IP)

Altera MAX10 FPGA provides an ADC IP which contains a hard IP block in the MAX10 device to deal with external inputs and soft logic through the Altera Modular ADC soft IP core which is our VHDL (VHSIC (very high speed integrated circuit) Hardware Description Language) code needed to interface with it. The ADC hard IP block has the magic piece "Sampling and Hold with 12 bit 1 Mbps ADC." This piece provides you the capability to translate analog voltage levels to digital numbers. The basic function is to provide a 12-bit digital value of the analog signal being observed. Figure 12-6 shows you the ADC analog inputs to the ADC hard IP block and the connection between the hard IP block and Altera modular ADC soft IP core.

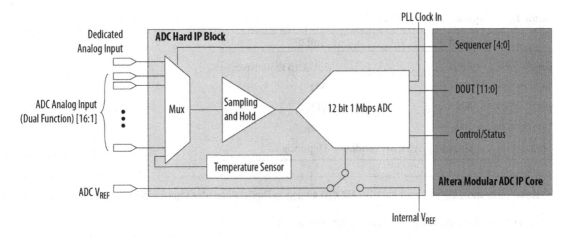

Figure 12-6. *ADC in MAX10 FPGA—source from Altera MAX10 Handbook*

12.4.1 Hard IP

By the way, the term "IP core" in FPGA means a block of logic that is used in making an FPGA. If the IP physically exists inside the FPGA before the user programs it (like the logic inside the ADC hard IP block, logic element, internal RAM, and I/O block), then we call it hard IP core. Most of the time, FPGA vendors only provide the name of the module for you to call when you need to use it. They may only provide a simulation model for you to do the simulation but not the detail of how those logic blocks are built. It is their secret recipe (integrated circuit mask layout) to build the FPGA chip and sell it to you. This also means that you cannot change it after you get the FPGA. The good thing about using hard IP is that you can use it as is.

12.4.2 Soft IP

Soft IP can be changed after the FPGA has left the manufacturer. Often soft IP is in the form of HDL (Hardware Description Language). It means that you can simulate it and know what is happening inside the IP. You can get soft IP from the FPGA vendor or some other company that only provides soft IP for FPGAs. Using soft IP involves a lot more work than hard IP. You need to make sure the soft IP gets synthesized correctly. This means that it is NOT plug and play. You need to spend some time on it. Most of the free soft IPs come with the design VHDL files. You can go to the following web site to get some free VHDL IP. It's worth noting, however, that soft IP, while more time-consuming and complex than hard IP, is most likely a lot easier and faster to use than trying to create your own from scratch. Soft IP is then a great way to leverage others' expertise so that you can focus on the problem at hand.

■ **Note** Web sites for free soft IP sources:

Open Cores: `http://opencores.org/`

Gaisler SOC library: `www.gaisler.com/index.php/products/ipcores/soclibrary`

Most of the time we only configure hard IP in the FPGA design, and soft IP needs to be generated by the FPGA vendor tools or tools from the third-party company that provided you with the VHDL code. Table 12-1 summarizes the differences between hard and soft IP in FPGA.

Table 12-1. *Hard vs. Soft IP in FPGA*

	Hard IP	Soft IP
Cost	FREE	FREE to Expensive
Easy to use	YES	NO
Flexibility	NO	YES
Changeable	NO	YES
Speed	Guaranty by FPGA vendor	Depends

■ **Note** For more detail about the ADC MAX10 Analog to Digital Converter User Guide link, see

www.altera.com/literature/hb/max-10/ug_m10_adc.pdf.

12.4.3   How to Configure Your First IP

Step 1: Create a new bank Quartus project in a manner similar to the way we did it in Chapter 4.

Step 2: In the IP Catalog, search for ADC, select the Altera Modular ADC core, and double-click it as shown in Figure 12-7.

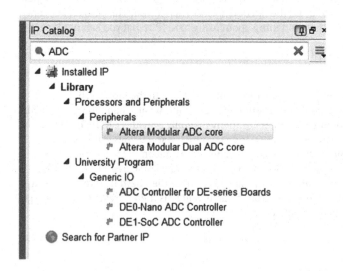

Figure 12-7. *IP Catalog search for ADC*

Step 3: A new IP variation window will appear as Figure 12-8. Enter **adc_interface** in Entity name. The Save in folder location is your project folder location. You don't need to change the family and device setting. Click **OK**.

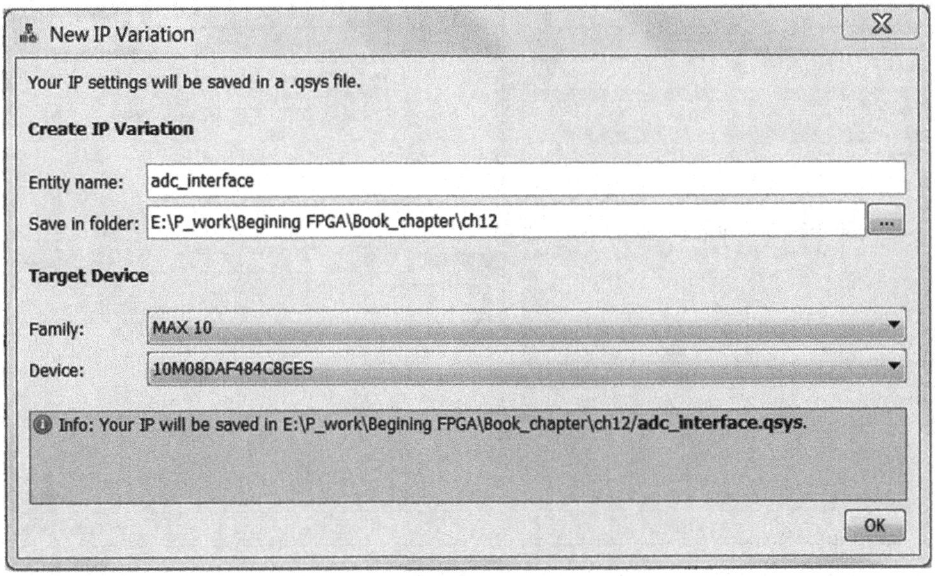

Figure 12-8. New IP variation window for ADC interface IP

Step 4: A new IP Parameter Editor window will appear as Figure 12-9 and we can set our preferred parameters. We want it to constantly send out ADC samples and we want to check and control the IP's status and command registers, so we should select the Core Variant to be **Standard sequencer with external sample storage** on the General tab. For this design we are only interested in channel 4 which is connected to the photo sensor on the BeMicro Max10 board. Check **Use Channel 4** in the Channels tab and CH4 tab. Figure 12-9 shows the setting.

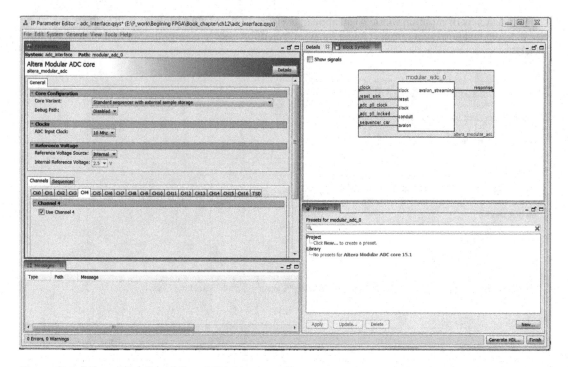

Figure 12-9. *Altera Modular ADC core IP parameter editor*

Step 5: The sequencer tab settings default to no channel, so make sure you select **CH 4** where the number of slots used is **1**. Figure 12-10 shows the setting.

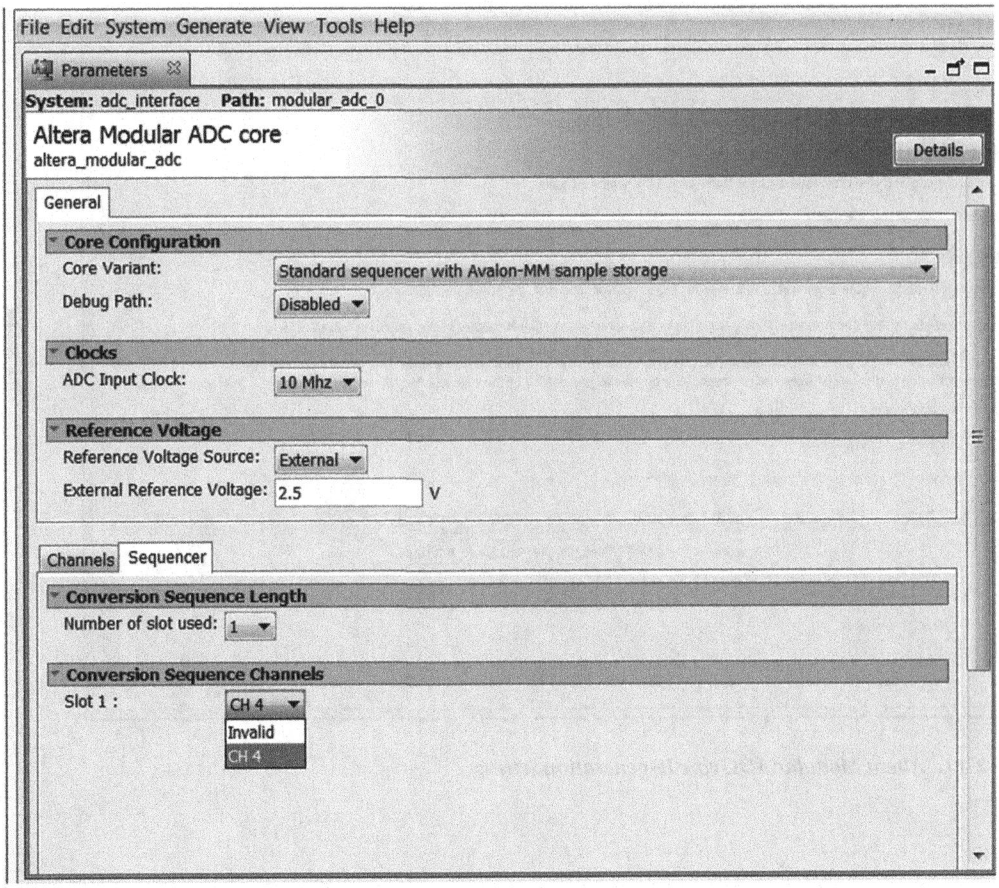

Figure 12-10. *Altera Modular ADC core IP parameter editor—sequencer tab*

Step 6: Click **Generate HDL...** and Figure 12-11 window will pop up. Select **VHDL** for synthesis and the path for storing the generated IP VHDL files. Click **Generate**. Figure 12-12 will pop up when generation is going to begin.

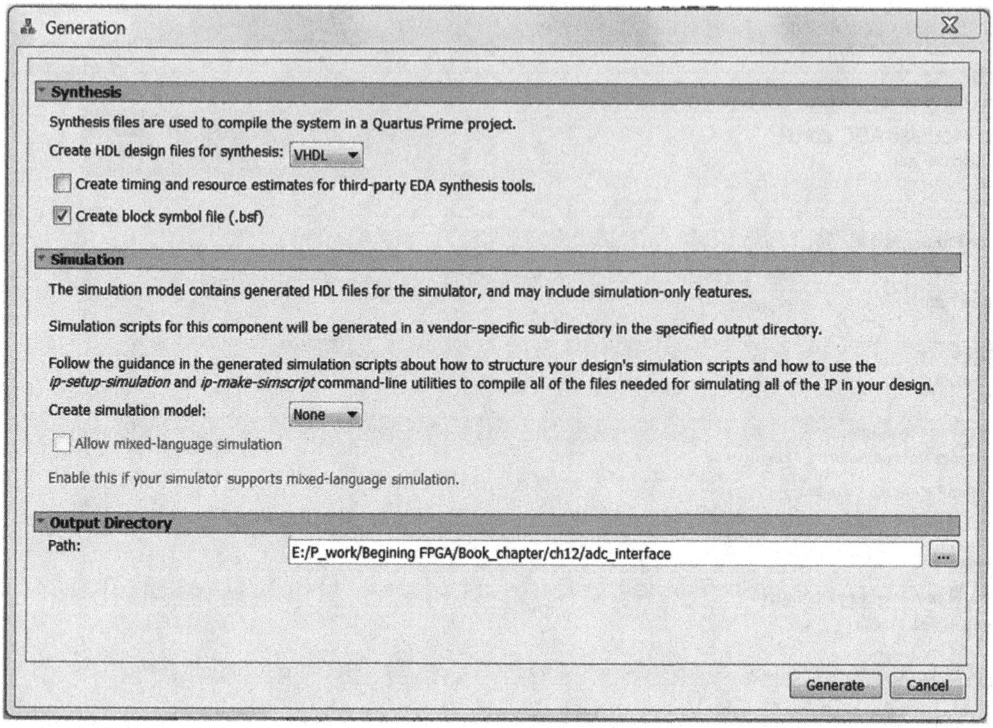

Figure 12-11. *Altera Modular ADC core IP generation setting*

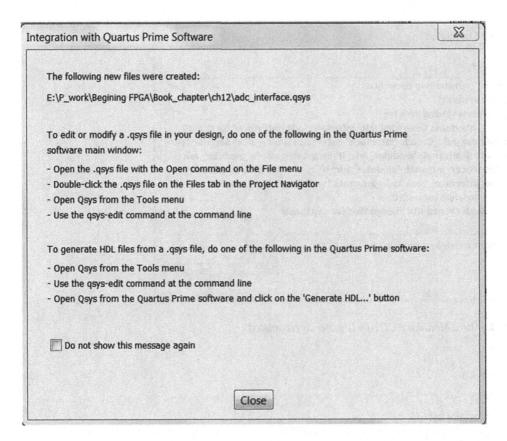

Figure 12-12. Message shows up after generation is finished

Step 7: Generate Completed window (Figure 12-13) will show up after you click the generation in the last step. Next click **Close** on the Generate Completed window and click **Finish** in the IP parameter editor window. Figure 12-14 shows all the files generated by the Altera IP tools. The name of the generated IP is adc_interface.

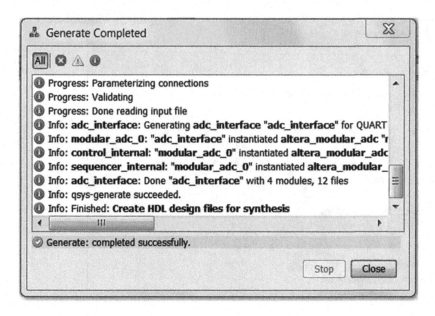

Figure 12-13. *Altera Modular ADC core IP generate completed*

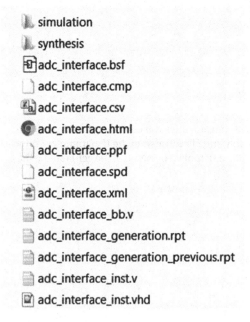

Figure 12-14. *ADC interface—Altera Modular ADC core IP generated file list*

12.5   FPGA IP—Altera PLL IP

Altera PLL IP can generate a very wide range of clock frequencies. A phase-locked loop (PLL) is a closed-loop frequency-control system based on the phase difference between the input clock signal and the feedback clock signal of a controlled oscillator. It has a lock pin output to indicate that the output clock is stable and ready to use. We use this lock output as an active low reset to our system.

We need to create two PLL Clock IPs for the Altera ADC IP. This is because the MAX10 FPGA's ADC requires a specific PLL inside the FPGA as its clock source. It is called adc_pll in the diagram below (Figure 12-15). The BeMicroMax10 board's 50MHz clock source can only drive directly into the other PLL. We called it cascade_pll in this design. Two PLLs need to connected, as in Figure 12-15, to provide the clock for the ADC (adc_pll C0 output)

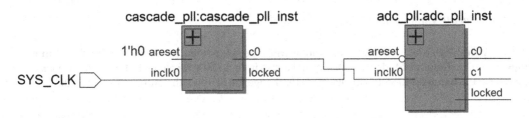

Figure 12-15. *Altera PLL cascade connection*

12.5.1   Generate ADC PLL IP

Step 1: In the IP Catalog, search for **altpll**, select the **ALTPLL,** and **double-click** it as shown in Figure 12-16.

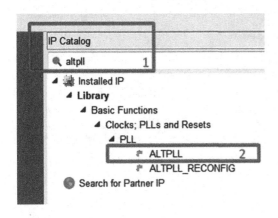

Figure 12-16. *IP Catalog—Altera PLL IP*

Step 2: A new IP variation window will appear as in Figure 12-17. Enter **adc_pll** at the end of the IP variation file name. Select **VHDL**. Click **OK**.

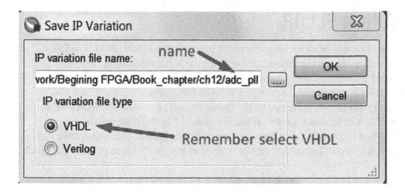

Figure 12-17. Save IP Variation for adc_pll

Step 3: A MegaWizard Plug-In Manager window will appear as in Figure 12-18. Under the **1: Parameter Settings** tab, on the **General/Modes** tab, change the inclk0 input to **50 MHz** which is the on board clock frequency. On the **Bandwidth/SS** tab in Figure 12-19, change the Bandwidth Setting to **Preset High**.

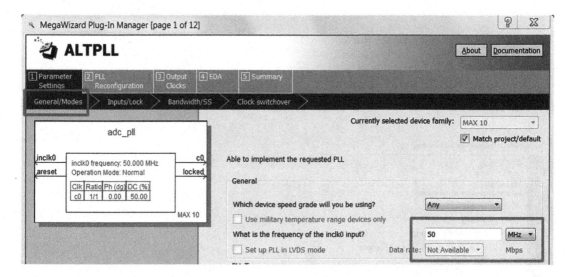

Figure 12-18. MegaWizard Plug-In Manager for ADC IP—1

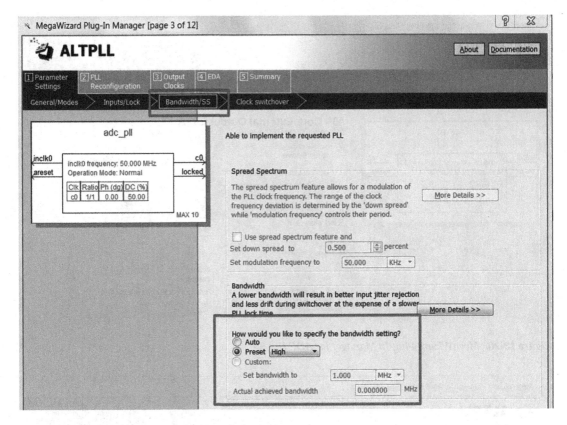

Figure 12-19. *MegaWizard Plug-In Manager for ADC IP—2*

Step 4: Under the **3: Output Clocks** tab, the ADC requires a 10 MHz clock from the c0 output of PLL_1 on our BeMicro Max10 board. On the **clk c0** tab in Figure 12-20, change the division factor to **5**. On the **clk c1** tab in Figure 12-21, tick the **Use this clock** checkbox and leave the rest of the parameters at their defaults.

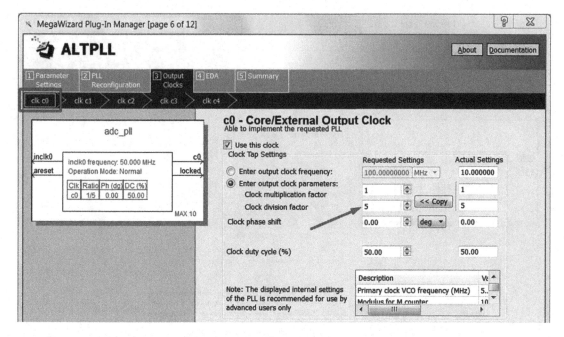

Figure 12-20. *MegaWizard Plug-In Manager for ADC IP—3*

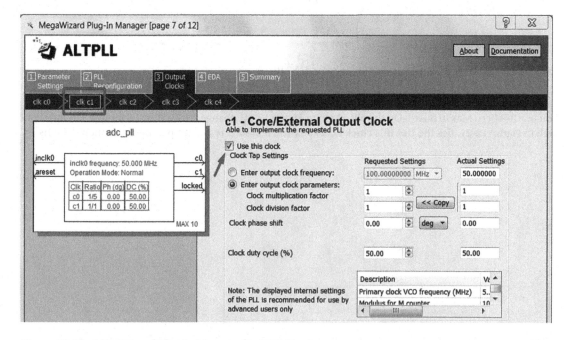

Figure 12-21. *MegaWizard Plug-In Manager for ADC IP—4*

Step 5: Click the **Finish** button in Figure 12-22, It may pop up another sub-window. Click the **Finish** button on the sub-window and note that the resulting files were added to the Files tab of the Project Navigator.

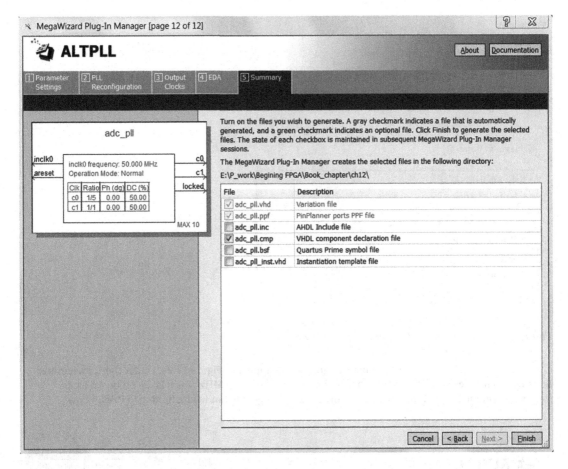

Figure 12-22. *MegaWizard Plug-In Manager for ADC IP—5*

12.5.2   Generate Cascade PLL IP

Step 1: In the IP Catalog, search for **altpll**, select **ALTPLL,** and **double-click** it as shown in Figure 12-23. A new IP variation window pops up. Enter **cascade_pll** at the end of the IP variation file name. Select **VHDL**. Click **OK**

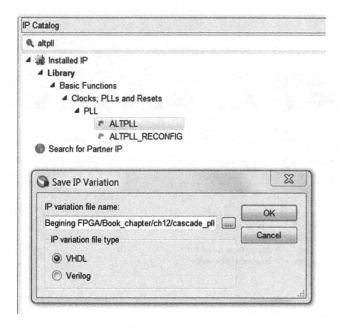

Figure 12-23. *IP Catalog—Altera PLL IP for cascade*

Step 2: A MegaWizard Plug-In Manager window will appear as Figure 12-24. Under the **1: Parameter Settings,** on the **General/Modes** tab, change the inclk0 input to **50 MHz** which is the on board clock frequency. On the **Bandwidth/SS** tab in Figure 12-25, change the Bandwidth Setting to **Preset Low**.

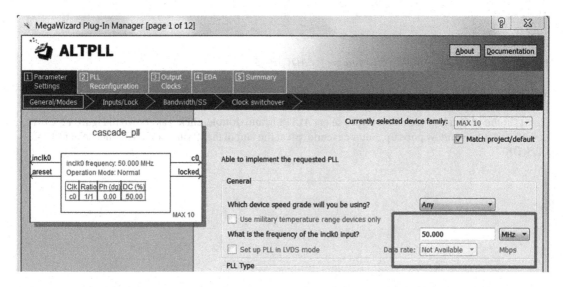

Figure 12-24. *MegaWizard Plug-In Manager for Cascade IP—1*

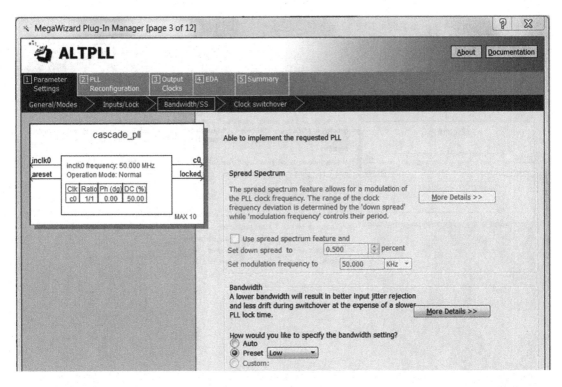

Figure 12-25. *MegaWizard Plug-In Manager for Cascade IP—2*

Step 3: Under the **3: Output Clocks** tab, the ADC PLL requires a 50 MHz clock. On the **clk c0** tab in Figure 12-26, change the division factor to **1** and click **Finish**. Figure 12-27 will show up. Click **Finish**. All of the IP files will be added to the project.

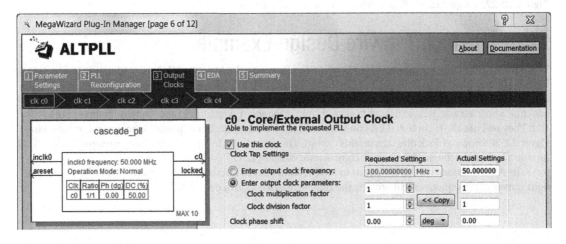

Figure 12-26. *MegaWizard Plug-In Manager for Cascade IP—3*

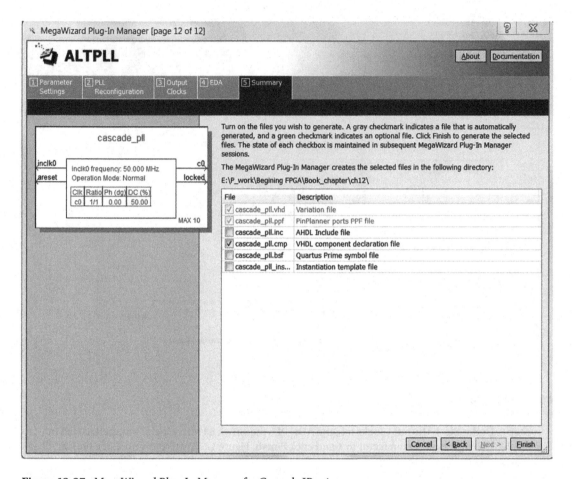

Figure 12-27. *MegaWizard Plug-In Manager for Cascade IP—4*

12.6 Hi-Tech Tripwire Design Example

The purpose of this design example is to become familiar with the Max10's ADC and with using IP functions as well as integrating them into VHDL. The most important part is of course having fun with the FPGA!

The Hi-Tech Tripwire design includes five VHDL files: `light_sensor_top.vhd`, `adc_interface.vhd`, `adc_pll.vhd`, `cascade_pll.vhd`, `light_sensor_adc_sequencer.vhd`, and `light_sensor_counter_led.vhd`. They will use the eight user-LEDs on the board to show the number of people who passed the tripwire. Figure 12-28 shows a block diagram on this design. The eight LEDs form an 8-bit binary unsigned value. This function is done by the module name "Light sensor counter LED."

The ADC interface (Altera IP) needs to have a controller to turn on the ADC conversion operation. The light sensor ADC sequencer will provide the right sequence to turn on the ADC.

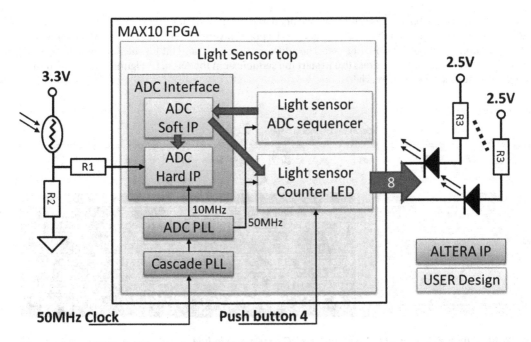

Figure 12-28. *Hi-Tech Tripwire design block diagram*

12.6.1   Light Sensor ADC Sequencer Module

The ADC interface Altera IP needs a module to send a turn on command to it. Please open the generated adc_interface.vhd file under the folder adc_interface/synthesis/; then the first few lines show the adc_interface module port list (Figure 12-29). The ADC sequencer interface includes four inputs and one output from ADC_interface side. They are Altera's Avalon-Memory Map interface. It means that we need to have a module which has four inputs and one output to match it.

```
entity adc_interface is
    port (
        adc_pll_clock_clk       : in  std_logic                          := '0';
        adc_pll_locked_export   : in  std_logic                          := '0';
        clock_clk               : in  std_logic                          := '0';
        reset_sink_reset_n      : in  std_logic                          := '0';
        response_valid          : out std_logic;
        response_channel        : out std_logic_vector(4 downto 0);
        response_data           : out std_logic_vector(11 downto 0);
        response_startofpacket  : out std_logic;
        response_endofpacket    : out std_logic;
        sequencer_csr_address   : in  std_logic                          := '0';
        sequencer_csr_read      : in  std_logic                          := '0';
        sequencer_csr_write     : in  std_logic                          := '0';
        sequencer_csr_writedata : in  std_logic_vector(31 downto 0) := (others => '0');
        sequencer_csr_readdata  : out std_logic_vector(31 downto 0)
    );
end entity adc_interface;
```

Figure 12-29. *Port list of adc_interface module*

We need to find out what address and value we need to write into the adc_interface to start the ADC. You can get the information from the MAX10 Analog to Digital Converter User Guide: Altera Modular ADC Register Definitions—Sequencer Core Register. The address offset is 0x0 and bit 1 is the Run bit. It means that we only need to write 0x1 to address 0x0 to start the sequencer in the Altera IP. Figure 12-30 is the output from light_sensor_adc_sequencer.vhd.

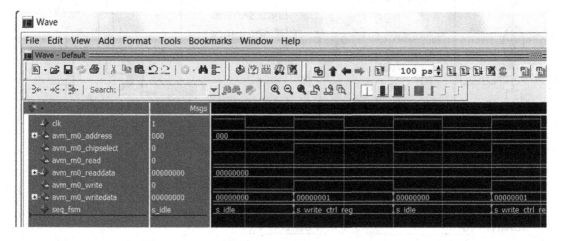

Figure 12-30. *Simulation result of the light sensor ADC sequencer module*

The FSM (seq_fsm) is jumping between idle state and write control register state. It will set writedata bit 0 to 1 when in the write control register state with chipselect and write set High to create a write operation to address 0x0 with value 0x1 to the adc_interface.

In Figure 12-31, line 18, it defines two states for the FSM: s_idle and s_write_ctrl_reg. It is used by the line 19 seq_fsm. Lines 22-34 are the sequential process with the state jump between s_idle and s_write_ctrl_reg. Lines 38-62 in Listing 12-1 defined the outputs which are only depends on the seq_fsm (current state).

Using state machine to build this light_sensor_adc_sequencer.vhd is a little bit of overkill. You can go to open the RTL viewer for the light_senssor_adc_sequencer after you copy my code into your machine. You will find it only uses one register and some wire connections. It is only used for demonstrating FSM design.

```
18 ┌   type seq_fsm_type is (s_idle, s_write_ctrl_reg);
19 └   signal seq_fsm : seq_fsm_type := s_idle;
20  ⊟begin
21  │
22  ⊟  sequences_proc : process(clk)
23  │   begin
24  ⊟    if rising_edge(clk) then
25  ⊟      case seq_fsm is
26  │        when s_idle =>
27  │          seq_fsm <= s_write_ctrl_reg;
28  │        when s_write_ctrl_reg =>
29  │          seq_fsm <= s_idle;
30  │        when OTHERS =>
31  │          seq_fsm <= s_idle;
32 ─      end case;
33 ─    end if;
34    end process;
```

Figure 12-31. *light sensor ADC sequencer VHDL code (part of it)*

12.6.1.1   Code for Light Sensor ADC Sequencer

Listing 12-1 shows the VHDL code for light sensor ADC sequencer.

Listing 12-1. light_sensor_adc_sequencer.vhd

```vhdl
library ieee;
use ieee.std_logic_1164.all;
use ieee.numeric_std.all;

entity light_sensor_adc_sequencer is
  port(
    clk                 : in std_logic := '0';
    avm_m0_address      : out std_logic_vector(9 downto 0);
    avm_m0_chipselect : out std_logic;
    avm_m0_read         : out std_logic;
    avm_m0_readdata   : in std_logic_vector(31 downto 0) := (OTHERS => '0');
    avm_m0_write        : out std_logic;
    avm_m0_writedata  : out std_logic_vector(31 downto 0)
    );
end light_sensor_adc_sequencer;

architecture arch of light_sensor_adc_sequencer is
  type seq_fsm_type is (s_idle, s_write_ctrl_reg);
  signal seq_fsm : seq_fsm_type := s_idle;
begin

  sequences_proc : process(clk)
  begin
    if rising_edge(clk) then
      case seq_fsm is
        when s_idle =>
          seq_fsm <= s_write_ctrl_reg;
        when s_write_ctrl_reg =>
          seq_fsm <= s_idle;
        when OTHERS =>
          seq_fsm <= s_idle;
      end case;
    end if;
  end process;

  process(seq_fsm)
  begin
    case seq_fsm is
      when s_idle =>
        avm_m0_address <= std_logic_vector(to_unsigned(16#0000#, avm_m0_address'length));
        avm_m0_chipselect <= '0';
        avm_m0_read <= '0';
        avm_m0_write <= '0';
        avm_m0_writedata <= (OTHERS => '0');

      -- Set RUN bit of CMD reg
      when s_write_ctrl_reg =>
        avm_m0_address <= std_logic_vector(to_unsigned(16#0000#, avm_m0_address'length));
```

```
        avm_m0_chipselect <= '1';
        avm_m0_read <= '0';
        avm_m0_write <= '1';
        avm_m0_writedata <= x"00000001";

    when others =>
        avm_m0_address <= (OTHERS => '0');
        avm_m0_chipselect <= '0';
        avm_m0_read <= '0';
        avm_m0_write <= '0';
        avm_m0_writedata <= (OTHERS => '0');
    end case;
  end process;

end;
```

12.6.2 Light Sensor Counter LED

This counter will only increment by one when the ADC value (the light intensity) changes from a high value to a low value, which indicates that someone blocked the laser beam. The counter LED will reset to zero when the button is pushed. Figure 12-32 shows that the design will be armed when the ADC value is higher than the HIGH_BOUNDARY value. The HIGH_BOUNDARY is a generic value for the design. There is another generic value for the design which is LOW_BOUNDARY and the number of LEDs (Figure 12-34, lines 9-11). Figure 12-33 shows that when the ADC data changes from 4072 to 8, it will trigger and increment the count_number of trip counter and the output LED will change too. Figure 12-34 and Listing 12-2 show the code for the light sensor counter LED.

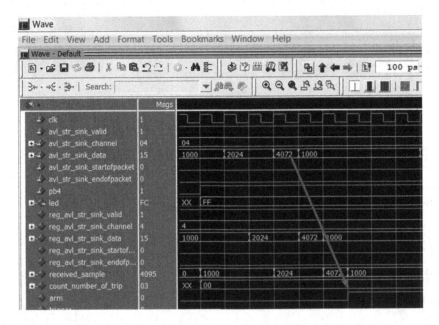

Figure 12-32. *arm set to high when ADC value equal to 4072*

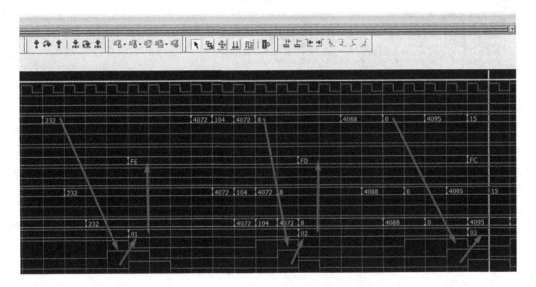

Figure 12-33. *light_sensor_counter_led.vhd increments the counter three times*

12.6.2.1   Code for Light Sensor Counter LED

```vhdl
1    library ieee;
2    use ieee.std_logic_1164.all;
3    use ieee.numeric_std.all;
4
5    entity light_sensor_counter_led is
6      generic(
7        -- Adjust sensitivity and offset with these two parameters.
8        -- Find the right Low boundary Higher than ROOM lighting and adjust the trigger point
9        LOW_BOUNDARY   : integer := 1000;
10       HIGH_BOUNDARY  : integer := 3000;
11       NUM_LEDS       : integer := 8
12       );
13     port(
14       clk                        : in  std_logic;
15       avl_str_sink_valid         : in  std_logic;
16       avl_str_sink_channel       : in  std_logic_vector(4 downto 0);
17       avl_str_sink_data          : in  std_logic_vector(11 downto 0);
18       avl_str_sink_startofpacket : in  std_logic;
19       avl_str_sink_endofpacket   : in  std_logic;
20       pb4                        : in  std_logic;  -- when push the button, this go Low
21       led                        : out std_logic_vector(NUM_LEDS-1 downto 0)
22       );
23   end light_sensor_counter_led;
24
25   architecture arch of light_sensor_counter_led is
26
27     -- Input registers
28     signal reg_avl_str_sink_valid         : std_logic;
29     signal reg_avl_str_sink_channel       : std_logic_vector(avl_str_sink_channel'range);
30     signal reg_avl_str_sink_data          : std_logic_vector(avl_str_sink_data'range);
31     signal reg_avl_str_sink_startofpacket : std_logic;
32     signal reg_avl_str_sink_endofpacket   : std_logic;
33
34     signal received_sample     : std_logic_vector(11 downto 0);
35     signal count_number_of_trip : unsigned(7 downto 0); -- Counter
36
37     signal arm         : std_logic := '0'; -- Go High when the received_sample is High value
38     signal trigger     : std_logic := '0'; -- Trigger only when change from High to Low value
39     signal trigger_dly : std_logic := '0';
40
41   begin
42
43     process(clk)
44       variable received_sample_int : integer range 0 to 2**received_sample'length-1;
45     begin
46       if rising_edge(clk) then
47         -- Load the input registers
48         reg_avl_str_sink_valid         <= avl_str_sink_valid;
49         reg_avl_str_sink_channel       <= avl_str_sink_channel;
50         reg_avl_str_sink_data          <= avl_str_sink_data;
51         reg_avl_str_sink_startofpacket <= avl_str_sink_startofpacket;
52         reg_avl_str_sink_endofpacket   <= avl_str_sink_endofpacket;
53
54         -- Get the data from ADC channel 4, which is the photo sensor
55         if reg_avl_str_sink_channel = "00100" then -- channel 4
56           if reg_avl_str_sink_valid = '1' then
57             received_sample <= reg_avl_str_sink_data;
58           end if;
59         end if;
60
61         received_sample_int := to_integer(unsigned(received_sample));
62
63         --Arm when the ADC input is high
64         if(trigger = '1' or pb4 = '0') then
65           arm <= '0';
66         elsif((received_sample_int > HIGH_BOUNDARY) and arm = '0')then
67           arm <= '1';
68         end if;
69
70         if((received_sample_int < LOW_BOUNDARY) and arm = '1')then
71           trigger <= '1';
72         else
73           trigger <= '0';
74         end if;
75
76         trigger_dly <= trigger;
77
78         -- Increnment the LED counter evertime the trip trigger
79         -- The LED counter will clear by push button 1
80         if(pb4 = '0') then
81           count_number_of_trip <= (others => '0');
82         elsif (trigger_dly = '0' and trigger = '1') then -- rising edge of the trigger
83           if (count_number_of_trip < 255) then -- Count to the MAX = 255 (2^12 -1)
84             count_number_of_trip <= count_number_of_trip + 1;
85           end if;
86         end if;
87
88       end if;
89     end process;
90
91     -- convert unsigned value to std logic vector
92     led <= not(std_logic_vector(count_number_of_trip));
93
94   end;
```

Figure 12-34. *Light sensor counter LED design*

Listing 12-2 is text version for easy copying.

Listing 12-2. light_sensor_counter_led.vhd

```vhdl
library ieee;
use ieee.std_logic_1164.all;
use ieee.numeric_std.all;

entity light_sensor_counter_led is
  generic(
    -- Adjust sensitivity and offset with these two parameters.
    -- Find the right Low boundary Higher than ROOM lighting and adjust the trigger point
    LOW_BOUNDARY  : integer := 1000;
    HIGH_BOUNDARY : integer := 3000;
    NUM_LEDS      : integer := 8
    );
  port(
    clk                       : in  std_logic;
    avl_str_sink_valid        : in  std_logic;
    avl_str_sink_channel      : in  std_logic_vector(4 downto 0);
    avl_str_sink_data         : in  std_logic_vector(11 downto 0);
    avl_str_sink_startofpacket : in  std_logic;
    avl_str_sink_endofpacket  : in  std_logic;
    pb4                       : in  std_logic;  -- when push the button, this go Low
    led                       : out std_logic_vector(NUM_LEDS-1 downto 0)
    );
end light_sensor_counter_led;

architecture arch of light_sensor_counter_led is

  -- Input registers
  signal reg_avl_str_sink_valid         : std_logic;
  signal reg_avl_str_sink_channel       : std_logic_vector(avl_str_sink_channel'range);
  signal reg_avl_str_sink_data          : std_logic_vector(avl_str_sink_data'range);
  signal reg_avl_str_sink_startofpacket : std_logic;
  signal reg_avl_str_sink_endofpacket   : std_logic;

  signal received_sample       : std_logic_vector(11 downto 0);
  signal count_number_of_trip  : unsigned(7 downto 0); -- Counter

  signal arm         : std_logic := '0'; -- Go High when the received_sample is High value
  signal trigger     : std_logic := '0'; -- Trigger only when change from High to Low value
  signal trigger_dly : std_logic := '0';

begin

  process(clk)
    variable received_sample_int : integer range 0 to 2**received_sample'length-1;
  begin
    if rising_edge(clk) then
      -- Load the input registers
      reg_avl_str_sink_valid          <= avl_str_sink_valid;
```

```
        reg_avl_str_sink_channel        <= avl_str_sink_channel;
        reg_avl_str_sink_data           <= avl_str_sink_data;
        reg_avl_str_sink_startofpacket <= avl_str_sink_startofpacket;
        reg_avl_str_sink_endofpacket    <= avl_str_sink_endofpacket;

        -- Get the data from ADC channel 4, which is the photo sensor
        if reg_avl_str_sink_channel = "00100" then  -- channel 4
          if reg_avl_str_sink_valid = '1' then
            received_sample <= reg_avl_str_sink_data;
          end if;
        end if;

        received_sample_int := to_integer(unsigned(received_sample));

        --Arm when the ADC input is high
        if(trigger = '1' or pb4 = '0') then
          arm <= '0';
        elsif((received_sample_int > HIGH_BOUNDARY) and arm = '0')then
          arm <= '1';
        end if;

        if((received_sample_int < LOW_BOUNDARY) and arm = '1')then
          trigger <= '1';
        else
          trigger <= '0';
        end if;

        trigger_dly <= trigger;

        -- Increnment the LED counter evertime the trip trigger
        -- The LED counter will clear by push button 1
        if(pb4 = '0') then
          count_number_of_trip <= (others => '0');
        elsif (trigger_dly = '0' and trigger = '1') then -- rising edge of the trigger
          if (count_number_of_trip < 255) then -- Count to the MAX = 255 (2^12 -1)
            count_number_of_trip <= count_number_of_trip + 1;
          end if;
        end if;

    end if;
  end process;

  -- convert unsigned value to std logic vector
  led <= not(std_logic_vector(count_number_of_trip));

end;
```

12.6.3   Light Sensor Top Level

This module is used to connect all of the IPs and the two modules we created in this chapter. It also provides inputs and outputs to connect to the external world (anything not inside the FPGA). Examine the code in Listing 12-3. It defines an entity, which are the inputs and outputs as well as some parameters. Tables 12-2 and 12-3 show the generic and port functions in the design.

Table 12-2. *Generic Parameters Functions*

Generic Name	Function
LOW_BOUNDARY	Define the ADC expected value in room normal light brightness
HIGH_BOUNDARY	Define the ADC expected value of laser beam on the photo sensor
NUM_LEDS	Number of LEDs. Set to 8 our system.

All three of the generics (parameters) are directly used by `light_sensor_counter_led.vhd`.

Table 12-3. *Port Names Functions*

Port Name	Function
SYS_CLK	Input: BeMicro MAX10 on board clock and the frequency is 50MHz
USER_LED	Output: All eight LEDs connection
PB	Input: All four user push button connection. In this design we only use the number 4 push buttons.

SYS_CLK is connected to the `cascade_pll.vhd` clock input: `inclock0`. USER_LED and PB(4) are connected to `light_sensor_counter_led.vhd`.

The `light_sensor_top.vhd` file declares some components and signals which will be used by the top-level design. After the BEGIN statement, all modules: cascade_pll, adc_pll, adc_interface, light_sensor_adc_sequencer, and light_sensor_counter_led are stitched together as we saw in Figure 12-28.

In the code in Listing 12-3, we added a NOT gate in the design. Following is the VHDL code of that NOT gate:

```
pll_cascade_locked_reset_wire_n <= not pll_cascade_locked_reset_wire;
```

We would like to keep the second PLL (adc_PLL) in reset when the first PLL (cascade_pll) is NOT locked. The right-hand side of the code statement (pll_cascade_locked_reset_wire) is connected to the first PLL lock output and left-hand side is using it as a reset signal for the second PLL. We need to add a NOT gate between the two signals because the second PLL reset is active HIGH reset. When the first PLL is locked (High), then the second PLL reset is LOW (NOT reset).

12.6.3.1   Code for Light Sensor Top Level

Listing 12-3. light_sensor_top.vhd

```vhdl
library ieee;
use ieee.std_logic_1164.all;

entity light_sensor_top is
  generic(
    LOW_BOUNDARY  : integer := 1800;     -- May vary from board to board...
    HIGH_BOUNDARY : integer := 2600;     -- May vary from board to board...
    NUM_LEDS      : integer := 8
    );
  port(
    SYS_CLK  : in  std_logic;            -- inclk0
    USER_LED : out std_logic_vector(NUM_LEDS downto 1);
    -- pushbutton switch ins
    PB       : in  std_logic_vector(4 downto 1)  -- Only use the PB 4
    );
end light_sensor_top;

architecture arch of light_sensor_top is
  component cascade_pll is
    port
      (
        areset : in  std_logic := '0';
        inclk0 : in  std_logic := '0';
        c0     : out std_logic;
        locked : out std_logic
        );
  end component;

  component adc_pll
    port(inclk0 : in  std_logic;
         areset : in  std_logic;
         c0     : out std_logic;
         c1     : out std_logic;
         locked : out std_logic
         );
  end component;

  component adc_interface is
    port (
      adc_pll_clock_clk     : in  std_logic := '0';     -- adc_pll_clock.clk
      adc_pll_locked_export : in  std_logic := '0';     -- adc_pll_locked.export
      clock_clk             : in  std_logic := '0';     -- clock.clk
      reset_sink_reset_n    : in  std_logic := '0';     -- reset_sink.reset_n
```

```vhdl
    response_valid            : out std_logic;                          -- response.valid
    response_channel          : out std_logic_vector(4 downto 0);   -- .channel
    response_data             : out std_logic_vector(11 downto 0); -- .data
    response_startofpacket    : out std_logic;                          -- .startofpacket
    response_endofpacket      : out std_logic;                  -- .endofpacket
    sequencer_csr_address     : in  std_logic := '0'; -- sequencer_csr.address
    sequencer_csr_read        : in  std_logic := '0'; --                    .read
    sequencer_csr_write       : in  std_logic := '0'; --                    .write
    sequencer_csr_writedata : in  std_logic_vector(31 downto 0) := (others => '0');
--.writedata
    sequencer_csr_readdata  : out std_logic_vector(31 downto 0)  -- endofpacket
    );
  end component adc_interface;

  component light_sensor_adc_sequencer
    port
      (
        clk                 : in  std_logic;
        avm_m0_address      : out std_logic_vector(9 downto 0);
        avm_m0_chipselect : out std_logic;
        avm_m0_read         : out std_logic;
        avm_m0_readdata     : in  std_logic_vector(31 downto 0);
        avm_m0_write        : out std_logic;
        avm_m0_writedata    : out std_logic_vector(31 downto 0)
        );
  end component;

  component light_sensor_counter_led
    generic (LOW_BOUNDARY  : integer;
             HIGH_BOUNDARY : integer;
             NUM_LEDS       : integer
             );
    port(clk                        : in  std_logic;
        avl_str_sink_valid         : in  std_logic;
        avl_str_sink_channel       : in  std_logic_vector(4 downto 0);
        avl_str_sink_data          : in  std_logic_vector(11 downto 0);
        avl_str_sink_startofpacket : in  std_logic;
        avl_str_sink_endofpacket   : in  std_logic;
        pb4                        : in  std_logic;
        led                        : out std_logic_vector(NUM_LEDS-1 downto 0)
        );
  end component;

  signal pll_adc_clk_50m_wire                 : std_logic;
  signal pll_cascade_c0_wire                  : std_logic;
  signal pll_adc_c0_wire                      : std_logic;
  signal adc_pll_locked_wire                  : std_logic;
  signal pll_cascade_locked_reset_wire        : std_logic;
  signal pll_cascade_locked_reset_wire_n : std_logic;
```

```
signal wire_avm_m0_address      : std_logic_vector(9 downto 0);
signal wire_avm_m0_chipselect   : std_logic;
signal wire_avm_m0_read         : std_logic;
signal wire_avm_m0_waitrequest  : std_logic;
signal wire_avm_m0_readdata     : std_logic_vector(31 downto 0);
signal wire_avm_m0_write        : std_logic;
signal wire_avm_m0_writedata    : std_logic_vector(31 downto 0);


signal wire_avl_str_adc_counter_valid         : std_logic;
signal wire_avl_str_adc_counter_channel       : std_logic_vector(4 downto 0);
signal wire_avl_str_adc_counter_data          : std_logic_vector(11 downto 0);
signal wire_avl_str_adc_counter_startofpacket : std_logic;
signal wire_avl_str_adc_counter_endofpacket   : std_logic;

begin

-- The ADC in 10M08DAF484 needs to be fed by the c0 output of PLL_1 in the device.
-- The input clock source SYS_CLK on the BeMicro Max10 board is unfortunately placed on
the dedicated input to PLL_2 and can not feed PLL_1
-- Therefore we need to cascade the clock source via PLL_2, which is called "cascade_pll"
in this case.
cascade_pll_inst : cascade_pll
   port map (
      areset => '0',
      inclk0 => SYS_CLK,
      c0     => pll_cascade_c0_wire,
      locked => pll_cascade_locked_reset_wire
      );

-- The ADC sample clock must use the c0 output of PLL_1
adc_pll_inst : adc_pll
   port map(
      inclk0 => pll_cascade_c0_wire,
      areset => pll_cascade_locked_reset_wire_n,
      c0     => pll_adc_c0_wire,
      c1     => pll_adc_clk_50m_wire,
      locked => adc_pll_locked_wire
      );

pll_cascade_locked_reset_wire_n <= not pll_cascade_locked_reset_wire;

-- This module is created with Qsys
adc_inst : adc_interface
   port map (
      clock_clk             => pll_adc_clk_50m_wire, -- System clock
      reset_sink_reset_n    => '1',
      adc_pll_clock_clk     => pll_adc_c0_wire,      -- ADC clock
      adc_pll_locked_export => adc_pll_locked_wire,  -- PLL lock condition

      sequencer_csr_readdata  => wire_avm_m0_readdata,
      sequencer_csr_writedata => wire_avm_m0_writedata,
```

```vhdl
    sequencer_csr_address    => wire_avm_m0_address(0),
    sequencer_csr_write      => wire_avm_m0_write,
    sequencer_csr_read       => wire_avm_m0_read,

    response_valid           => wire_avl_str_adc_counter_valid,
    response_channel         => wire_avl_str_adc_counter_channel,
    response_data            => wire_avl_str_adc_counter_data,
    response_startofpacket   => wire_avl_str_adc_counter_startofpacket,
    response_endofpacket     => wire_avl_str_adc_counter_endofpacket
    );

-- This module writes a "run" command into the ADC's CSR register
-- Default address in Qsys was placed on 0x0000_0000. Make sure it corresponds!
sequencer_inst : light_sensor_adc_sequencer
  port map (
    clk                  => pll_adc_clk_50m_wire,
    avm_m0_address       => wire_avm_m0_address,
    avm_m0_chipselect    => wire_avm_m0_chipselect,
    avm_m0_read          => wire_avm_m0_read,
    avm_m0_readdata      => wire_avm_m0_readdata,
    avm_m0_write         => wire_avm_m0_write,
    avm_m0_writedata     => wire_avm_m0_writedata
    );

-- This module take the ADC data and detect the lost of light from laser beam
-- Counter number of lost and output the count value to LEDs
counter_led_inst : light_sensor_counter_led
  generic map(
    LOW_BOUNDARY    => LOW_BOUNDARY,
    HIGH_BOUNDARY   => HIGH_BOUNDARY,
    NUM_LEDS        => NUM_LEDS
    )
  port map(
    clk                      => pll_adc_clk_50m_wire,
    avl_str_sink_valid       => wire_avl_str_adc_counter_valid,
    avl_str_sink_channel     => wire_avl_str_adc_counter_channel,
    avl_str_sink_data        => wire_avl_str_adc_counter_data,
    avl_str_sink_startofpacket => wire_avl_str_adc_counter_startofpacket,
    avl_str_sink_endofpacket => wire_avl_str_adc_counter_endofpacket,
    pb4                      => PB(4),
    led                      => USER_LED
    );

end arch;
```

12.6.4   Add All Files to the Project and Create the Tripwire Device

You need to add two Altera IPs to the project. Please take the following steps:

Step 1: Right-click the File icon (Figure 12-35) and click **Add/Remove Files in Project...** or, from the Project menu, select **Add/Remove Files in Project**.

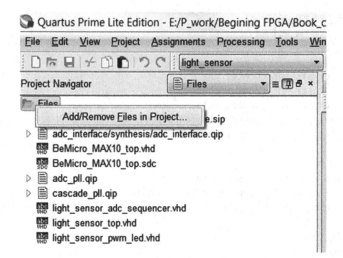

Figure 12-35. *Add/Remove Files in Project*

Step 2: Browse ➤project_directory➤\adc_interface\synthesis\ and select **adc_interface.qip**. Click **Open** and then **Add** (Figure 12-36).

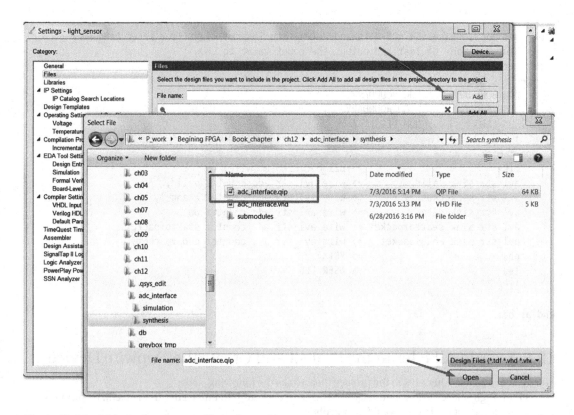

Figure 12-36. *Add adc_interface.qip file to the project*

Step 3: After you have added the adc_pll.qip and cascade_pll.qip files, Figure 12-37 shows all the files in the correct order. You can use the Up or Down button to move the file order up or down. Please follow this file order, as it is very important for simulation. The top-level design file (light_sensor_top.vhd) must be the last one.

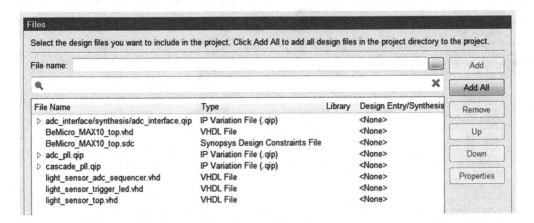

Figure 12-37. *File list for the light sensor—tripwire design*

Step 4: When all the files are ready, select the light_sensor_top.vhd file as the top-level entity. Right-click the light_sensor top.vhd file and select **Set as Top-Level Entity**.

Step 5: Click the ▶ or select **Start Compilation** from the **Processing** menu. You should see Figure 12-38 as your result. In the Task window (lower left), it should have all green checks, a 100% progress bar, and no red errors in the Message window. At this point, you are ready to upload the design to the MAX10 FPGA.

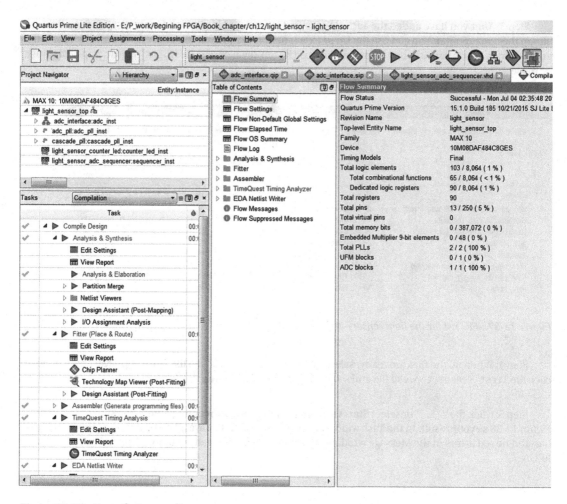

Figure 12-38. *Compilation result*

Now you have all of the files in the project and you can start simulating the design one block at a time. You need to make sure the project is compiled and the Project Navigator shows the Hierarchy as in Figure 12-38 before you move to the simulation section.

Let me show you a trick to generate a TCL script in ModelSim.

We need to open the ModelSim (click Tools ➤ Run Simulation Tools ➤ RTL Simulation) and start the simulation using the following script in the Transcript window or right-click the light_sensor_counter_led and click Simulate (Figure 12-39).

```
vsim work.light_sensor_counter_led
```

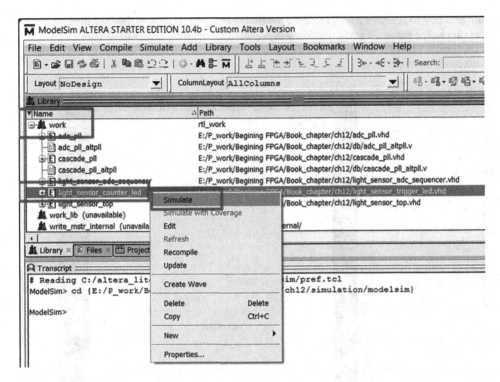

Figure 12-39. *Start simulation from ModelSim GUI interface*

After you run the script or click the simulate selection, the light_sensor_counter_led simulation is started. You can add all of the design signals to the wave window by right-clicking the target instance in the sim window and selecting **Add Wave** (Figure 12-40).

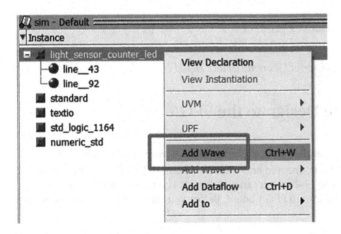

Figure 12-40. *How to add wave from the ModelSim GUI interface*

The second tip is how to generate a script to force a signal or generate a clock. Right-click the target signal and select **Clock...** or Force... A small window will pop up a for defining a clock or forcing a signal. After you click OK (Figure 12-41), the script will be generated in the transcript window (Figure 12-42) and you only need to copy it and use it later.

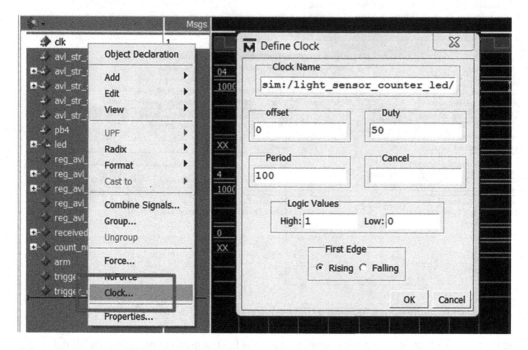

Figure 12-41. *Use ModelSim Wave window to generate script*

```
run
VSIM 52> run
force -freeze sim:/light_sensor_counter_led/clk 1 0, 0 {50 ps} -r 100
```

Figure 12-42. *Transcript window generates the script for create a clock signal*

12.6.5   Program the Tripwire Design to the FPGA

Step 1: Open the Quartus Prime programmer window from the Tools menu (Figure 12-43) or click from the toolbar. If the BeMicro Max10 board is connected and the USB-Blaster II device driver has been installed successfully on your computer (Figure 12-44), you can go to step 2. If your programmer is shown as in Figure 45, you need to plug in your BeMicro Max10 FPGA board. Before you can go to step 2, you need to follow the steps in Figure 12-45.

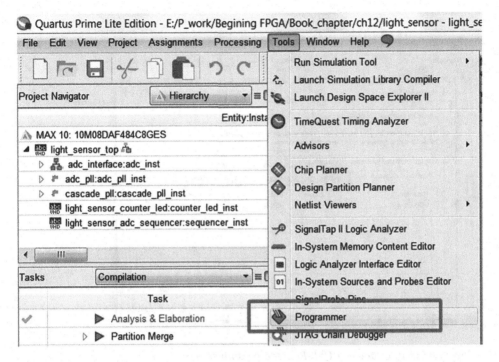

Figure 12-43. Open programmer in Quartus Prime

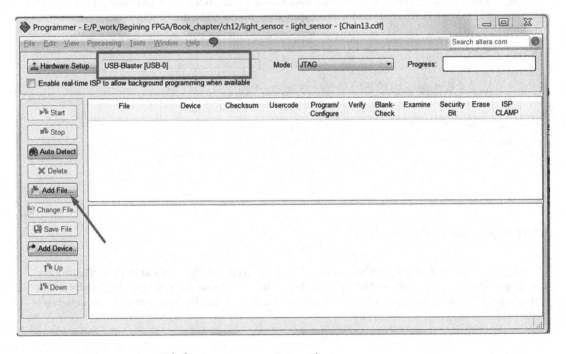

Figure 12-44. Programmer with the correct programmer setting

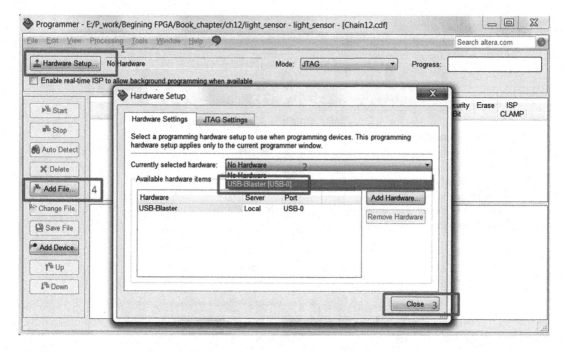

Figure 12-45. *Programmer setting for a new USB-Blaster programmer*

Step 2: You can point to the newly created configuration file by clicking the **Add File** button and selecting the light_sensor.sof file under the **output_files** directory (Figure 12-46).

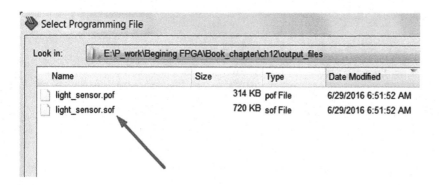

Figure 12-46. *Select file light_sensor.sof*

Step 3: Make sure the Program/Configure check box is ticked and click the **Start** button (Figure 12-47). The Progress bar will go to 100% and turn green. This means the programming process has finished. Now you should try to use the laser pointer to point to the photo resistor and then put something in between to check out the design.

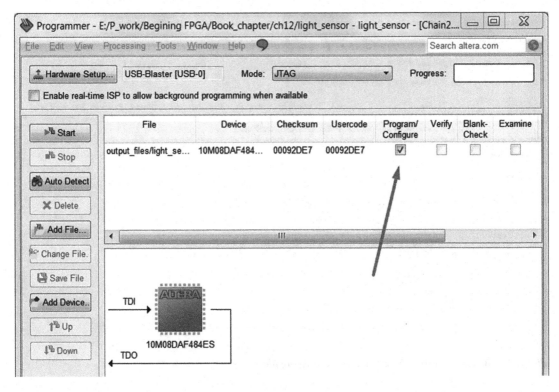

Figure 12-47. *Start programming the design*

Step 4: If you want to make the design able to reload after power is lost on the board, you need to select light_sensor.pof file. This file will ask the programmer to program the file to the flash memory which is nonvolatile. Figure 12-48 shows the difference when you select a .pof file. I suggest you use the .sof file to try out a couple of times and tune the high boundary and low boundary values. You can use the .pof file to program the FPGA when it is close to the final design. Remember to check the **Program/configure** box before you click the **Start** button.

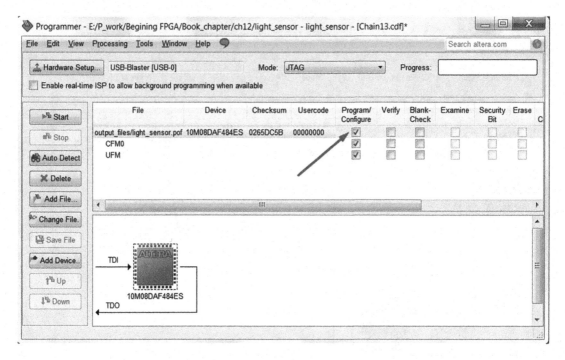

Figure 12-48. *Start to program the design with the .pof file*

12.6.5.1 My Tripwire Setup

I use masking tape to stick my BeMicro Max10 on one side and a laser pointer on another side. Anyone passing through my door will trigger the counter and I will know many people go into (or leave) my room. Figure 12-49 is what my setup looks like and Figure 12-50 is a close look on the BeMicro MAX10 with a laser beam on the photo resistor.

Figure 12-49. *My tripwire setup*

Figure 12-50. Close look at the BeMicro MAX10

12.7   Summary

This chapter shows you how to configure and generate two Altera IPs—ADC IP and PLL IP. You know how easy it is to employ something useful without knowing how it really works (like driving a car without knowing how an engine moves your car forward or backward). We only need to know the interface to the IPs and how to handle it. These two IPs are very useful for the next chapter because we will reuse all of them and add more fun (design) to them.

The light sensor ADC sequencer shows you a simple FSM. It only has two states and every clock cycle the state changes to another state.

We demo one more time how to create a counter and flip-flop in the light sensor counter led module with generic settings. The top-level design (`light_sensor_top.vhd`) is a good top module example. It should only have connections and instantiation designs. You should minimize putting combination logic and sequential logic in the top-level file.

We hope you enjoyed this tripwire design and we will use a third-party IP and add more interesting designs in the next chapter.

■ **Note**   Due to an ADC offset issue, the ADC output always has an offset 0.8V, which is around 1300 from the ADC output value. That is the reason my low boundary value is set to higher than the value 1300.

"Projects we have completed demonstrate what we know—future projects decide what we will learn."

—Dr. Mohsin Tiwana

CHAPTER 13

Temperature Sensors: Is It Hot in Here, or Is It Just Me?

13.1 Introduction

You would like to build a system with communication (bus) capability. The communication can be between modules, integrated circuit (IC), or even a PC. What kind of kind of bus or communication system do you think an IC can use to send data to a PC? The answer is UART (universal asynchronous receiver/transmitter)! UART is one of the most common and timeless interfaces because it's easy to design the hardware and the software for this communication interface. Figure 13-1 shows the BeMicro MAX10 board with user-defined UART interfaces—two pins: one transmit (Tx) and one receive (Rx). We will show you how to connect it to your PC in the design example.

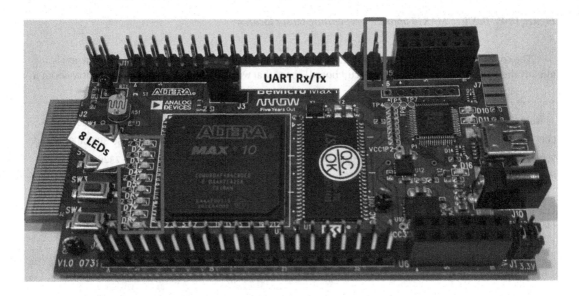

Figure 13-1. BeMicro MAX10 board—UART interface pin and LEDs

© Aiken Pang and Peter Membrey 2017

A. Pang and P. Membrey, *Beginning FPGA: Programming Metal*, DOI 10.1007/978-1-4302-6248-0_13

I2C is another very common communication interface between ICs. You can tell from the name inter-integrated circuit. This chapter will use a super-high accuracy temperature sensor to sense the environment temperature. It can sense the difference between 16.0425°C and 16.0347°C. The sensor provides an I2C bus interface for other ICs to read out the temperature. The same I2C interface can be used to change the sensor settings too. Figure 13-2 shows that the sensor IC is located at the back of the board.

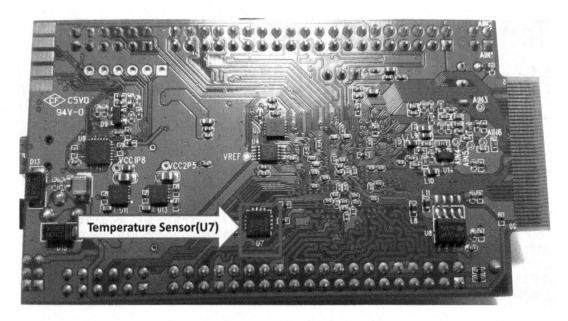

Figure 13-2. *BeMicro MAX10 board—temperature sensor location*

The connection between the temperature sensor and the FPGA (field-programmable gate array) is already there inside the PCB (printed circuit board) so we that we don't need to do a thing or worry about it.

■ **Note** UART to USB cable: You can buy one from Amazon or another electronic shop. This is the design for connect Raspberry Pi. The part's name is TTL-232-R-PRI. Remember to use the 3.3V. Don't use any other voltage version. Datasheet: `www.ftdichip.com/Support/Documents/DataSheets/Cables/DS_TTL-232R_RPi.pdf`.

Figure 13-3 shows the cable used in this chapter. The orange-colored one is TX and the yellow-colored one is RX. Remember to connect the USB cable TX to the FPGA input(RX) and USB cable RX to the FPGA output(TX).

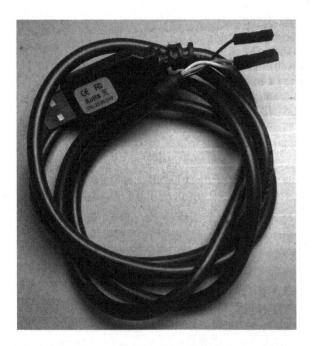

Figure 13-3. *USB to UART cable—TTL-232R-3V3/TTL-232R-RPI*

13.2   UART with Control Memory Map

Any time we talk about connections between PCs and FPGAs, UART is the simplest way to achieve that. UART communication mainly uses two pins for data transfer, and these are Tx, which is the transmit data pin used to send data, and Rx, which is the receive data pin used to get data. Each time UART sends data, it sends the data as a data packet. You can easily find the format of the UART packet on the web site.

■ **Note**   The following Basic UART tutorial link is a good starting point for beginners: www.ocfreaks.com/ uart-tutorial-basics/.

We are going to download a UART IP from the web so that we do not need to design one at this time. You don't need to fully understand the UART to use the IP (Internet Protocol). All you need to know is that we are going to use the UART to send or receive one byte at a time.

13.2.1 UART IP

The name of the IP is uart_fpga_slow_control. It is designed for using the UART interface to control the FPGA at slow speeds. The slow speed in here is compared with other interfaces like PCIe, USB, or Ethernet. The IP is from opencores.org. You need to register as a limited account to download the IP from them. The site manually approves new accounts; you might like to register it as early as possible.

■ **Note**   UART download link: `http://opencores.org/project,uart_fpga_slow_control`.

After you log in to opencore.org and use the above link to access that page, it should show up as in Figure 13-4. Download the file `uart_fpga_slow_control_latest.tar` and open it. We are only going to use the files under the uart_fpga_slow_control/trunk/code as shown in Figure 13-5. We will need these files in our design example later in this chapter.

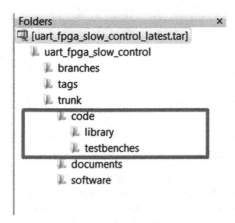

Figure 13-4. *The folder structure of the UART IP*

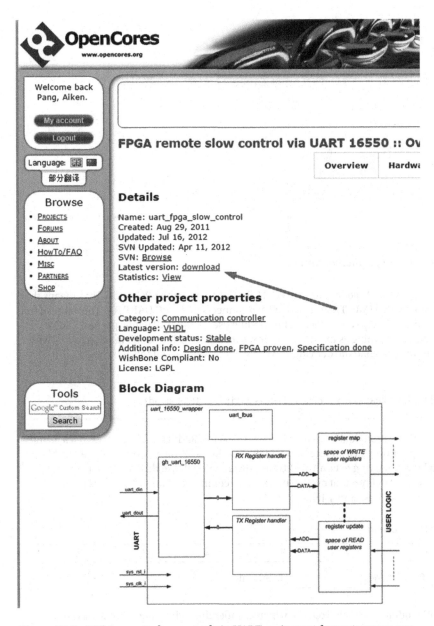

Figure 13-5. *FPGA remote slow control via UART main page from opencores.org*

Let's open the IP design file. The file is under the code folder and the name is ab_uart_16550_wrapper. vhd. Figure 13-6 shows the first part of the file—the port list.

```
|entity uart_16550_wrapper is
|  port(
   -- general purpose
   sys_clk_i           : in std_logic;  -- system clock
   sys_rst_i           : in std_logic;  -- system reset
   -- TX/RX process command line
   echo_en_i           : in std_logic;  -- Echo enable (byte by byte) enable/disable = 1/0
   tx_addr_wwo_i       : in std_logic;-- control of TX process With or WithOut address W/WO=(1/0)
   -- serial I/0 side
   uart_din_i          : in std_logic;   -- Serial data INPUT signal (from the FPGA)
   uart_dout_o         : out std_logic;  -- Serial data OUTPUT signal (to the FPGA)
   -- parallel I/0 side
   s_br_clk_uart_o     : out std_logic;      -- br_clk clock probe signal
   -- RX part/control
   v_rx_add_o          : out std_logic_vector(15 downto 0); -- 16 bits full addr ram input
   v_rx_data_o         : out std_logic_vector(31 downto 0); -- 32 bits full data ram input
   s_rx_rdy_o          : out std_logic;      -- add/data ready to be write into RAM
   s_rx_stb_read_data_i : in std_logic;      -- strobe signal from RAM ...
   -- TX part/control
   s_tx_proc_rqst_i    : in std_logic;       -- stream TX process request 1/0 tx enable/disable
   v_tx_add_ram_i      : in std_logic_vector(15 downto 0); -- 16 bits full addr ram output
   v_tx_data_ram_i : in std_logic_vector(31 downto 0); -- 32 bits full data ram output
   s_tx_ram_data_rdy_i : in std_logic;       -- ram output data ready and stable
   s_tx_stb_ram_data_acq_o : out std_logic -- strobe ram data/address output acquired 1/0 acquired/not acquired
      );
|end entity;
```

Figure 13-6. ab_uart_16550_wrapper module port list

The signals uart_din_i and uart_dout_o are the UART Rx and Tx from the FPGA side. This means that the uart_din_i connects to the PC UART TX and uart_din_o connects to the PC UART RX. The name of this IP is 16650 as it is one of the UART IC part numbers. This module uses another IP name, gh_uart_16550. vhd. The IP is doing the exact same thing as the IC 16650. Texas Instruments Inc. is still making this IC with the name PC16550D. You can download the datasheet to understand more about this IC.

■ **Note**   UART 16650 datasheet link: www.ti.com/lit/ds/symlink/pc16550d.pdf.

The ab_uart_16550 converts 8-bit data from the gh_uart_16550 to a 32-bit interface (v_rx_data_o and v_tx_data_ram_i). The wrapper provides an interface which looks like a 32-bit wide memory read/write interface. This helps us a lot when trying to control FPGA hardware. We will use this interface to control the LED and I2C module. This IP defines that every 6 bytes is one command. Table 13-1 shows the 6-byte command format. It has 2-byte address and 4-byte (32-bit) data.

Table 13-1. UART Command Format

Bytes	1	2	3	4	5	6
Name	16 bit Address		32 bit Data			

There is another vhdl module called ab_top.vhd which is under the code folder. We will base our modifications on this file to get our example design done.

13.2.2   UART PC Software

If you don't have any experience writing software to control the PC UART interface, then you can use RealTerm. It is an open source program from sourceforge.net. It is very powerful and flexible to use. We used this software to test our FPGA temperature sensor. Figure 13-7 is the download page of RealTerm and Figure 13-8 show the GUI (graphical user interface). Mincom in Linux should work for you too.

■ **Note** REALTERM Download link: http://sourceforge.net/projects/realterm/files/

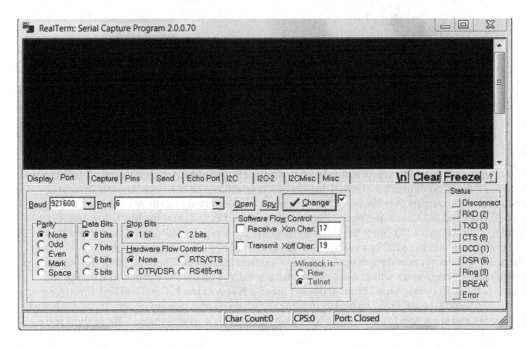

Figure 13-7. *RealTerm download page*

Figure 13-8. *RealTerm GUI window*

13.3 I2C Communication

I2C is pronounced I-Squared-C. The I2C bus was developed in the late 1970s for Philips consumer products. It is now a worldwide industry standard and used by all major IC manufacturers.

It is a multi-master and multi-slave communication bus that only requires two wires! Figure 13-9 shows an example of using the I2C bus with two masters/transmitters (MCU and FPGA) and two slaves/receivers (the ADC and LCD driver). It does not require separate select lines as some other communication buses do. I2C is a standard bus, which means you can find the specifications very easily on line. The best one I found is the original one from Philips (now called NXP). The document name is UM10204.

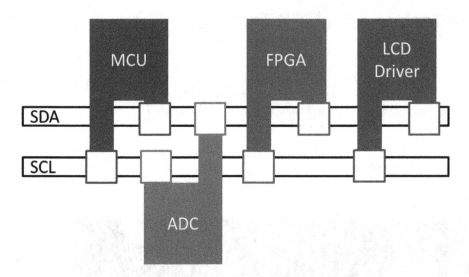

Figure 13-9. *Example of an I2C bus configuration*

13.3.1 Basic I2C

I2C is built for simplicity and therefore it only has two wires: SDA and SCL. SDA (Serial Data) is bidirectional which means that I2C communication is half duplex. SCL (Serial Clock) is the clock line. It is used to synchronize all data transfers over the bus. These two wires are connected to all devices on the bus (as in Figure 13-9). SDA and SCLK lines are "open-drain" which means they can drive the line to low voltage (0 V) but not to high voltage (3.3V). Since the I2C is open-drain, it will require pull-up resistors in order to function correctly. It is like the I2C bus in Figure 13-12, which has two 10k pull-up resistors.

There are only two types of devices on an I2C bus—masters and slaves. I2C allows multiple bus masters. Our design has only one master, which is the FPGA, and one slave, which is the temperature sensor. I2C is designed to be easily built in an IC, but that doesn't mean it is easy to use it. Don't feel bad, if you have trouble understanding the I2C bus. The beauty of using IP is that you only need to understand the interface that IP provides and know how to connect the IP to your design. This is what we would like to show you in this chapter.

13.3.2 I2C Master

Let's look at I2C Master IP first. You can download the I2C Master IP from the web site link. Figure 13-10 shows the I2C Master IP page. Click i2c_master.vhd (version 2.2) to download the IP. This is a very small design such that it only contains one file: i2c_master.vhd.

■ **Note** I2C Master IP web site link: www.eewiki.net/pages/viewpage.action?pageId=10125324.

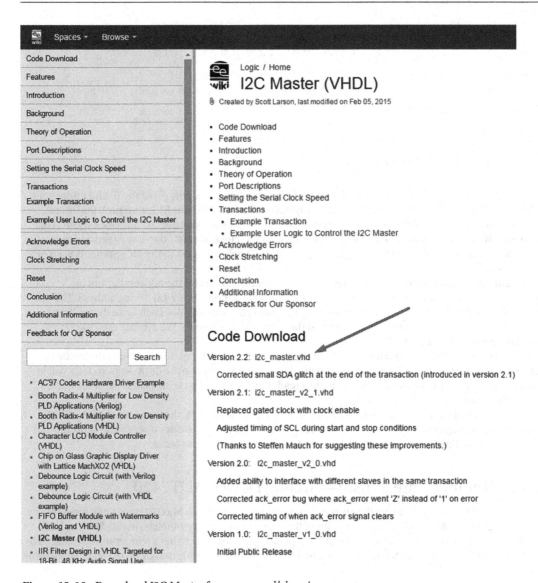

Figure 13-10. Download I2C Master from www.eewiki.net

It is time to open the I2C Master VHDL file. You can use Notepad ++ or Altera Quartus Prime. Figure 13-11 is the port list of the I2C Master VHDL file. The designer of the I2C master did a good job of writing this IP. It is a very good vhdl example for you.

```
]ENTITY i2c_master IS
]  GENERIC(
      input_clk : INTEGER := 50_000_000; --input clock speed from user logic in Hz
      bus_clk   : INTEGER := 400_000);    --speed the i2c bus (scl) will run at in Hz
]  PORT(
      clk       : IN     STD_LOGIC;                          --system clock
      reset_n   : IN     STD_LOGIC;                          --active low reset
      ena       : IN     STD_LOGIC;                          --latch in command
      addr      : IN     STD_LOGIC_VECTOR(6 DOWNTO 0);       --address of target slave
      rw        : IN     STD_LOGIC;                          --'0' is write, '1' is read
      data_wr   : IN     STD_LOGIC_VECTOR(7 DOWNTO 0);       --data to write to slave
      busy      : OUT    STD_LOGIC;                          --indicates transaction in progress
      data_rd   : OUT    STD_LOGIC_VECTOR(7 DOWNTO 0);       --data read from slave
      ack_error : BUFFER STD_LOGIC;                          --flag if improper acknowledge from slave
      sda       : INOUT  STD_LOGIC;                          --serial data output of i2c bus
      scl       : INOUT  STD_LOGIC);                         --serial clock output of i2c bus
END i2c_master;|
```

Figure 13-11. *I2C Master IP VHDL port list*

You will know what we need to connect to the IP after you look at the port list of the IP and understand the basic operation of I2C. The I2C master is the only device that can drive the SCL wire such that there are generics in the i2c_master for input clock speed, send to i2c_master, and the I2C bus clock speed. The IP itself doesn't know the input clock (clk) and the expected I2C clock. It needs the user to provide the information (generics) to do the I2C clock (SCL) generation. The first process in the I2C_master is used to generate the SCL.

A multi-slave bus needs to use addresses to select a specific device and the address cannot be duplicated on the same I2C bus. Each slave device has a unique address. It is 7-bit device address. The master will send out the target device address at the beginning of a transaction. Each slave device listens— if the device address matches the internal address, then the device responds. We provide the 7-bit target device address to the addr port.

I2C is a byte transfer bus, which means the basic unit is 8 bits (one byte). If you want to do a write transfer (I2C master write to I2C slave), then you need to provide the data to the data_wr port. Data will be ready on the data_rd read port when you initiate a read transfer. The IP is taking care of all of the frames signals, arbitration, and clock generation.

If you'd like to get more info about the IP and/or I2C Master Operation, then you can read the I2C Master download page, when you download the i2c_master.vhd file. It provides a very good short tutorial on I2C. By the way, the web site www.eewiki.net is a very good hardware resource.

13.3.3   Temperature Sensor—Analog Device ADT7420

We need a temperature sensor to get the current temperature. The BeMicro Max10 board has a temperature sensor IC. Figure 13-12 shows the block diagram of the temperature sensor which is Analog Devices Inc.'s ADT7420. The ADT420 is a high-accuracy digital temperature sensor. It contains a temperature sensor, a 16-bit ADC to monitor and digitize the temperature to 0.0078°C. In our example design we use the default value of 13 bits.

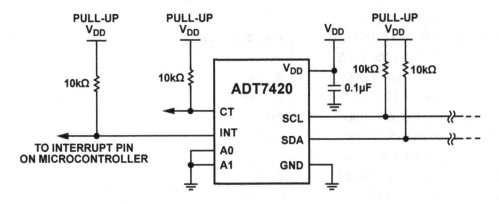

Figure 13-12. *Temperature sensor block diagram*

The most important thing is that it provides an I2C slave interface and it is connected to the FPGA pins with two pull-up resistors. The I2C interfaces for external control and sends out the temperature data. That is all we need to get the temperature data and control the sensor. Figure 13-13 shows the sensor registers. We are going to use registers 0x00, 0x01, 0x03, 0x08, and 0x2F. Figure 13-14 shows the binary data mapping to temperature.

Register Address	Description	Power-On Default
0x00	Temperature value most significant byte	0x00
0x01	Temperature value least significant byte	0x00
0x02	Status	0x00
0x03	Configuration	0x00
0x04	T_{HIGH} setpoint most significant byte	0x20 (64°C)
0x05	T_{HIGH} setpoint least significant byte	0x00 (64°C)
0x06	T_{LOW} setpoint most significant byte	0x05 (10°C)
0x07	T_{LOW} setpoint least significant byte	0x00 (10°C)
0x08	T_{CRIT} setpoint most significant byte	0x49 (147°C)
0x09	T_{CRIT} setpoint least significant byte	0x80 (147°C)
0x0A	T_{HYST} setpoint	0x05 (5°C)
0x0B	ID	0xCB
0x2F	Software reset	0xXX

Figure 13-13. *Temperature sensor register map*

Temperature	Digital Output (Binary) Bits[15:3]	Digital Output (Hex)
−40°C	1 1101 1000 0000	0x1D80
−25°C	1 1110 0111 0000	0x1E70
−0.0625°C	1 1111 1111 1111	0x1FFF
0°C	0 0000 0000 0000	0x000
+0.0625°C	0 0000 0000 0001	0x001
+25°C	0 0001 1001 0000	0x190
+105°C	0 0110 1001 0000	0x690
+125°C	0 0111 1101 0000	0x7D0
+150°C	0 1001 0110 0000	0x960

Figure 13-14. *13 bits of data map to temperature in degrees C*

We will use the quick guide from the ADT7420 datasheet to get the data through I2C and send it back to the PC.

The following steps are based on the quick guide for reading temperatures from the ADT7420:

1. After powering up the ADT7420, verify the setup by reading the device ID from the address 0x0B. It should be 0xCB.

2. Write to configuration register address 0x03 with value 0x80. This will set up the ADC and provide 13-bit data.

3. Read the temperature value MSB register from address 0x00 and read the LSB register from address 0x01. This should provide us with the temperature measurement. If the data read-back is 0x190, then the temperature is 25°C.

These three steps will be translated to a UART command and sent from the PC to the BeMicro Max 10 board. Since the ADT7420 temperature sensor works as an I2C slave/receiver device, we will use the I2C master to send the commands to the sensor. In the next section we will download another IP which is also an I2C slave from another web site. It is only used for simulation. We need the I2C slave IP to simulate the temperature sensor.

13.3.4   I2C Slave

For simulation, we need to have an I2C Slave to work and look like the ADC I2C interface. We found an easy-to-use one from GitHub. It is really surprising to us that GitHub hosted VHDL (VHSIC (very high speed integrated circuit) Hardware Description Language) code hosted on it! The following note shows the download link. We need to use a specific revision from GitHub. Don't download the master version.

■ **Note**   I2C slave link: https://github.com/oetr/FPGA-I2C-Slave/blob/
bd7833a8cb663f2d9d756be50567fd613c919aa8/I2C_slave.vhd.

We only need one file—I2C_slave.vhd—from GitHub. Figure 13-15 shows the web site screenshot and the port list of the I2C slave module.

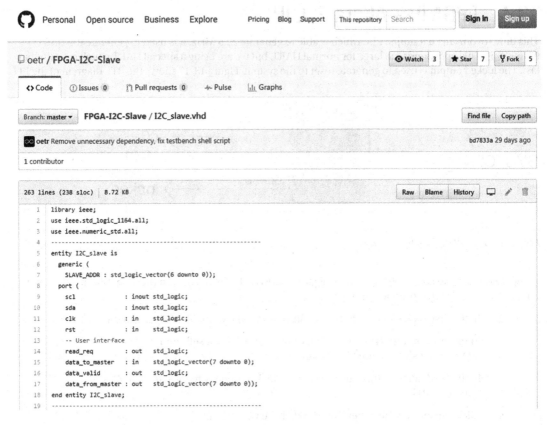

Figure 13-15. *Download I2C slave IP from GitHub*

The port list in Figure 13-16 has scl and sda. They form the I2C interface and the user interface as a simple read/write register interface. Figure 13-16 shows the port list of the I2C slave module. We will set the SLAVE_ADDR to 0x48 in the simulation which is the exact address used by ADT7420. The user interface section shows the read or write operation from the master with the data in or out.

```
entity I2C_slave is
  generic (
    SLAVE_ADDR : std_logic_vector(6 downto 0));
  port (
    scl               : inout std_logic;
    sda               : inout std_logic;
    clk               : in    std_logic;
    rst               : in    std_logic;
    -- User interface
    read_req          : out   std_logic;
    data_to_master    : in    std_logic_vector(7 downto 0);
    data_valid        : out   std_logic;
    data_from_master  : out   std_logic_vector(7 downto 0));
end entity I2C_slave;
```

Figure 13-16. *I2C Slave IP VHDL port list*

279

13.4   FPGA IP—Altera PLL IP

This time we only need a simple PLL which is able to generate 29.5 MHz. It is used to generate the UART 921600 bps. This bps sounds too large for normal UART, but we are using a special UART which can run that fast. The locked output is used to generate reset to the system. Figure 13-17 shows the RTL diagram of the PLL.

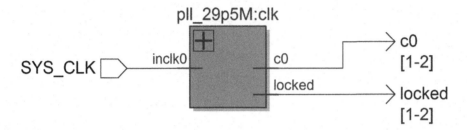

Figure 13-17. *Altera PLL block diagram*

Give the PLL the name pll_29p5M (see Figure 13-18) and select VHDL. In the MegaWizard of the PLL (Figure 13-19), execute the following steps

1.   In the first tab (General/Mode), set the inclk0 equal to 50 MHz (Figure 13-19).

2.   In the first tab (Inputs/Lock), uncheck the Create an "areset" input to asynchronously reset the PLL (Figure 13-20).

3.   In the third tab (clk c0), enter the output clock frequency request to 29.5 MHz (Figure 13-21).

4.   Click Finish two times; then you should have your PLL IP.

Figure 13-18. *Name the PLL pll_29p5M.vhd*

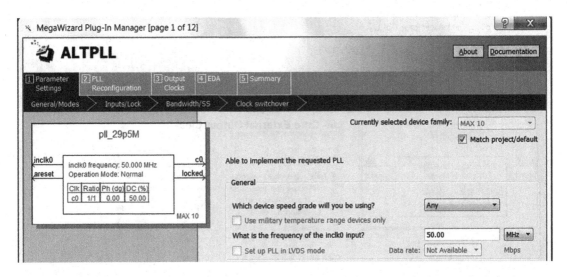

Figure 13-19. *Set the inclk0 input to 50.00 MHz*

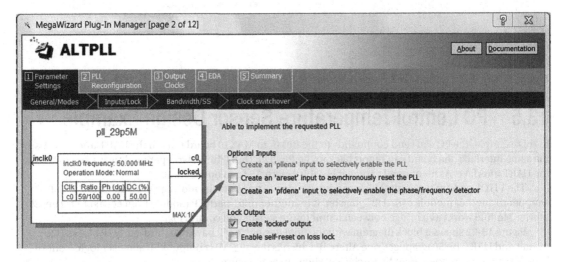

Figure 13-20. *Uncheck the Create an "areset" input to asynchronously reset the PLL*

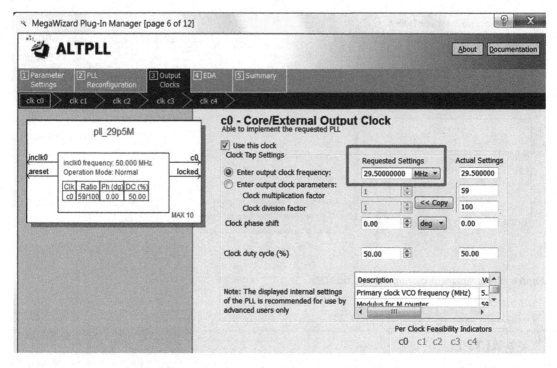

Figure 13-21. *Enter output clock frequency equal to 29.5 MHz*

13.5   PC Control Temperature Sensor Design Example

In this example, the PC can send commands to the BeMicro MAX10 board though the UART interface. Using the same interface, the board can report back to the PC. The UART 16550 wrapper module is used to handle the UART interface. As mentioned earlier, it is a third-party IP from opencores.org.

The VHDL code in the control logic module is used to translate the message from the UART 16550 wrapper to another module called i2C_master. It is another third-party IP module from eewiki.net. The I2C Master Module works as a bridge between temperature sensor and control logic.

Figure 13-22 shows a block diagram with the final design. It will have two third-party IP blocks (i2c master and UART 16650 wrapper), one Altera IP which is the 29.5 MHz output PLL and user logic/control logic. In the Quartus, the design hierarchy will show up as in Figure 13-23.

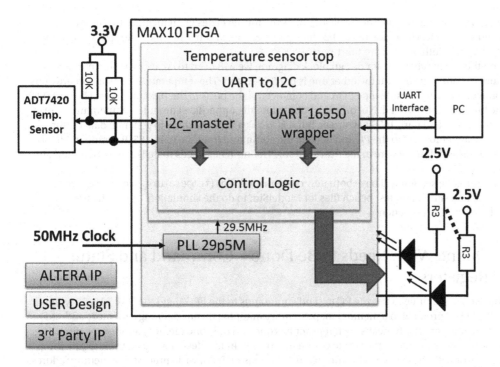

Figure 13-22. *Temperature sensor design block diagram*

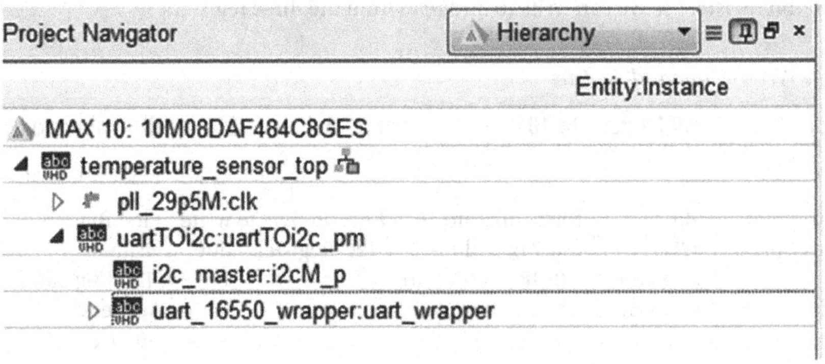

Figure 13-23. *Temperature sensor design structure*

Figure 1223 shows that temperature_sensor_top is the top-level design. It includes two modules: pll_29p5M and uartTOi2c. Under the uartTOi2c module, there are another two modules: i2c_master and uart_16550_wrapper. Both of them are third-party IPs.

Based on the temperature sensor design block diagram, we will need to create two more modules. One is temperature_sensor_top.vhd and the other one is uartTOi2c.vhd. The temperature_sensor_top provides all of the connections from outside the FPGA and connects all the ports to the right modules. The uartTOi2c. vhd is a little bit more complicated. Not only is it connecting the upper-level module (temperature_sensor_ top) to the i2c_master and uart_16550_wrapper, but it also has a state machine to generate data for the UART_16550_wrapper to send to the PC and decode the command from the uart_16550_wrapper. All the command and status definitions are in the next section, "Define What Needs to Be Done—Command and Status Registers."

The example code section will have both new design .vhdl files (`temperature_sensor_top.vhd` and `uartTOi2c.vhd`) and simulation test bench files for ModelSim to do the simulation. This is the first time we are using .vhdl files as a test bench.

13.5.1 Define What Needs to Be Done—Command and Status Registers

We know that we are planning to use the PC to send commands to the FPGA and the UART 16650 wrapper can decode the UART protocol to a memory map. Memory mapping means defining a memory address location for each register, which means each register has one and only one memory address location. The UART IP section already mentions the 6-byte command format. In this design we need to configure the temperature sensor with the correct value through the I2C master. It is a write process to a memory address in the temperature sensor (I2C slave). We need to read back the configuration and temperature data and send to the PC too. This is a read process.

Let's define the three 32-bit registers so we can write to and read from the three registers.

Table 13-2. PC UART 6-Byte Write Command Register

Address	Bit 31 downto 24			Bit 23 downto 16		Bit 15 downto 8	Bit 7 downto 0
0x0000	Not use						LED 7 downto 0
0x0010	Bit 31 I2C ena	Bit 30 2Bytes I2C CMD	Not used	Bit 23 I2C rw 1= Read 0 = Write	Bit 22 downto 16 I2C 7 Bit Address = 0x48 (ADT7420)	Second Byte to write "I2C Register Value"	First Byte to write "I2C Register Address" (Figure 13-5a)
0x8000	Need to set to all zeroes to read back three registers						

Table 13-3. PC UART 6-Byte Read Status Registers

Address	Bit 31 down to 24	Bit 23 down to 16	Bit 15 down to 8	Bit 7 downto 0
0x0000	Not use			LED 7 downto 0
0x0010	Last command to I2C Master			
0x0011	Temperature value in degrees Celsius			Raw temperature value read from ADT7420

In the command register table, we defined that the register at memory address location 0x0000 can turn on or off the external 8 LED lights.

The register at memory address location 0x0010 (Table 13-2) is used to send a command to the I2C Master to create I2C commands to ADT7420. The IC2 command includes read/write (bit 23), I2C slave address (bit 22 to 16), and two bytes (bit 15 to 0). The I2C slave address for ADT7420 is 0x48, which is from the ADT7420 datasheet. We will have examples later to show you how to use this command.

The last command at memory address location 0x8000 is used to request that all of the status registers (Table 13-3) are read back from the BeMicro MAX 10.

13.5.2   Example Design Codes

13.5.2.1   Temperature_sensor_top.vhd Code

The code in Listing 13-1 is a top-level design file for this project. It has the system clock (50 MHz) input, ADT7420 IC interfaces (which include I2C SCL and SDA wire), USER_LED, which is included for fun, and UART TX and RX pins. The purpose of this module is to connect all the external wires to the correct modules and generate the correct clock (29.5 MHz) for the uartTOi2c module. Please read the comments to get a more detailed feel of the design. We will simulate the design later, which will give you some hands-on experience with how it works.

Listing 13-1. Temperature Sensor Top-Level Design vhdl File

```vhdl
library ieee;
use ieee.std_logic_1164.all;

entity temperature_sensor_top is
  port(
    -- Clock ins, SYS_CLK = 50MHz
    SYS_CLK : in std_logic;

    -- Temperature sensor, I2C interface (ADT7420)
    ADT7420_CT  : in    std_logic; -- NOT USE
    ADT7420_INT : in    std_logic; -- NOT USE
    ADT7420_SCL : inout std_logic;
    ADT7420_SDA : inout std_logic;

    -- LED outs
    USER_LED : out std_logic_vector(8 downto 1);

    GPIO_J3_39 : out std_logic;        -- UART TX
    GPIO_J3_40 : in  std_logic         -- UART RX
    );

end entity temperature_sensor_top;

architecture arch of temperature_sensor_top is

  signal locked, clk_uart_29MHz_i, uart_rst_i : std_logic:= '0';
  signal delay_8: std_logic_vector(7 downto 0);

begin
```

```
clk : entity work.pll_29p5M
  port map
  (
    inclk0 => SYS_CLK,         -- 50MHz clock input
    c0      => clk_uart_29MHz_i,-- 29.5MHz clock output
    locked => locked           -- Lock condition, 1 = Locked
    );

dealy_p:  process(SYS_CLK)
  begin
  if(rising_edge(SYS_CLK) )THEN
  delay_8 <= delay_8(6 downto 0)&locked; -- create active LOW reset
END IF;
END PROCESS;

uart_rst_i <= delay_8(7);
  uartT0i2c_pm : entity work.uartT0i2c
    port map(
      clk_uart_29MHz_i    => clk_uart_29MHz_i,
      uart_rst_i          => uart_rst_i,
      uart_leds_o         => USER_LED,
      clk_uart_monitor_o => open,
      uart_dout_o         => GPIO_J3_39,        -- yellow color wire
      uart_din_i          => GPIO_J3_40,        -- orange color wire
      i2c_scl             => ADT7420_SCL,
      i2c_dat             => ADT7420_SDA);

end architecture arch;
```

13.5.2.2   uartTOi2c.vhd Code

This is the major design in this example (Listing 13-2). This is because it does all of the decoding of commands from the UART and generates status updates to the UART. It also translates the commands from the PC and sends the correct operation sequence for the i2C Master module. There are three processes in this module: register_map, i2c_data_p, and register_update.

The register_map process works as a command decoder. It decodes the s_uart_rx_add when s_uart_rx_rdy is high and copies the 32-bit s_uart_rx_data to the correct registers (e.g., 0x0000 is mapped to r_leds).

The second process is i2c_data_p. It copies data from the I2C Master byte read output to reg02 in the lower 16 bits (15 down to 0). It is a special shift register, which is similar to the 8-bit shift register which shifts 1 bit at a time in Chapter 10. This special shift register shifts 8 bits at a time such that two 8 bytes (16 bits) from the i2c_Master can be stored in one 32-bit register. This process will translate the 13-bit ADC data from the temperature sensor to degrees Celsius. This simple bit shift to the left for 9 bits happens every clock cycles. Figure 13-14 shows that the 25°C digital output bit (15:3) is "0000110010000." The 2-byte (16 bits) output bits should look like "0000110010000000." If we shift the 2-byte version 9 bits to left, then we will get a 4-byte "0000000000011001 0000000000000000." The higher 2-byte binary value is "0000000000011001," which equals 25 in unsigned value. This shows that we can use the shift register to do the math.

The last process is register_update. It is actually a small state machine. It is used to generate a sequence of register reads by the command address in 0x8000 with the value all zero and to send the Table 13-3 values to the uart_16550_wrapper.

There is one simple design trick in this design for generating a pulse when it detects a signal change from low to high (which is a rising edge of a signal). The signal name in the design is i2c_busy_01.

■ **Tip**   Edge detection of a signal can be done by using the delayed version of the signal with a NOT gate and an AND gate.

Rising Edge = (the org. signal) and NOT (delayed one clock cycle signal)

Falling Edge = NOT (the org. signal) and (delayed one clock cycle signal)

Listing 13-2. uartTOi2c.vhd vhdl

```vhdl
library ieee;
use ieee.std_logic_1164.all;
use ieee.numeric_std.all;

entity uartTOi2c is
  port(
    clk_uart_29MHz_i   : in    std_logic;
    uart_rst_i         : in    std_logic;
    uart_leds_o        : out   std_logic_vector(7 downto 0);
    clk_uart_monitor_o : out   std_logic;
    ------------UART TX & RX---------------------------
    uart_dout_o        : out   std_logic;
    uart_din_i         : in    std_logic;
    -----------I2C interface---------------------------
    i2c_scl            : inout std_logic;   -- serial clock
    i2c_dat            : inout std_logic);  -- serial data

end uartTOi2c;

architecture rtl of uartTOi2c is
  --
  -- Internal signal declaration
  --
  signal s_rst      : std_logic;            -- main reset
  signal s_clk_uart : std_logic;            -- slow (29 MHz) clock
  -- uart control signals
  signal s_uart_br_clk           : std_logic;  -- unused clock monitor
  signal s_uart_rx_add           : std_logic_vector (15 downto 0);
  signal s_uart_rx_data          : std_logic_vector (31 downto 0);
  signal s_uart_rx_rdy           : std_logic;
  signal s_uart_rx_stb_read_data : std_logic;
  signal s_update                : std_logic;
  signal s_uart_tx_add           : std_logic_vector (15 downto 0);
  signal s_uart_tx_data          : std_logic_vector (31 downto 0);
  signal s_uart_tx_data_rdy      : std_logic;
  signal s_uart_tx_req           : std_logic;
  signal s_uart_tx_stb_acq       : std_logic;
  signal s_tx_complete           : std_logic;
```

```vhdl
-- address decoder signals
signal r_config_addr_uart : std_logic_vector (1 downto 0);
signal r_leds             : std_logic_vector (7 downto 0);   -- 0x0000
signal reg01              : std_logic_vector (31 downto 0);  -- 0x0010
signal reg02              : std_logic_vector (31 downto 0);  -- 0x0001
----------------------------------
-- singals for i2c Master block --
----------------------------------
signal s_rst_n            : std_logic;
signal i2c_busy           : std_logic;
signal i2c_busy_dly       : std_logic;
signal i2c_busy_01        : std_logic;   -- rising edge of i2c_busy
signal i2cByte1           : std_logic;
signal i2c_2bytes         : std_logic;
signal data_wr            : std_logic_vector(7 downto 0);
signal data_rd            : std_logic_vector(7 downto 0);
-------------------------
-- State Machine states --
-------------------------
type t_tx_reg_map is (IDLE, WAIT_A_BYTE, LATCH, TRANSMIT);
signal s_tx_fsm           : t_tx_reg_map;

begin

    s_rst   <= not uart_rst_i;          -- Change to active high reset
    s_rst_n <= uart_rst_i;              -- active low reset
    uart_leds_o <= not r_leds;          -- Output LED with '1' mean on
    s_clk_uart         <= clk_uart_29MHz_i;  -- UART system clock 29.4912 MHz
    clk_uart_monitor_o <= s_uart_br_clk;
    i2c_busy_01 <= i2c_busy and not i2c_busy_dly;
    i2c_2bytes  <= reg01(30);           -- This i2c command has 2 bytes
    -- Data write to the I2C Master depends on # of bytes operations
    data_wr <= reg01(7 downto 0) when i2cByte1 = '0' else reg01(15 downto 8);

    -- UART simple register map : UART to BeMicro MAX10
    register_map : process (s_rst, s_clk_uart)
    begin
      if s_rst = '1' then               -- reset all registers here
        s_uart_rx_stb_read_data <= '0';
        s_update                <= '0';
        r_leds                  <= (others => '0');
        r_config_addr_uart      <= "10";
        reg01                   <= (others => '0');
        i2c_busy_dly            <= '0';
        i2cByte1                <= '0';
      elsif rising_edge(s_clk_uart) then
        i2c_busy_dly <= i2c_busy;
        if s_uart_rx_rdy = '1' then
          case (s_uart_rx_add) is
            -- Address 0x00 0x00
            when X"0000" => r_leds   <= s_uart_rx_data(7 downto 0);
            -- Address 0x00 0x10
```

```vhdl
        when X"0010" => reg01    <= s_uart_rx_data;
        -- Address 0x80 0x00
        when X"8000" => s_update <= '1';  -- register update self clearing
        when others  => null;
      end case;
      s_uart_rx_stb_read_data <= '1';
    else
      s_uart_rx_stb_read_data <= '0';
      s_update                <= '0';       -- register update self clearing
      -- Last byte send out to the i2C Master, then clean up data bits
      if(i2c_busy_01 = '1' and i2cByte1 = '0' and i2c_2bytes = '0') then
        reg01(29 downto 0) <= (others => '0');
      end if;
      -- After send the command to the I2C Master, then clean up command bits
      if(i2c_busy_01 = '1' and (i2cByte1 = i2c_2bytes)) then   -- 11 or 00 condition
        reg01(31 downto 30) <= (others => '0');
      end if;

      if (s_uart_rx_stb_read_data = '1') then
        i2cByte1 <= '0';  -- reset the condition after UART read request
      elsif(i2c_2bytes = '1' and i2c_busy_01 = '1') then
        -- Toggle every time i2C_busy change from low to high and two bytes operations
        i2cByte1 <= not i2cByte1;
      end if;

    end if;
  end if;
end process;

i2c_data_p : process (s_rst, s_clk_uart)
begin
  if s_rst = '1' then
    reg02(29 downto 0) <= (others => '0');
  elsif rising_edge(s_clk_uart) then
    -- when the busy is change from 1 to 0
    if(i2c_busy = '0' and i2c_busy_dly = '1') then
      -- copy the I2C data_rd to reg02(7 downto 0)
      -- and copy reg02(7 downto 0) to reg02(15 dwonto 0)
      reg02(15 downto 0) <= reg02(7 downto 0) & data_rd;
    end if;
    -- bit 15 to 3 is the 13 bit temperature
    -- each 1 equal 0.0625 and 0x0 equal to 0'C
    -- Only need bit 15 to 7 to read out in integer
    -- shift bits to upper bytes for easy read in degree C
    reg02(24 downto 16) <= reg02(15 downto 7);

  end if;
end process;

register_update : process (s_rst, s_clk_uart)
  variable v_uart_tx_add : unsigned (15 downto 0);
  variable v_count       : unsigned (15 downto 0);
```

```vhdl
begin
  if s_rst = '1' then                      -- reset all registers here
    s_uart_tx_data_rdy <= '0';
    s_uart_tx_req      <= '0';
    v_uart_tx_add      := (others => '0');
    v_count            := (others => '0');
    s_uart_tx_data     <= (others => '0');
    s_uart_tx_add      <= (others => '0');
    s_tx_fsm           <= IDLE;
  elsif rising_edge(s_clk_uart) then
    case s_tx_fsm is
      when IDLE =>
        if s_update = '1' then
          s_tx_fsm <= WAIT_A_BYTE;
        else
          s_tx_fsm           <= IDLE;
          s_uart_tx_data_rdy <= '0';
          s_uart_tx_req      <= '0';
          v_uart_tx_add      := (others => '0');
          v_count            := (others => '0');
          s_uart_tx_data     <= (others => '0');
          s_uart_tx_add      <= (others => '0');
        end if;
      when WAIT_A_BYTE =>
        s_uart_tx_data_rdy <= '0';
        v_count            := v_count + 1;
        if v_count = X"0900" then
          v_uart_tx_add := v_uart_tx_add + 1;
          s_tx_fsm      <= LATCH;
        else
          s_tx_fsm <= WAIT_A_BYTE;
        end if;
      when LATCH =>
        if s_uart_tx_stb_acq = '0' then
          s_uart_tx_req <= '1';
          s_uart_tx_add <= std_logic_vector (v_uart_tx_add);
          case v_uart_tx_add is
            when X"0001" => s_uart_tx_data (7 downto 0) <= r_leds;
                            s_tx_fsm <= TRANSMIT;
            when X"0010" => s_uart_tx_data <= reg01;
                            s_tx_fsm <= TRANSMIT;
            when X"0011" => s_uart_tx_data <= reg02;
                            s_tx_fsm <= TRANSMIT;
            -- End Of Transmission register = last register + 1
            when X"0012" => s_tx_fsm        <= IDLE;  -- end of transmission
            when others  => s_uart_tx_data <= (others => '0');
                            v_uart_tx_add      := v_uart_tx_add + 1;
                            s_uart_tx_data_rdy <= '0';
                            s_tx_fsm           <= LATCH;
          end case;
        else
```

```
            v_count  := (others => '0');
            s_tx_fsm <= WAIT_A_BYTE;
          end if;
        when TRANSMIT =>
          s_uart_tx_data_rdy <= '1';
          v_count            := (others => '0');
          s_tx_fsm           <= WAIT_A_BYTE;
        when others =>
          s_tx_fsm <= IDLE;
      end case;
    end if;
  end process;

  uart_wrapper : entity work.uart_16550_wrapper
    port map(
      sys_clk_i                => s_clk_uart,
      sys_rst_i                => s_rst,
      echo_en_i                => r_config_addr_uart(0),
      tx_addr_wwo_i            => r_config_addr_uart(1),
      uart_din_i               => uart_din_i,
      uart_dout_o              => uart_dout_o,
      s_br_clk_uart_o          => s_uart_br_clk,
      v_rx_add_o               => s_uart_rx_add,
      v_rx_data_o              => s_uart_rx_data,
      s_rx_rdy_o               => s_uart_rx_rdy,
      s_rx_stb_read_data_i     => s_uart_rx_stb_read_data,
      s_tx_proc_rqst_i         => s_uart_tx_req,
      v_tx_add_ram_i           => s_uart_tx_add,
      v_tx_data_ram_i          => s_uart_tx_data,
      s_tx_ram_data_rdy_i      => s_uart_tx_data_rdy,
      s_tx_stb_ram_data_acq_o  => s_uart_tx_stb_acq
      );

  i2cM_p : entity work.i2c_master
    generic map(
      input_clk => 29_491_200,  --input clock speed from user logic in Hz
      bus_clk   => 100_000)     --speed the i2c bus (scl) will run at in Hz
    port map(
      clk      => s_clk_uart,       --system clock
      reset_n  => s_rst_n,          --active low reset
      ena      => reg01(31),        --latch in command
      addr     => reg01(22 downto 16),  --address of target slave
      rw       => reg01(23),        --'0' is write, '1' is read
      data_wr  => data_wr,          --data to write to slave
      busy     => i2c_busy,         --indicates transaction in progress
      data_rd  => data_rd,          --data read from slave
      ack_error => reg02(30),       --flag if improper acknowledge from slave
      sda      => i2c_dat,          --serial data output of i2c bus
      scl      => i2c_scl);         --serial clock output of i2c bus

end architecture rtl;
```

13.5.3   Example Simulation Codes

This is the first time we have a simulation test bench. It is working as a "test bench" for the design files. Most of the time the test bench files can run only in simulation but NOT in real hardware. This is because the test bench not only includes the design files but also has to simulate the external world. In this case, they are physical UART interfaces, ADT7420 I2C interfaces, LEDs, and 50 MHz clock sources.

13.5.3.1   tb_temp_sensor_top.vhd Code

This test bench includes an i2c slave model (i2c_slave) and the temperature_sensor_top design, which we call the unit under test in the test bench. We use test_data as an array of bytes to send to the UART interface. There is a new std_logic value "H" which is used in this test bench for the I2C bus scl (serial clock) and sda (serial data) signals. This "H" value means a weak pull-up (10K ohm) resistor on the bus which is used to simulate the I2C bus 10k pull-up resistor on the board (Figure 13-22). There is a VHDL 2008 new method that gets used in this test bench. Following is that piece of code:

```
s_br_clk_uart_o <= << signal  .tb_temp_sensor_top.uut.uartTOi2c_pm.s_uart_br_clk : std_
logic >>
```

This VHDL code means the s_uart_br_clk value, which is in the uartTOi2c_pm module that is assigned to s_br_clk_uart_o in the top level of the design.

Following is the VHDL code:

```
library ieee;
use ieee.std_logic_1164.all;
use ieee.std_logic_unsigned.all;
use ieee.numeric_std.all;

entity tb_temp_sensor_top is
end tb_temp_sensor_top;

architecture behavior of tb_temp_sensor_top is

  --Inputs
  signal sys_clk_i    : std_logic := '0';
  signal uart_din_emu : std_logic := '0';
  signal uart_rst_emu : std_logic := '0';

  --Outputs
  signal uart_dout_emu  : std_logic;
  signal s_br_clk_uart_o : std_logic;
  signal uart_leds_emu  : std_logic_vector (7 downto 0);

  --i2c slave
  signal rst             : std_logic;
  signal read_req        : std_logic;
  signal data_to_master  : std_logic_vector(7 downto 0) := (others => '0');
  signal data_valid      : std_logic;
  signal data_from_master : std_logic_vector(7 downto 0);

  signal scl, sda : std_logic := 'H';   -- 'H' is to simulate Pull up resistors
```

```vhdl
constant system_clock_period : time := 20 ns;
constant uart_clock_period : time := 34 ns;                    -- 29.5MHz
constant bit_period         : time := uart_clock_period*32;  -- 921600bps

type sample_array is array (natural range<>) of std_logic_vector (7 downto 0);

constant test_data : sample_array :=
  (
    -- READ TDA7420 ID CMD -1: Write 0xb to I2C address 0x48
    X"00",                        -- BYTE1
    X"10",                        -- BYTE2
    X"80",                        -- BYTE3
    X"48",                        -- BYTE4
    X"00",                        -- BYTE5
    X"0b",                        -- BYTE6
    -- READ ID CMD -2:  Read from I2C
    X"00",                        -- BYTE1
    X"10",                        -- BYTE2
    X"80",                        -- BYTE3
    X"C8",                        -- BYTE4
    X"00",                        -- BYTE5
    X"00",                        -- BYTE6
    -- DUMMY for waiting
    X"00",                        -- BYTE1
    X"20",                        -- BYTE2
    X"00",                        -- BYTE3
    X"00",                        -- BYTE4
    X"00",                        -- BYTE5
    X"00",                        -- BYTE6
    -- DUMMY for waiting
    X"00",                        -- BYTE1
    X"20",                        -- BYTE2
    X"00",                        -- BYTE3
    X"00",                        -- BYTE4
    X"00",                        -- BYTE5
    X"00",                        -- BYTE6
    -- Read registers to UART
    X"80",                        -- BYTE1
    X"00",                        -- BYTE2
    X"00",                        -- BYTE3
    X"00",                        -- BYTE4
    X"00",                        -- BYTE5
    X"00",                        -- BYTE6
     -- DUMMY for waiting
    X"00",                        -- BYTE1
    X"20",                        -- BYTE2
    X"00",                        -- BYTE3
    X"00",                        -- BYTE4
    X"00",                        -- BYTE5
    X"00",                        -- BYTE6
     -- DUMMY for waiting
```

```
    X"00",                          -- BYTE1
    X"20",                          -- BYTE2
    X"00",                          -- BYTE3
    X"00",                          -- BYTE4
    X"00",                          -- BYTE5
    X"00",                          -- BYTE6
    -- Reset the ADC write 0x00 to ADT7420 register offset:0x2F
    X"00",                          -- BYTE1
    X"10",                          -- BYTE2
    X"C0",                          -- BYTE3
    X"48",                          -- BYTE4
    X"00",                          -- BYTE5
    X"2F",                          -- BYTE6
    -- Write 0x80 to offset 0x03 to ADT7420 to set 13bit
    X"00",                          -- BYTE1
    X"10",                          -- BYTE2
    X"C0",                          -- BYTE3
    X"48",                          -- BYTE4
    X"80",                          -- BYTE5
    X"03",                          -- BYTE6
    -- dummy
    X"00",                          -- BYTE1
    X"20",                          -- BYTE2
    X"00",                          -- BYTE3
    X"00",                          -- BYTE4
    X"00",                          -- BYTE5
    X"00",                          -- BYTE6
    -- Read two byte - 1 From I2C address 0x48
    X"00",                          -- BYTE1
    X"10",                          -- BYTE2
    X"80",                          -- BYTE3
    X"48",                          -- BYTE4
    X"00",                          -- BYTE5
    X"00",                          -- BYTE6
    -- Read two byte - 2
    X"00",                          -- BYTE1
    X"10",                          -- BYTE2
    X"C0",                          -- BYTE3
    X"C8",                          -- BYTE4
    X"00",                          -- BYTE5
    X"00",                          -- BYTE6
    -- dummy  Waiting
    X"00",                          -- BYTE1
    X"20",                          -- BYTE2
    X"00",                          -- BYTE3
    X"00",                          -- BYTE4
    X"00",                          -- BYTE5
    X"00",                          -- BYTE6

    -- Read back from I2C
    X"80",                          -- BYTE1
```

```
    X"00",                          -- BYTE2
    X"00",                          -- BYTE3
    X"00",                          -- BYTE4
    X"00",                          -- BYTE5
    X"00"                           -- BYTE6
    );

begin

  -- Instantiate the Unit Under Test (UUT)
  uut : entity work.temperature_sensor_top port map(
    SYS_CLK      => sys_clk_i,
    USER_LED     => uart_leds_emu,
    GPIO_J3_39   => uart_dout_emu,
    GPIO_J3_40   => uart_din_emu,
    ADT7420_CT   => '0', -- Not use
    ADT7420_INT  => '0', -- NOt use
    ADT7420_SCL  => scl, -- I2C SCL
    ADT7420_SDA  => sda  -- I2C SDA
    );

  i2c_slave : entity work.I2C_slave
    generic map(
      SLAVE_ADDR => "1001000") -- address 0x48
    port map(
      scl               => scl,
      sda               => sda,
      clk               => sys_clk_i,
      rst               => rst,
      -- User interface
      read_req          => read_req,
      data_to_master    => data_to_master,
      data_valid        => data_valid,
      data_from_master  => data_from_master);

  scl <= 'H';
  sda <= 'H';

  s_br_clk_uart_o <= << signal
.tb_temp_sensor_top.uut.uartTOi2c_pm.s_uart_br_clk : std_logic >>;

  i2c_data : process(sys_clk_i)
  begin
    if(rising_edge(sys_clk_i)) then
      if read_req = '1' then -- the read back value increment by one every read
        data_to_master <= std_logic_vector(unsigned(data_to_master) +1);
      end if;
    end if;
  end process;

  uart_clock_process : process
```

```vhdl
  begin
    sys_clk_i <= '0';
    wait for system_clock_period/2;
    sys_clk_i <= '1';
    wait for system_clock_period/2;
  end process;

  rst_p : process
  begin
    rst <= '1';
    wait for 200 ns;
    wait until rising_edge(sys_clk_i);
    rst <= '0';
    wait;
  end process;

  -- Stimulus process
  stim_proc : process
  begin
    -- hold reset
    wait for 50 ns;
    wait for system_clock_period*10;
    -- insert stimulus here
    uart_din_emu <= '1';

    wait for 10 us;

    -- look through test_data
    for j in test_data'range loop
      -- tx_start_bit
      uart_din_emu <= '0';
      wait for bit_period;

      -- Byte serializer
      for i in 0 to 7 loop
        uart_din_emu <= test_data(j)(i);
        wait for bit_period;
      end loop;

      -- tx_stop_bit
      uart_din_emu <= '1';
      wait for bit_period;
      wait for 5 us;
    end loop;

    wait;
  end process;

end;
```

13.5.3.2   i2c_slave.vhd Code

We downloaded this .vhdl IP file from github.com and we need to make the following change to this IP. All of those that are sda and scl with a status of '1' need to change to have a status of 'H'. The following shows the line number that needs to be changed. Line 50 and line 262 are added to the vhdl.

```
Line 50:  signal sda_i : std_logic;
Line 65:      if scl_prev_reg = '0' and scl = 'H' then
Line 69:      if scl_prev_reg = 'H' and scl = '0' then
Line 76:      if scl = 'H' and scl_prev_reg = 'H' and
Line 77:        sda_prev_reg = 'H' and sda = '0' then
Line 83:      if scl_prev_reg = 'H' and scl = 'H' and
Line 84:        sda_prev_reg = '0' and sda = 'H' then
LINE 117: addr_reg(6-bits_processed_reg) <= sda_i;
LINE 120: cmd_reg              <= sda_i;
LINE 161: data_reg(6-bits_processed_reg) <= sda_i;
LINE 163: data_from_master_reg <= data_reg & sda_i;
Line 194:          if sda = 'H' then          -- nack = stop read

Line 261:    read_req        <= read_req_reg;
Line 262:    sda_i <= '1' when sda = 'H' else '0';
Line 263: end architecture arch;
```

13.5.4   Create Temperature Sensor Project Design and Program It

We will start creating a project from a project template: BeMicro MAX 10 Kit Baseline Pinout.

1.   Project ➤ Add / Remove Files in the project and add all of the files from the uart_16660_wrapper IP (under the core Figure 13-24 and core/library Figure 13-25)

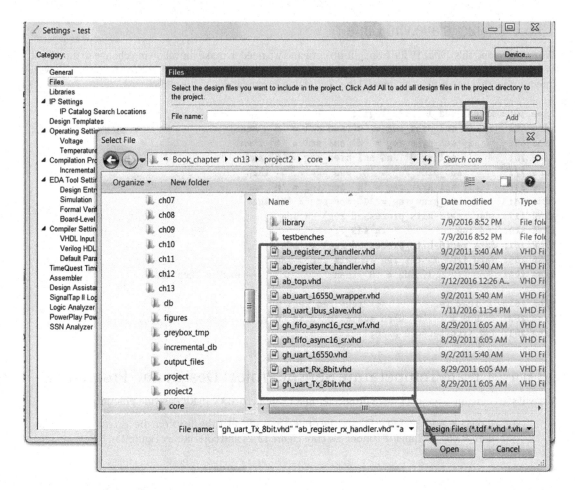

Figure 13-24. *File list of UART 1650 IP core*

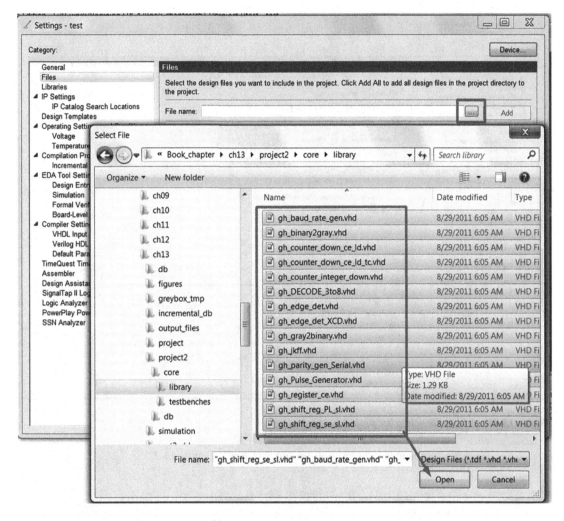

Figure 13-25. *File list of UART 1650 IP library*

2. Project ➤ Add / Remove Files in the project and add i2c_master.vhd, uartTOi2c.vhd, and temperature_sensor_top.vhd files in the project.

3. Add Altera PLL IP—pll_29p5M.vhd as shown in the FPGA IP—Altera PLL IP section

4. Set up simulation tool and test bench. Assignment ➤ Settings... ➤ EDA Tool Settings / Simulation ➤ Select Compile test bench and click Test Benches... (Figure 13-26)

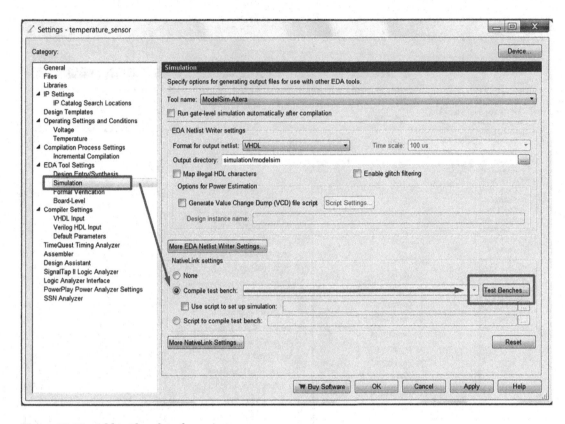

Figure 13-26. *Add test bench to the project*

    5.   Open the Test Benches window pop-up and click New... (Figure 13-27)

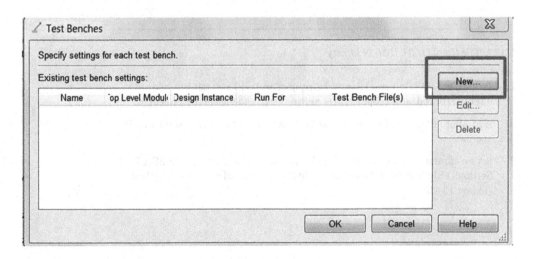

Figure 13-27. *Test Benches list*

6. In the New Test Bench Settings window, please follow Figure 13-28 and click OK and OK again. You will add two .vhd files under Create new test bench settings: I2C_slave.vhd and tb_temp_sensor_top.vhd.

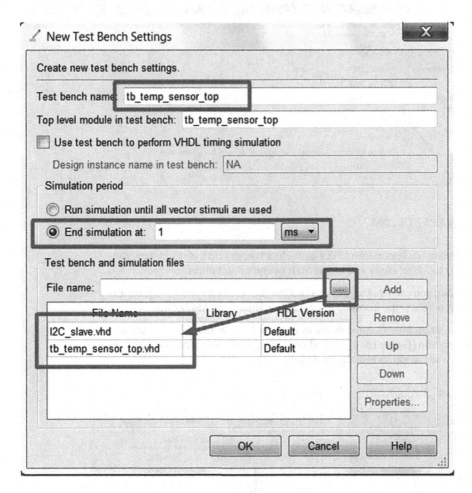

Figure 13-28. *New Test Bench Settings*

■ **Note** Only add the tb_temp_sensor_top.vhd under test bench settings but NOT the project file section.

---

7. In the Compiler Setting ➤ VHDL Input, select VHDL 2008. Figure 13-29 shows the setting.

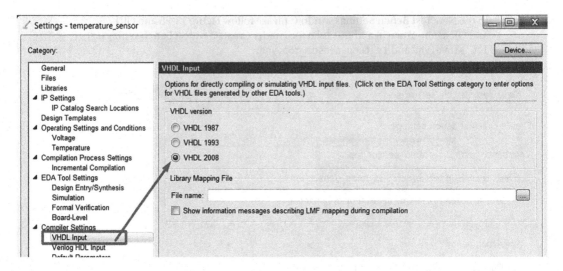

Figure 13-29. *Setting for VHDL 2008*

8. In the Project Navigator, select Files and select `temperature_sensor_top.vhd` and set as top-level entity and hit the Start compilation button.

9. At this point you can use the same method as shown in Chapter 12 to program the FPGA or follow the next step to start a simulation with ModelSim.

10. Start simulation from Quartus Prime by clicking Tools ➤ Run Simulation tool ➤ RTL simulation (Figure 13-30). This should bring us to the ModelSim with the test bench as the top level of the simulation.

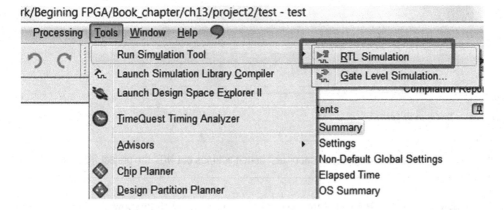

Figure 13-30. *Start RTL simulation*

■ **Note** Starting the ModelSim from Quartus takes around 30 seconds.

11. The ModelSim should start like Figure 13-31 and the sim instance list shown in Figure 13-32. It will run for 1 mS.

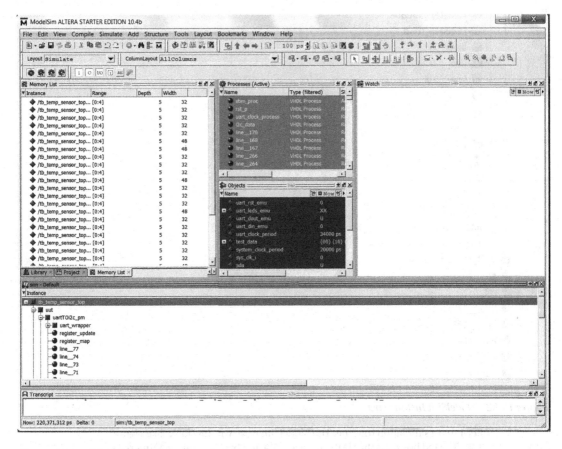

Figure 13-31. *ModelSim with test bench*

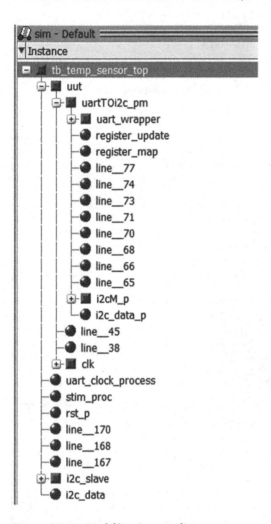

Figure 13-32. *ModelSim Instance list*

12. After 1 ms of simulation runtime. The ModelSim wave window looks like Figure 13-33. The red box # 2 is the UART interface. The red back # 1 is the I2C interface.

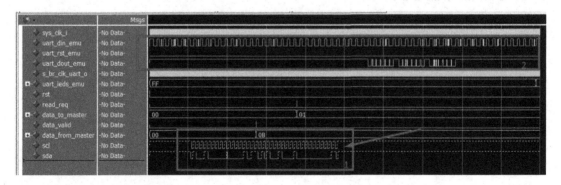

Figure 13-33. *Simulation result*

13.5.5   Hardware Setup for the Temperature Sensor Project Design

1. Connect the UART to the USB cable as in Figure 13-34. Connect the black (GND) to the pin 30, orange to pin 40 and yellow to pin 39.

2. You can now connect the programmer USB cable to directly upload the image to the FPGA.

3. Connect the USB side of the USB to UART cable to the PC.

4. Connect the FPGA programmer.

5. The next step is to ready the PC side software; please follow the next section to do so.

Figure 13-34. *Connection to the USB UART*

13.5.6   UART Software Setup—RealTerm

Please follow the setup as displayed in Figure 13-35 and set up the port as in Figure 13-36. Remember the baud rate is 921600. The USB to UART cable can do much faster than normal UART speed.

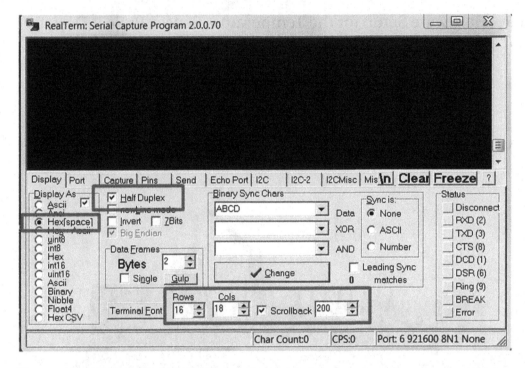

Figure 13-35. *RealTerm display setup*

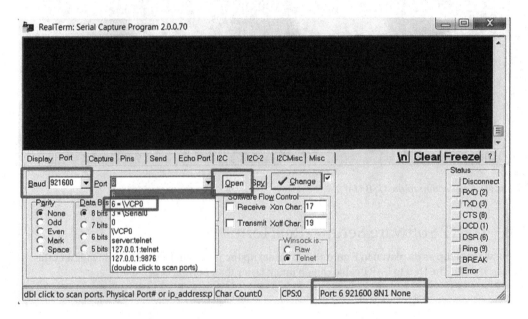

Figure 13-36. *RealTerm port setup*

13.5.7   Command Your FPGA to Read the Temperature

In RealTerm, check that the right low corner setting is correct. It should be 921600 8N1 None. In the Send tab, type 0x80 0x00 0x00 0x00 0x00 0x00 in the box number 1 and click box number 2 (Figure 13-37). This should send out the command to request reading back three registers.

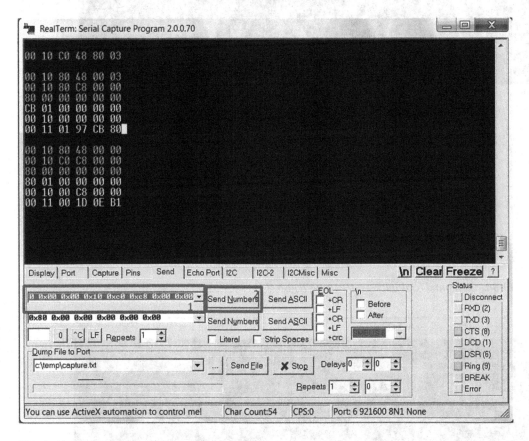

Figure 13-37. How to send command to the FPGA

In the terminal, all of the data sent out to the FPGA is in green and all received data from the FPGA is in yellow. Figure 13-37 shows two separate read request commands in green (80 00 00 00 00 00 in lines 4 and 11) followed by three yellow 6-byte lines.

Each of the 6 bytes of yellow data sent from the FPGA has its own meaning. The first line of the last byte (last on the right-hand side) is the 8 LED condition. The second line reports the last command sending to the I2C master module. The last line reports the data read from the I2C slave (ADT7420) though I2C master.

Figures 13-38 and 13-39 show a command read-back of three status registers.

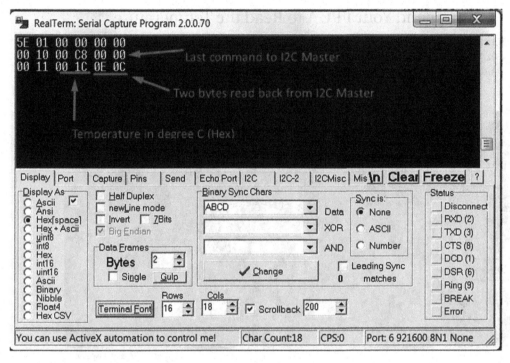

Figure 13-38. Command read-back—three status registers

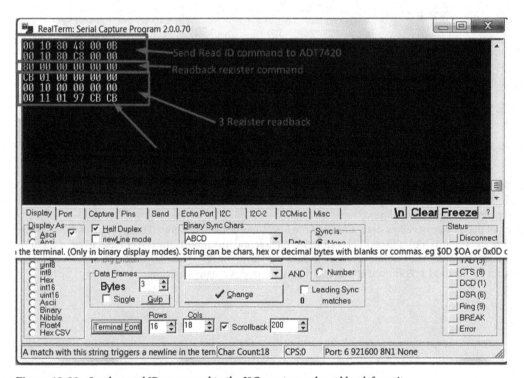

Figure 13-39. Send a read ID command to the I2C master and read back from it

13.5.7.1   Read Temperature Sensor ID and Set Up the Chip

The command we need to send to the UART is the following:

1. 0x00 0x10 0x80 0x48 0x00 0x0b 0x00 0x10 0x80 0xc8 0x00 0x00

The line includes two commands and sends them back to back. The first 6 bytes (command 0x00 0x10 0x80 0x48 0x00 0x0b) are used to send a write command to the I2C address 0x48 which is ADT7420 with a byte value equal to 0xb. From the ADT7420 datasheet, the 0xb (the last byte of the command) is the offset address for the next command read offset address. The second 6-byte command (0x00 0x10 0x80 0xc8 0x00 0x00) is used to send a read command to the I2C address 0x48 to read one byte.

The FPGA will report the I2C read data to the PC by receiving the following command from the PC:

2. 0x80 0x00 0x00 0x00 0x00 0x00

The FPGA will report three lines and each line has 6 bytes registered to the PC as shown in the first three yellow lines in Figure 13-40.

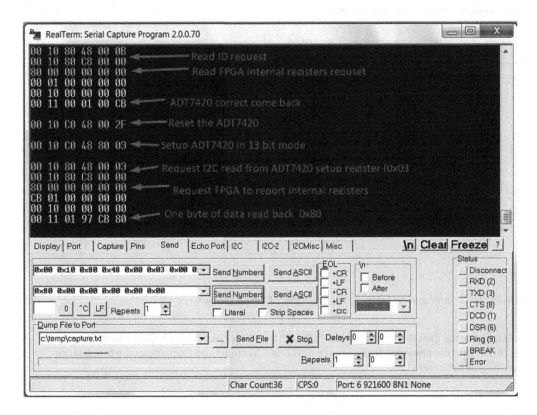

Figure 13-40. *Commands sent to the FPGA and FPGA responses*

The next step is to reset the ADT7420 chip by sending the following command shown in Figure 13-40 the 4th green line:

3. 0x00 0x10 0xC0 0x48 0x00 0x2f

Now we need to set up the ADT7420 chip in 13-bit mode by setting the IC register address 0x03 with the value of 0x80. This is done by sending the following command (shown in Figure 13-40 5th green line).

309

4.   0x00 0x10 0xC0 0x48 0x80 0x03

To read back the value we just write into the IC register address 0x03. We need to send the following command to the I2C Master and follow with an FPGA internal register read-back request:

5.   0x00 0x10 0x80 0x48 0x00 0x03 0x00 0x10 0x80 0xc8 0x00 0x00

6.   0x80 0x00 0x00 0x00 0x00 0x00

13.5.7.2   Read Temperature from Temperature Sensor

After the last step, the ADT7420 is ready to report temperature data. The temperature request also comes with two commands. The first one is to set the IC register address 0x00 and the second one is to request a 2-byte read. According to the I2C specification, this will allow us to read register addresses 0x00 and 0x01 which are the temperature registers' most significant and least significant bytes (Figure 13-41).

1.   0x00 0x10 0x80 0x48 0x00 0x00 0x00 0x10 0xc0 0xc8 0x00 0x00

2.   0x80 0x00 0x00 0x00 0x00 0x00

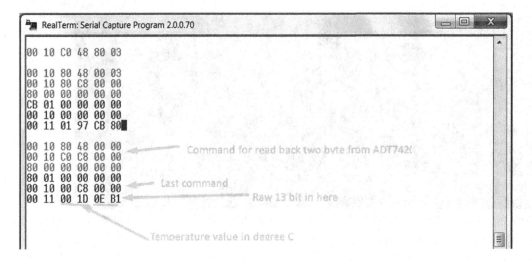

Figure 13-41. Command and status for read temperature from the sensor

The last line of the data read-back (00 11 00 1D 0E B1) includes two types of information. The last two bytes (0E B1) are the raw value read from the ADT7420. The third and fourth bytes are forming one temperature value in degrees C.

13.6 Summary

After this chapter, you should know how to download and use free IP from the Internet. You learned about two new communication links, UART and I2C bus. The example design shows you how to transmit and receive meaningful data (command and status) between the FPGA and the PC though a simple protocol which only has six bytes.

This chapter also showed you an example of how to do simulations with the VHDL code as a test bench which generates UART messages to the unit under test which is our `temperature_sensor_top.vhd`. Using VHDL as a verification method is very powerful so it is really beneficial to take the time to learn how to use it.

We hope you are now confident in trying out others IPs. You can learn a lot of things simply by using others IPs, and, as an added bonus, you also get the job done faster. In the next chapter we will build our first IP: SPI interface.

■ **Note** There is one more command in the FPGA which is 0x00 0x00 0x00 0x00 0x00 0x??. The ?? is the value of the 8-bit LED on/off switches. Try to turn on/off some LEDs on the board.

"Do or do not. There is no try."

—Yoda

CHAPTER 14

■ ■ ■

How Fast Can You Run? Ask the Accelerometer!

14.1   Introduction

The FPGA (field-programmable gate array) design in this chapter, based on the one in Chapter 13, adds a new design block—a Serial Peripheral Interface master. The new block will "talk" to an accelerometer IC (integrated circuit) on the BeMicro Max10 board. We will design the block in this chapter. This chapter will show you the steps needed to build an interface module.

The setup for this chapter is exactly the same as that for Chapter 13 (see Figure 14-1). We will use the PC to control the board through the UART (universal asynchronous receiver/transmitter). The LED (light-emitting diode) on the MicroMAX10 board will be used to show the acceleration conditions. The connection between the accelerometer sensor and FPGA is already there inside the PCB (printed circuit board), so we don't need to touch that either!

Figure 14-1. *Exactly the same setup used in Chapter 13*

© Aiken Pang and Peter Membrey 2017
A. Pang and P. Membrey, *Beginning FPGA: Programming Metal*, DOI 10.1007/978-1-4302-6248-0_14

14.2   Steps to Build Your First Interface Module

Steps 1 through 3 illustrate a simple design flow for an SPI master module.

14.2.1   Understanding the SPI

In Chapter 13, we used the I2C (inter-integrated circuit) bus third-party IP (Internet Protocol) to communicate with the IC. This time we will use another interface—the Serial Peripheral Interface (SPI) to talk with the IC and we are going to create the SPI master modules to talk to the Accelerometer. It is a very common communication protocol used for two-way communication between two ICs. A standard SPI bus contains four wires: clock (SCLK), chip select (CS), master in slave out (MISO), and master out slave in (MOSI). An SPI bus has only one master and one or more slaves. The master can talk to any slave on the bus and the slave can talk to the master too. There is no direct communication between slaves.

SPI is a synchronous bus, which means that it uses separate lines for data and clock. It is not like the UART interface which only sends and receives data. The receiver needs to guess the bit location from the data which is an asynchronous bus. You can get more detail about UART from Chapter 13. Although SPI uses one more wire to transmit or receive data, it can run faster than the UART interface because the SPI don't need to guest the data bit location. The master uses SCLK to let the slave know when data is ready for it to copy. SPI can easily run at 8 MHz without a problem, if both master and slave are on the same circuit board or within ten feet .

SPI uses CS (assuming it is active Low) from not active (High) to active (Low) to indicate a start of transfer. The transfer is terminated by changing CS from active (Low) to not active (High)

Basically, SPI has four signals: clock, chip select, and two single direction data lines. The Accelerometer on the BeMicro MAX10 board needs an SPI master with the four signals interface to control it. Figure 14-2 shows the Accelerometer.

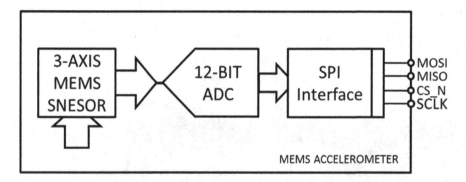

Figure 14-2. *Accelerometer block diagram*

14.2.2   What Do You Need for an SPI Master Module?

We need the port list for the SPI master module so that other modules can talk to the master SPI and the master SPI can respond. The master SPI port list needs to include the three-wire serial protocol with chip select/enable described in Figure 14-3.

The port list is like a software API (application programming interface) or a function's input and output. We need to ask ourselves a few questions before we design the port list. What do we need the master SPI to do for the slave? And how do we want to control the master SPI? We can connect all four wires to a 4-bit register and let the PC read/write on the 4-bit register to simulate the SPI interface. This design only includes one 4-bit register which is a very simple FPGA design. We can go to another extreme and fully automate with a tailor-made design for our slave SPI interface. This will include more than one state machine in the FPGA design. In this example, we will go for somewhere in between.

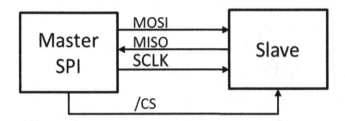

Figure 14-3. *SPI master typical usage*

Following are the requirements for the master SPI module to allow the user to control it and send/receive bytes from the slave.

1. User can control the master clock (SCLK) speed. It is useful for reusing the same module for a different slave.

2. User can control the master clock polarity (CPOL) and phase (CPHA) (Figure 14-4 shows the CPOL and CPHA).

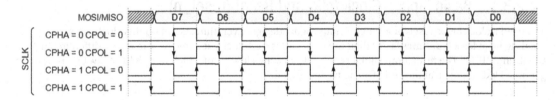

Figure 14-4. *SPI clock timing setting*

3. User can start a transfer/receive and end a transfer/receive by controlling the CS (see Figure 14-5).

4. Each time user provides an 8-bit piece of data to send to or receive from the slave (see Figure 14-5).

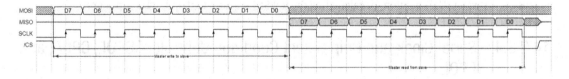

Figure 14-5. *SPI write and read byte timing*

14.2.3   Create the SPI Master Module Entity Port List

From step 2, we will have the following entity (Figure 14-6) for the SPI master block. This section describes each port.

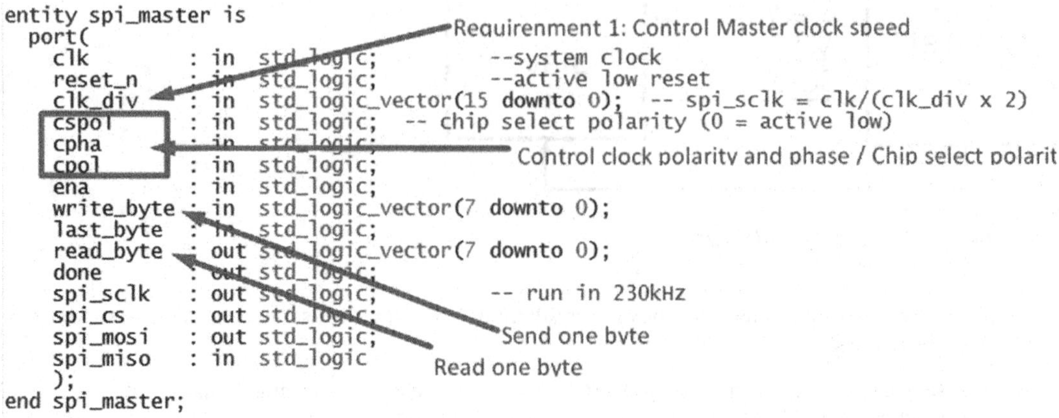

```
entity spi_master is
  port(
    clk         : in  std_logic;                        --system clock
    reset_n     : in  std_logic;                        --active low reset
    clk_div     : in  std_logic_vector(15 downto 0);    -- spi_sclk = clk/(clk_div x 2)
    cspol       : in  std_logic;    -- chip select polarity (0 = active low)
    cpha        : in  std_logic;
    cpol        : in  std_logic;
    ena         : in  std_logic;
    write_byte  : in  std_logic_vector(7 downto 0);
    last_byte   : in  std_logic;
    read_byte   : out std_logic_vector(7 downto 0);
    done        : out std_logic;
    spi_sclk    : out std_logic;                        -- run in 230kHz
    spi_cs      : out std_logic;
    spi_mosi    : out std_logic;
    spi_miso    : in  std_logic
  );
end spi_master;
```

Requirement 1: Control Master clock speed

Control clock polarity and phase / Chip select polarit

Send one byte

Read one byte

Figure 14-6. *SPI master module entity port map*

14.2.3.1   Basic Inputs: Clock (clk) and Reset (reset_n)

You need a clock and a reset for a synchronous digital design. Everything is run on this clock. This clock needs to be at least four times faster than the target SPI serial clock such that we can create different SPI CPOL and CPHA. The reset input signal reset_n is an active low input which means logic low ('0') is reset. In general, I like to put _n at the end of an active low signal.

14.2.3.2   SPI Interface: SPI_SCLK, SPI_CS, SPI_MOSI, & SPI_MISO

We need these four signals for a three-wire SPI with CS interface. SPI_SCLK, SPI_CS, and SPI_MOSI are outputs and SPI_MISO is an input.

14.2.3.3   Serial Clock Speed Control: clk_div

We create an input port (clk_div) to provide a way to control the SPI serial clock speed. The name clk_div means clock divider. The equation for calculating the SPI SCLK is next to the clk_div input port.

14.2.3.4   Serial Clock and Chip Select Condition Controls: CSPOL, CPHA, and CPOL

The chip select will be active low when chip select polarity (CSPOL) is LOW. The functions are shown in Figure 14-4. Figures 14-7, 14-8, 14-9, and 14-10 are the actual outputs from the SPI master with different combinations of CPHA and CPOL.

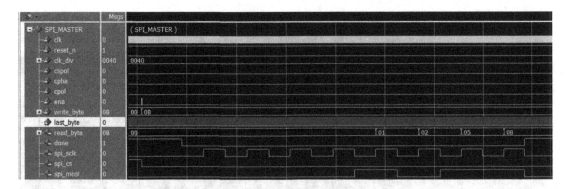

Figure 14-7. *SPI master sclk and mosi when cpha = 0 and cpol = 0*

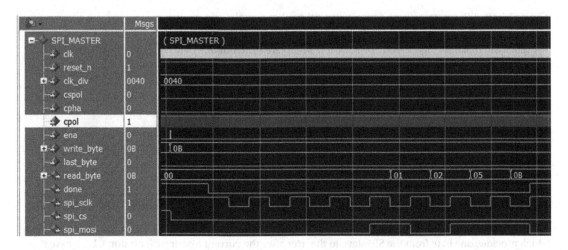

Figure 14-8. *SPI master sclk and mosi when cpha = 0 and cpol = 1*

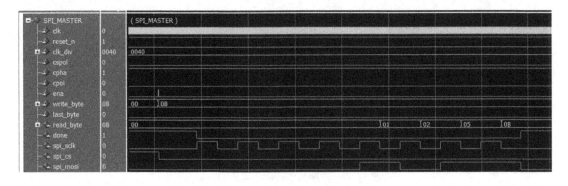

Figure 14-9. *SPI master sclk and mosi when cpha = 1 and cpol = 0*

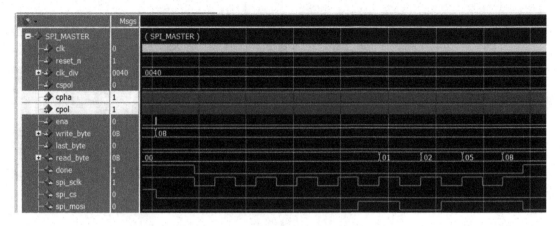

Figure 14-10. *SPI master sclk: and mosi when cpha = 1 and cpol = 1*

Each SPI masters (Figure 14-7, 14-8, 14-9 & 14-10) are send out one byte with value equal to 0x0b serially on the spi_mosi with the clk_div equal to 63 (Hex 0x0040)

14.2.3.5 Request the SPI Master Does Something: ena

The SPI master module needs an input port like ena from the SPI master module port map to kick-start the SPI operation. In Figure 14-10, all of the chip select, spi clock, and spi mosi start operating after the ena pulse is received.

14.2.3.6 One Byte Input and Output: Write_byte, Read_byte, and Last_byte

Write_byte is an 8-bit input port for the user to provide one byte to send and read_byte is an 8-bit output port which provides one byte from the SPI slave to the user after the current byte transfer is done. Last_byte is a 1-bit input port to let the SPI master know when it should set or clear the chip select.

14.2.3.7 Done Is Done

The last one is the DONE output. Every time the user requests that the SPI master do something, DONE bit goes low until it is finished. It will go high again until the next request from the user. We may not use this bit in this design but it is very useful when you try to make the SPI send data faster. You can build a simple finite state machine (FSM) to run this interface.

14.2.4 Create Processes in VHDL for the Requirements

In step 2, we had four requirements for the SPI master.

14.2.4.1 Control the Master Clock (SCLK) Speed, Polarity, and Phase

We are going to generate an SPI SCLK which has a 50% duty cycle; this means that 50% of the time is spent high and 50% is spent low. We need to have a counter to count a value from zero to clk_div x 2 such that we can create the duty cycle (half high, half low clock). In VHDL (VHSIC (very high speed integrated circuit)

Hardware Description Language), it is easy to multiply by 2. VHDL only needs to "add" a '0' at the end of the unsigned. It is because adding one more bit at the end of a binary number creates an effect of double the value (e.g., binary number "111" is 6; "1110" is 14). Line 37 in Figure 14-11 shows that clk_div is doubled by "& '0'" at the end of the unsigned(clk_div). This code doesn't need to be within the process block because it is not going to change every clock cycle. We don't expect the user will change it once the SPI master is generating the SCLK.

There is a clk_gen_p process with clk and reset_n in the sensitivity list (Figure 14-11, lines 40 to 74). It generates spi_sclk which is SPI SCLK. The count on lines 43 and 47-51 is the counter for creating the slower spi_sclk clock. It is a free-running counter with the maximum value of clk_div times 2 minus 1. When it hits the maximum value (clk_div x 2 - 1), it will roll over to zero.

```
37    clk_div2 <= unsigned(clk_div) & '0';   -- double the clk_div value to clk_div2
38
39    --generate the timing for the spi clock (spi_sclk) and the data clock (data_clk)
40    clk_gen_p : process(clk, reset_n)
41    begin
42       if(reset_n = '0') then                 --reset asserted
43          count    <= (others => '0');
44          spi_sclk <= '0';
45          data_clk <= '0';
46       elsif rising_edge(clk) then
47          if(count = clk_div2-1) then          --end of timing cycle
48             count <= (others => '0');         --reset timer
49          else
50             count <= count + 1;               --continue clock generation timing
51          end if;
52
53          if(running = '1' and bit_count < 8) then
54             if(count < unsigned(clk_div)) then      --first 1/2 cycle of clocking
55                if(cpha = cpol) then                 -- both equal 0 or 1
56                   spi_sclk <= '0';
57                else
58                   spi_sclk <= '1';
59                end if;
60                data_clk <= '0';
61             elsif(count >= unsigned(clk_div)) then  --second 1/2 cycle of clocking
62                if(cpha = cpol) then
63                   spi_sclk <= '1';
64                else
65                   spi_sclk <= '0';
66                end if;
67                data_clk <= '1';
68             end if;
69          else
70             spi_sclk <= cpol;
71             data_clk <= '0';
72          end if;
73       end if;
74    end process;
```

Figure 14-11. *spi_master.vhd part-1*

The SPI master needs to have one internal clock which is used to manage the data output and input timing and one external clock for the SPI interface to use which is spi_sclk. The internal clock is data_clk in Figure 14-6. The data_clk timing is NOT affected by chpa or cpol. The spi_sclk depends on chpa and cpol for setting high and low. Running and bit_count are used to indicate the SPI is sending out data (8-bit).

14.2.4.2   Start a Transfer/Receive and End a Transfer/Receive with Chip Select

The process running_p is the main timekeeper for the whole SPI master. It sets running = '1' to start the SPI master operation and how long SPI master should run for (when to end the operation, the process set running = '0'). It is using two counters: one is the count from the clk_gen_p and another one is inside the running_p: bit count.

The operation starts when running_p detects a rising edge on ena and the free running count is equal to the maximum value (Figure 14-12, line 87). The operation will stop (running = '0') when the bit_count is equal to 8 (line 91). bit_count counts the number of clock cycles generated. Our application transfers only one byte per request (ean = '1') so the operation is completed when the bit_count is equal to 8.

```
75  ⊢
76  ⊟    running_p : process (clk, reset_n)
77  |    begin
78  ⊟      if (reset_n = '0') then
79  |         bit_count <= (others => '0');
80  ⊢         running    <= '0';
81  ⊟      elsif(rising_edge(clk)) then
82  ⊟         if(running = '1') then              -- Clear when running
83  ⊢            ena_dly <= '0';
84  ⊟         elsif(ena = '1') then
85  |            ena_dly <= '1';
86  ⊢         end if;
87  ⊟         if(ena_dly = '1' and count = clk_div2-1) then   -- wait for the right
88  |                                                          -- start time
89  ⊢            running <= '1';
90  ⊟         else
91  ⊟            if(bit_count = 8) then            -- stop running after 8 bit send out
92  |               running <= '0';
93  ⊢            end if;
94  |         end if;
95  ⊢
96  ⊟         if(running = '1' and count = clk_div2-1) then
97  ⊟            if (bit_count < 8) then
98  ⊢               bit_count <= bit_count + 1;
99  ⊟            else
100 |               bit_count <= (others => '0');
101 ⊢            end if;
102 ⊟         else
103 ⊟            if(bit_count = 8) then
104 |               bit_count <= (others => '0');
105 ⊢            end if;
106 ⊢         end if;
107 ⊢      end if;
108 |    end process;
109 |
```

Figure 14-12. spi_master.vhd part-2

There is another process called cs_p which is for generating the correct polarity and timing for the chip select. Line 116 in Figure 14-13 shows the conditions for setting the spi_cs to not active.

```
110
111  ⊟  cs_p : process (clk, reset_n)
112  |  begin
113  ⊟    if (reset_n = '0') then
114  ⊢      spi_cs <= '1';
115  ⊟    elsif(rising_edge(clk)) then
116  ⊟      if(running = '0' and bit_count = 0 and last_byte = '1' and ena = '0' and ena_dly = '0') then
117         spi_cs <= not cspol;        -- chip select is not active after the
118  ⊢                                   -- last byte send/receive
119  ⊟      elsif(ena = '1') then        --Chip select is active when start to
120  |                                   --send/ receive data
121         spi_cs <= cspol;
122  ⊢    end if;
123  ⊢    end if;
124     end process;
125  ⊢
```

Figure 14-13. *spi_master.vhd part-3*

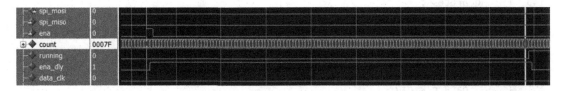

Figure 14-14. *ena to running timing—start running when count is equal to 0x7F which is the maximum value of the count*

14.2.4.3   Transfer and Receive One Byte at a Time

We are using data_out_p and data_in_p processes to shift the data in and out. The data_out_p shift register is reg_shift_out. It loads the shift register value with write_byte when ena is equal to '1' (Figure 14-15, lines 134-135). The shift register starts to shift left 1 bit when ena is equal to '0,' running is High, and count = 0, which is the time to change the output data on the SPI MOSI. The most significant bit of the shift register is connected to the spi_mosi output.

The data_in_p is shifting bit by bit into shift register reg_shift_in from spi_miso which is the SPI slave output. These shift register values get reset to zero when ena = '1' (Figure 14-15, line 155). It starts shifting left when running is equal to '1' and there is a rising edge on data_clk. The whole 8-bit shift register is connected to the output port of read_byte.

```
126    |----------------------------------------------------------------
127    |-- Data sending out to the MOSI is using shift register
128    |----------------------------------------------------------------
129    data_out_p : process (clk, reset_n)
130    begin
131      if (reset_n = '0') then
132        reg_shift_out <= (others => '0');
133      elsif(rising_edge(clk)) then
134        if(ena = '1') then
135          reg_shift_out <= '0'& write_byte;
136        else
137          if(running = '1' and count = 0) then
138            reg_shift_out <= reg_shift_out(7 downto 0)& '0';
139          end if;
140        end if;
141      end if;
142
143    end process;
144
145    |----------------------------------------------------------------
146    |-- Data receiving from SPI slave is shifted into shift register
147    |----------------------------------------------------------------
148    data_in_p : process (clk, reset_n)
149    begin
150      if (reset_n = '0') then
151        data_clk_dly <= '0';
152        reg_shift_in <= (others => '0');
153      elsif(rising_edge(clk)) then
154        data_clk_dly <= data_clk;
155        if(ena = '1') then
156          reg_shift_in <= (others => '0');
157        else
158          if(running = '1' and data_clk_dly = '0' and data_clk = '1') then
159            -- only shift when SPI clock is rising edge
160            reg_shift_in <= reg_shift_in(6 downto 0)& spi_miso;
161          end if;
162        end if;
163      end if;
164
165    end process;
166
167    spi_mosi    <= reg_shift_out(8);
168    read_byte   <= reg_shift_in;
```

Figure 14-15. spi_master.vhd part-4

14.3   PC Control Accelerometer Sensor Design Example

As mentioned earlier, this example is based on the design from Chapter 13 and adds an SPI master module to it. We can clone the design from Chapter 13 and rename it for this chapter. We will use the PC to generate commands to the BeMicro MAX10 board though the UART interface. The VHDL code in the control logic module is updated with new control logic for the SPI master. The SPI Master Module acts as a bridge between the accelerometer sensor and the control logic. Figure 14-16 shows a block diagram of the accelerometer sensor design. The design hierarchy in the Quartus will show up as in Figure 14-17.

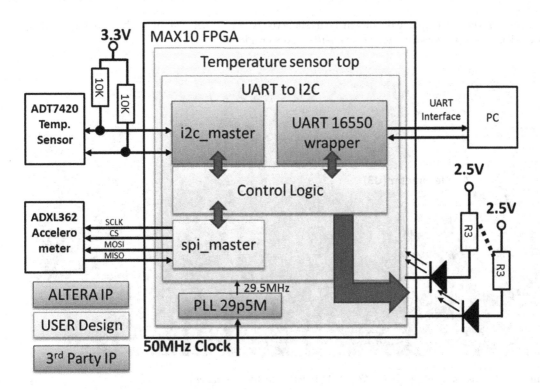

Figure 14-16. *Accelerometer sensor design block diagram*

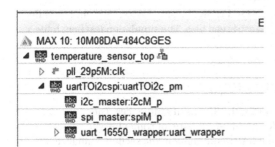

Figure 14-17. *Temperature sensor design structure*

In Figure 14-17 you can see that temperature_sensor_top is the top-level design. The top-level design replaces the uartTOi2c (from the example in Chapter 13) with the uartTOi2cspi module. The new uartTOi2cspi module is the uartTOi2c module with SPI master module (spi_master).

We are going to update the Chapter 13 design to include the Accelerometer. We will start from the lowest-level module which is uartTOi2c. We need to update three things on this module.

1. Add spi_master to the uartTOi2c.vhd

2. Add new control and status registers for the UART to control the SPI master

3. Save as a new file with a new entity name of uartTOi2cspi.vhd with the new port list (SPI)

Before moving on to update the design, let us show you where the accelerometer chip is on the BeMicro MAX10. Figure 14-18 shows the back of the board and the location of the chip.

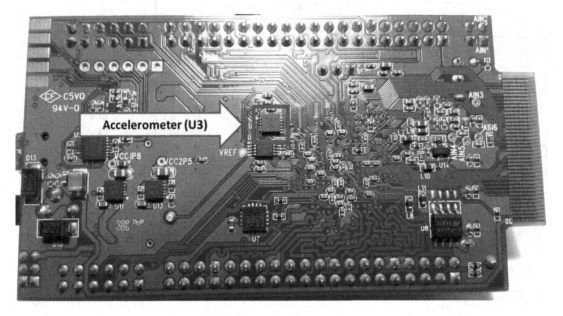

Figure 14-18. *The back side of the BeMicro MAX10 with the Accelerometer*

All of the commands and status definition are in the next.

In the example code section we will have both a new design VHDL file (`spi_master.vhd`) and modified versions of the `temperature_sensor_top.vhd` and `uartTOi2cspi.vhd` files. The simulation test bench file will be updated as an exercise for you.

14.3.1   Add New Command and Status Registers

We need two new commands and three new status registers for the SPI master interfaces. The two new command address locations are 0x0100 and 0x0101. Tables 14-1 and 14-2 are for someone who wants to get deeper into designing FPGAs. We will provide the initial UART command in the section "Initialize the Accelerometer—ADXL362."

Table 14-1. *PC UART 6-Byte Write Command Register version 2*

Address	Bit 31 downto 24			Bit 23 downto 16		Bit 15 downto 8	Bit 7 downto 0
0x0000							LED 7 downto 2
0x0010	Bit 31 I2C ena	Bit 30 2Bytes I2C CMD	Not use	Bit 23 I2C rw 1= Read 0 = Write	Bit 22 downto 16 I2C 7 Bit Address = 0x48 (ADT7420)	Second Byte to write "I2C Register Value"	First Byte to write "I2C Register Address"
0x0100				Bit 22 cpol Bit 21 CPHA Bit 16 CSPOL		Bit 15 downto 0 Clock diver	
0x0101	ENA					Bit 8 1 = Last byte	Bit 7 downto 0 Write Byte
0x8000	Need to set all zero to read back three registers						

Table 14-2. *PC UART 6-Byte Read Status Register version 2*

Address	Bit 31 downto 24	Bit 23 downto 16	Bit 15 downto 8	Bit 7 downto 0
0x0000	Not use			LED 7 downto 0
0x0010	Last command to I2C Master			
0x0011	Temperature value in degree Celsius		Raw Temperature value read from ADT7420	
0x0100	Bit 22 CPOL	Bit 21 CPHA Bit 16 CSPOL	Bit 15 downto 0 Clock divider	
0x0101	Last command to SPI Master			
0x0110		Last Read Byte	Last Read Byte	Current Read Byte

In Table 14-1, we defined that the register with the address 0x0000 can control the external LED and turn it on and off. The register gets updated to control only the top six LEDs. The low two LEDs (1 and 0) are connected to the SPI slave INT 1 and INT 2. So LED 1 and LED 0 are used to indicate the interrupts from the Accelerometer.

The register 0x0100 is used to set up the SPI master module clock speed, polarity, and clock phase. It is reported back to the status section.

The register 0x0101 is used to request the SPI master to send/receive one byte. Bit 31 is set to '1' to indicate a valid request with the write value in the bit 7 to 0. If this request is the last byte to write/read, bit 8 (the last byte) also needs to be set HIGH. This register will report back to the status section too.

The register 0x0110 status reports three bytes. These three bytes are the last three times read result from the acceleration sensor. It works like a byte shift register. On every new read request from the acceleration sensor (register 0x0101), this register will shift left by one byte (8 bits), which means that it will show the last three read bytes from the acceleration sensor. This three bytes read back are used to report the value of three axis acceleration from teh Accelerometer.

The section "Example Design Codes" will show all of the foregoing updates.

14.3.2   Create the Temperature Sensor Project Design and Program It

Copy the Chapter 13 project into a new directory and copy the following new SPI_master, uartTOi2cspi, and temperature_accelerometer_sensor_top vhdl files into the project. You should use the same method you used in Chapter 13 to build the project for the FPGA.

■ **Note**   Remember to select the temperature_accelerometer_sensor_top.vhd as the top entity design file in the project before compiling the project.

14.3.3   Example Design Codes

14.3.3.1   SPI_MASTER.VHD code

Listing 14-1 is the SPI master main module design.

Listing 14-1. spi_master.vhd

```
library ieee;
use ieee.std_logic_1164.all;
use ieee.numeric_std.all;

entity spi_master is
  port(
    clk        : in  std_logic;          --system clock
    reset_n    : in  std_logic;          --active low reset
    clk_div    : in  std_logic_vector(15 downto 0);  -- spi_sclk = clk/(clk_div x 2)
    cspol      : in  std_logic;  -- chip select polarity (0 = active low)
    cpha       : in  std_logic;
    cpol       : in  std_logic;
    ena        : in  std_logic;
    write_byte : in  std_logic_vector(7 downto 0);
```

```vhdl
      last_byte  : in  std_logic;
      read_byte  : out std_logic_vector(7 downto 0);
      done       : out std_logic;
      spi_sclk   : out std_logic;          -- run in 230kHz
      spi_cs     : out std_logic;
      spi_mosi   : out std_logic;
      spi_miso   : in  std_logic
      );
end spi_master;

architecture rtl of spi_master is

   signal ena_dly                : std_logic;
   signal running                : std_logic;
   signal count                  : unsigned(16 downto 0);  --timing for clock generation
   signal data_clk, data_clk_dly : std_logic;
   signal bit_count              : unsigned(3 downto 0);
   signal reg_shift_out          : std_logic_vector(8 downto 0);
   signal reg_shift_in           : std_logic_vector(7 downto 0);
   signal clk_div2               : unsigned(16 downto 0);
begin

   clk_div2 <= unsigned(clk_div) & '0';  -- double the clk_div value to clk_div2

   --generate the timing for the spi clock (spi_sclk) and the data clock (data_clk)
   clk_gen_p : process(clk, reset_n)
   begin
     if(reset_n = '0') then               --reset asserted
       count    <= (others => '0');
       spi_sclk <= '0';
                 data_clk <= '0';
     elsif rising_edge(clk) then
       if(count = clk_div2-1) then         --end of timing cycle
         count <= (others => '0');         --reset timer
       else
         count <= count + 1;               --continue clock generation timing
       end if;

       if(running = '1' and bit_count < 8) then
         if(count < unsigned(clk_div)) then      --first 1/2 cycle of clocking
           if(cpha = cpol) then                  -- both equal 0 or 1
             spi_sclk <= '0';
           else
             spi_sclk <= '1';
           end if;
           data_clk <= '0';
         elsif(count >= unsigned(clk_div)) then  --second 1/2 cycle of clocking
           if(cpha = cpol) then
             spi_sclk <= '1';
           else
             spi_sclk <= '0';
           end if;
```

```vhdl
          data_clk <= '1';
        end if;
      else
        spi_sclk <= cpol;
        data_clk <= '0';
      end if;
    end if;
  end if;
end process;

running_p : process (clk, reset_n)
begin
  if (reset_n = '0') then
    bit_count <= (others => '0');
    running   <= '0';
  elsif(rising_edge(clk)) then
    if(running = '1') then              -- Clear when running
      ena_dly <= '0';
    elsif(ena = '1') then
      ena_dly <= '1';
    end if;
    if(ena_dly = '1' and count = clk_div2-1) then  -- wait for the right
                                                   -- start time
      running <= '1';
    else
      if(bit_count = 8) then           -- stop running after 8 bit send out
        running <= '0';
      end if;
    end if;

    if(running = '1' and count = clk_div2-1) then
      if (bit_count < 8) then
        bit_count <= bit_count + 1;
      else
        bit_count <= (others => '0');
      end if;
    else
      if(bit_count = 8) then
        bit_count <= (others => '0');
      end if;
    end if;
  end if;
end process;

cs_p : process (clk, reset_n)
begin
  if (reset_n = '0') then
    spi_cs <= '1';
  elsif(rising_edge(clk)) then
    if(running = '0' and bit_count = 0 and last_byte = '1' and ena = '0' and ena_dly =
    '0') then
      spi_cs <= not cspol;             -- chip select is not active after the
                                       -- last byte send/receive
```

```vhdl
      elsif(ena = '1') then                    --Chip select is active when start to
                                       --send/ receive data
         spi_cs <= cspol;
      end if;
    end if;
  end process;


  --------------------------------------------------------------------------
  -- Data sending out to the MOSI is using shift register
  --------------------------------------------------------------------------
  data_out_p : process (clk, reset_n)
  begin
    if (reset_n = '0') then
      reg_shift_out <= (others => '0');
    elsif(rising_edge(clk)) then
      if(ena = '1') then
        reg_shift_out <= '0'& write_byte;
      else
        if(running = '1' and count = 0) then
          reg_shift_out <= reg_shift_out(7 downto 0)& '0';
        end if;
      end if;
    end if;

  end process;

  --------------------------------------------------------------------------
  -- Data receiving from SPI slave is shifted into shift register
  --------------------------------------------------------------------------
  data_in_p : process (clk, reset_n)
  begin
    if (reset_n = '0') then
          data_clk_dly <= '0';
      reg_shift_in <= (others => '0');
    elsif(rising_edge(clk)) then
      data_clk_dly <= data_clk;
      if(ena = '1') then
        reg_shift_in <= (others => '0');
      else
        if(running = '1' and data_clk_dly = '0' and data_clk = '1') then
          -- only shift when SPI clock is rising edge
          reg_shift_in <= reg_shift_in(6 downto 0)& spi_miso;
        end if;
      end if;
    end if;

  end process;

  spi_mosi  <= reg_shift_out(8);
  read_byte <= reg_shift_in;
  done      <= not running;

end rtl;
```

14.3.3.2 uartTOi2cspi.vhd code

This module is copied from Chapter 13's uartTOi2c.vhd file with modifications to support the SPI master. It added some commands and status registers which are described in the section "Add New Command and Status Registers." This new updated uartTOi2cspi code in Listing 14-2 also includes the new spi_master.vhd file

Listing 14-2. uartTOi2cspi.vhd vhdl

```vhdl
library ieee;
use ieee.std_logic_1164.all;
use ieee.numeric_std.all;

entity uartTOi2cspi is
  port(
    clk_uart_29MHz_i  : in   std_logic;
    uart_rst_i        : in   std_logic;
    uart_leds_o       : out  std_logic_vector(7 downto 0);
    clk_uart_monitor_o : out std_logic;
    ------------UART TX & RX----------------------------
    uart_dout_o       : out  std_logic;
    uart_din_i        : in   std_logic;
    -----------I2C interface----------------------------
    i2c_scl           : inout std_logic;   -- serial clock
    i2c_dat           : inout std_logic;  -- serial data
    -----------SPI Master interface--------------------
    spi_sclk          : out  std_logic;
    spi_csn           : out  std_logic;
    spi_mosi          : out  std_logic;
    spi_miso          : in   std_logic;
    spi_int1          : in   std_logic;
    spi_int2          : in   std_logic
    );
end uartTOi2cspi;

architecture rtl of uartTOi2cspi is
  --
  -- Internal signal declaration
  --
  signal s_rst      : std_logic;          -- main reset
  signal s_clk_uart : std_logic;          -- slow (29 MHz) clock

  -- uart control signals
  signal s_uart_br_clk          : std_logic;  -- unused clock monitor
  signal s_uart_rx_add          : std_logic_vector (15 downto 0);
  signal s_uart_rx_data         : std_logic_vector (31 downto 0);
  signal s_uart_rx_rdy          : std_logic;
  signal s_uart_rx_stb_read_data : std_logic;
  signal s_update               : std_logic;
  signal s_uart_tx_add          : std_logic_vector (15 downto 0);
  signal s_uart_tx_data         : std_logic_vector (31 downto 0);
  signal s_uart_tx_data_rdy     : std_logic;
  signal s_uart_tx_req          : std_logic;
```

```vhdl
signal s_uart_tx_stb_acq      : std_logic;
signal s_tx_complete          : std_logic;

-- address decoder signals
signal r_config_addr_uart : std_logic_vector (1 downto 0);
signal r_leds             : std_logic_vector (7 downto 0);    -- 0x0000
signal reg01              : std_logic_vector (31 downto 0);   -- 0x0010
signal reg02              : std_logic_vector (31 downto 0);   -- 0x0001
signal reg_spi_control    : std_logic_vector (31 downto 0);   -- 0x0100
signal reg_spi_write      : std_logic_vector (31 downto 0);   -- 0x0101
signal reg_spi_read       : std_logic_vector (31 downto 0);   -- 0x0110
----------------------------------
-- singals for i2c Master block --
----------------------------------
signal s_rst_n            : std_logic;
signal i2c_busy           : std_logic;
signal i2c_busy_dly       : std_logic;
signal i2c_busy_01        : std_logic;   -- rising edge of i2c_busy
signal i2cByte1           : std_logic;
signal i2c_2bytes         : std_logic;
signal data_wr            : std_logic_vector(7 downto 0);
signal data_rd            : std_logic_vector(7 downto 0);


----------------------------------
-- signals for SPI Master block --
----------------------------------
signal spi_done      : std_logic;
signal spi_done_dly  : std_logic;
signal spi_firstbyte : std_logic;
signal spi_read      : std_logic_vector(7 downto 0);
--------------------------
-- State Machine states --
--------------------------
type t_tx_reg_map is (IDLE, WAIT_A_BYTE, LATCH, TRANSMIT);
signal s_tx_fsm      : t_tx_reg_map;

begin

  s_rst   <= not uart_rst_i;            -- Change to active high reset
  s_rst_n <= uart_rst_i;                -- active low reset

  uart_leds_o <= not r_leds;            -- Output LED with '1' mean on

  s_clk_uart        <= clk_uart_29MHz_i; -- UART system clock 29.4912 MHz
  clk_uart_monitor_o <= s_uart_br_clk;

  i2c_busy_01 <= i2c_busy and not i2c_busy_dly;
  i2c_2bytes  <= reg01(30);                    -- This i2c command has 2 bytes

  -- Data write to the I2C Master depends on # of bytes operations
  data_wr <= reg01(7 downto 0) when i2cByte1 = '0' else reg01(15 downto 8);
```

```vhdl
-- UART simple register map : UART to BeMicro MAX10
register_map : process (s_rst, s_clk_uart)
begin
  if s_rst = '1' then                      -- reset all registers here
    s_uart_rx_stb_read_data <= '0';
    s_update                 <= '0';
    r_leds                   <= (others => '0');
    r_config_addr_uart       <= "10";
    reg01                    <= (others => '0');
    i2c_busy_dly             <= '0';
    i2cByte1                 <= '0';
    reg_spi_control          <= x"00000040";
    reg_spi_write            <= (others => '0');
  elsif rising_edge(s_clk_uart) then
    r_leds(1) <= spi_int2;
    r_leds(0) <= spi_int1;  -- LED0 will up when the motion detected

    i2c_busy_dly <= i2c_busy;
    if s_uart_rx_rdy = '1' then
      case (s_uart_rx_add) is
        -- Address 0x00 0x00  -- Removed the lower two bit for spi int
        when X"0000" => r_leds(7 downto 2) <= s_uart_rx_data(7 downto 2);
        -- Address 0x00 0x10
        when X"0010" => reg01               <= s_uart_rx_data;
        -- Address 0x00 0x100
        when X"0100" => reg_spi_control     <= s_uart_rx_data;
        -- Address 0x00 0x101
        when X"0101" => reg_spi_write       <= s_uart_rx_data;
        -- Address 0x80 0x00
        when X"8000" => s_update            <= '1';  -- register update self clearing
        when others  => null;
      end case;
      s_uart_rx_stb_read_data <= '1';
    else
      s_uart_rx_stb_read_data <= '0';
      s_update                <= '0';  -- register update self clearing
      -- Last byte send out to the i2C Master, then clean up data bits
      if(i2c_busy_01 = '1' and i2cByte1 = '0' and i2c_2bytes = '0') then
        reg01(29 downto 0) <= (others => '0');
      end if;
      -- After send the command to the I2C Master, then clean up command bits
      if(i2c_busy_01 = '1' and (i2cByte1 = i2c_2bytes)) then   -- 11 or 00 condition
        reg01(31 downto 30) <= (others => '0');
      end if;

      if (s_uart_rx_stb_read_data = '1') then
        i2cByte1 <= '0';  -- reset the condition after UART read request
      elsif(i2c_2bytes = '1' and i2c_busy_01 = '1') then
        -- Toggle every time i2C_busy change from low to high and two bytes operations
        i2cByte1 <= not i2cByte1;
      end if;
```

```
      -- Generate a ena pulse for SPI Master
      reg_spi_write(31) <= '0';

    end if;
  end if;
end process;

i2c_data_p : process (s_rst, s_clk_uart)
begin
  if s_rst = '1' then
    reg02(29 downto 0) <= (others => '0');
  elsif rising_edge(s_clk_uart) then
    -- when the busy is change from 1 to 0
    if(i2c_busy = '0' and i2c_busy_dly = '1') then
      -- copy the I2C data_rd to reg02(7 downto 0)
      -- and copy reg02(7 downto 0) to reg02(15 downto 0)
      reg02(15 downto 0) <= reg02(7 downto 0) & data_rd;
    end if;
    -- bit 15 to 3 is the 13 bit temperature
    -- each 1 equal 0.0625 and 0x0 equal to 0'C
    -- Only need bit 15 to 7 to read out in integer
    -- shift bits to upper bytes for easy read in degree C
    reg02(24 downto 16) <= reg02(15 downto 7);

  end if;
end process;

spi_data_p : process (s_rst, s_clk_uart)
begin
  if s_rst = '1' then
    reg_spi_read  <= (others => '0');
    spi_firstbyte <= '1';
  elsif rising_edge(s_clk_uart) then
    spi_done_dly <= spi_done;
    if(spi_done = '1' and spi_done_dly = '0') then
      if(spi_firstbyte = '1') then    -- First byte
        reg_spi_read(31 downto 8) <= (others => '0');
        reg_spi_read(7 downto 0)  <= spi_read;
      else
        reg_spi_read <= reg_spi_read(23 downto 0) & spi_read;
      end if;

      if(reg_spi_write(8) = '1') then  -- last byte
        spi_firstbyte <= '1';  -- ready for next spi read as first byte
      else
        spi_firstbyte <= '0';
      end if;
    end if;

  end if;
end process;
```

```vhdl
register_update : process (s_rst, s_clk_uart)
  variable v_uart_tx_add : unsigned (15 downto 0);
  variable v_count       : unsigned (15 downto 0);
begin
  if s_rst = '1' then                  -- reset all registers here
    s_uart_tx_data_rdy <= '0';
    s_uart_tx_req      <= '0';
    v_uart_tx_add      := (others => '0');
    v_count            := (others => '0');
    s_uart_tx_data     <= (others => '0');
    s_uart_tx_add      <= (others => '0');
    s_tx_fsm           <= IDLE;
  elsif rising_edge(s_clk_uart) then
    case s_tx_fsm is
      when IDLE =>
        if s_update = '1' then
          s_tx_fsm <= WAIT_A_BYTE;
        else
          s_tx_fsm           <= IDLE;
          s_uart_tx_data_rdy <= '0';
          s_uart_tx_req      <= '0';
          v_uart_tx_add      := (others => '0');
          v_count            := (others => '0');
          s_uart_tx_data     <= (others => '0');
          s_uart_tx_add      <= (others => '0');
        end if;
      when WAIT_A_BYTE =>
        s_uart_tx_data_rdy <= '0';
        v_count            := v_count + 1;
        if v_count = X"0900" then
          v_uart_tx_add := v_uart_tx_add + 1;
          s_tx_fsm      <= LATCH;
        else
          s_tx_fsm <= WAIT_A_BYTE;
        end if;
      when LATCH =>
        if s_uart_tx_stb_acq = '0' then
          s_uart_tx_req <= '1';
          s_uart_tx_add <= std_logic_vector (v_uart_tx_add);
          case v_uart_tx_add is
            when X"0001" => s_uart_tx_data (7 downto 0) <= r_leds;
                            s_tx_fsm <= TRANSMIT;
            -- ####################
            -- declare more registers here to READ
            -- ####################
            when X"0010" => s_uart_tx_data <= reg01;
                            s_tx_fsm <= TRANSMIT;
            when X"0011" => s_uart_tx_data <= reg02;
                            s_tx_fsm <= TRANSMIT;
            when X"0100" => s_uart_tx_data <= reg_spi_control;
                            s_tx_fsm <= TRANSMIT;
```

```vhdl
            when X"0101" => s_uart_tx_data <= reg_spi_write;
                            s_tx_fsm <= TRANSMIT;
            when X"0102" => s_uart_tx_data <= reg_spi_read;
                            s_tx_fsm <= TRANSMIT;
            -- End Of Transmission register = last register + 1
            when X"0103" => s_tx_fsm          <= IDLE;  -- end of transmission
            when others  => s_uart_tx_data <= (others => '0');
                            v_uart_tx_add       := v_uart_tx_add + 1;
                            s_uart_tx_data_rdy <= '0';
                            s_tx_fsm            <= LATCH;
          end case;
        else
          v_count  := (others => '0');
          s_tx_fsm <= WAIT_A_BYTE;
        end if;
      when TRANSMIT =>
        s_uart_tx_data_rdy <= '1';
        v_count            := (others => '0');
        s_tx_fsm           <= WAIT_A_BYTE;
      when others =>
        s_tx_fsm <= IDLE;
    end case;
  end if;
end process;

uart_wrapper : entity work.uart_16550_wrapper
  port map(
    sys_clk_i               => s_clk_uart,
    sys_rst_i               => s_rst,
    echo_en_i               => r_config_addr_uart(0),
    tx_addr_wwo_i           => r_config_addr_uart(1),
    uart_din_i              => uart_din_i,
    uart_dout_o             => uart_dout_o,
    s_br_clk_uart_o         => s_uart_br_clk,
    v_rx_add_o              => s_uart_rx_add,
    v_rx_data_o             => s_uart_rx_data,
    s_rx_rdy_o              => s_uart_rx_rdy,
    s_rx_stb_read_data_i    => s_uart_rx_stb_read_data,
    s_tx_proc_rqst_i        => s_uart_tx_req,
    v_tx_add_ram_i          => s_uart_tx_add,
    v_tx_data_ram_i         => s_uart_tx_data,
    s_tx_ram_data_rdy_i     => s_uart_tx_data_rdy,
    s_tx_stb_ram_data_acq_o => s_uart_tx_stb_acq
    );

i2cM_p : entity work.i2c_master
  generic map(
    input_clk => 29_491_200,  --input clock speed from user logic in Hz
    bus_clk   => 100_000)     --speed the i2c bus (scl) will run at in Hz
  port map(
    clk        => s_clk_uart,          --system clock
```

```
      reset_n  => s_rst_n,              --active low reset
      ena      => reg01(31),            --latch in command
      addr     => reg01(22 downto 16),  --address of target slave
      rw       => reg01(23),            --'0' is write, '1' is read
      data_wr  => data_wr,              --data to write to slave
      busy     => i2c_busy,             --indicates transaction in progress
      data_rd  => data_rd,              --data read from slave
      ack_error => reg02(30),    --flag if improper acknowledge from slave
      sda      => i2c_dat,              --serial data output of i2c bus
      scl      => i2c_scl);             --serial clock output of i2c bus

  spiM_p : entity work.spi_master
    port map(
      clk        => s_clk_uart,
      reset_n    => s_rst_n,
      clk_div    => reg_spi_control(15 downto 0),
      cspol      => reg_spi_control(16),  -- chip select polarity (0 = active low)
      cpha       => reg_spi_control(21),
      cpol       => reg_spi_control(22),
      ena        => reg_spi_write(31),
      write_byte => reg_spi_write(7 downto 0),
      last_byte  => reg_spi_write(8),
      read_byte  => spi_read,
      done       => spi_done,
      spi_sclk   => spi_sclk,           -- run in 230kHz
      spi_cs     => spi_csn,
      spi_mosi   => spi_mosi,
      spi_miso   => spi_miso);

end architecture rtl;
```

14.3.3.3   Temperature_accelerometer_sensor_top.vhd Code

The code in Listing 14-3 is the top-level design file for this project. It has the system clock (50 MHz) input and ADT7420 IC interfaces which include I2C SCL and SDA wires. The USER_LED is included for fun. The purpose of this module is to connect all of the external wires to the correct modules and to generate the correct clock (29.5 MHz) for the uartTOi2c module. Please read the comments to better understand the details of the design. We will simulate the design later and so you should have a better idea how it works after that.

Listing 14-3. Temperature Sensor Top-Level Design VHDL File

```
library ieee;
use ieee.std_logic_1164.all;

entity temperature_accelerometer_sensor_top is
  port(
    -- Clock ins, SYS_CLK = 50MHz
    SYS_CLK : in std_logic;

    -- Temperature sensor, I2C interface (ADT7420)
```

```
    ADT7420_CT  : in    std_logic; -- NOT USE
    ADT7420_INT : in    std_logic; -- NOT USE
    ADT7420_SCL : inout std_logic;
    ADT7420_SDA : inout std_logic;
    -- The following is added for chapter 14 SPI interface
    -- Accelerometer, 3-Axis, SPI interface (ADXL362)
    ADXL362_CS : out std_logic;
    ADXL362_INT1 : in    std_logic;
    ADXL362_INT2 : in    std_logic;
    ADXL362_MISO : in    std_logic;
    ADXL362_MOSI : out std_logic;
    ADXL362_SCLK : out std_logic;
    -- LED outs
    USER_LED : out std_logic_vector(8 downto 1);

    GPIO_J3_39 : out std_logic;         -- UART TX
    GPIO_J3_40 : in  std_logic          -- UART RX
    );

end entity temperature_ ACCELEROMETER_sensor_top;

architecture arch of temperature_ ACCELEROMETER_sensor_top is

  signal locked, clk_uart_29MHz_i, uart_rst_i : std_logic:= '0';
  signal delay_8: std_logic_vector(7 downto 0);

begin

  clk : entity work.pll_29p5M
    port map
    (
      inclk0 => SYS_CLK,          -- 50MHz clock input
      c0     => clk_uart_29MHz_i,-- 29.5MHz clock ouput
      locked => locked            -- Lock condition, 1 = Locked
      );

 dealy_p:  process(SYS_CLK)
  begin
  if(rising_edge(SYS_CLK) )THEN
  delay_8 <= delay_8(6 downto 0)&locked; -- create active LOW reset
END IF;
END PROCESS;

uart_rst_i <= delay_8(7);
-- Replace the module uartTOi2c with uartTOi2cspi for chapter 14
  uartTOi2c_pm : entity work.uartTOi2cspi
    port map(
      clk_uart_29MHz_i    => clk_uart_29MHz_i,
      uart_rst_i          => uart_rst_i,
      uart_leds_o         => USER_LED,
      clk_uart_monitor_o => open,
```

```
    uart_dout_o       => GPIO_J3_39,      -- yellow colour wire
    uart_din_i        => GPIO_J3_40,      -- orange colour wire
    i2c_scl           => ADT7420_SCL,
    i2c_dat           => ADT7420_SDA ,
    spi_sclk          => ADXL362_SCLK,
    spi_csn           => ADXL362_CS,
    spi_mosi          => ADXL362_MOSI,
    spi_miso          => ADXL362_MISO,
    spi_int1          => ADXL362_INT1,
    spi_int2          => ADXL362_INT2
    );
```

```
end architecture arch;
```

14.3.4   Hardware Setup for the Accelerator Sensor Project Design

1.   Use the exact same hardware setup as in Chapter 13. Follow the section "Hardware Setup for the Temperature Sensor Project Design" in Chapter 13 if you need a reminder or if you skipped that chapter.

2.   You can now connect the programmer USB cable to directly upload the image to the FPGA.

3.   Connect the USB side of the USB to UART cable to the PC.

4.   Connect the FPGA programmer.

5.   The next step is to use RealTerm to send requests to the SPI and read-back registers

14.3.5   Initialize the Accelerometer—ADXL362

Step 1: Send a status request command to the board to check that the connection is set up correctly.
    Command = 0x80 0x00 0x00 0x00 0x00 0x00
    You should able to see the read-back as in Figure 14-19.

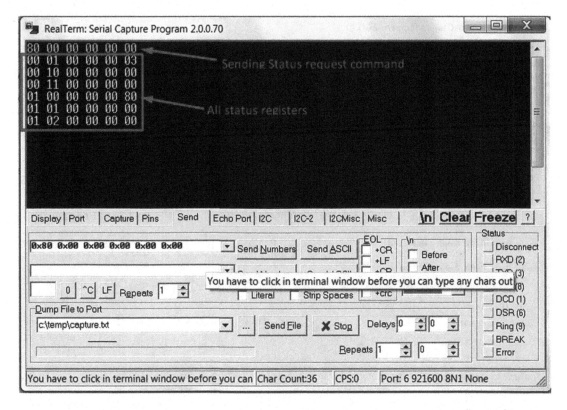

Figure 14-19. *Send a status request command and see the status coming back*

Step 2: Set the SPI master clock speed, clock polarity, and phase. Figure 14-20 shows the setup command and status being read back.

Command = 0x01 0x00 0x00 0x00 0x00 0x40

This command setting the clk_div is 0x40. By the equation we shared earlier in the chapter, the SPI SCLK will run at 230.5 kHz.

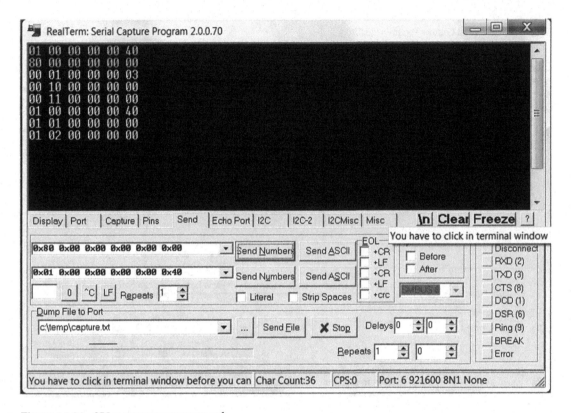

Figure 14-20. *SPI master setup commands*

Step 3: This step is based on the ADXL362 datasheet to enable "applications information autonomous motion switch" with startup routine.

Following is the command list to program the ADXL362 register from 0x20 to 0x26 (Figure 14-21 shows the commands):

1. 0x01 0x01 0x80 0x00 0x00 0x0a 0x01 0x01 0x80 0x00 0x00 0x20 0x01
    0x01 0x80 0x00 0x00 0xFA

2. 0x01 0x01 0x80 0x00 0x00 0x00 0x01 0x01 0x80 0x00 0x00 0x02 0x01
    0x01 0x80 0x00 0x00 0x96

3. 0x01 0x01 0x80 0x00 0x00 0x00 0x01 0x01 0x80 0x00 0x00 0x1E 0x01
    0x01 0x80 0x00 0x01 0x00

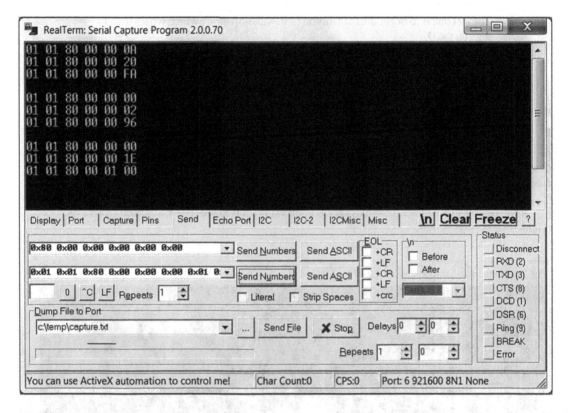

Figure 14-21. *SPI master setup commands—2*

4. Write 0x3F to Register 0x27 which configures motion detection in loop mode and enables referenced activity and inactivity detection.

    0x01 0x01 0x80 0x00 0x00 0x0a 0x01 0x01 0x80 0x00 0x00 0x27 0x01
    0x01 0x80 0x00 0x01 0x3f

5. Write 0x00 to register 0x28 and 0x80 to register 0x29 to configure FIFO.

    0x01 0x01 0x80 0x00 0x00 0x0a 0x01 0x01 0x80 0x00 0x00 0x28 0x01
    0x01 0x80 0x00 0x00 0x00 0x01 0x01 0x80 0x00 0x01 0x80

6. Write 0x40 to register 0x2a and 0x01 to register 0x2b to map AWAKE bit to the INT2.

    0x01 0x01 0x80 0x00 0x00 0x0a 0x01 0x01 0x80 0x00 0x00 0x2a 0x01
    0x01 0x80 0x00 0x00 0x40 0x01 0x01 0x80 0x00 0x01

7. Write 0x13 to register 0x2c to configure general device settings.

    0x01 0x01 0x80 0x00 0x00 0x0a 0x01 0x01 0x80 0x00 0x00 0x2c 0x01
    0x01 0x80 0x00 0x01 0x13

8. The last one is to begin the measurement in wake-up mode which writes 0x0a to register 0x2D.

```
0x01 0x01 0x80 0x00 0x00 0x0a 0x01 0x01 0x80 0x00 0x00 0x2d 0x01
0x01 0x80 0x00 0x01 0x0a
```

Five seconds after the last command, all of the LEDs should be off. You can to shake the board to see what happens. LED 0 will turn on when the device is AWAKE.

Send the following command:

```
0x01 0x01 0x80 0x00 0x00 0x0b 0x01 0x01 0x80 0x00 0x00 0x08 0x01 0x01 0x80 0x00 0x00 0x00
0x01 0x01 0x80 0x00 0x00 0x00 0x01 0x01 0x80 0x00 0x01 0x00
0x80 0x00 0x00 0x00 0x00 0x00
```

It will be able to read back three axis acceleration values. A is X-axis, B is Y-axis, and C is Z-axis (Figure 14-22).

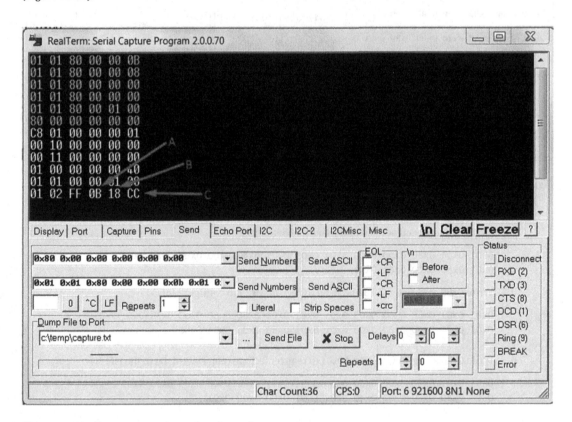

Figure 14-22. Request xyz-axis acceleration value

14.4   Summary

In this chapter, we showed you the steps to create your own interface IP and we created a complicated command list for the SPI from the UART interface. It is important to define the requirements first and then define the port list. The last step is going to create the VHDL process (sequential and combination logic) based on the requirements.

We created a generic SPI master interface module. It supports a very wide range of SPI clock frequencies and it is programmable at runtime. The module only does one byte at a time, which is the basic unit for SPI interfaces. This allows higher-level software/hardware to create different read/write operations for different SPI slaves.

In the SPI master module, we only used one 17-bit counter, one 4-bit counter, two 8-bit shift registers, and some registers. This helps to demonstrate that creating an interface module is not all that difficult.

"The only way to do great work is to love what you do."

—Steve Jobs

PART IV

Taking It Further: Talking to the Raspberry Pi and LED Displays

■ ■ ■

## CHAPTER 15

Two-Way Communications with Your Raspberry Pi: SPI

15.1 Introduction

We are going to use the Raspberry PI SPI (Serial Peripheral Interface) master to control the BeMicro MAX10 LEDs (light-emitting diodes). We need to design an SPI slave interface in the FPGA (field-programmable gate array) to let the Raspberry PI control the LEDs on the board. In the following section, we will show you how to connect a Raspberry Pi to BeMicro MAX10 board, design an SPI slave for the FPGA, and write a simple Python script to run on the Raspberry Pi that will do two-way communication on the SPI interface.

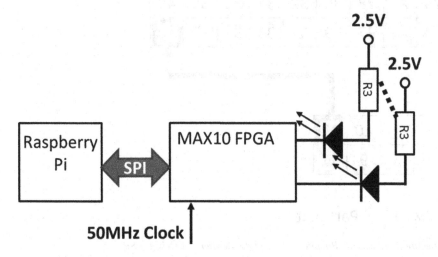

Figure 15-1. SPI two-way communication between Raspberry Pi and MAX10 FPGA block diagram

15.2 Define Our SPI Slave Interface for the Raspberry Pi

We are going to design a four-pin SPI slave device for the FPGA. The four pins are clock, slave select (or chip select), MOSI (master output slave input), and MISO (master input slave output). In Chapter 13, we had the same signals but in reverse. In this design, the clock, slave select, and MOSI are inputs to the FPGA and MISO is an output from FPGA.

There are some general purpose input/output pins (GPIO) on the BeMicro MAX10 board labeled pin header 5 (J5). We need to find four pins available from J5 for the SPI to use. Table 15-1 shows the pins we selected from the FPGA and Raspberry Pi. We will use the Raspberry Pi SPI0 CE1 Master to talk with the FPGA SPI slave on J5. Figure 15-2 shows both the FPGA and Raspberry Pi pin locations with color codes. Black is the ground. It is very important to connect the ground pins first before you make another pin connection. Yellow is the CLOCK. Orange is the SLAVE SELECT. RED is the MOSI. BROWN is the MISO. The same color jumper wires are used to connect them to the breadboard. There is one more color, BLACK, in Figure 15-2.

Table 15-1. *Pin Definition on Both FPGA and Raspberry*

	FPGA J5	Raspberry PI Pin
CLOCK	GPIO _01 - Pin 1	SPI0 SCLK - Pin 23
SLAVE SELELCT	GPIO _03 - Pin 3	SPI0 CE1 - Pin 26
MOSI	GPIO _02 - Pin 2	SPI0 MOSI - Pin 19
MISO	GPIO _04 - Pin 4	SPI0 MISO - Pin 21
GROUND	Pin 12	Pin 39

Raspberry Pi Pin Out - Part of it

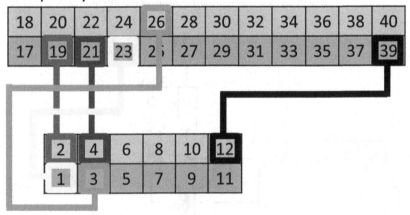

BeMicro MAX10 J5 – Part of it

Figure 15-2. *Cable connection between the Raspberry Pi and the BeMicro MAX10 for SPI*

■ **Note** Before making any connection between two boards, make sure both of them are powered off and connect the ground between the two boards first! The jumper J1 and jumper J9 on the BeMicro MAX10 board provide a selection of 2.5V or 3.3V for the pin header 5 (J5). Both of them need to be set to 3.3V. (Figure 15-3 in the lower right corner shows the correct jumper locations: near the edge of the board.) Pin 39 on the Raspberry Pi and J5 pin 12 on the BeMicro MAX10 are both grounds.

Figure 15-3. *SPI slave example wires set up with Raspberry Pi SPI 0 CE1 Master*

15.3 Design SPI Slave in FPGA

We are going create a new project from the BeMax10 template which is from the section "Write Code" in Chapter 4, and it is similar to Chapter 14. This design will have three modules: (1) SPI slave module which is a new design (spi_slave.vhd); one Altera PLL IP (pll_29p5M), which is the same PLL (phase-locked loop) from Chapter 13; and a new top-level module which is raspberryPi_spi_top.vhd. Figure 15-4 shows all the modules need for this chapter design. We are going to describe how to design the new SPI slave module in this chapter. First we have to define what we need to design in the SPI slave (the requirements) and then we can design it in next section.

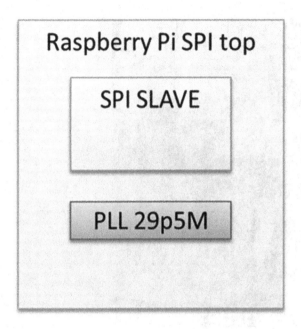

Figure 15-4. Modules needed in this chapter

We are going to define the SPI slave input and output ports, review Raspberry Pi SPI master, and then define the detail requirements for the SPI slave.

15.3.1   New SPI Slave Module Port List

The new SPI slave (spi_slave.vhd) is used to receive SPI-formatted messages from the Raspberry Pi SPI master and translate them to READ or WRITE commands. Therefore, the spi_slave module needs to have an SPI slave with 4-pin ports and a read/write register interface. Table 15-2 shows the basic port list names and functions. Figure 15-5 is the actual VHDL port list.

Table 15-2. spi_slave.vhd Port List

Name	Type	Function
sys_clock	std_logic	29.5 MHz clock
sys_rst	Std_logic	Active Low reset (logic 0 is reset)
rspi_sclk	Std_logic	SPI interface clock
rspi_ss	Std_logic	SPI interface slave select
rspi_mosi	Std_logic	SPI interface master out slave in
rspi_miso	Std_logic	SPI interface master in slave out
wr_enable	Std_logic	Back-end byte write enable Data_out is valid when wr_enable is High (1)
data_out	Std_logic_vector(7 downto 0)	Back-end byte write data
data_in	Std_logic_vector(7 downto 0)	Back-end byte read data

```
1    library IEEE;
2    use IEEE.STD_LOGIC_1164.all;
3    use IEEE.STD_LOGIC_ARITH.all;
4    use IEEE.STD_LOGIC_UNSIGNED.all;
5
6  ⊟entity spi_slave is
7  ⊟  port(
8        -- general purpose
9        sys_clock : in std_logic; -- system clock
10       sys_rst : in std_logic;   -- system reset active low
11       -- serial I/O side
12       rspi_sclk : in  std_logic; -- SPI clock from raspberry SPI Master
13       rspi_ss   : in  std_logic; -- SPI chip select from raspberry SPI Master
14       rspi_mosi : in  std_logic; -- SPI data from raspberry SPI Master
15       rspi_miso : out std_logic; -- SPI data to raspberry SPI Master
16       -- Register read/write interface
17       wr_enable : out std_logic; -- Write Enable: Data_out data is valid
18       data_out  : out std_logic_vector(7 downto 0); -- 8 Bit data from raspberry
19       data_in   : in  std_logic_vector(7 downto 0)  -- 8 bit data read back
20       );
21   end entity;
```

Figure 15-5. *Port list for the new SPI slave module*

15.3.2   Raspberry Pi SPI Master 0 Default Setting and Data Format

The Raspberry Pi Python SPI library (SPIDEV) has the following default settings: clock speed is 500 kHz, slave select is active low, data change is clock falling edge, and data capture is rising edge. Figure 15-6 shows the default settings of the Raspberry Pi SPI master. In this example we added a simple protocol for READ and WRITE on top of the simple SPI byte transfer.

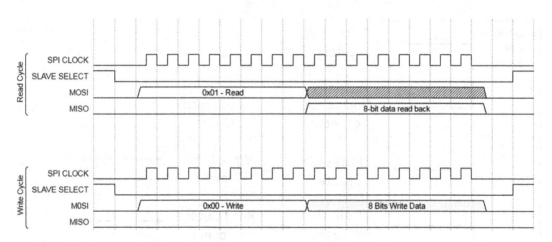

Figure 15-6. *Raspberry Pi SPI Master 0 interface*

Figure 15-6 also shows the protocols. The top one shows a read cycle. The SPI master (Raspberry Pi) first byte is 0x01 and the SPI slave (FPGA) needs to send out one byte with the following eight clock cycles. The bottom of Figure 15-6 shows a write cycle. The first and second bytes are sent from the SPI master (Raspberry PI). The first byte is 0x0 to indicate a write cycle and the second byte is the byte from Raspberry Pi written to the FPGA. We will use this byte to control the onboard LEDs.

351

15.3.3   Writing VHDL for the SPI Slave

The SPI slave has two functions. The first is receiving two bytes from the SPI master and sending a one-byte status during the read cycle. The second is generating a pulse with one-byte data from Raspberry which is used by another module to control the LEDs. The pulse is set high when the data from Raspberry is valid.

We will divide the SPI slave into the following six processes (functions):

1.   SPI clock edge detection which is used to generate a one-clock cycle pulse when an SPI clock rising edge or falling edge occurs.

2.   SPI clock cycle counter which is used to count 16 cycles (two bytes).

3.   SPI in which an 8-bit shift register is used to shift one bit of SPI master data into the FPGA when the rising edge of SPI clock occurs.

4.   Read/write cycle which is used to detect write cycles or read cycles after the first eight bits from from the SPI master are received.

5.   Write input process which generates a pulse (wr_enable), registers the byte from Raspberry SPI master, and sends it to the other module through output port data_out.

6.   Read output is an 8-bit shift register to shift out one bit to the SPI master when the falling edge of the SPI clock occurs.

Figure 15-7 shows the block diagram of the SPI slave design.

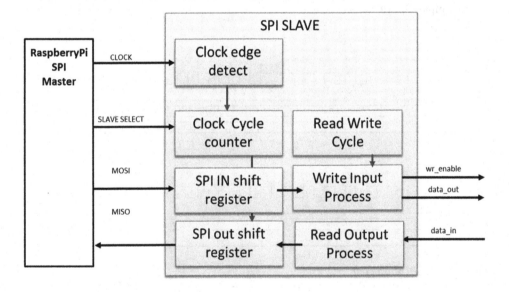

Figure 15-7. SPI slave block diagram

We will need to create seven signals in the spi_slave module and we need to put the code in between architecture and begin. Figure 15-8 shows all seven of the signals and their definitions.

```
27  architecture arch of spi_slave is
28
29      signal spi_clk_rising_edge   : std_logic;
30      signal spi_clk_falling_edge  : std_logic;
31      signal spi_write_cycle       : std_logic;
32      signal spi_clk_dly_line      : std_logic_vector(2 downto 0);
33      signal spi_clk_count         : unsigned(5 downto 0);   -- count # of clock cycles
34      signal spi_datain_shifter    : std_logic_vector(7 downto 0);
35      signal spi_dataout_shifter   : std_logic_vector(7 downto 0);
36
37  begin
```

Figure 15-8. Signals needed for SPI slave design

15.3.3.1   SPI Clock Edge Detection

In a lot of applications, we will not directly use the clock from outside the FPGA. If the outside clock is four times slower than the FPGA clock, then we can use the following method to generate a virtual clock edge inside the FPGA. We don't need to have a reset for this process because the outputs of this process (spi_clk_rising_edge and spi_clk_falling_edge) are not going to create trouble for other logic in this module. Figure 15-9 is the clock edge detection logic process VHDL (VHSIC (very high speed integrated circuit) Hardware Description Language).

```
39  -- edge detection process
40  -- This method require sys_clock is at least 4 times faster than spi clock
41  spi_clk_edge_detect_p : process(sys_clock)
42      begin
43      if(rising_edge(sys_clock)) then
44          -- delay spi_clk three system clock cycles
45          spi_clk_dly_line <= spi_clk_dly_line(1 downto 0) & rspi_sclk;
46
47          -- Rising edge detected when two clock cycles low and then two clock cycles High
48          if(spi_clk_dly_line(2) = '0' and spi_clk_dly_line(1) = '0' and
49              spi_clk_dly_line(0) = '1' and rspi_sclk = '1') then
50              spi_clk_rising_edge <= '1';
51          else
52              spi_clk_rising_edge <= '0';
53          end if;
54          -- Falling edge detected when two clock cycles high and then two clock cycles Low
55          if(spi_clk_dly_line(2) = '1' and spi_clk_dly_line(1) = '1' and
56              spi_clk_dly_line(0) = '0' and rspi_sclk = '0') then
57              spi_clk_falling_edge <= '1';
58          else
59              spi_clk_falling_edge <= '0';
60          end if;
61      end if;
62  end process;
63
```

Figure 15-9. SPI clock edge detection VHDL code

On line 45, we use a 3-bit shift register (spi_clk_dly_line) to sample the rspi_sclk by sys_clock. When the change of the rspi_sclk is sampled and stored in the shift register we can do all the clock edge detection logic in sys_clock domain. Figure 15-10 shows that the rising edge detection pulse is delayed two sys_clock clock cycles. It is expected when we use a fast clock to sample a slow clock and do the clock edge detection. The spi_clk_dly_line (2), (1), and (0) are storing the history of the rspi_sclk. We defined the rising edge as when (2) and (1) are logic low and at the clock cycle (0) and rspi_sclk are logic high.

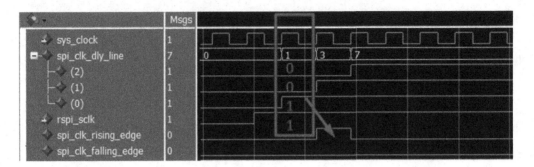

Figure 15-10. Rising edge detection simulation

Figure 15-11 shows the falling edge detection simulation. It uses the same concept of edge detection as rising edge. It only changes the logic value.

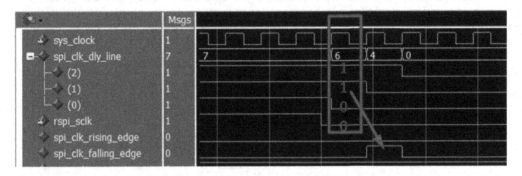

Figure 15-11. Falling edge detection simulation

This clock edge logic works like a clock tick for the rest of the logic.

15.3.3.2   SPI Clock Cycle Counter—Simple Counter

We know that every SPI transfer is started by the slave select (spi_ss) and each transfer is going to have 16 clock cycles, which means 16 rising edges. Figure 15-12 shows that the counter (spi_clk_count) gets reset to zero when slave select is logic High. The counter starts counting when slave select is Low and SPI clock rising edge happens. It will count to 16 and then reset to zero. We will use this counter to detect when the first byte (counter value is 8) or second byte (counter value is 16) is done.

```
64   spi_clock_cycles_counter_p : process(sys_clock)
65   begin
66      if(rising_edge(sys_clock)) then
67         if(rspi_ss = '1') then  -- reset counter to zero when not chip select
68            spi_clk_count <= (others =>'0');
69         else
70            if(spi_clk_rising_edge = '1') then  -- every rising edge add one
71               if(spi_clk_count = 16) then
72                  spi_clk_count <= (others => '0');
73               else
74                  spi_clk_count <= spi_clk_count + 1;
75               end if;
76            end if;
77         end if;
78      end if;
79   end process;
80
```

Figure 15-12. *SPI clock cycle counter VHDL code*

15.3.3.3   SPI Data in 8-Bit Shift Register

The Raspberry Pi SPI master changes the MOSI data line when SPI clock is falling edge, which means the MOSI data is not stable at that time. We wait a half clock cycle to let the MOSI stabilize so we should shift in the data when SPI clock is rising edge, which is stable for shift data in. Figure 15-13 shows the spi_in_p process shift rspi_mosi data in to the spi_datain_shifter register when spi_clk_rising_edge is equal to '1.' We don't need to clear the spi_datain_shifter because we only use it when the spi_clk_count is equal to 8.

```
81   -- Every time SPI chip select go low, it will have 16 bit data (Read/Write(8bit)+data(8it)
82   spi_in_p : process(sys_clock)
83   begin
84      if(rising_edge(sys_clock)) then
85         if(spi_clk_rising_edge = '1') then
86            spi_datain_shifter <= spi_datain_shifter(6 downto 0) & rspi_mosi;
87         end if;
88      end if;
89   end process;
90
```

Figure 15-13. *SPI data in 8-bit shift register VHDL code*

15.3.3.4   Read/Write Cycle

Once the first eight bits of SPI DATA are in the shift register (spi_datain_shifter), we can design it is a read cycle or write cycle. We need to make this decision when the spi_clk_counter is equal to 8 and the spi_clk_falling_edge is '1.' This allows us enough time before the ninth rising clock edge comes in. Figure 15-14 shows the VHDL code that will set the spi_write_cycle equal to '1' when we receive a byte value of 0x00 in the first byte from the Master SPI. The spi_write_cycle value will remain stable until the slave select is equal to '1' which is when the cycle is finished.

```
91   read_write_cycle_p: process(sys_clock, sys_rst)
92   begin
93   if(sys_rst = '0') then
94       spi_write_cycle <= '0';
95   elsif(rising_edge(sys_clock))then
96       if(rspi_ss = '1') then
97           spi_write_cycle <= '0';
98       elsif(spi_clk_count = 8 and spi_datain_shifter = x"00" and spi_clk_falling_edge = '1') then
99           spi_write_cycle <= '1';
100      end if;
101  end if;
102  end process;
103
```

Figure 15-14. *Read/write cycle VHDL code*

15.3.3.5   Write Input Process

The second eight bits from MOSI will continue to shift in to the spi_datain_shifter after read_write_cycle_p decides whether the current cycle is a write or read cycle. When the current cycle is a write cycle (spi_write_cycle = '1') and all of the second eight bits are shifted in to the spi_datain_shifter (line 112 in Figure 15-15), write_input_p will generate a pulse on wr_enable and copy the spi_datain_shifter 8-bit data to the data_out port. data_out will keep the value until the next write cycle. Figure 15-15 shows one of the ways to create this write input process.

```
104  write_input_p: process(sys_clock, sys_rst)
105  begin
106      if(sys_rst = '0') then
107      wr_enable <= '0';
108      data_out   <= (others =>'0');
109      elsif(rising_edge(sys_clock))then
110          if(rspi_ss = '1') then
111              wr_enable <= '0';
112          elsif( spi_clk_count = 16 and spi_write_cycle = '1' and spi_clk_falling_edge = '1') then
113              wr_enable <= '1';
114              data_out <= spi_datain_shifter;
115          else
116              wr_enable <= '0';
117          end if;
118      end if;
119  end process;
120
```

Figure 15-15. *Write input process VHDL code*

15.3.3.6   Read Output

If the first byte from Raspberry Pi, which is stored in spi_datain_shifter, is equal to 0x01(hex), which means read cycle, then it is time to provide a byte to Raspberry Pi. It copies the FPGA data (data_in) from other logic to an 8-bit shift register (spi_dataout_shifter).

In Figure 15-16, lines 130-131, shift the data to the left (high bit) when SPI clock is falling edge after it copied the FPGA data_in to the shift register. Line 136 connects the most significant bit of the shift register (bit 7) to the rspi_miso pin which connected to Raspberry Pi 3 SPI data input.

```
121 ┌  read_output_p : process(sys_clock, sys_rst)
122 │  begin
123 ┌    if(sys_rst = '0') then
124 ├      spi_dataout_shifter    <= (others => '0');
125 ┌    elsif(rising_edge(sys_clock))then
126 │
127 ┌      if(spi_clk_count = 8 and spi_datain_shifter = x"01" and spi_clk_falling_edge = '1') then
128 │        spi_dataout_shifter <= data_in;
129 │
130 ┌      elsif(spi_clk_falling_edge = '1') then
131 │        spi_dataout_shifter <= spi_dataout_shifter(6 downto 0)& '0';
132 ├      end if;
133 ├    end if;
134 │  end process;
135 │
136 │  rspi_miso <= spi_dataout_shifter(7);  -- msb send to the SPI master
137 │
138 │ end arch;
139 └
```

Figure 15-16. *Read output process VHDL code*

Listing 15-1 provides the whole spi_slave module VHDL design file.

Listing 15-1. spi_slave.vhd

```
library IEEE;
use IEEE.STD_LOGIC_1164.all;
use IEEE.STD_LOGIC_ARITH.all;
use IEEE.STD_LOGIC_UNSIGNED.all;

entity spi_slave is
  port(
    -- general purpose
    sys_clock : in std_logic; -- system clock
    sys_rst : in std_logic;   -- system reset active low
    -- serial I/O side
    rspi_sclk : in  std_logic; -- SPI clock from raspberry SPI Master
    rspi_ss   : in  std_logic; -- SPI chip select from raspberry SPI Master
    rspi_mosi : in  std_logic; -- SPI data from raspberry SPI Master
    rspi_miso : out std_logic; -- SPI data to raspberry SPI Master
    -- Register read/write interface
    wr_enable : out std_logic; -- Write Enable: Data_out data is valid
        data_out  : out std_logic_vector(7 downto 0); -- 8 Bit data from raspberry
        data_in   : in  std_logic_vector(7 downto 0)  -- 8 bit data read back
    );
end entity;


--===============================================================================
-- architecture declaration
--===============================================================================


architecture arch of spi_slave is

  signal spi_clk_rising_edge  : std_logic;
  signal spi_clk_falling_edge : std_logic;
  signal spi_write_cycle      : std_logic;
  signal spi_clk_dly_line     : std_logic_vector(2 downto 0);
```

```vhdl
  signal spi_clk_count         : unsigned(5 downto 0);  -- count # of clock cycles
  signal spi_datain_shifter    : std_logic_vector(7 downto 0);
  signal spi_dataout_shifter   : std_logic_vector(7 downto 0);

begin

-- edge detection process
-- This method require sys_clock is at least 4 times faster than spi clock
  spi_clk_edge_detect_p : process(sys_clock)
  begin
    if(rising_edge(sys_clock)) then
          -- delay spi_clk three system clock cycles
      spi_clk_dly_line <= spi_clk_dly_line(1 downto 0) & rspi_sclk;

              -- Rising edge detected when two clock cycles low and then two clock cycles
                High
              if(spi_clk_dly_line(2) = '0' and spi_clk_dly_line(1) = '0' and
                spi_clk_dly_line(0) = '1' and rspi_sclk = '1') then
        spi_clk_rising_edge <= '1';
      else
        spi_clk_rising_edge <= '0';
      end if;
              -- Falling edge detected when two clock cycles high and then two clock
                cycles Low
      if(spi_clk_dly_line(2) = '1' and spi_clk_dly_line(1) = '1' and
                spi_clk_dly_line(0) = '0' and rspi_sclk = '0') then
        spi_clk_falling_edge <= '1';
      else
        spi_clk_falling_edge <= '0';
      end if;
    end if;
  end process;

  spi_clock_cycles_counter_p : process(sys_clock)
  begin
    if(rising_edge(sys_clock)) then
      if(rspi_ss = '1') then  -- reset counter to zero when not chip select
        spi_clk_count <= (others =>'0');
      else
        if(spi_clk_rising_edge = '1') then  -- every rising edge add one
          if(spi_clk_count = 16) then
            spi_clk_count <= (others => '0');
          else
            spi_clk_count <= spi_clk_count + 1;
          end if;
        end if;
      end if;
    end if;
  end process;
```

```vhdl
-- Every time SPI chip select go low, it will have 16 bit data (Read/Write(8bit)+data(8it)
  spi_in_p : process(sys_clock)
  begin
    if(rising_edge(sys_clock)) then
      if(spi_clk_rising_edge = '1') then
        spi_datain_shifter <= spi_datain_shifter(6 downto 0) & rspi_mosi;
      end if;
    end if;
  end process;

  read_write_cycle_p: process(sys_clock, sys_rst)
  begin
  if(sys_rst = '0') then
                spi_write_cycle <= '0';
        elsif(rising_edge(sys_clock))then
                if(rspi_ss = '1') then
                        spi_write_cycle <= '0';
                elsif(spi_clk_count = 8 and spi_datain_shifter = x"00" and spi_clk_falling_
                edge = '1') then
                        spi_write_cycle <= '1';
                end if;
        end if;
  end process;

  write_input_p: process(sys_clock, sys_rst)
  begin
    if(sys_rst = '0') then
     wr_enable <= '0';
          data_out  <= (others =>'0');
    elsif(rising_edge(sys_clock))then
     if(rspi_ss = '1') then
                        wr_enable <= '0';
          elsif( spi_clk_count = 16 and spi_write_cycle = '1' and spi_clk_falling_edge =
          '1') then
          wr_enable <= '1';
                        data_out <= spi_datain_shifter;
      else
          wr_enable <= '0';
      end if;
    end if;
  end process;

  read_output_p : process(sys_clock, sys_rst)
  begin
    if(sys_rst = '0') then
      spi_dataout_shifter      <= (others => '0');
    elsif(rising_edge(sys_clock))then

      if(spi_clk_count = 8 and spi_datain_shifter = x"01" and spi_clk_falling_edge = '1')
      then
        spi_dataout_shifter <= data_in;
```

```
      elsif(spi_clk_falling_edge = '1') then
        spi_dataout_shifter <= spi_dataout_shifter(6 downto 0)& '0';
      end if;
    end if;
  end process;

  rspi_miso <= spi_dataout_shifter(7);   -- msb send to the SPI master

end arch;


--==============================================================================
-- architecture end
--==============================================================================
```

15.4   Create the FPGA Top-Level Design

We need to have a top-level design to use the output from the SPI slave to control the LEDs on the BeMicro MAX10 board. The top-level design should look like Figure 15-17. The top design includes the SPI slave, SPI data register, and the Altera PLL IP (Internet Protocol).

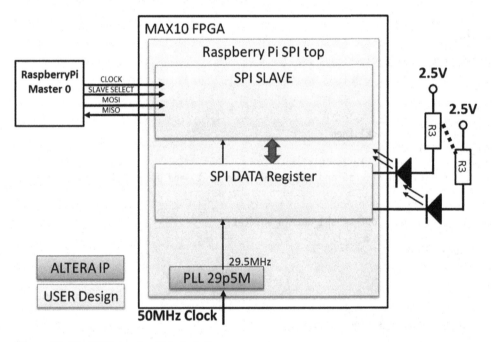

Figure 15-17. *FPGA top-level block design*

We will reuse the same PLL from Chapter 13 which is 50 MHz in and generate a 29.5 MHz clock out. The SPI slave and SPI data register will directly use this output clock as a system clock.

The SPI DATA register is updated by the SPI slave wr_enable output. The value of the register will be used to drive the LED outputs.

15.4.1   Top-Level Design VHDL Code

Figures 15-18 and 15-19 are the top-level design. Lines 12 to 15 are the port list for the SPI to the Raspberry Pi. The top-level design included an Altera PLL IP—pll-29p5M (see Chapter 13).

```
1    library ieee;
2    use ieee.std_logic_1164.all;
3
4    entity raspberryPi_spi_top is
5      port(
6        -- Clock ins, SYS_CLK = 50MHz
7        SYS_CLK : in std_logic;
8
9        -- LED outs
10       USER_LED : out std_logic_vector(8 downto 1);
11
12       GPIO_01 : in  std_logic;            -- SPI CLOCK
13       GPIO_02 : in  std_logic;            -- SPI MOSI
14       GPIO_03 : in  std_logic;            -- SPI SLAVE SELECT (Active low)
15       GPIO_04 : out std_logic             -- SPI MISO
16       );
17   end entity raspberryPi_spi_top;
18
19   architecture arch of raspberryPi_spi_top is
20
21     signal locked, clk_29MHz_i, rst_i : std_logic := '0';
22     signal data_out, SPI_DATA          : std_logic_vector(7 downto 0);
23
24     signal rspi_clk  : std_logic;
25     signal rspi_mosi : std_logic;
26     signal rspi_miso : std_logic;
27     signal rspi_ss   : std_logic;
28
29     signal wr_enable : std_logic;
30
31   begin
32
33     clk : entity work.pll_29p5M
34       port map
35       (
36         inclk0 => SYS_CLK,               -- 50MHz clock input
37         c0      => clk_29MHz_i,          -- 29.5MHz clock ouput
38         locked => locked                 -- Lock condition, 1 = Locked
39       );
```

Figure 15-18. *Raspberry Pi SPI top-level design Part 1*

We use the locked signal from the PLL as an active low reset (rst_i). The signal will go high when the PLL output is stable. This reset (rst_i) and output clock (clk_29Mz_i) are used in the rest of the logic.

SPI_DATA register is updated with data_out when the spi_slave, which is instantiated as spi_slave_pm output wr_enable, is high. The LED outputs are an inverted version of the SPI_DATA (line 72) because the LEDs are active low logic outputs.

```
40        . .
41        rst_i <= locked;
42
43    spi_slave_pm : entity work.spi_slave
44      port map(
45        sys_clock => clk_29MHz_i,
46        sys_rst   => rst_i,
47        rspi_sclk => rspi_clk,      -- SPI clock from raspberry SPI Master
48        rspi_ss   => rspi_ss,       -- SPI chip select from raspberry SPI Master
49        rspi_mosi => rspi_mosi,     -- SPI data from raspberry SPI Master
50        rspi_miso => rspi_miso,     -- SPI data to raspberry SPI Master
51        wr_enable => wr_enable,
52        data_out  => data_out,
53        data_in   => SPI_DATA
54        );
55
56    spi_data_p : process(clk_29MHz_i, rst_i)
57    begin
58      if(rst_i = '0') then
59        SPI_DATA <= (others => '0');
60      elsif(rising_edge(clk_29MHz_i)) then
61        if (wr_enable = '1') then
62          SPI_DATA <= data_out;
63        end if;
64      end if;
65    end process;
66
67    rspi_clk  <= GPIO_01;
68    rspi_mosi <= GPIO_02;
69    rspi_ss   <= GPIO_03;
70    GPIO_04   <= rspi_miso;
71
72    USER_LED <= not SPI_DATA;
73
74  end architecture arch;
```

Figure 15-19. *Raspberry Pi SPI top-level design Part 2*

The RTL design view in Quartus looks like Figure 15-20 when you compile the design and select the RTL view from the top-level design (see section "Using Altera Quartus to Understand the FSM," in Chapter 11, for more information on how to use the RTL view).

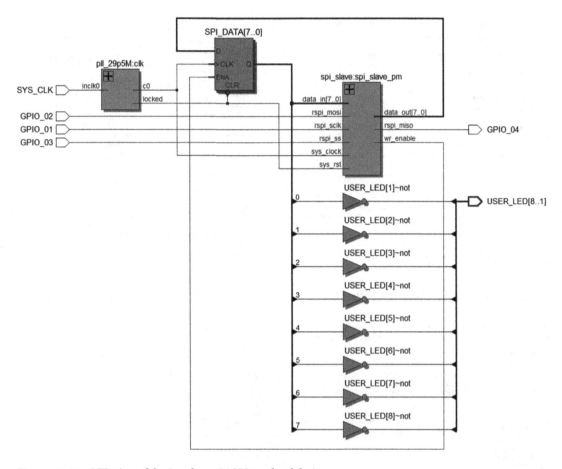

Figure 15-20. RTL view of the Raspberry Pi SPI top-level design

15.4.2   Generate and Program the FPGA

You can create the project in the same way you did in Chapter 13, or you can add the two new VHDL design files (spi_slave.vhd and raspberryPi_spi_top.vhd) under the same project from that chapter and set raspberryPi_spi_top.vhd as the top-level entity. Your Altera Quartus Project Navigator should look like figure 15-21 (box 1) after you set the top level as raspberryPi_spi_top.vhd.

   Figure 15-21 shows the steps (Box 2 and Box 3) to generate the bit file (.sof file) and start programming the design. Figure 15-22 shows the steps for selecting the SOF file and starting to program the FPGA. All you need to do is follow the arrow steps in the figure. After you have programmed the FPGA, it only has the red LED on. The green LEDs are not blinking because the Raspberry Pi SPI master is not running. Let's go to the next section to get the SPI master running.

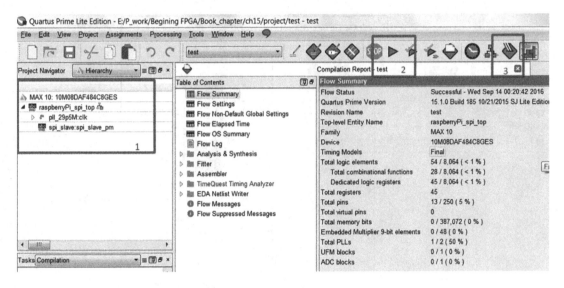

Figure 15-21. *Generate the bit file for the FPGA*

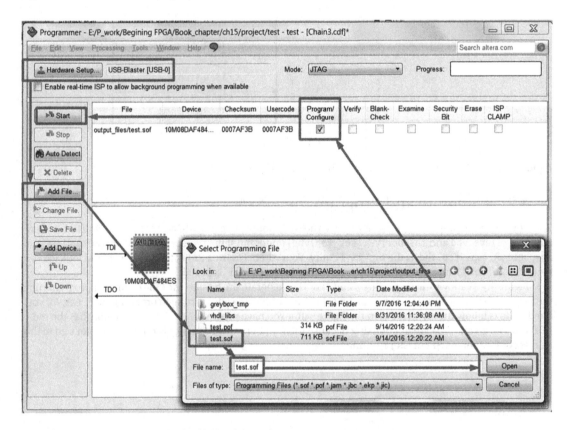

Figure 15-22. *Programming the bit file for the FPGA*

15.5   How to Use Raspberry Pi SPI Master Interface

Here we will only show the basic steps to make the Raspberry Pi SPI master work. We have provided some web site links later in the chapter if you want to explore further.

We can use the Raspberry Pi Python SpiDev() to control the SPI master. Run the following commands on your Raspberry Pi:

```
$ sudo apt-get update sudo apt-get install python-dev
$ git clone git://github.com/doceme/py-spidev
$ cd py-spidev
$ sudo python setup.py install
```

The following link provides more info on thee SPIDEV modules: www.100randomtasks. com/simple-spi-on-raspberry-pi.

15.5.1   Python Code to Read and Write SPI Master

You can use the Python code shown in Figure 15-23 to test your FPGA slave SPI. The code enables Master 0 on the Raspberry Pi and uses CE1 which is connected to the FPGA GPIO_03 to select the SPI slave.

```
max10spi_simple.py ✕
1    import spidev
2    import time
3    import binascii                      Open Master 0 CE 1 SPI interface
4
5    spi=spidev.SpiDev()
6    spi.open(0,1)  ◄───────────          SPI Clock is 500kHz
7    spi.max_speed_hz=500000  ◄──────
8    ⊟while True:                          READ operation
9        resp = spi.xfer2([0x01,0x00])  ◄─
10       print binascii.hexlify(bytearray(resp))
11       time.sleep(1)                     WRITE 0xFF to turn on all LEDs
12       resp = spi.xfer2([0x00,0xff])  ◄─
13       print ''        Wait 1 second
14       time.sleep(1)  ◄───
15
16       resp = spi.xfer2([0x01,0x00])
17       print binascii.hexlify(bytearray(resp))
18       time.sleep(1)
19       resp = spi.xfer2([0x00,0x55])
20       print ''
21       time.sleep(1)
22
23       resp = spi.xfer2([0x01,0x00])
24       print binascii.hexlify(bytearray(resp))
25       time.sleep(1)
26       resp = spi.xfer2([0x00,0xaa])
27       print ''
28       time.sleep(1)
29
30       resp = spi.xfer2([0x01,0x00])
31       print binascii.hexlify(bytearray(resp))
32       time.sleep(1)
33       resp = spi.xfer2([0x00,0x00])
34       print ''
35       time.sleep(1)
```

Figure 15-23. Python code for controlling SPI master in Raspberry Pi

Run the Python code as follows. Figure 15-24 shows the result from the Raspberry Pi. The LEDs on the BeMicro MAX10 board will start blinking when the code is running. The LED is on and off as the value shown in the Raspberry PI.

```
$ python max10spi_simple.py
```

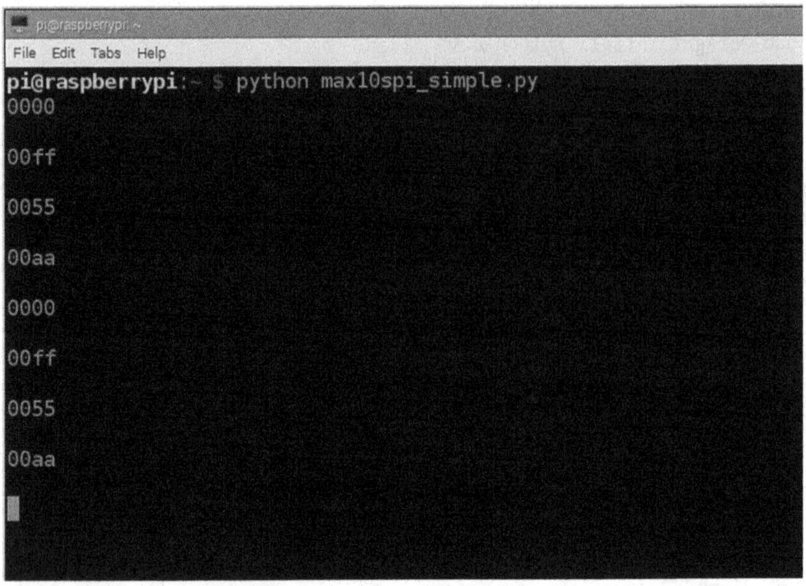

Figure 15-24. Running the Python code max10spi_simple.py

Following are additional web sites with information about the SPI in Raspberry Pi:

```
http://raspberrypi-aa.github.io/session3/spi.html
```

```
www.raspberrypi-spy.co.uk/2014/08/enabling-the-spi-interface-on-the-raspberry-pi/
```

15.6 Summary

This chapter shows you how to do two-way communication with your Raspberry Pi. We created our own two-byte protocol for reading and writing.

We have also provided detailed design explanations on the spi_slave. You should now know the function of all six processes in the design and the connection between them. This example illustrates (clock edge detection) how to deal with the number-one issue of external communication—clock in the communication link. The example shows you how to use shift registers to send and receive data.

It is not that hard to send and receive data to and from the FPGA though standard interfaces.

> *"As an engineer I'm constantly spotting problems and plotting how to solve them."*

—James Dyson

CHAPTER 16

■ ■ ■

Up in Lights: How to Drive LED Segment Displays

16.1   Introduction

In this chapter we will introduce a 7 segment display counter design. The counter counts from 0 to 9 and then resets to 0 and starts again. The Raspberry Pi can also send a control message to force the counter to have a particular value. We will re-use all of the VHDL code from Chapter 15 and add a 7 segment display counter module.

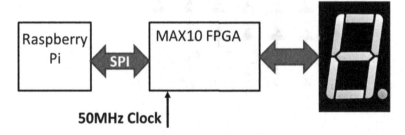

Figure 16-1. *7 segment displays system block diagram with Raspberry Pi*

16.2   How to drive a 7 segment display

In the last couple of chapters, the BeMicro MAX10 was only able to use the onboard 8 LEDs to display some binary information. To improve information display from the FPGA, we can use a 7 segment display. 7 segment displays look like the one in Figure 16-2. The name 7 segments comes from the fact that it has 7 LEDs. What's special though is that the arrangement of the 7 LEDs can be used to display decimal numbers, 0 to 9. Figure 16-3 shows a schematic of a common cathode 7 segment display that we will be using. It shows which pins map to which LED. For example, the pin 7 is used to control the segment A. If we provide voltage on Pins 6 & 4 and ground pins 3 & 8, the the LED segment B and C will light up. Together, this looks like a "ONE". There is another type of 7 segment display which is referred to as common anode. We only show how to connect common cathode 7 segment display in our example. The reason of using cathode version is because we can turn on the LED by output logic high and user will not damage the FPGA by driving the LED with external voltage source which is possilbe too high for the FPGA. For common anode 7 segments display, change the connections of pin 3 and 8 from ground to 3.3V pin (Pin 11 on J5).

© Aiken Pang and Peter Membrey 2017

A. Pang and P. Membrey, *Beginning FPGA: Programming Metal*, DOI 10.1007/978-1-4302-6248-0_16

Figure 16-2. *7 segment display block*

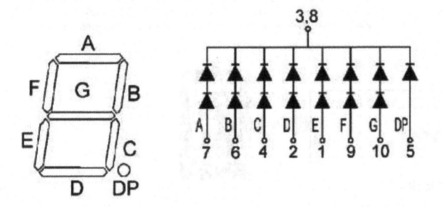

Figure 16-3. *Pins mapping on the 7 segment display*

16.2.1   Connecting 7 segment display to FPGA

In our example, we will connect the 7 segment to the BeMicro MAX10 board connector J5. Figure 16-4 shows the connections between the 7 segment display and the connector. We need to add a 1~5k ohm resistor between connector and 7 segment display pins connection. The resistor is used to protect the LEDs and the FPGA output drivers.

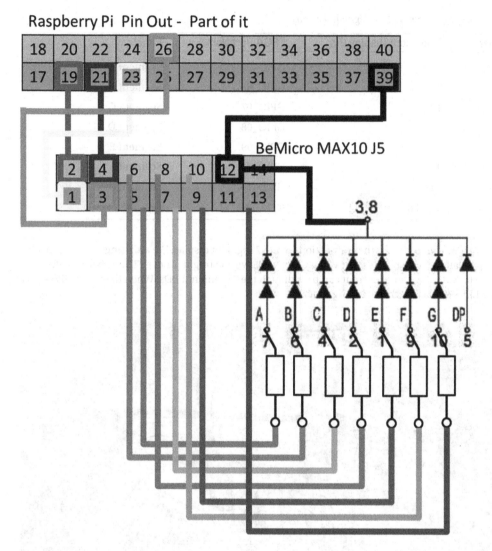

Figure 16-4. Pins mapping on the 7 segment display

The connections should look like the following table mapping on the FPGA side. We will use the FPGA port names in the VHDL design.

Table 16-1. *FPGA pins mapping to 7 Segment display*

J5 Pin Number	7 Segment Display Pin	FPGA Port Name	Function
5	7	GPIO_05	Segment A
6	6	GPIO_06	Segment B
7	4	GPIO_07	Segment C
8	2	GPIO_08	Segment D
9	1	GPIO_09	Segment E
10	9	GPIO_10	Segment F
13	10	GPIO_11	Segment G
12	3 and 8	N/A	Ground

Figure 16-5 shows our setup for the connections of the 7 segment display. We are using 5k ohm resistor for our setup. You can use a smaller resistor value which will give you brighter LEDs. This is because the smaller the resistor value, the more current can pass though the 7 segment LEDs. When the FPGA GPIO pins drive high, the LEDs on the 7 segment will light up.

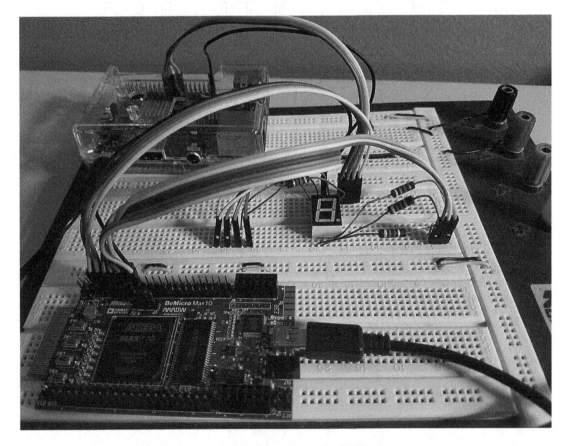

Figure 16-5. *Connection between 7 segment display and Be Micro MAX 10*

If you power up the BeMicro MAX10 FPGA, the 7 segment display may partially light up. It is because any non-programed pin from FPGA may have lower than the 2.5V voltage come out from the pin. The next section will create the VHDL design to actually driving it.

16.3   Designing the 7 segment display counter

We are going to design a 7 segment counter in the FPGA. We need to have two sections for this counter. The first is a simple counter and the second is decoding the counter value to display on the 7 segment display which is human readable. Table 16-2 shows the port list for the 7 segments display counter. It has a 29.5 MHz clock and reset inputs, counter update input ports, current value report output and 7 segment display output ports. Figure 16-6 shows the first section of the VHDL design: Libraries, entity with port list and architecture with the name arch.

Table 16-2. *seven_segment_counter.vhd port list*

Name	Type	Function
sys_clock	std_logic	29.5MHz clock
sys_rst	Std_logic	Active Low reset (logic 0 is reset)
data_in	Std_logic_vector(7 downto 0)	Updated counter value
current_value	Std_logic_vector(7 downto 0)	Current counter value output
segments_a2g	Std_logic_vector(0 to 6)	7 segment display: A to G LEDs outputs

```
1    library IEEE;
2    use IEEE.STD_LOGIC_1164.all;
3    use IEEE.STD_LOGIC_ARITH.all;
4    use IEEE.STD_LOGIC_UNSIGNED.all;
5
6    entity seven_segment_counter is
7       port(
8          -- general purpose
9          sys_clock : in std_logic; -- system clock
10         sys_rst : in std_logic;    -- system reset active low
11         -- serial I/O side
12         data_in : in std_logic_vector(7 downto 0);
13         data_valid: in std_logic;
14         current_value: out std_logic_vector(7 downto 0);
15         -- 7 Segment display interface
16         segments_a2g: out std_logic_vector(0 to 6)
17
18         );
19   end entity;
20
21   architecture arch of seven_segment_counter is
22
23      signal data_in_reg: std_logic_vector(7 downto 0);
24      signal counter_0to9: unsigned(3 downto 0);
25      signal second_count: unsigned(24 downto 0);
26      signal second_tick: std_logic;
27
28   begin
29
```

Figure 16-6. *seven_segment_counter entity and architecture signal section*

16.3.1   Simple counter design section

Since we have one 7 segment display, the counter will only allow us to count 0 to 9. The simple counter will count from 0 to 9 and then start from 0 again. We should slowly increment the counter value such that we can see the update one by one. This counter should provide an interface for updating the current value such that the counter value can start from any value we select.

1.   Data input process for update the current counter value

2.   One second internal counter for slowly updating the 7 segment display counter

3.   4 bit counter with value from 0 to 9 and loading input port

16.3.1.1   Data input process

This process is synchronous to sys_clock which is 29.5MHz. It will update the data_in_reg value when data_valid is equal to '1'. It is a simple 8 bit register. Figure 16-7 shows this data input registers process. The default value of the data_in_reg after power on is 0xFF such that the 7 segment display counter will start to count automatically.

```
30    -- Register the data_in value to internal registers
31    -- when data_valid go high
32    data_input_p: process(sys_clock, sys_rst)
33    begin
34       if(sys_rst = '0') then
35          data_in_reg   <= (others =>'1');
36       elsif(rising_edge(sys_clock))then
37          if(data_valid = '1') then
38                data_in_reg <= data_in;
39          end if;
40       end if;
41    end process;
42
```

Figure 16-7. *data input process*

16.3.1.2   One second counter

This is a counter with a max value equal to 29.5M such that we can count one second duration. The binary value of 29.5M has 25 bits. We need to have a counter (second_count) with the same number of bit to counter one second. This counter starts from 0 and counter all the way up to 29499999. It will generate a tick (second_tick) when it is equal to 29.5M - 1, which is one second when the counter is clocked by 29.5MHz. Figure 16-8 shows this one second counter design process.

```
43     -- One second counter
44     one_sec_counter_p : process(sys_clock, sys_rst)
45     begin
46       if(sys_rst = '0') then
47         second_count  <= (others =>'0');
48         second_tick <= '0';
49       elsif(rising_edge(sys_clock))then
50         if(unsigned(data_in_reg ) < 10) then
51           second_count <= (others =>'0');
52           second_tick <= '0';
53         else
54           if(second_count = 29499999) then
55             second_count <= (others =>'0');
56             second_tick <= '1';
57           else
58             second_count <= second_count +1;
59             second_tick <= '0';
60           end if;
61         end if;
62       end if;
63     end process;
64
```

Figure 16-8. One second counter

16.3.1.3   4 Bit Counter with value from 0 to 9

This is a counter with a max value much less than the last one. It only counts from 0 to 9. This counter is controlled by the input value (data_in_reg). The counter will start increment by one when the data_in_reg value is bigger than 9. If the data_in_reg value is smaller or equal to 9, then the counter value (counter_0to9) will be updated by the data_in_reg value and freeze which means the counter will not incremented. Figure 16-9 shows the design of this 4 bit counter (counter_0to9)

```
65     -- 0 to 9 counter with load value
66     -- Load value from data_in_reg when it is smaller
67     -- or equal to 9
68     -- counter start incrnment counting when bigger than 9
69     counter_with_load_p : process(sys_clock, sys_rst)
70     begin
71       if(sys_rst = '0') then
72         counter_0to9  <= (others =>'0');
73       elsif(rising_edge(sys_clock))then
74         if(unsigned(data_in_reg ) > 9 ) then
75           if( second_tick = '1' ) then
76             if(counter_0to9 = 9) then
77               counter_0to9 <= (others =>'0');
78             else
79               counter_0to9 <= counter_0to9 +1;
80             end if;
81           end if;
82         else
83           counter_0to9 <= unsigned(data_in_reg(3 downto 0));
84         end if;
85       end if;
86     end process;
87
```

Figure 16-9. 4 bits counter with load

In line 74, we use unsigned(data_in_reg) to convert the std_logic_vector to an unsigned value such that we can compare it with 9.

16.3.2   7 segment decoder section

The output from the simple counter is a binary number. We need to translate the 4 bit binary number to 7 bit segment display LEDs output. In this design we are using a common cathode LED which means we need to output '1' to make the LED on. We can use a simple case statement in VHDL to map these 4 bit binary inputs to 7 bit segment outputs.

16.3.2.1   Case statement for 7 Segment decoder

This decoder is a pure combinational logic design which uses case statements. This is a good example of how to use a case statement as part of combinational logic. Counter_0to9 is the case inputs. We only need to decode the value between 0 to 9. The 7 segment display will NOT output anything when the counter_0to9 value are not equal to valid range (0 ~ 9) which is in the case statement "others"(Figure 16-10 line 103). Remember to add the counter_0to9 to the sensitive list. Line 107 and 108 connect the counter_0to9 value externally. This example shows you how to create combinational logic without any logic gate design. All of the logic gates are created by the Altera tools.

```
88      -- 7 segment decode
89      decode_7seg_display_p: process(counter_0to9)
90      begin
91       case counter_0to9 is
92                                          --abcdefg--
93          when "0000" => segments_a2g <= "1111110";
94          when "0001" => segments_a2g <= "0110000";
95          when "0010" => segments_a2g <= "1101101";
96          when "0011" => segments_a2g <= "1111001";
97          when "0100" => segments_a2g <= "0110011";
98          when "0101" => segments_a2g <= "1011011";
99          when "0110" => segments_a2g <= "1011111";
100         when "0111" => segments_a2g <= "1110000";
101         when "1000" => segments_a2g <= "1111111";
102         when "1001" => segments_a2g <= "1111011";
103         when others => segments_a2g <= "0000000";
104       end case;
105     end process;
106
```

Figure 16-10. *7 Segment decoder case statements*

16.3.3   End of the counter design

Each VHDL module design has entity (line 6 to 19) and architecture (line 21 to 110). Figure 16-3e shows the last three line of VHDL code. The lower four bits of current_vlaue is connected to the counter_0to9 (the 4 bit counter) and the upper four bits are all set to zero. This current_value is an output port of the 7 segment display counter module. The port value will be used to report the value back to Raspberry Pi (when it sends a read back command) and output to drive the one board LEDs.

The last line (line 110) in the Figure 16-11 is the end of the counter design. It defines the end of the architecture: arch.

```
107  current_value(3 downto 0) <=   std_logic_vector(counter_0to9);
108  current_value(7 downto 4) <= (others =>'0');
109
110  end arch;
111
```

Figure 16-11. *end of the architecture deisgn of the 7 segment display counter*

16.4   7 Segment display example design

Every FPGA design needs a top level design to connect all of the modules together and to the outside world (the board connections). This 7 segment display example also needs a top level design.

We will re-use the SPI slave and PLL design from chapter 15 (Two-way communications with your raspberry Pi: SPI) and add the 7 segment display counter module from the last section. Figure 16-12 shows all of the modules within the design and their connections.

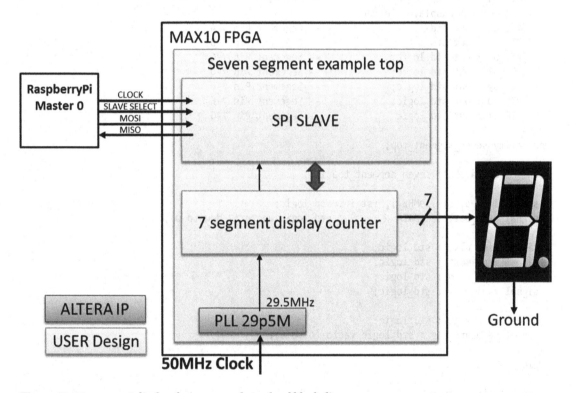

Figure 16-12. *segment display design example top level block diagram*

16.4.1   Code for the top level design

You can copy the following code from Listing 16-1 and save to a file called seven_segment_top.vhd file. Add this file to the last chapter's project and select it as top level design by right clicking on the seven_segment_top.vhd file in the Project navigator "FILES" and select Set as Top-level Entity.

Listing 16-1. seven_segment_top.vhd 7 segment example top level design

```vhdl
library ieee;
use ieee.std_logic_1164.all;

entity seven_segment_top is
  port(
    -- Clock ins, SYS_CLK = 50MHz
    SYS_CLK : in std_logic;
    -- LED outs
    USER_LED : out std_logic_vector(8 downto 1);
    -- SPI Interface to Raspberry Pi
    GPIO_01 : in  std_logic;           -- SPI CLOCK
    GPIO_02 : in  std_logic;           -- SPI MOSI
    GPIO_03 : in  std_logic;           -- SPI SLAVE SELECT (Active low)
    GPIO_04 : out std_logic;           -- SPI MISO
    -- 7 Segment display interface
    GPIO_05 : out std_logic;           -- Segement Pin 7-A
    GPIO_06 : out std_logic;           -- Segement Pin 7-B
    GPIO_07 : out std_logic;           -- Segement Pin 7-C
    GPIO_08 : out std_logic;           -- Segement Pin 7-D
    GPIO_09 : out std_logic;           -- Segement Pin 7-E
    GPIO_10 : out std_logic;           -- Segement Pin 7-F
    GPIO_11 : out std_logic            -- Segement Pin 7-G
    );
end entity seven_segment_top;

architecture arch of seven_segment_top is

  signal locked, clk_29MHz_i, rst_i : std_logic;
  signal data_out, SPI_DATA         : std_logic_vector(7 downto 0);

  signal rspi_clk  : std_logic;
  signal rspi_mosi : std_logic;
  signal rspi_miso : std_logic;
  signal rspi_ss   : std_logic;

  signal wr_enable : std_logic;
  signal segments_a2g : std_logic_vector(0 to 6);

begin

  clk : entity work.pll_29p5M
    port map
    (
      inclk0 => SYS_CLK,               -- 50MHz clock input
      c0     => clk_29MHz_i,           -- 29.5MHz clock ouput
      locked => locked                 -- Lock condition, 1 = Locked
      );
```

```vhdl
  rst_i <= locked;

  spi_slave_pm : entity work.spi_slave
    port map(
      sys_clock => clk_29MHz_i,
      sys_rst   => rst_i,
      rspi_sclk => rspi_clk,              -- SPI clock from raspberry SPI Master
      rspi_ss   => rspi_ss,       -- SPI chip select from raspberry SPI Master
      rspi_mosi => rspi_mosi,             -- SPI data from raspberry SPI Master
      rspi_miso => rspi_miso,             -- SPI data to raspberry SPI Master
      wr_enable => wr_enable,
      data_out  => data_out,
      data_in   => SPI_DATA
      );

  rspi_clk  <= GPIO_01;
  rspi_mosi <= GPIO_02;
  rspi_ss   <= GPIO_03;
  GPIO_04   <= rspi_miso;


  USER_LED <= not SPI_DATA;                 -- Output binary counter value to on
                                            -- board LEDs

  seven_segment_counter_pm : entity work.seven_segment_counter
    port map(
      -- general purpose
      sys_clock     => clk_29MHz_i,
      sys_rst       => rst_i,
      -- serial I/O side
      data_valid    => wr_enable,
      data_in       => data_out,
      current_value => SPI_DATA,
      -- 7 Segment display interface
      segments_a2g  => segments_a2g
      );

  GPIO_05 <= segments_a2g(0);             -- Segement Pin 7-A
  GPIO_06 <= segments_a2g(1);             -- Segement Pin 7-B
  GPIO_07 <= segments_a2g(2);             -- Segement Pin 7-C
  GPIO_08 <= segments_a2g(3);             -- Segement Pin 7-D
  GPIO_09 <= segments_a2g(4);             -- Segement Pin 7-E
  GPIO_10 <= segments_a2g(5);             -- Segement Pin 7-F
  GPIO_11 <= segments_a2g(6);             -- Segement Pin 7-G

end architecture arch;
```

16.4.2   Generate and program the FPGA

We create the project in the same way as chapter 15 or you can add the two new VHDL design files (seven_segment_counter.vhd and seven_segment_top.vhd) to the same project and set seven_segment_top.vhd as top-level entity. You can get the Altera Quartus Project Navigator look like figure 16-13.

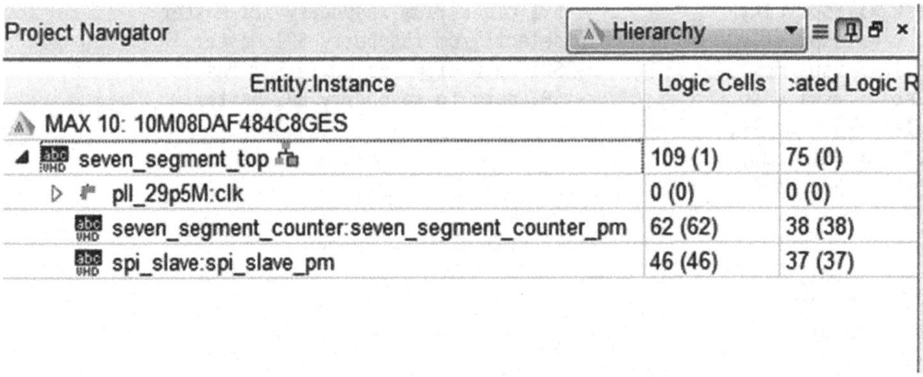

Project Navigator	Hierarchy		
Entity:Instance		Logic Cells	:ated Logic R
MAX 10: 10M08DAF484C8GES			
seven_segment_top		109 (1)	75 (0)
pll_29p5M:clk		0 (0)	0 (0)
seven_segment_counter:seven_segment_counter_pm		62 (62)	38 (38)
spi_slave:spi_slave_pm		46 (46)	37 (37)

Figure 16-13. *Seven Segment Top Altera Quartus Project Navigator*

You can follow the same method as we used in Chapter 15 to generate the bit file and program the FPGA for this example design.

After the bit file is uploaded to the FPGA, the 7 segment display should start to count from 0 to 9. We can control the counter from Raspberry PI SPI master interface.

16.5   Control the 7 segment counter from Raspberry Pi

Based on the setup from Chapter 15 for the Raspberry Pi, we should be able to run the following Python script to get the 7 segment counter to count 3, 2, 1, 2,3,4,5,6,7,8,9,0…etc.

```
max10spi_7s_count.py ✕
1    import spidev
2    import time
3    import binascii
4
5    spi=spidev.SpiDev()
6    spi.open(0,1)                          Set the 7 segment display to "3"
7    spi.max_speed_hz=500000
8  ⊟while True:
9        resp = spi.xfer2([0x01,0x00])
10       print binascii.hexlify(bytearray(resp))
11       time.sleep(1)
12       resp = spi.xfer2([0x00,0x03])
13       print ''                          Set the 7 segment display to "2"
14       time.sleep(1)
15
16       resp = spi.xfer2([0x01,0x00])
17       print binascii.hexlify(bytearray(resp))
18       time.sleep(1)
19       resp = spi.xfer2([0x00,0x02])
20       print ''
21       time.sleep(1)                      Set the 7 segment display to "1"
22
23       resp = spi.xfer2([0x01,0x00])
24       print binascii.hexlify(bytearray(resp))
25       time.sleep(1)
26       resp = spi.xfer2([0x00,0x01])
27       print ''
28       time.sleep(1)
29
30       resp = spi.xfer2([0x01,0x00])
31       print binascii.hexlify(bytearray(resp))
32       time.sleep(1)
33       resp = spi.xfer2([0x00,0x0A])  ◄── 7 segment count start to increnment
34       print ''                           for 20 seconds
35       time.sleep(20)  ◄────────────
```

Figure 16-14. *Python script for running the counter example*

16.6   Summary

In this chapter, we designed a special version of the 7 segment counter. The counter module includes some register design, a second counter and combination logic for decoding the 7 segment display. All three elements are very basic and useful for most of the design. The seven_segment_top.vhd shows most of what all top level designs do - connect all of the modules to the outside world.

After this chapter, you should know to handle the design flow for a FPGA design which is like the following.

- Define clock and reset

- Define the input and output requirements

- Create the port list

- Separate the design requirements into multiple stages/steps

- Design each stage/step with one process with VHDL code

The second step should be simulating it with ModelSim after you get your design done. ModelSim can show a lot of things that are very helpful when debuging the design.

The idea of this design flow is to allow us to understand what we want to build first before we start to write the VHDL code. This is important for you to create hardware.

We hope this book provided you with enough information to kick start your learning about FPGA and VHDL. You have just started FPGA and VHDL journey. The follow websites are ideal for continuing the learning process for both FPGA and VHDL.

One more BeMicro MAX10 example design from Altera

```
https://cloud.altera.com/devstore/platform/15.1.0/become-an-fpga-designer-in-4-
hour-lab-solution/
```

Huge collections of VHDL and FPGA stuff

```
http://members.optusnet.com.au/jekent/FPGA.htm
```

A lot of good free IP and tutorial for different interfaces

```
http://www.fpga4fun.com/
```

"What I cannot build, I do not understand"

— Richard Feynman

Index

© Aiken Pang and Peter Membrey 2017
A. Pang and P. Membrey, *Beginning FPGA: Programming Metal*, DOI 10.1007/978-1-4302-6248-0

▓ V, W, X, Y, Z

Get the eBook for only $4.99!

Why limit yourself?

Now you can take the weightless companion with you wherever you go and access your content on your PC, phone, tablet, or reader.

Since you've purchased this print book, we are happy to offer you the eBook for just $4.99.

Convenient and fully searchable, the PDF version enables you to easily find and copy code—or perform examples by quickly toggling between instructions and applications.

To learn more, go to http://www.apress.com/us/shop/companion or contact support@apress.com.

Printed in the United States
By Bookmasters